PHAEDRA FISHER

VODKA

DIPLOMACY

AND OTHER ADVENTURES AND LESSONS

IN THE NEW RUSSIA

Vodka Diplomacy: And Other Adventures and Lessons in the New Russia

By Phaedra Fisher
Vodka Diplomacy: And Other Adventures and Lessons in the New Russia

Copyright: Phaedra Fisher
Published: May 2013
ISBN: 978-0-9895178-1-2

Contents

PREFACE

Every generation of university graduates believes they are going to change the world. My classmates and I took things one step further and really tried.

The Soviet Union had collapsed in late 1991. The future was not yet written. There were no correct answers. Anything could happen.

On this raw new frontier, anyone in academia or politics or business who tried to posture as an "expert" was really just guessing as best as they could. My classmates and I who studied Russian language and economics found ourselves graduating at the precise moment in history when these skills were highly valued. I leaped into the thick of the post-Soviet era in August 1993, delirious with naïve optimism, a thirst for adventure, and a mission to make a difference.

An underlying theme for my experience in Russia was established literally on my first day working in Moscow, when an American businessman offered the simple explanation for his astonishing actions as "In Russia there are no laws – only suggestions." At first this mantra was exhilarating. I charged into my role with various aid projects energized that with enough creativity, any obstacle could be overcome. Anything was possible and of course we would be successful.

I passionately believed in the stated objectives of my projects. Establishing local consulting centers throughout Russia would build the business skills of Russians and help the newly privatized enterprises overhaul their operations, attract foreign investors, and become growing hubs of employment and opportunity. Automating and streamlining the real estate title registration processes would provide a key to help Russians build their economic independence through buying and selling property and facilitating using their property as collateral for loans. I firmly believed in these stated goals and I was proud to be part of the effort to secure the first steps towards economic freedom for people who had been oppressed for far too long.

But then over time I came to realize that the definition of "success" has as many variations as there are participants. USAID, the Russian government, and the local officials I worked with all held different views of the desired outcomes – shaped by personal and political influences. With this, the mantra "No laws – only suggestions" began to take on a more ominous overtone. In a society not bound by rules, one is left naked to the whims of benevolence or force of others. I could use this concept to solve some logistical problems and enjoy a bit of adventure along the way, with my brand of "success" as a beacon. But others with a different view of success were also able to force their agenda as well. And "force" an agenda, I increasingly learned, was not just an abstract concept, but alarmingly real.

This book is not an academic tome. Do not read this looking for meticulous citations or broad analytical theories. I am offering a personal adventure through a chaotic time in world history and my own lessons learned along the way. I was one of hundreds, if not thousands, of American and European expats who were thrust onto the front lines of the change that was in motion throughout the former Soviet Union in the mid 1990s. My story is not unique and should not be read as such.

This is not a historical account of particular people and events. The narrative of this book is based on actual events, to the best of my memory, but the participants have been thrown into the blender of literary license. The characters are composites of many elements of different people and everyone has been baptized with new names. Of course, some characters are presented in a negative light and some in a positive light. My goal is not to critique anyone as individuals or to point at specific issues with particular projects or government agencies. We were all pioneers, charting new ground to the best of our abilities. We all had our own way of approaching the very real challenges that we faced. This is my story and therefore it is told from my perspective. Any one of my former colleagues (Americans, Russians, and a few Brits) could write a similar story from their own vantage point. And honestly, for the sake of adding greater texture to the records of this important time in history, I hope that they do.

I left Russia in June 1996 much older than the few short years would imply. By the standards of USAID, all of my projects were completed successfully – on time, on budget, with all the major milestones signed off. Each was even granted a follow on "phase two" – an implicit stamp of approval for a job well done. On paper we were successful, but in reality what had changed? Were our efforts resulting in empowering individuals to pursue economic independence – or entrenching the political insiders further?

The next generation of optimistic bright-eyed kids are now embarking on their own crusades to change the world – to save the environment, reduce third-world poverty, improve the economic opportunities for women, and so on. Their energy is refreshing. The passion to "do *something*" is admirable. I can only hope that among the next generation is at least a few individuals who will look beyond the headlines declaring success or failure for their initiatives and ask the deeper question of what *really* happened.

This book is my response to that question. Some will read my account as simply a rollicking wild ride on the roller coaster of the post-Soviet era. That is fine by me. I believe that everyone can learn something from my experience – academics studying the post-Soviet period, those interested in the realities of life in a society without a solid rule of law, policy-makers examining what really happens on aid projects, or just curious casual readers in search of a good adventure. But most of all I hope that I am helping future generations to be inspired to not just undertake their own adventures in the name of "doing something to help X cause," but to look beyond the simplified statements of headline news and the historical record – and to gain the wisdom to challenge their own views as well.

☆

1 FIRST LESSON

June 1994 – Moscow Russia

"Surely you must understand! In Russia we have no rules, only suggestions!"

After delivering these words of wisdom, the American businessman seated next to me lifted his glass with a silent salute and drank his double shot of vodka in one polished move. It was nine o'clock in the morning.

I stared at my travelling companion in astonishment. Partly at the fact that he was doing vodka shots early in the morning. But more so by what he had just told me he intended to do next.

We were chatting to pass the time while our plane was delayed on the tarmac of Sheremyetovo II airport waiting for an arrival gate during a torrential downpour. After the first hour of delay, the flight attendants had decided to roll out the beverage carts in an attempt to calm down the agitated passengers. The American businessman had been briefing me on what to expect with customs and the arrivals area of Sheremyetovo. He was a seasoned expat, returning to Moscow after a bit of shore leave back in the United States, whereas I was arriving at this airport for the first time. He was drinking vodka. I was drinking Diet Coke.

"Once you are released from here, it will take you at least three hours to get through immigration," he predicted. "And that will be only if you successfully claw yourself to the front of the pack like a rabid animal."

"*You*, not *We?*" I had asked. "Won't you be in the passport control line as well?"

No, he answered. He would not be waiting in the immigration line. His long term work visa had expired, and his renewal had not been processed in time for his return from the latest visit to the US. Given the fact that he already knew that he was going to be detained by immigration, he had decided that he would simply charge the border as quickly as possible after landing. He had organized for his "fixer" to be ready to organize his release from custody as necessary. The immigration officers would certainly intercept and detain him regardless of whether he charged the border or waited in line. Why wait three hours at immigration just for the same result? Quite likely his fixer would have the situation sorted and he would be on his way out of the airport faster than the three hours or so I would spend following the "official" process.

This American was truly a seasoned expat. He was *planning* to violate the stated official process. Where most people would be alarmed by the prospect of being detained by Russian immigration, this American just accepted that it would happen and simply set about planning the most efficient way to deal with it.

The American saw my wide eyed amazement and laughed and delivered the line that I would repeat many times myself in the years to come: "Surely you must understand. In Russia there are no rules, only suggestions."

I was on my third assignment in the former Soviet Union and I was still a novice by comparison.

The predictions from the American businessman proved to be entirely accurate. No we were not allocated a jet way. Eventually stairs were located to release us into the driving rain – before our plane ran out of alcohol but after two other international flights had unloaded their passengers. Once we were allowed to escape, the several hundred jet-lagged and fatigued passengers sprang to life with astonishing vigor. I was swept along in a stampeding herd charging towards passport control. The weak and the slow would be trampled to a pulp or cast aside. The strong would emerge victorious. It was the Russian system at work.

Exposed wires and cables cascaded from concrete ceilings. Light fixtures dangled precariously – some working, but most not. Interior finishings like ceiling tiles, wall paint, or even signage were almost completely absent. A single ancient escalator funneled the churning torrent of passengers into the dungeon of passport control. There was no evidence that it ever had been operational.

The sea of humanity pushed forward and people vigorously attempted to defend their positions. Ethnically the room was only about one quarter Russian, but this was obvious only by looking at people's clothing and complexions, not their behavior. Back at JFK airport or in Frankfurt, this same group of western businessmen would probably grump about passport control but behave peacefully in line, waiting to be processed in turn. Here, however, they were awakened into a primal struggle for survival. New Russians, wearing the mandatory uniform of bottle green jackets with gold chains and a decorative thin silent *devushka* at their side, would push themselves aggressively through the crowd straight to the passport control booth. The trampled would sometimes voice a protest, but this would be met by silent indifference from the New Russians. The several hundred bodies from my flight were all soaked and unwashed, so a wet dog smell thickened the air as we grunted and pushed forward.

Through the crowd I managed to catch a glimpse of my travelling companion well in front of me. Exactly as planned, he was charging up to the border control. Without breaking his stride, the American confidently vaulted over a low barrier and then, as predicted, was immediately seized. Although his arms were now pinned by multiple immigration officers, he somehow managed to turn around and spot me in the crowd to give me a cheerful smile and nod goodbye. All was well. I shouldn't worry.

Good grief. I was raised as a rule abiding good girl in the American Midwest. Did I have what it would take to work effectively in this country?

Hours later I found my mental state lunging from trepidation to euphoria. My self-confidence had received an enormous boost as I undertook my own first illicit adventure in Moscow. After three hours of battling my way through passport and customs control I had then fought my way through the churning sea of the arrivals hall. Scruffily dressed men pounced on new arrivals offering rides to the city. Drivers with signs were lost in the fray. Theoretically I had a driver to meet me – but my flight had landed five hours earlier. He had certainly given up waiting by now and I was on my own with all my worldly possessions for the next two years trying to figure out how to get from Sheremyetovo airport to the Aerostar hotel with no obvious sign of taxi service or public transportation. The only option appeared to be a churning mass of scruffy men all pressing against me and saying that they would give me a lift wherever I wanted to go. The reality sank in that I was going to have to hitchhike under the worst of circumstances – with a mountain of luggage and the obvious glassy-eyed look of a newcomer to the city.

I had selected a man from the mob who appeared to be the least likely to leave my dismembered body on the side of the road. We agreed at $40 for the ride from the airport to the hotel Aerostar and, with minimal additional drama, we were underway.

The rain had cleared. The thick smog of Moscow had been temporarily subdued. The air was momentarily clean and the sky was a deep blue. An absolutely astonishing triple rainbow was painted in technicolor over the city. A fitting symbol to launch a new chapter of my life.

I leaned back in the seat and relaxed for the first time in hours and allowed myself a quiet smile. I was deeply pleased with my life at the moment. I had passed my first test and managed to enter the country and get a ride to the hotel by myself. They were small accomplishments, but fed my confidence.

At the age of 26 I had been hired as a manager into a "Big Six" consulting firm to serve as deputy project manager for a multi-million dollar USAID project based in Moscow. I would have responsibility, a challenge, use my education, and live in the exotic, but relatively civilized, city of Moscow. I had tasted expatriate life for short nips in Kamchatka and Kazakhstan and now I was plunging into the experience more deeply for the next two years or so.

My driver was glad to accept $40 from me in crisp US currency. But he definitely was not pleased that yet another American had arrived in Moscow with intentions to stay for a while. He cursed the Russian government for being weak and condemned the foreign aid programs. The strength of Russia can be re-built only by Russians! Yeltsin was succumbing to the foreign imperialists! Foreigners are in Russia only with the objective of weakening the country. If foreigners were serious about helping Russia re-build, then they would simply hand the aid money over to Russians and walk away. Only Russians know what is best for Russia!

My driver emphatically waved his smoldering cigarette stub in the direction of the World War II memorial on the outskirts of Moscow. (Or, to the Russians, the Great Patriotic War.) Giant anti-tank barricades memorialize the point of the German army's closest advance to Moscow. The memorial is within sight of the primary outer suburbs – just 23 kilometers from the Kremlin walls. Far too close for comfort.

My driver was fiercely proud of this point. "We turned back the Germans with force! But now look at what is happening today. We are letting the foreigners into the country to steal from us all!" The driver took a long drag from his cigarette and contemplated the ruin of his nation. An absolutely putrid Russian cigarette, I might add, that was visibly disintegrating in his nicotine-stained fingers.

Given the fact that all my worldly possessions were in the trunk of his car and the back seat, I decided not to start an argument with this driver. Of course, I did not agree that the foreigners were intent on plundering the riches of Russia. I firmly believed that the presence of young enthusiastic foreigners could only help Russia. We would bring in the western work ethic. We would convey basic concepts of capitalism and management based on meritocracy not political influence. We would teach newly privatized companies the basics of business planning.

Of course, this is what I had believed when I arrived in Kazakhstan as well. That project, I believed, had been foiled due to poor planning on the part of the project design team and the fact that no senior people were actually on the ground with us in Kazakhstan. I still sincerely believed that aid and privatization projects could work in Russia. Improved project management and more senior resources on the ground would certainly be the key to success.

I was convinced that this new project was bound to be an immense improvement upon the wreckage I had left behind in Kazakhstan. For starters, the firm had committed senior level managers and partners to the project full time on the ground with us in Moscow. They would see for themselves what was going on. I was joining the project close to its inception, so I could help with the design process – and live with my own mistakes. I was thoroughly pleased – even by the prospect of the inevitable poor decisions to come. I would rather suffer and learn from my own mistakes than have to endure the consequences of another's.

So my driver may not want me in Russia. The grumpy clerks at immigration may not want me in Russia. The airport offered no illusion of a warm welcome. But I felt strong and energized and ready to overcome all obstacles that may be put in my path to achieve what was best for the country. The sun was shining, the brilliant rainbow arched dramatically over the city, and I was pleasantly deluded that a new day was dawning on Russia. The sensation was lovely while it lasted.

Although it did not register in my mind at the time, within hours of landing in Moscow, my driver had already given me the key to a major source of my angst for the next two years – Russians firmly believe they know what is best for Russia. It is a matter of fierce national pride. And, of course, the entire premise of aid projects is that economic analysts in sitting back in their air-conditioned offices in Washington DC hold the true knowledge of what is best for Russia. Clearly these are two incompatible points of view.

Actually, the term "point of view" is a serious understatement. These were two incompatible fundamental philosophies about how to guide the future of the nation. As in any situation with a built-in contradiction, the underlying tensions would only continue to build until they were either addressed or stress reached the point of explosion. Since the underlying tensions were not acknowledged by anyone, it was practically inevitable that the two philosophies would collide in a dramatic spectacle. I was too naive to see this then. Hindsight, of course, allows the luxury of perfect vision.

From the first moment I walked in the project office in Moscow, it was clear that this project was going to be significantly different from the one I had left in Kazakhstan. Moscow was indeed the promised land – the project teams from all the firm's aid projects had set up camp in a set of conference rooms in the Aerostar Hotel. Sheer luxury. I was awestruck. The rooms were carpeted and filled with folding tables and conference chairs and power strips connected to extension cords. Everyone had their own computer, even the Russians. People had enough space to stack papers or type quietly at their keyboards.

I was filled with an immense surge of optimism. Yes, Moscow was light-years ahead of Kazakhstan. People had space to work. The Russians looked like they actually knew how to use the computers and everyone was busy and focused. There were laser printers in operation and multiple phones ringing. The productivity of this office was going to be astonishing!

"Sorry about the crap offices we have right now," the American responsible for office operations, Robert, introduced himself. "We're working on finalizing a lease to move into more permanent accommodation."

"This is sheer luxury!" I beamed with delight. "Do you have any idea what normal working conditions are like anywhere else in the former Soviet Union?"

Robert waved his arms at the conference room. "How could working conditions possibly be worse than this? We are stacked on top of each other in a conference room. We don't have cabling for a network set up here. There aren't enough phones to go around. If we need to have a private conversation, we have to go outside. This is simply unsustainable!"

I looked at the conference room again. Yes, from the perspective of an American manager arriving for his first overseas project, this was certainly a step down. Especially given the luxury suites that the Big Six firms typically occupy in the urban metropolises across the United States. This was the ultimate open-plan office, but before open plan offices became all the vogue. It did not achieve the standard that the Americans expected, and therefore it was unsatisfactory and would be tolerated, but never appreciated.

I glanced sideways at Robert who was now grumping about the fact he did not have his own office here. In Kazakhstan our project had been strained due to the fact that the senior project planners and personnel were based in Washington DC. I had convinced myself that Russia would be different. If the senior managers and partners were on the ground with the rest of the team then certainly they would have a more realistic understanding of what was feasible and the sorts of challenges we faced. But now listening to the complaints from this American (you cannot even find a decent cup of coffee anywhere in Moscow!), I started to wonder if bringing non-Russian speaking managers into Moscow would help or hinder our cause.

I had signed on to be deputy project manager. But was I in fact condemned to a role such as cultural liaison? Was I doomed to be crushed between two worlds that were colliding within the walls of this conference room? All would be revealed over time.

At least Robert was not on my project team. I could only hope that he was not representative of what I would have to deal with in the months and years to come. Yes, work conditions in Moscow will be tougher than what you are used to in the United States. If you expect America, then you should stay in America. And yes, it is difficult to maintain a positive attitude when things aren't going your way. But I had a real issue with him starting my introduction to the Moscow office on that note. Shouldn't we start from an optimistic point of view? If we can't see the sunny side of life now at the beginning of the project, then how will it be possible later as we face more serious challenges than whether we can find a decent cup of coffee?

We were working in the conference rooms of the Hotel Aerostar and we were temporarily living in the tiny hotel rooms of the Hotel Aerostar. Breakfast was included in my room rate, so I would have breakfast in the Hotel Aerostar as well. Those who know Moscow know that this hotel is far from the center of the city. And actually, even if we were in the center of the city, lunch prospects were limited to about seven restaurants that would meet an American expectation of a "lunch spot" – in a city of 11 million people, mind you. I would not be able to face another minute inside the hotel at lunch and would usually stroll the street near the Metro station and find a sausage or some other bit of charred flesh cooked over a burning oil drum for lunch. Anything to get out of the hotel.

Life felt quite sterile, to say the least. We were protected within the walls of the hotel for the entire day and night, escaping only at mealtimes. With eager anticipation, I looked forward to my first weekend in Moscow. Finally an opportunity to see a bit of what the city had to offer.

So what was my first cultural expedition in Moscow? A walking tour of the Kremlin? A night at the Bolshoi theater? Dinner at a Georgian restaurant? Dancing the night away at a Moscow *diskotek*? All that would come later. The first major cultural experience was watching a game of football between the Moscow Mustangs and the Kiev Destroyers.

Football. Real American grid iron football. Not soccer. And yes, the teams really were the Moscow Mustangs and the Kiev Destroyers. For reasons I do not understand to this day, a small league of football clubs was launched in 1994 across Russia and some of the other former Soviet states. No, American football does not have a large following in Russia or, to my knowledge, anywhere outside the United States. This fact, however, did not stop the formation of the club.

Stephen, one of the managers in our office, had seen the small notice in the *Moscow Times* advertising the upcoming weekend match. Of course we were intrigued.

The day of the match was a gorgeous afternoon for football. The sun was shining and about a hundred bewildered spectators speckled the benches of the Dinamo stadium. The people I was with represented possibly the only Americans in the crowd and, almost certainly, the only spectators who actually understood the rules of the game.

The announcer read the names of the players over the loudspeaker. Vladimir Dmitreevich Zaslavski – quarterback, Sergei Ivanovich Yablokov – wide receiver, Igor Mikhailovich Kuznetsev – fullback. Pockets of reserved cheers indicated where the players' family and friends were huddled in the stands.

The team captains shook hands and the two teams retreated to their respective benches to prepare for the first quarter of play. The announcer began, in Russian, to explain the rules of the game as the teams positioned themselves for the opening kickoff.

"The kickoff will determine where the offense team will begin their attack towards the goal line," he explained in clear simple language. "One member from the defending team will kick the football and the offense team will return the ball until the ball carrier is tackled to the ground."

The place kicker for the Kiev Destroyers carefully placed the football on the 35 yard line. His teammates lined up beside him, eagerly anticipating his next move.

"The opening kickoff takes place on the 30 yard line," the announcer declared in a reprimanding tone.

The place-kicker glanced around him and sought advice from his teammates. After a bit of a conference the players must have agreed that the announcer was correct. The football was relocated to the 30 yard line. The team lined up ready for the opening kick-off. Then the place-kicker trotted up to the ball, gave it a good soccer-style boot, and play was underway.

The spectators watched the opening kickoff in baffled silence. Clusters of women, who were most likely the mothers of the players, conferred earnestly in hushed whispers. They had come to support their boys, but they were not exactly sure what would constitute an appropriate moment to cheer.

A shout erupted from three women near the center of the stands: "Oleg! Throw the ball!" They cheered and called out advice to their boy who was now at the center of the action.

Oleg ran and dodged several tackles before finally passing the ball on to another team member further downfield. Oleg's friends cheered and the teammates were enthusiastic. They had gained at least 30 yards on the play.

"Forward passing is permitted only by the quarterback behind the line of scrimmage!"The announcer brought a quick halt to the celebration on the field. "Other players may pass the ball, but in a backwards direction, away from the goal line. Penalty on the Moscow Mustangs."

A referee blew a whistle and picked up the football, intent on implementing the necessary penalty. He sat the football down on the Kiev Destroyers' 45 yard line and blew his whistle again to resume play. An outburst now from the Moscow Mustangs. A shouting match between the referee and the Moscow team on the correct number of yards for the penalty. Finally the Moscow team's coach waved from the sidelines that the penalty was appropriate and order was re-established. At least momentarily.

The announcer continued to clarify the rules of play for the benefit of the spectators and players alike. Penalties mounted rapidly. Referee whistles were followed by vigorous on-field debates about the rules. A strict instruction from the announcer would usually settle the dispute and play would resume. Moscow fans cheered and then were abruptly silenced by their friends, once they realized the play was actually to the Kiev team's benefit.

Okay, this was not exactly the San Francisco 49ers in action. But what the players lacked in talent or training they made up for in enthusiasm. The defenders vigorously pounced into the offensive line. The running backs darted in a mad frenzy up the field. Professional players in the United States make the game look so easy, as their moves are practiced, assured, and confident. Every gesture of the Moscow Mustangs, however, suggested that these kids had been pulled together for their first training session just a week or so ago. They exploded with youthful enthusiasm – sometimes even in the same direction.

We were thoroughly amused.

Finally half-time. We were in Russia, not America, so of course there was no half-time entertainment. At least no organized entertainment. We didn't mind – we were thoroughly enjoying the spectacle in its natural raw state. At the break the Moscow Mustangs climbed up into the stands to join their friends and family. Picnics were quickly produced and beer and vodka appeared. All the friends had to try on the helmets and (of course) thump each other on the head, while the team members sat down and accepted the vodka shots and sausages offered to them.

Rounds of shots were poured, toasts made, and congratulations and slaps on the back to the players in each of the small circles of friends and family. We were apparently one of the few groups of spectators that had not come as direct supporters for one of the team members. *Babushkas* wearing battered heads carves and dusty brown floral dresses fussed over their sons – or grandsons. Have some more dried fish and cucumbers and bread! You must be starving after such hard work. You must have your strength for the second half of the game!

Watching the families fussing over their sons, we started to develop a theory for what was really underpinning the day's activity. Why would Russia have a league of American football? Logically this made virtually no sense at all. It was as culturally foreign to Russia as dried fish snacks are to America. One lone photographer with a massive fluffy Orthodox beard made a bored attempt to take a few photographs from the sidelines. Why would these young Russian men be so maniacally enthusiastic in their play when no one in the stands understood what was happening in the slightest? Why were the families out in full force for an event that few others even knew existed?

Perhaps they were all daydreaming that a top recruiter from some NFL team was secretly watching them in the stands. There were a few solitary men sitting in the stands wearing non-descript grey overcoats, blending into the crowds. Perhaps here on a muddy field in the dilapidated Dinamo stadium was the new top secret source of fresh young athletes for some scout working for the Miami Dolphins. The mystery recruiter could offer American dollars. A contract that would offer a level of wealth so fantastic that it was simply incomprehensible.

A futile pipe dream? Perhaps. At face value you could simply make a crass statement: "oh give it up, what are the odds that you will become a superstar?" But you could say the same thing about the young kids in inner city ghettos relentlessly determined to become basketball stars. This dream must be viewed in the context of their brutal lives. What if you lived in a three room apartment with ten family members of assorted generations? What if your family could afford to buy meat once a month? What if ten years of hard study for a medical degree led to a government hospital position where you could go for months at a time without a paycheck?

And then what if someone then said to you: "Hey Viktor, you run fast. You can catch a ball. You could become an American football player." I'll bet you would grasp on this thread, no matter how fragile. Perhaps it is a futile pipe dream. At least this pipe dream offers a shred of hope to an otherwise desperate life. The odds are that none of these kids will ever be seen by the mythical American recruiters. But what if one – just one of them – managed a contract to warm a bench for the Washington Redskins? Then the dream would be real. Hope would be renewed. A kid from the crumbling housing projects of Moscow could break away from the burden of history and hold the key to the new life of his choice. Hope is essential to survival. No matter how fragile the final thread of hope, it must be preserved. If these Russians dreamed of a future with an American football contract, then let them have their dream.

Then again, that was all conjecture. I have absolutely no idea what was actually motivating these players. I watched the Moscow Mustangs toss back their final shots of vodka and finish off their dried fish snacks. The players then vaulted the barrier from the stands onto the field and were ready to start the second half.

We all turned to Stephen to congratulate him for having found this amazing event in the *Moscow Times*. Please Stephen, what other marvelous sources of local entertainment do we have to look forward to? Stephen was deep in thought reading a very compelling article in the *Moscow Times*. He was oblivious to our discussion. We gave him a friendly shove and asked for him to share with us the latest. The *Moscow Times* was the primary source of news and gossip for the expatriate community. The latest restaurants, the hippest nightclubs. Heck you could even learn who...

"One of the American consultants was shot dead in his own bathtub last week," Stephen summarized in one sharp sentence.

Our mindless babble was brought to an abrupt halt. What exactly was Stephen talking about? Quickly everyone crowded around the newspaper to read for themselves. Stephen's summary was accurate. An American manager for one of the major consultancies had been found shot dead – naked in his own bathtub, in his apartment in an exclusive building in Moscow. We read further. We knew that violence surrounded us. Violence was the underlying theme of the former Soviet Union. Law and order was non-existent. Yes, we expected street violence. But being found dead with a gunshot wound to the head and naked in your own bathtub was far beyond street violence.

"Mafia connections are suspected," Stephen read aloud. Of course. We all breathed a sigh of restrained relief. Mafia connections. Street violence will stay on the street where it belongs. This young American manager (rest his soul) died of other causes – mafia connections. We nodded knowingly at each other. That manager had brought the situation upon himself. He was involved in grey market operations. He should have considered the consequences. He was American. He had been a manager with one of the Big Six firms. But that was where the connection ended. He did not deserve our sympathy. He had brought a bad taste to the whole of the American expatriate community. How dare he taint American business with mafia connections! We were here to help these people, not to perpetuate the system.

We folded the newspaper in disgust and cast it aside. The world of the *Moscow Times* article had nothing to do with us. On to more amusing matters. The third quarter of our football match was about to begin.

2 REMONT

July 1994 — Moscow, Russia

Remont. What a classic Russian concept. Linguistically the term is borrowed from the French language and literally means "repair" or "renovation". But the Russians have so completely adapted the concept into their own cultural situation that these French origins are wholly inappropriate. Early in my tour of duty in Kazakhstan I heard one of our Kazakh team members discuss the ongoing *remont* of his apartment with my friend and colleague, Maria, who is a native French speaker. Andrei paused to ensure his listener was following the full meaning of the discussion.

"You understand the term *remont*, yes?" Andrei asked Maria.

"Of course," she nodded. "It is the same as the French — to repair."

Andrei, who was university-educated and sophisticated enough to understand major conceptual differences between the languages, just laughed and shook his head. "No. The French verb implies 'to repair' or 'to renovate' as a simple project with a beginning and an end. *'Remont'* in the Russian sense, is a state of mind. A phase of your life. It does not have a definite beginning or end. And sometimes it is not even a deliberate choice. You just find yourself in a state of existence of *remont*."

Maria and I laughed and were entertained by the amusing stories of *remont* from our Russian and Kazakh team. Everyone had some anecdote to support Andrei's assertion that *remont* in the former Soviet Union was an ordeal unlike anything the Americans could possibly understand. Sasha explained that he had such difficulties attempting to secure an electrician that he had finally started to study electrical wiring himself. Andrei added that his entire apartment block was without water for over a week earlier in the year when one apartment owner decided to renovate his bathroom. Soviet-era apartment blocks were designed in complete adherence to principles of central planning, so work on one bathroom required the water to be turned off for the entire building. Kiril had rolls of new wallpaper cluttering his apartment for months while he was on a hunt to find decent wallpaper paste. He was not satisfied with anything he had seen for the last year, but was certain that with supply chains opening to the West, he might find some satisfactory materials soon.

Their message was clear — *remont* involved suffering and patience and perseverance. *Remont* was not for the weak or faint-hearted. *Remont* would test your soul and only the strong would survive. I listened to their stories and nodded agreement and sympathy. But obviously I did not fully understand. If I had truly comprehended the depth of their suffering and frustration, then I would have taken appropriate steps to avoid such a situation myself. Ah yes, I was a naive, arrogant American who, in a fit of misguided superiority, believed that my western management skills would enable me to control a renovation project much more effectively than any of the Russians I had met. The price I paid for my arrogance was that I now found myself entrenched deep in the bottom-less, murky quagmire of Russian *remont*.

Oh, the different choices we would make if we had perfect knowledge of the future implications of our foolish actions. Like all decisions, my choice of apartment and the plan to renovate had seemed sensible at the time. I was living and working in the hotel Aerostar and craved an existence where I would be able to differentiate my work life from my personal life. As a pathologically organized person, I was definitely starting to crack under the strain of living with all my worldly possessions and my cat in a small hotel room. The room was slightly larger than the double bed, with only the tiniest of clothes racks. Without room to unpack properly, I was reduced to living in a state of complete anarchy, hunting continuously through my trunks just to find a clean pair of socks. The cost of laundry at hotels is, of course, ludicrous. (I was still too new to the American corporate scene to seriously consider submitting $200 laundry bills for reimbursement on a weekly basis.) So I hand washed everything in my bathtub and strung clotheslines from the curtain rod at the window to the clothes rails near the door.

I was a corporate executive living like a refugee. A well-clothed and fed refugee, but a refugee nonetheless. My dear cat (and faithful companion) arrived a few weeks in Moscow after me. She was visibly upset about the confines of her new temporary home in my four star slum. And now I had her food dishes and litter box to contend with as well in the shoe box of a room. The effect of the squalor on my mind was debilitating.

I desperately needed serenity — a haven of my own. This craving was reinforced as I started to work on the plan for our project. Even in these early weeks I already knew that I would be traveling extensively throughout the country. The scope of work called for activities and local staff in up to thirty cities scattered throughout the country. The prospect of weekly trips to remote outposts like Tyumen, Krasnoyarsk, and Rostov filled me with excitement and anxiety. From my experience in Kazakhstan I already knew that business travel in Russia would be rough and raw. But it also could be a rewarding experience — if I had the right frame of mind.

In order to be able to approach the impending months of full immersion in Russian business development with something resembling a positive attitude, I knew that I would have to have a refuge on weekends where I could recharge and regain my strength for the week ahead. This perfectly rational thought is what started me down the slippery slope into the *remont* abyss. And of course the perverse effect of it was that my time in the four-star refugee camp of the Hotel Aerostar was extended far beyond the limits of my endurance.

I needed an apartment – a pleasant, serene apartment – and quickly. In Russia in 1994 there were precious few ways to find such a thing as an apartment. Classifieds in the newspaper were simply non-existent and formal property management companies were only in their infancy. Kazakhstan had taught me that post-Soviet landlords had only a shaky grasp of rudimentary property management and tenant relationship concepts. I would need a reliable local guide to help me navigate the urban jungle to identify and secure a suitable apartment.

Through a friend of a friend I was introduced to Andrew, who explained his profession with the brief summary that he was "in the property business." Andrew, mind you, not the Russian "Andrei". Andrew spoke English flawlessly, but not as a native speaker. Similarly I heard him negotiate in Russian effortlessly, but that was not his native tongue either. I could only make a wild guess at his ethnic origins and developed the theory that his family found its roots with some fair-skinned nationality in northern Africa or the Middle East. Idle curiosity and casual questioning provided no further illumination. Andrew's personal situation was to remain his own business.

But still the curiosity was maddening. What would drive a person to immigrate *into* Russia in the early 1990s? What sort of a situation had he left behind that Moscow was seen as an improvement over his prior existence? How did he come to have such a substantial network of contacts that he was able to run a flourishing trade in rental properties? I mentally catalogued Andrew in with those I had met in Kamchatka and Kazakhstan who certainly led dual existences. But then doesn't everyone lead a dual existence between public life and one's private life? The real question is one of degree, and in Russia everything always seemed to take on extreme proportions.

Andrew collected me from the Hotel Aerostar for a driving tour of Moscow and visits to rental properties on offer. His battered yellow Lada gasped with raspy metallic breath as it reluctantly came to life. Each crunch of the gears changing suggested that the clutch was well beyond its "use by" date. The door on the passenger side of the car swung open if he took left turns a bit too quickly.

Andrew's driving philosophy was be the aggressor or be the crushed. He carved his way through traffic, giving only a cursory nod to traffic signals. "Suggestions, not rules" he noted quietly to me, while I held onto the door in a silent gesture of self-preservation. He would make aggressive hook turns onto Sadovoye Koltso – a style of turn where to turn left onto a street, the driver first turns right, then makes a violent U turn to cut in front of the traffic waiting at the light on the cross street. Lawyers and safety regulations ensures that nothing of the sort exists in the United States. In Moscow, however, the hook turn was standard practice. As much as I enjoy driving, I was happy being simply a passenger on the aggressive chaotic streets of Moscow.

Occasionally the GAI would wave their batons at the car, and Andrew would be pulled over for a traffic stop. Of course the stop had nothing to do with any actual traffic violation, but more an opportunity for the GAI to demand a bit of cash as a fine. I had barely even been aware of the GAI in Kazakhstan, and now I fully understood my Kazakh driver's assertions about the benefits of a nicer car. The dilapidated Ladas were pulled over by the GAI. The shiny black Mercedes and Volgas of the elite were even more aggressive with their blatant disregard of traffic lights, curbs, center lines, speed limits – but were quickly waved on. You never could tell who would be in the back seat of such a vehicle and the GAI did not want to find out. With the rusted Lada, however, one could easily demand a cash fine on the spot – for whatever infringement the officer devised. No actual physical ticket. No recourse available. A protest would result in a higher fine. And definitely the American would have to keep her mouth closed. Foreigners have deeper pockets – so the fines would be higher.

So I would sit in silence and frustration as Andrew paid a "fine" to the GAI for some invented infraction. The transaction would be quick and quiet and only a few thousand rubles would trade hands (only a few dollars). Andrew would keep the words to a minimum. The transaction would be complete in under a minute. I was furious about the lack of justice. Who could we protest to? But of course there was no one. If the police themselves are the ones stopping people randomly and asking for money, then who do you appeal to?

After a dizzying spin through the twisting backstreets of Moscow, I was completely disoriented to our location but relieved to be stepping out of the car onto solid ground.

How to accurately describe apartment-hunting in Moscow in the early 1990s? Think of your worst stereotypes of public housing urban decay. Ensure that the apartment blocks in your mental image are thoroughly unattractive and identical. The architect's mandate was one of expediency rather than beauty or function. Roughen this picture with dirt, grime, decaying rubbish, crumbling concrete, and collapsing balconies. The only exterior colors are concrete grey and muddy brown/black. No other colors at all, not even a splash of colorful graffiti or a plot of grass. Just dirt and concrete.

This was Soviet-era housing in Moscow. Seventy five years of communism and state provided infrastructure resulted in the creation of an endless ghetto of decayed public housing. There were a few dramatic exceptions from the exterior, like the bombastic forms of the seven Stalin buildings – built at the peak of the Stalinist era to promote a visual image of power and strength. A few samples of 19th century architecture survived the ravages of the Communist era as well, but these are the exception rather than the rule in Moscow. In general the back neighborhood streets of Moscow were filled with block after block after block of decaying concrete jungle.

One advantage of Moscow's public housing over the United States in 1994 was the apparent absence of drugs or gang violence. Rats scampered down dimly lit hallways and years of dirt on the concrete floors ground grittily under my feet, but at least there were no discarded needles, graffiti, or other alarming indications of drug-related activity. Cockroaches and rats would take a bit to get used to, but they were far more appealing neighbors to me than street gangs.

Okay, I just said that I would be able to live with cockroaches and rats. I knew that both were permanent fixtures of Moscow life. Then there is a small matter of degree. The first apartment Andrew showed me had a large family of cockroaches swarming on the kitchen wall directly over the stove, in full daylight. The landlord was not flustered in the least by this. He stirred a pot of potatoes simmering on the stove and then left the pot to escort us around the apartment. I restrained a compulsive urge to find a lid for the pot to prevent additional bits of meat from being added to his stew. I may have to accept cockroaches in my apartment, but I had to draw the line on cohabitating with colonies of insects that showed no fear of humans.

Now, I would like to believe that I was not being overly fussy. Perhaps I was. Every apartment Andrew showed me that week had some absolutely fatal issue that I could not get beyond. One landlord said that the second bedroom would remain locked – he would retain the key because he needed to use the room for storage. Did he intend on coming in and out while I was living there? Of course! It was his apartment! I had to pass.

At another apartment, a couple greeted us enthusiastically at the door and said that they had recently completed their renovation and they hoped I would like it. The tiny living room had been converted into an outrageous replica of a salon from the Winter Palace. The room was white with elaborate plaster cornices and gold gilding and even a massive chandelier that swung dangerously low in the center of the room. The bedroom had no windows and the walls were painted all black, with mirrors on the ceiling. The setting was completed with fluffy pink shag carpeting throughout the entire apartment. The couple was beaming with pride at their handiwork. I was stupefied into silence.

Most of the apartments we visited, however, were completely unrenovated and in their natural state of total disrepair. Brown linoleum bubbled up on the floor, sheets of slimy brown and green wallpaper hung limply on the walls, the plumbing in the bathroom was completely rusted through and shook violently as I tested it. And everywhere the floor plans demonstrated a criminal carelessness on behalf of the architect.

Typically the main bedroom was placed into an alcove of the living room, in a window-less corner, or in a line with the second bedroom to the bathroom. Privacy was not possible in any of these apartments. Just let me have a bedroom where the door closes and guests can have their own space and we can all use the restroom without trotting through each other's bedrooms! But that seemed to be an unreasonable request.

In June 1994 the influx of western consultants was in high gear. The demand for housing sent the market into an insane spiral upwards. The apartments I was looking at were offered at about $1500 per month – complete with cockroaches, gas stoves that were blackened from minor explosions, and gritty brown linoleum floors. After $2000 per month, the kitchens started to be a bit cleaner and the bathrooms a bit less alarming. $2500 could buy you a fully renovated and furnished apartment, complete with polished floorboards and freshly painted white walls. For $3000 per month there would even be stainless steel German appliances.

I sighed and looked longingly at an apartment that was nearly double my budget. Spacious, serene, a wonderful big bathtub that just beckoned me to soak in it. I fanta-sized about snuggling up in my own private oasis during the heart of winter. But it was not to be. My budget was around $1500 per month. The decor at that price range was strictly orange, brown and green – and various combinations thereof. The floors were painted or crusty linoleum, and ratty carpets were hung on the walls.

This was Russia. This was the way Russians lived. I was working in Russia on a US government-sponsored privatization and aid program, so shouldn't I live like the Russians as well? How deep into the local culture was I willing and able to go? It is so politically correct to state the very naive declaration that you are going to immerse yourself fully in the local way of life and "live like a native." But really everyone chooses their own comfort level and no one truly goes native – at least not while you are expected to achieve western business standards during the day.

No American expatriate, no matter how devoted to the idea of "going native" would seriously consider living with eleven relatives in a two room apartment. You would not spend two hours or more each day hunting through the street markets to find fresh bread, vegetables, and dried meat to take home. And, most critically, your salary would certainly be higher than the Moscow standard of $100 per month. Why would an American expatriate live in a typical Russian apartment? The Russians did not live in a state of squalor voluntarily – the fact that everyone was in some stage of *remont* attested to this.

The Russians, like most people, craved to improve their living conditions as their income allowed. With a clear conscience, I could not say that I was intending to live like a Russian. To state that would be hypocritical. We had charmed lives in comparison to the Russians. I could not possibly conceive of what life would be like as a young Russian woman in Moscow in 1994. Therefore I concluded that the intellectually honest path forward would be to face this fact openly. I am American – I need an environment at home that will keep me comfortable.

But realistically as much as I knew I was not Russian, I also knew that I was not an American of the breed that has their homes photographed for *Architectural Digest*. Besides, the cool sleek glamour of spa baths and marble counter tops felt incongruous with the world of near anarchy that was just outside the front door. It was one thing to need a refuge to gain some breathing space and recovery time, but an entirely different matter to seal off any acknowledgement that I was in Russia at all.

I would be working squarely in the middle between American management and Russian bureaucracy. Therefore, I concluded, I should live somewhere between *Architectural Digest* and a roach haven. Rather general guidelines. I continued my apartment quest with the confidence that suitable basic accommodation was a reasonable request.

Next Andrew showed me a two bedroom apartment that was in the midst of renovation. Not some strange Russian interpretation of renovation, but the mastermind behind the plan must have had some western influence. The walls had been freshly plastered and were painted white. The kitchen featured fresh cabinets that looked suspiciously like they had been procured from Ikea. A box of dark blue slate tiles was stacked next to new ceramic fixtures and fittings that were awaiting installation in the bathroom.

This apartment was perfect – nearly. Of everything I had seen so far, I was most tempted into the possibility of leasing this apartment under renovation. Every room featured a wonderful airy balcony overlooking a courtyard. One fatal flaw paused my enthusiasm: The apartment was on the first floor of the apartment building. The tenant would have access to this wonderful balcony from the apartment, but so would every petty criminal in Moscow. Moscow was already dangerous enough for foreigners. I did not need to deliberately make it easier for criminal elements to find me.

Still, the property was beautiful and in my price range. I stalled and wavered and enjoyed fantasizing what life here would be like – minus the easy access from the balcony, of course. Andrew was clearly tiring of escorting this fussy American around Moscow. Once he saw that I was vaguely interested, he started lobbying me to lease the apartment.

The renovation would be finished in a week or two, so I should be able to move in quickly. How did he know that the work would be finished so quickly? I asked, a bit dubious, looking at all the bathroom fixtures and fittings that were still to be assembled. Andrew explained that he was serving as the general contractor for the renovation and therefore he had total confidence that it would be completed in a timely manner. So wait – Andrew had the connections and abilities to be a general contractor for a renovation? I suddenly grasped the implications of this statement. I could do the city of Moscow a favor by providing American financing for the improvement of at least one apartment. The world could be a better place for everyone.

Andrei's voice echoed in the back of my mind, warning me that his family had been in the midst of *remont* for over ten years. But certainly I would be able to avoid such a debacle. Here was evidence before my own eyes that a general contractor could manage a *remont* project successfully. My eyes skimmed over the materials piled in the hallway awaiting installation in the bathroom and focused on the kitchen that was pristine and inviting. Andrew obviously had the connections to accomplish all this — he seemed to be a relatively honest and reliable person —therefore, why not?

I was enthralled by the dreamy vision of a private sanctuary in the midst of the chaos of Russia and pressed the urgent whispers from Andrei out of my mind. A haunting voice scolded me *"nyet! nyet! nyet!"*. If I knew what was best for me then I would say *nyet* to renovation. But then I turned my back on Andrei's scolding. I decided to interpret *"nyet"* to be an opinion rather than a definitive statement. I would do as I pleased.

A suitable apartment for renovation was identified shortly thereafter. All the fundamentals for the apartment were quite positive: The entrance to the building was reasonably clean, without any visible signs of rats. The apartment had a practical floor plan and closet space — a big plus. The location was sensational — just a few steps away from the pleasant pedestrian walking street of the Old Arbat and three different stops on the wonderful Moscow subway. With a bit of imagination, I could claim to have a "view". If I stood at the far left edge of my balcony and leaned out, I could see the white and gold bell tower of the Kremlin framed perfectly between two crumbling Soviet era apartment towers.

The best feature of the apartment was, however, the landlord, Dmitri. He appeared to be a very docile man who accepted all the terms I proposed for the lease. The terms of my expatriate allowance covered rent only, but with a bit of creativity I was able to negotiate a mutually beneficial agreement with Dmitri to rent the apartment, amortize the cost of renovation, and purchase furnishings all for a total of $1500 per month. I gained a cozy apartment fully furnished and he received the benefits and income of a renovated flat.

In its raw state, the apartment certainly was not a pretty sight to the American eye. The green, brown and orange floral wallpaper was tumbling off the walls in large slimy strips. Under the wallpaper, newspapers from the 1960s were the next layer, providing an interesting archeological discovery. In places the newspapers were peeling off as well, revealing crumbling plaster. Beneath the plaster was a metal grid. I reached out to poke the exposed metal out of curiosity — but the landlord and Andrew barked at me quickly in alarm to stop. The grid was apparently crossed with the live electrical wiring in the apartment and I would have received a 220v reminder that safety standards in Russia are a bit behind those in the United States.

I looked around the apartment and smiled. Yes, the walls were alarming, but that just required stripping and plastering. The big project would be to gut the bathroom, but besides that the work was all cosmetic. The kitchen cabinets were holding together reasonably well and actually only needed a solid cleaning. A new stove and fridge were essential, but Andrew assured me he could easily secure new Russian appliances of reasonable quality for less than $100 each. New doors would be fitted for all the rooms and closets and the parquet floors had to be sanded and sealed. I looked around the apartment and considered myself to be incredibly fortunate at the find. And for furnishings? I should be able to order what I needed from Ikea.

I bounced into our office-conference rooms at the Hotel Aerostar the next day bubbling with excitement about my new apartment. The Russian staff were thoroughly impressed by the location and the layout of my apartment as I described it. They were a bit more skeptical, however, when I outlined my scope for *remont*. They exchanged knowing smiles and rolled their eyes when I stated that I would be moving into my new apartment in four weeks' time. Did Andrew have a source for all the necessary materials? Did he have reliable subcontractors? Did he have other clients that would distract him? Why did I believe him when he said it would be ready for move in after only four weeks?

Of course, the Russians could see what would happen next while I was happily riding a blissful wave of naïve optimism.

The first setback was procuring furniture. No, Ikea had not yet arrived in Moscow, I had simply assumed that Andrew would be able to help me place an order for Ikea furniture to be delivered from Sweden to me in Moscow. This was the first of many lessons that absolutely *nothing* should be assumed.

Andrew was able to put an Ikea catalogue in my hands, together with the fax number in Sweden where orders could be placed. He warned me, however, that if I placed the order this way that the total value of my purchase would be subject to an import duty of at least 65%, plus shipping costs and additional taxes and fees. Sixty five percent import duty! Although the country was more open than under the Soviet period, this still was prohibitively high for most people to buy anything other than the Russian-made Salvation-army style furniture. If I wanted imported furniture, after taxes and shipping I would pay at least double the price of what was presented in the catalogue. My heart sank. The dream of a fresh new bed with clean Scandinavian design was slipping from my reach. I was facing the prospect of scavenging for Russian furniture.

But of course, for every problem there are alternate solutions. And in the case of import duty, the alternate answer was found with diplomatic privilege. Through the expat network I met Alex, an American about my age working in the Moscow US Embassy. Although his passport read that he was American, his parents were Russian and he had definitely been born and raised with the Russian attitude that *nyet* was just an opinion, not a binding restriction. My order was placed under Alex's name and with his diplomatic privilege the import duty was waived – and the cost of the furniture once again became a bit more reasonable.

Although Alex's diplomatic privilege could help me with the furniture, for the renovations, however, I was completely dependent upon Andrew.

The day after the lease was signed, Andrew retrieved me from the Hotel Aerostar and compelled me to draw up more firm specifications for the scope of work. What about security? The front door of the building did not lock. This was true for 99% of the buildings in Russia at the time, so I had not included this in my selection criteria. However, as anyone could walk in off the street and up to my apartment on the eleventh floor, I really needed to replace the thin wood panel with a steel door and frame. Good security is essential – especially for foreigners, Andrew coached me. He then asked if I had heard about the American consultant who had been assassinated in his own bathtub. Cripes news travels fast. Okay, valid point. Let's include an improved steel door and frame.

Then what about the floor in the kitchen? The linoleum there is coming up in massive patches and is a hazard. And what about the position of the stove in the kitchen? If the gas fittings were moved just a few feet, then the layout of the kitchen would be significantly more convenient. And this is how the scope for projects starts to creep up. Every addition is just a minor bit of work. But it is additional procurement, additional subcontractors, additional scheduling, additional time and additional budget. I was digging my own grave, one spoonful of sand at a time.

Andrew insisted that I accompany him on every expedition in search of bathroom tiles, a stove and refrigerator, paint and plaster, doors and door handles, a bathtub and sink and related fittings. In the United States can any homeowner honestly imagine undertaking a serious renovation project without Home Depot being there to provide assistance at every step of the way? What if the Yellow Pages didn't exist? (This was before all the modern miracles of the internet.) How would you know where to find plumbing supplies, plaster, or that difficult odd sized door for the hall closet? And when you finally tracked down these elusive shops, what if they were only open 10 am to 4pm Monday through Friday and located in scattered points throughout the city so that each trip required at least three hours' absence from work? Finally, what if each home improvement supply shop were about the size of your typical 7-11 in the United States and the dusty shelves featured battered unlabeled boxes of random sizes? Oh the things we take for granted.

Yes, in the United States we are blessed or cursed with choice, depending on your perspective. Years ago in Moscow, my life was much simpler when I surveyed the three choices for floor tiles in the bathroom – white with orange flowers, green with a brown cross hatch, or gray. Of course I had to go with the gray. Anything but the continuous bombardment of green, orange, and brown! With tiles now safely in the trunk of the car, Andrew was ready to take me across town to a place that sold bathroom fittings and fixtures. I, however, had already been missing from the office for nearly two hours and only had the tiles to show for it. The bathroom fittings would have to wait for another day.

The route back to the Hotel Aerostar passed near my apartment, so we paused to drop off the tiles and check on the work in progress. We were greeted at the door by a hulk of a man covered in dust and holding a sledgehammer. I instinctively took a step backwards, but Andrew stepped forward through the doorway then greeted the man as an old friend.

"Phaedra, let me introduce Igor. He helps me with managing the subcontractors as needed."

With a grunt and a nod, Igor brushed off the grime then took my hand in his large paw, only once I had stepped into the apartment. Bad karma to shake hands across the threshold. It was not difficult to imagine that Igor could be a very compelling general manager, although his methods would probably not be endorsed by American business schools.

I looked around the apartment in disbelief. Two weeks into the four week job I found the apartment in just about the same condition as the day I leased it – with one notable exception: the parquet floors had been sanded and sealed. I had never undertaken a renovation project before in my life but at least I knew the very basic principle that the floors are always the last to be completed.

"Why! Why! Why!" I demanded of Andrew. "The floors are beautiful now, but will certainly be demolished when the walls are stripped, plastered, and painted!"

Andrew just shrugged. "The guys were the best floor sanders and polishers around. I already had them arranged to do the other apartment, so I had them do the work here while they were available."

Yes, the floors were spectacular, but I already knew that I would never see them in this virginal condition again. I was in agony at the futility of the situation.

"Don't worry. Igor is chasing down the other subcontractors," Andrew gestured to the goliath who was now carrying the sledgehammer to the bathroom, presumably to commence his demolition work.

My gaze darted from the sledgehammer to the beautiful floors and I let out an involuntary sigh. Here in Russia the rule was crush or be crushed. The GAI would carefully select who they would extract the fines from. Igor would be a very convincing foreman of the subcontractors. The lesson here was that I would have to learn how to pick and choose my arguments.

This was week two and my Russian *remont* experience was only beginning.

3 CHISTIYE PRUDI

July 1994 — Moscow, Russia

While I was battling the *remont* dramas at my apartment, Robert was suffering a parallel torture. The firm had just concluded contracts to manage four massive projects for USAID. The total budget for these projects probably approached $30 million. Additional project managers were arriving from the United States to assist. Hiring of a local Russian team was moving into high gear. Our conference rooms at the Hotel Aerostar were bursting at the seams. Robert had identified suitable permanent accommodation for our group in the Chistiye Prudi area of Moscow. The move was long overdue and he carried a haggard grimace from the continuous barrage of abuse he was receiving from the American managers. The reason for the delays, of course, was that the office space was undergoing *remont*.

Apparently August 10 was the magic date. Andrew had cited this date to me as the point I could plan to move into my apartment. In his parallel world, Robert had been given the same date for when the office space would be ready for occupancy. A quiet office pool started among the Russians, placing wagers on which project would be finished first and what the actual move-in date would be. All the Russians chose dates in late September and October. I was a bit more optimistic and selected a date in early September.

Nikolai, who was running the pool, took my rubles and shook his head with a half smile. "*Devushka*, you have so much to learn."

None of us, with the exception of Robert as the office manager, had actually seen the office space at Chistiye Prudi. Nikolai was so smug with his confidence that the move in date would be no earlier than October, that I desperately wanted him to be proven wrong. I decided to make an inspection of the construction site myself. The nominal reason for the visit was to ensure the fit out for my project area would be appropriate for my team's requirements. But in reality, of course, I had to see if there was any possibility I would win the office pool or at least prepare myself for the chiding I would get from Nikolai if we did, in fact, move in October.

The fastest way to travel from the Hotel Aerostar to Chistiye Prudi is on the Moscow Metro. So far in my narrative, I know I have lodged complaint after complaint about the state of Soviet-era buildings and the quality of the infrastructure. I must, however, offer nothing but praise and admiration for the Moscow Metro. In the midst of a sea of catastrophic architecture and complete absence of quality standards, the Metro shines a ray of hope that all Russian construction projects are not doomed from the start. The subway system is a monument of impressive design and engineering, function, and breathtaking beauty.

The Moscow Metro is one of the most-used subway systems in the world – second only to Tokyo. Close to seven million passengers travel daily throughout the system in one continuous flow of humanity. The process is a bit intimidating to the novice, but even the Americans who cannot read Russian found themselves appreciating the network very quickly. A subway token when I first arrived was 100 rubles, or about five cents. This plastic token gave me entrance through the man-eating gates and into the bowels of the system for as far as I wanted to travel.

The sea of humanity crushes forward through the toll gates into the station. The loud grinding engine of the escalators beats a deafening rhythm – even over the stampede of the masses. The escalator moves at an astonishing rate, scooping up *babushki,* pensioners, gypsies, *devushki,* and anyone else in its path and carries them downwards at a speed more akin to a controlled crash than a leisurely escalator ride. At the bottom you must move quickly out of the way. Any hesitation will result in five, ten, fifteen people rapidly being deposited unceremoniously on top of you – thrashing and cursing at those stupid enough to pause at the bottom of the escalator.

But it is natural to pause at the foot of the escalator, especially in the inner city stations. On the streets of Moscow in 1994, virtually every modern building was a grey concrete box. Some were short grey concrete squares and some a bit taller, thinner grey concrete towers, but the theme remained definitely the same. Soviet era architects lacked creativity or at least the freedom to express their creativity. The Metro system, however, was one of the very few public venues where the artists and architects were unleashed – just a bit – to enable them to create a living, functional gallery of design and sculpture.

Each station is a unique artistic achievement. Graceful arches, soaring ceilings, indulgent chandeliers – and stunning displays of Soviet realist art. My favorite is Ploschad Revolutsii – Revolution Square – in the center of the city. This station features massive bombastic sculptures glorifying the great heroes of the Soviet Revolution. Industrial workers striding forward carrying hammers. Strong young peasant women gracefully carrying armfuls of wheat. Men bent over anvils absorbed in their work. It represents the epitome of Soviet realist art – strong, healthy proletariats and peasants united in building the future of the nation. The faces of the sculptures resonate with strength and youthful vigor and utter dedication to the industrial or agricultural tasks that they are engrossed in.

At the feet of these grand figures, the huddled masses of Muscovites swarm through the station platform without a glance at the statues. Looking at the reality of modern Russia, I had to wonder if such glorious handsome dedicated figures ever existed at any time in the history of the Soviet Union. Such people certainly did not exist in 1994.

In modern reality, the battle-weary figures scuttled through the station and crowded to the edge of the platforms. *Babushki* were hunched over carrying plastic bags of vegetables scavenged from somewhere. The men were uniformly grey and brown – the clothing may have started out more vibrant colors, but after years of exposure to the thick sludge of the Moscow air and washing by hand in sinks, all clothing had become the same dusty color. Faces reflected the hard years of pain endured so far – Stalinist era torment, struggle for survival during the siege on Moscow in Great Patriotic War, years of deprivation, years of fear to speak one's mind. Eyes were stoic and weary with the world. Never a smile or a casual friendly glance. It is safer to keep opinions to oneself and not offer any gesture that would be distinguished a crowd. The tortured history of the nation was written on every older face.

At the end of every platform was a large digital display that ticked off the time since the previous train passed through. So much could be criticized about Soviet design, architecture and technology, but the efficiency of the Moscow subway was completely beyond reproach. Once on the platform, all faces instinctively turned to the digital timer. Only thirty seconds after the previous train has left the station, all eyes started to scour the tunnel for signs of an incoming train. At one minute the crowds began to get restless. At two minutes there were grumblings in the crowd as *babushki* muttered that this was yet another sign that the country was falling to pieces ever since the firm leadership of Communism was ousted. If a train had not arrived in four minutes, the platform became outright dangerous, as the throngs of passengers continued to be discharged from the churning escalator into the subterranean holding pen. Fortunately the train usually arrived after about two and a half minutes – the throngs pushed forward into the antique subway cars and we were swept away into the labyrinth of the Metro.

When I exited from the Chistiye Prudi station the first time, I had to laugh. Wary eyes darted in my direction. Clearly she was a foreigner, smiling in public and (most outrageously) laughing on her own, for no obvious reason.

"So this is Chistiye Prudi", I nearly exclaimed.

In Russian the phrase means "clean ponds". This name was as misleading as the statues in the Ploschad Revolutsii station. The typical citizen was certainly not strong, healthy and enthusiastically building the great industrial future. Similarly, Chistiye Prudi featured two murky algae-infested puddles in the traffic median in the middle of a boulevard. Discarded vodka bottles littered the edge of the puddle and a foul stench of decay thickened the air. It was a stretch to call even call these features "ponds" and they certainly were not "clean." The great Russian propaganda machine lives on.

I found our new office space relatively quickly. With great satisfaction I noted that we would be only steps away from the Metro station. A wonderful convenience for everyone, especially the future staff that I was recruiting. Private cars were very rare among typical Russians and certainly no one would consider the luxury of driving to work. In addition, I had never seen either a parking lot or a gas station.

Immediately I was charmed by our new building. It was a classic period structure from the mid-19th century, complete with soaring arched windows and an exterior that was aging gracefully rather than crumbling to bits. The interior, however, was more akin to a bomb site than office accommodation. The interior was an open cavern of stone and rubble and not much else. No signs of electrical wiring, flooring, or telephones. In the United States this would be a "hard hat only" zone, restricted to all but official construction personnel. In Moscow I was simply able to state that I was a representative of the firm commissioning the building works and I was waved into the site without a second question.

I picked my way over chunks of plaster and rubble and consulted the floor diagram sketch provided by the office manager. Cubicles. Well, why not. If we were going to impose American business standards on our Russian project team, we had might as well take the approach to its logical conclusion. What more fitting demonstration of the American management's mindset than to take a gorgeous gem of nineteenth century Russian architecture – gut it and insert a rabbit warren of identical sea foam colored cubicles with ergonomic chairs. It would soon be an interesting social experiment to see what would happen when we introduced our Russian staff to this controlled and color coordinated environment.

That introduction would have to wait a while longer. Apparently the demolition work was nearing completion here at Chistiye Prudi, but I could not see any evidence that the construction crews had yet started their work. This was mid-July. The August 10 deadline would certainly breeze by. But surely the work would be completed by my guess of 10 September? I had 1,000 rubles riding on the outcome. Okay, that was less than one dollar, but I had my reputation to consider.

When I returned to the office, Nikolai and the other Russian staff plied me with questions about the office space. How close was the building to the Metro? Was there a market nearby to pick up meat and potatoes for dinner? Would there be a kitchen where everyone could cook their lunch? And, most critically, what was the state of the *remont*? When I relayed that the demolition was apparently nearing completion, but no actually construction works had started, they exchanged meaningful glances and winks. Nikolai had my 1,000 rubles. With a wink he told me to call him "Kolya" – the informal nickname for Nikolai. He smiled and said that I would be held to my statement of 10 September. The moment of truth, however, was still nearly two months away.

Renovations of office space and cubicles were not the only indicator that my consultancy was serious about a professional work environment for the team. We also were to have access to the latest modern invention – "electronic mail." We were advised by the DC-based team that we needed to adopt this new tool to stay in touch with the home office. No one on the team, not even the Americans, had sent an electronic mail message before and we had no idea how to get started. We had no formal IT support team of our own, so one day Robert organized an external technical consultancy to come in and meet with us and get us going.

Our "electronic mail" introduction was led by a Russian consultant, Vladimir, with his American colleague, Sarah, looking on. Although our office space was modern in comparison to what I had seen in Kazakhstan, we still were well short of all the things we take for granted today – projectors, white boards, even flip charts. Therefore the Americans and Russians in our office huddled around Vladimir as he sketched in a notebook and attempted to explain the process of sending an electronic letter. His narrative was in Russian. Kolya, as the official team interpreter, attempted to translate for Robert and my project director, Raymond.

"Every computer has a unique Internet Protocol address. The address is created by the internet service provider at the time of connection. The connection occurs through a dial up from a modem through a telephone line to the internet service provider. The computer requires an email client software. An account on the POP server is also necessary. From there the message is relayed via routers…"

Kolya was doing his best to translate Vladimir's explanation of networking, the internet, and electronic mail. To him (and the rest of us) this was simply gibberish. Raymond, who had never even used a computer before in his life, was completely baffled. He eventually just stood up and turned to me and said that he was trusting that I would sort out how to send an "electronic letter" – clearly his generation was never intended to use such complex technology.

Certainly we did not need to have a sophisticated understanding of the foundation technology that made electronic mail work. I had heard rumors that this e-mail thing was easy to use and a great convenience, but now I was concerned. The Russian team was just becoming familiar with the whole concept of a mouse and keyboard. We really did not have the time or capacity to train everyone (myself included) on what a POP server was and how to connect to one. I turned to Vladimir's American counterpart, Sarah, and pleaded for her to help simplify the explanation.

Sarah popped open her own laptop on a table and demonstrated how to take a telephone cable from a phone and connect this to the modem. She showed how she established a dial up connection and then opened an email application – Microsoft Mail. She typed in a simple address in the "to" line like *Michael@consultant.com*, typed a quick "hello" and hit the send button. That was all there was to it. She would help us get the necessary people in the office signed up with an ISP and ensure we all received email addresses. She would also help us learn how to do the dial up process and ensure we had the list of dial up numbers. (Every city in Russia had a different dial up number, when travelling I would need to carry the list of numbers with me.) No, we did not need to know the technical background of how electronic mail actually worked.

I thanked Sarah profusely. In one step, she had helped me and my team leap into the modern technical age. In addition, just watching her and Vladimir's different styles with the same request for training gave me greater appreciation of the benefits that our project and American advisors could provide to the country. Where Vladimir was completely absorbed by the technology of *how* electronic mail worked, Sarah was truly client oriented and understood that we just needed to know how to use it.

Sarah was curious about our project and probed me with questions. With excitement I outlined the project to her. She had been in the country for at least two years already. Now I had a trusted friend and advisor to help me navigate the wilderness ahead.

When I was done with my narrative, Sarah smiled and shook her head with consolation. I had so much to learn. Yes, I was quite right to expect challenges in working with the Russian government counterparts, but had I really digested some of the other key points of our project? Namely we were expected to procure computer equipment and modernize the operations of offices across twelve cities in Russia. Did I really know what I was in for?

For starters, did I really understand the basic fact that USAID would not reimburse my company for any taxes or duties, yet the Russian government would be assessing a 40% import tax on all computer equipment brought into the country? Sourcing computer equipment in Russia was against USAID procurement rules, but paying the import duties also was not allowed. If we strictly followed the laws of both the Russian government and the US government, we would essentially be losing money with each computer that would be procured for the project. The consultancies were paid on the basis of cost plus a defined (small) margin for profit. What would make or break the profitability for any project was whether the expenses incurred could be reimbursed. And all that senior management back in Washington DC would be interested in was the bottom line of the project.

My heart sank and I fell into a depressed silence. Sarah smiled said that she had already been through the cruel hazing process of USAID procurement herself. For every rule there is always an alternate solution. It would just require a bit of creativity and nerves. She would be available to be a listening ear when I needed to vent my frustration to someone in the months ahead.

With this kind statement of support and encouragement, Sarah became my new best friend.

Before I was going to start the ordeal of USAID procurement, however I had to first hire staff for my project team. At this point I must say a few words about my Project Director and the project itself. Raymond was a retired partner with the firm. He had been enticed out of retirement to come to work in Moscow as the senior executive for the firm's USAID program office in Moscow. I learned that Raymond actually was accepted into the firm's partnership the year I was born. This gives you a sense not only of the age difference, but also the significant additional experience he had both with the firm and the ways of the "real" world. It was more than a bit intimidating to be hired as the right hand for such a senior level executive.

Our work relationship could have gone down two different paths. As a young kid fresh out of graduate school working with a senior executive, I could have either been treated as a glorified administrative assistant or as a true second in command with responsibilities far beyond my years. I will be eternally grateful to Raymond that he was inclined towards the second sort of approach. Although nearly forty years separated us in age, our relationship quickly developed into the most satisfying relationship I have ever had with a senior manager. Since Raymond and I parted ways, I have been eagerly looking forward to the next time I can work with an experienced retiree.

Raymond really was the best manager imaginable for the tumultuous scene of USAID privatization projects. He brought with him all the experience of over forty years of client service, but none of the psychological baggage of the aspiring partner that still has his eye on the next rung of the corporate ladder. He had already accomplished everything he had set out to do in his career and was now therefore in Moscow only for the sheer enjoyment of a challenge and the satisfaction that he could offer something constructive to Russia during this chaotic time. The firm's core motto of client service was "Think Straight, Talk Straight." For Raymond, this was not just a saying, but deeply embedded into the way he lived and worked. No political games – just direct to the point about what was on his mind.

Raymond was thrilled to have an over-excited young kid willing to handle the operations of the project. He had brought his wife, Rita, with him to Moscow and was determined to enjoy his retirement. He therefore was only too pleased to let me seize as much responsibility as I could possibly handle. Then when we found ourselves entangled in some political mess, he would ferociously defend me and the project team as needed at the highest levels of the Russian Privatization Center or USAID. We were all one team in his eyes. He did not play political games and he had no tolerance for those who attempted to do so.

Raymond's enlightened management approach was novel enough among the American managers. To the Russians, accustomed to their long-standing tradition of authoritarian control and central planning, he was a completely new species of animal.

Our project consisted of three primary components. First was a mandate to establish the local operations of the Russian Privatization Center in twelve cities (four regions of three cities each) across the country. This would involve basic logistics of renting office space, hiring staff, and providing computer equipment. Second, we were to send one long term American advisor to each regional center to teach the local Russian teams the basics of business consulting as well as to help coordinate other advisory and foreign investment outreach programs in the region. The third component then was to build a national database that would contain profiles of all the recently-privatized companies. The objective of this database was to enable foreign companies to identify potential Russian business partners. The work on this database would cover not only the twelve cities where we would be establishing local offices of the Russian Privatization Center, but ten additional cities where other consulting firms had been employed for a parallel support and advisory role. Although the Local Privatization Centers would start off as government entities that were fully funded by aid programs such as USAID, the objective was to establish consultancies that would eventually be able to offer their services for a fee and become self-sustaining private entities.

The work statement that was issued by USAID to describe these three activities was less than two pages long. It was up to Raymond and me to define the details in cooperation with the Russian Privatization Center. Nine million dollars was allocated for the project. We would be reimbursed for every expense to set up and operate the Local Privatization Centers – with the exception of any import duties, VAT, or other taxes which (USAID assured us) we were not legally obliged to pay.

Raymond took on the management of the business advisory services as well as the overall strategic direction of the project. I assumed the responsibility of managing the launch of the regional operations as well as the design and implementation of the database. Never mind that I had never designed or delivered a database before or set up office operations anywhere in the United States, needless to say across twelve cities in Russia – I would figure it all out somehow, with Raymond as my coach and mentor along the way.

I earnestly believed in the theory of the project. I was convinced that it would result in a significant step forward for Russian privatized companies. We would be providing

American management consultants to the firms to help them write business plans, develop product ideas, approach foreign markets, and attract foreign investors. The public access database was absolutely essential, as foreign companies had no organized way to identify potential Russian business partners. Although the centers would start off as wholly government funded entities, the goal was to establish a direction where they could be self-sustaining and eventually private. We were at the leading edge of post-privatization business transformation in Russia. Or, at least that is how we viewed ourselves.

The execution of the project, of course, would require significantly more staff than just Raymond and myself. Raymond undertook the recruitment of the American business advisors and I set about the daunting task of identifying and recruiting Russian staff for the project. The first task was to fill out our Moscow team with some accountants, administrative assistants, and an interpreter. After that, I would launch into the massive task of opening the privatization center operations in twelve cities and hiring data collectors in twenty one cities. As my project plan took shape, I found myself scheduling at least three days of traveling each week. I had not yet stepped on a domestic Aeroflot flight and already I longed for the promised refuge in my own apartment.

The process of hiring Russian staff in Moscow in 1994 for an American company was an educational experience, to say the least. Educational for the Americans as well as the Russians. I was pleased to learn that our consultancy intended to follow Russian employment laws – a huge improvement over my days in Kazakhstan handing out envelopes of cash and trying to be below the radar of the local authorities. Where our HR coordinator, Gloria, found all the candidates, I still don't know, but quickly I found myself submerged beneath a stack of applications for employment.

I say "employment applications" only for lack of a better term. The documents I received could not really be called that in an American sense. In fact, only the barest useful information was available on each candidate. The rest of the document was usually filled with data that had no relevance to the role and more often than not would have only provided fodder for a discrimination lawsuit in the United States.

"Natasha Dmitrieeva Afansayeva – 26 years old, married, two children, nationality: Georgian, secretarial experience – two years."

"Oksana Mikhailevna Radchenko – 24 years old, single, nationality: Ukrainian, secretarial experience – three years, driver's license, fluent in Russian, Ukrainian and English."

"Ekaterina Vasilievna Manzyukova – 26 years old, divorced, one child, nationality: Russian, secretarial experience – four years."

I shuffled through the papers and concluded that I would learn just about nothing from the employment applications. No review of skills or education. No identification of key strengths or career interests. In short, no evidence that any of these women had previous exposure to a western business environment or an understanding of what would be expected of them. Without any reasonable way to filter the employment applications, I was facing the prospect of inviting in a stampede of hopefuls for a few serious days of interviews and screening. With any luck I would be able to find some quality amongst the quantity.

Another small source of applicants was available as well through the other project teams. One of the projects had hired a few typists on a temporary basis to compile a massive report for the Ministry of Finance. This rush job was now reaching completion so I was encouraged to screen the temporary clerks. This prospect was less daunting than the possibility of facing a screening of twenty or more applicants, so, of course, I started my recruiting drive with the internal applicants.

The first woman I talked to was Tatiana. In the first few moments of our discussion I quickly learned that she had never worked on a computer before this temporary typing assignment, she could type in Russian, but had not yet used an English keyboard. Tatiana spoke English fairly well but lacked self-confidence and was continuously apologizing for her grammatical mistakes. Tatiana also highlighted the fact (unsolicited) that she was a single mother who also cared for her older mother and some other relatives in a one bedroom apartment, so she would not be able to work late nights.

Next I was directed to talk with Ingrid. I had noticed that she always arrived in the conference room precisely on time and slid into her chair at her computer without a word to anyone. She hunched over her keyboard all day, completely absorbed in her work. When one of the project managers spoke to her, she jumped nervously and shrunk lower into her chair. No one knew much about Ingrid other than she was the timid hard-working girl who hid in the corner.

I asked Ingrid if I could have a word alone with her. Her eyes filled with panic and she asked nervously, "what have I done wrong?"

"Nothing, Ingrid," I tried to calm the shuddering young woman.

She was about my age, but melted in fear of a conversation alone with me. Hopefully I wasn't coming across as being that alarming a character to the Russian girls, was I? Ingrid avoided eye contact and stared with determination at her tightly folded hands throughout our discussion. Involuntarily, my gaze followed hers to her hands. Years of stress and agitation had led her to chew her fingernails down to mutilated stumps. With a gasp, she noticed I was looking at her fingers. She quickly folded her arms to hide her hands, but now I could see that her wrists were bruised. Apparently she was a good typist, but would she die from shock in a western business environment?

I was not convinced that either Tatiana or Ingrid would be appropriate core team members for our project in Moscow, so I opened the floodgates to a sea of applicants. In the space of a few days, a marathon of interview sessions was quickly arranged by Gloria.

The open plan environment of the conference rooms ensured that Tatiana and Ingrid were quickly aware that I was looking at other candidates for our team. They silently watched as a parade of young women marched through our office space. I must note that over the next two years I would hire plenty of Russian men, but for some reason there was not a single male applicant in this first interview wave.

In order to gain a bit of privacy for our discussions, I commandeered a sofa in the elevator lobby. Curious hotel guests would look at us inquisitively, but still it was as much privacy as could be offered in our current accommodation. I had attempted to secure the fire escape off the conference rooms for my interview chamber, but the Russians from the other projects protested vigorously that this was needed for their cigarette breaks. So back to the elevator lobby I went.

What is it I wanted in an executive assistant for the team? A self-starter, a problem solver, someone with enough confidence and common sense to tackle basic issues on her own and did not seek continuous guidance. Someone who was comfortable with a computer and could type in English and Russian. Prior experience with a western company would be a huge bonus. Was I asking too much? Absolutely. Years of state-run enterprises and dictatorial management would not be easily eradicated from the business culture.

The first few discussions started to indicate the magnitude of the chasm between Russian reality and western expectations.

"So Galina," I looked at one woman's employment application. "You do realize that I am talking to about twenty other applicants today. Can you tell me what distinguishes you from the other women I will meet today?"

"Nothing," she answered meekly. "Nothing makes me different. I am exactly the same as everyone else."

My heart sank for her. How was it possible that Russian women had such a horribly low view of themselves? This message was reinforced in my next discussion:

"Ekaterina, your application says that you have four years of secretarial experience. Would you please describe your responsibilities in your most recent role?"

Ekaterina looked at me in shock. "You know what a secretary does," she retorted sharply. "I type and made tea." She glared at me like I was an absolute imbecile. What sort of a question was that? If I did not know what secretaries did then how would I possibly hire one?

Another interview proved to be a bit more positive.

"So Marina," I addressed the attentive young woman in front of me. "On your application you noted you have completed a 'business woman course'. Would you please tell me what was covered in your course and what were the most important things you learned in it?"

Marina beamed. She was clearly delighted to be asked about the 'business woman course'. She held herself with greater poise and self-confidence than any other candidate I had seen so far and presented an immaculate professional image. I was already impressed and our discussion had barely begun.

"Yes, I completed the business woman course last year. It was very instructive and provided all the basics every woman needs to know before entering a professional career. We learned how to serve tea properly and how to dress in a professional manner. We learned how to select appropriate executive gifts and how to organize restaurant bookings."

So this is what is expected of "business women" in modern Russia. And Marina was absolutely enthusiastic about how thoroughly the course had covered the essential material. She was delighted about the professional opportunities available to women in modern society in Russia.

"At least while we're young we'll have these opportunities," she added. She took it for granted that sooner or later she too would become a hunched toothless *babushka*. And she could not imagine the old *babushkas* working in a professional office or in any role other than sweeping the streets or minding a counter at a state store.

As a young enthusiastic American woman I found the day to be thoroughly depressing. It is easy back in the United States to read in newspapers that attempt to explain that in many parts of the world women are culturally excluded from equal participation in the workforce. It was another matter entirely to confront the reality of the situation head on in one-on-one discussions with women my own age. All these women were reasonably intelligent and university-educated, but conceptually lacked the ability to view themselves in any significant professional role. On my part, I was determined to serve as a good role model for my staff as a minimum and also to do anything in my power to help them overcome the enormous cultural barricades that had been built to limit them from achieving their potential. Or, at a minimum, I could help them believe that they had something resembling "potential" in the first place.

The sheer magnitude of this issue became even more clear during an interview later in the day. I was now talking with a beautiful petite blond girl named Oksana. I had finished my line of questioning with her and now I turned and asked if she had any questions for me.

"Yes I do," Oksana said very matter of fact. "Would you please tell me who I am expected to sleep with in this office?"

Excuse me? She could not have seriously asked this question. We were chatting in Russian. Perhaps I had misunderstood. "Please explain what you mean," I requested.

In every previous office situation, sexual favors had been an understood part of the employment arrangement. Usually just for her immediate boss, but at her last employer some of the other staff had placed demands on her as well. Not subtle demands either. When an executive traveled on business, they had usually requested that Oksana travel along as an "assistant" for the duration of the trip. She had resigned herself to the fact that this was part of the standard corporate scene, but she wanted to have a clear understanding of these expectations up front.

I was absolutely heartbroken. "Oksana, that is not how American companies operate. If anyone in a western company ever attempts to pressure you into sexual favors, go immediately to the office manager or a senior woman who you can trust." I could not believe that I was having this discussion.

"But my last employer was an American company. It was the American manager who I was asked to accompany on business trips," Oksana said in a simple matter-of-fact tone.

I was physically ill. Were Americans in Russia to help these people or just to perpetuate the system? I had no rational answer to her comment other than to swear sincerely that I would be her ally if she ever needed support.

At the end of the day I was back at the corner of a table which served as my desk compiling my interview notes when Raymond's wife, Rita, floated into the conference room. She radiated happiness and vigor. Rita moved gracefully and effortlessly and dressed simply but with elegant confidence. She was a naturally beautiful woman and touched her lips with just a bit of color to enhance her healthy glow. She was probably in her early-sixties – that is only a guess, however. Being a classic southern lady, Rita certainly would never have revealed her true age.

With a bubbly laugh and a gentle smile, Rita whisked Raymond out of the office to their dinner date that evening. As she made a graceful exit, I noticed that all the Russian women's eyes were firmly fixed on her – enraptured and stunned.

"Who was that?" Tatiana asked breathlessly after the couple had departed. "She looks like a movie star. She is so glamorous and vibrant."

I looked from Tatiana's astonished eyes to the doorway through which the captivating vision had just disappeared. And then I slowly realized the obvious implications of her comment – she had never seen a real live beautiful older woman before.

In the years that followed, every appearance of Rita was met with resounding enthusiasm by the Russian women in our office. They whispered to me that the image of Rita gave every younger Russian woman hope and strength to face the future. Now they knew that all women were not condemned to becoming toothless hags with gnarled hands and broken hair falling out by the handful. Somewhere in the world other women had experienced a better life, better food, and less stress and were able to resonate with a strong healthy glow even into their sixties. Perhaps they too could retain their own natural beauty for many years to come.

If our project accomplished nothing else, at least we gave a few young women a bit of optimism for their own futures. In the months to come, when we were engulfed in political battles or struggled to see any progress on our official project, I at least was able to enjoy the personal satisfaction that we were making a positive impact on a few young lives.

On other matters, I had not heard from Andrew for nearly a week and was starting to get anxious about the state of the *remont* on my apartment. The vision of Igor standing with his sledgehammer on my polished floors still haunted me. If the project was to be completed in a timely manner and with some degree of quality assurance, I was convinced that I would have to provide micromanagement. The only problem was that Andrew did not answer his phone and he did not call me.

Telecommunications were still in the dark ages in Moscow. No mobile phones. No voice mail. No answering machines. No call-back service. No roll-over to another extension if a phone went unanswered. If you needed to reach someone, you would have to dial the number (on a rotary phone) on an hourly basis and hope to find the person at their desk. Quite the shock to the American manager. And so convenient if you want to avoid someone.

Andrew was clearly avoiding me. Until this week he had been calling me every day to organize the design and procurement details for the apartment. And now there was nothing. Silence. I found this even more disturbing than his earlier demands that I take three hours out of the day to go shopping for door knobs with him.

After a week of deafening silence, I finally decided to visit the apartment again to see for myself what was going on. The lack of communication from Andrew had tipped me off that something was amiss, but nothing could have prepared me for the scene I found when I turned the key in the lock and walked through the front door.

Rubble. Masonry, tiles, plaster, plumbing, electrical parts, bathroom fixtures, you name it. The interior decor could only be called "post-apocalypse". To my despair, the rubble was all over the beautiful floorboards – not even a layer of newspapers had been laid down to protect them.

An astonishing amount of debris had somehow been created. I tiptoed through the rubble and discovered that the bathroom was the epicenter of the disaster. Actually "bathroom" is a bit of a misnomer. "The area that was formerly known as the bathroom" would be more accurate. Absolutely nothing recognizable remained in this cavern, just blackness and bits of plaster.

"Well good," I thought to myself and tried to be optimistic. "It looks like Igor has made progress on his demolition work at least."

In an inexplicable moment of foresight, I had brought along a flashlight. As nothing remained in the bathroom area, not even electrical wiring, I pulled the flashlight out of my handbag to have a closer inspection of the site. I shined the beam first on the ground to see more clearly what I was stepping over. The broken tiles looked familiar. I took a closer look and realized, in horror, that these were the very gray slate tiles that I had purchased with Andrew only two weeks earlier. They were now crumbled and battered beyond recognition.

What had happened here? I shined the flashlight at the black cavern at the end of the hall and had no immediate answers. The stench of stagnant Moscow tap water greeted me as I poked my nose inside the tomb. Cockroaches scuttled into the shadows. The tiles were still moist from some catastrophic plumbing explosion. Elsewhere I discovered the other fixtures I had purchased just weeks earlier – all in various degrees of demolition.

The ceiling offered the first clue for what had happened. Where there should have been plaster, I could see only a hodgepodge of boards, clumsily nailed together. Some explosion in the ceiling, it appeared. I honestly had never seen anything like it. I only knew that I certainly would not be moving into the apartment on 10 August and I would have to phone Andrew relentlessly until I extracted an answer from him.

There was nothing more I could do, so I gave a depressed farewell to my demolished floorboards and tiles and locked the door behind me.

I returned to the Hotel Aerostar on the Metro. I analyzed the faces of the women and came to the same conclusion that my American friends would all later observe – young Russian women are astonishingly beautiful, but something happened to them around age thirty. After thirty their eyes lost their fire, their faces sagged, their backs hunched and they lost all interest in dressing themselves fashionably. Life was a burden after thirty and a constant struggle for daily existence. This basic fact resonated in every face I examined.

But wait. That's a familiar face. Andrew! Of all amazing coincidences, Andrew had just entered my car on the Metro. In this city of eleven million people what are the chances that you will casually see someone you know on the Metro? Just about nil. I pounced at the opportunity to talk to him.

"Andrew, so good to see you," I started. "What is going on with my apartment?"

"Oh, everything's fine," he answered evasively. He edged toward the door to make a hasty exit at the next stop.

"Fine?" I was not going to let him off that easily. "Exactly what do you mean by fine? Have you seen the apartment recently?"

"We've had a few minor problems, but Igor is taking care of it." The train stopped and the doors opened. Andrew darted out onto the platform. I swiftly followed him. It wasn't my stop, but that didn't matter. I needed to talk to Andrew and another train would certainly be along in a few minutes anyway. I pursued him and told him that I would stalk him until he talked to me. After a bit of badgering, I finally extracted the details from him for what had happened.

The subcontractors had been working on the bathroom renovations for the past week –updating the electrical wiring and lighting, installing the new sink, toilet, bathtub, adding the taps, finishing the walls and laying the tiles. Then, just as they were finishing, the ceiling collapsed and the entire bathroom from the next level up fell into the pristine new bathroom in my apartment – demolishing every square inch of the fresh renovation.

"Everything we procured has been destroyed," Andrew advised. "All the labor has been wasted. But you will not need to pay for this again. Igor will obtain the money from the people that own the apartment upstairs. It was their fault that the ceiling collapsed."

I paused to think this through. "Are you certain it was their fault?" I thought of the hulking figure of Igor carrying his sledgehammer. If he knocked at the door of my neighbor's apartment demanding money, I had no doubt that he could be very convincing. But I then also wondered what my future relationship with my Russian neighbors would be like.

"Igor will take care of everything. Don't worry," Andrew insisted. He then turned and disappeared into the swarming crowd of the Metro station.

I had no choice but to accept that Andrew and Igor had the situation under control. This was Russia. Concepts like homeowner's insurance or small claims court were non-existent. Andrew and Igor would solve the problem the Russian way. But when would I be able to move into my apartment? Andrew had not offered any clues. I returned to my four star refugee camp at the Hotel Aerostar.

The next morning I arrived early in the project room to find Tatiana already engrossed in work at her computer. It was not even eight o'clock. A few Americans, mainly those still living in the Hotel Aerostar, arrived at this hour, but the Russians typically did not start work until nine. With her daughter and mother to care for, I was surprised to see Tatiana voluntarily putting in any extra time in the office.

"Good morning, Tatiana," I smiled. "Is the Ministry of Finance project team working you too hard?"

"No, not at all," she looked up briefly from her computer. "I just have concluded that if I'm going to improve with the computer then I need to come early and practice." Tatiana proudly showed me a bootleg copy of *Microsoft Word for Dummies* in Russian that she must have picked up the night before. She appeared to be working her way methodically through the first chapter.

I was seriously impressed and decided at that moment that she had to be part of my project team. Sure Tatiana could not type, she could barely use a computer, and she lacked self-confidence, but she was determined to improve herself. Above all things, however, I needed a team that was willing to learn and challenge themselves.

Our American office manager, Robert, questioned my judgment with this decision. "Don't we need people who actually have a secretarial skill base? And you know she's a single mom. She's going to be horribly distracted from her work."

"No," I said. "I have a good feeling about her. She has a great attitude. And I think that her being a single mom will actually be an asset. She needs this job desperately to support her family. She will be a dedicated worker."

Of course I made some hiring mistakes in the years to come, but not with Tatiana. She was one of the best hiring decisions of my life. I was proven right beyond my wildest dreams. She deeply appreciated the chance she was given and quickly became the most devoted and loyal employee anyone could possibly hope for. Her typing and computer skills slowly improved —never really to the level expected in America, but in the end that really did not matter to me. She attacked every new task with such enthusiasm and the quest to please that I could easily forgive the fact that inevitably I would have to plan time for corrections and coaching with every assignment.

Ingrid was another story. She arrived in the office that next morning wearing a headscarf and sunglasses. She tucked herself quietly into her corner chair and tried to make herself invisible. I walked over to say "good morning", and she quickly averted her face from me.

Not quick enough, however. Under her sunglasses I could see that her right eye was nearly swollen shut in an alarming purple and black pulp. Stunned, I took a step back. She refused to talk to me except over her shoulder, looking intently into the corner of the room.

Of course this explained her behavior. Why didn't I see it before? She had all the signs of domestic abuse plainly written on every inch of her body. She recoiled at any comment or criticism. Her fingers were mangled in stress and her wrists had been bruised from earlier struggles. Any self-confidence she may have had earlier in her life was shattered long ago. What was left was only a shadow of a shuddering insecure woman.

I turned Gloria, our HR manager. What could we do about Ingrid? We quickly agreed that it was absolutely horrific to see one of our staff members suffering from domestic abuse, but what to do next was unclear.

Domestic violence was still legal and widely practiced in Russia. The man had complete control over any relationship. If we tried to get her out of her domestic situation, then what would happen next? We could not expect her family to be supportive of her leaving her husband. Wife abuse was far too common. She would not be welcomed back with her parents. The rest of her family would already be packed in eight people to an apartment. One more would be a nuisance. The details of Ingrid's living situation would be inconsequential to the family – she had a place to stay and she should be satisfied with that. There certainly were not any social services available to battered women – halfway houses enabling the women to regain some sense of control over their own lives. She had been reduced to a state of insecurity and dependence that was heart wrenching to observe. She would not have the strength to leave this man on her own, but no one was there to help her make the step either. What if Gloria or I attempted to take her in personally... I was still living in my shoebox of a hotel room, so a roommate was completely out of the question. Even if I was living in my own apartment, like Gloria was, realistically what could we do then? We could provide a temporary home for a few weeks, but what next? I had absolutely no knowledge of her family or situation. Chances were that no one else would support the idea of her leaving her husband, so where would she go then? We would not be able to house her forever. The image of Igor with his sledgehammer convinced me that any disaffected people would certainly attempt to take matters into their own hands.

The futility of the situation was exhausting. Gloria and I were too young and inexperienced to have any rational idea for what to do next. We wanted to help, but we had no idea how.

The horrible situation was resolved unsatisfactorily a few days later. The temp agency advised that Ingrid was resigning, effective immediately. She did not offer any explanation, but suddenly simply ceased to appear in the office. Gloria and I were immediately concerned about her health and safety. Why had she suddenly resigned? How much worse had her home life become? But Ingrid had arrived as a mysterious temporary typist provided through an agency. She had left no forwarding contact information. We probably could have found her if we had put in a serious effort. But we were too young and too overwhelmed by the situation to arrive at a solution. We therefore found ourselves in the wholly unsatisfactory position of doing nothing.

So Ingrid faded from the project team and a wave of fresh young women arrived. Each new hire was greeted by attentive stares from the American men. The young single American men who never tired of talking about the beauty of Russian women and how feminine they were. I growled and bared my teeth like a protective mother bear – protecting her innocent cubs who were not yet able to fend for themselves.

"Lighten up, Phaedra," they said. "It's not like we're going to kidnap the girls. We'll ask them first."

And for my girls who had never been trained to say "no," that is exactly what I feared.

Moscow was already proving to be a city of extremes. Elegant graceful Rita coexisted in the same city as the abused Russian women and haggard worn *babushkas*. The incredible architectural achievement of the Moscow Metro stood in stark contrast to the depressing rubble of my apartment. The order and reliability of the Metro was calming in comparison to the pioneer justice of Igor or the domestic abuse suffered by Ingrid. Beauty was the exception rather than the rule. This made the Metro and Rita shine even brighter amid seemingly endless desolation and depression.

With Rita and the Metro system I found two bright beacons of hope for Russia's future. Without such guideposts lighting a possible path forwards, there is only darkness and despair. In the months to come I would find myself often referring back to these images for reassurance. Chistiye Prudi may be neither "clean" or "ponds" in reality, but at least we could create a hopeful image in our minds.

4 PET AMERICANS

August 1994 — Stavropol, Russia

The so-called "real" work of the project had begun. Or more accurately, in the name of mutual cooperation and business partnership I found myself struggling to down possibly my ninth shot of vodka for the evening.

I chided myself for whinging inside. Realistically there were two options for what could have happened that evening. Either my new Russian colleagues would subject me and my American colleague, Joseph, to an intense evening of team-bonding — Russian-style, or we would be simply disposed of at the Intourist Hotel for the evening. And, honestly taking the long-term view, the vodka-drenched team-bonding experience was the better option. If they had simply discarded us at the hotel, then we would have known that our relationship was off to a bad start.

Joseph and I found ourselves at a table of about twelve Russians that first evening in Stavropol. A few had been introduced to us as staff of the Local Privatisation Centre — the rest were local politicians or directors of local factories or god knows who. The director of the Local Privatisation Centre — a flamboyant man with the improbable name of Ivan Ivanovich Ivanov — was clearly in charge of the proceedings. He now had some pet Americans that he wanted to show off to the local dignitaries. Having Americans as guests was valuable currency in the political stakes of the mid 1990s. Ivan Ivanovich was determined to make the most of it.

So on that night we found ourselves at a table of twelve Russians. With Joseph and myself, this made fourteen. Fourteen people at table meant fourteen toasts of vodka — minimum. Then there would be extra glasses of champagne to start with and cognac to finish the meal.

I had been looking forward to launching into the "real" work of the project — helping to establish the operations of the local privatisation centres throughout Russia. In

Moscow I had trudged every night from the conference rooms on the fifth floor of the Hotel Aerostar to my four-star refugee camp on the third floor of the Hotel Aerostar, wondering when I would escape the false surroundings of Westernised Russia and return to the real thing. The longer I had been away from working in the "real" former Soviet Union, the more I had romanticised the idea. It had been nearly three months since I had set foot outside a major city (Moscow or Almaty). I had convinced myself that the next time I went out to the field that I would be able to hold a strict agenda of what was to be accomplished and to come back with my liver intact.

Oh how young and naïve I was.

For starters, although the Local Privatization Centers were funded via USAID and our consultancy had been engaged to operate them, the Russian director and staff were all appointed by the Russian Privatization Center. Our project's success would be wholly dependent upon political appointees. Raymond had immediately recognized the inherent problems here and raised the issue to USAID. How could we be asked to establish the operations of a consulting center when we had no governance over the leadership or staff of the center? USAID had simply responded saying that we needed to learn how to work with our Russian partners. Like in Kamchatka and Almaty, in the absence of a formal client or commercial relationship, we would be wholly dependent upon the whims and interests of these local political appointees overlapping with our own project goals.

In short, I could arrive in Stavropol with a nice plan for what I wanted to discuss and accomplish. And none of this would really matter, unless somehow it amused the local partner. And right now, all that Ivan Ivanovich cared about was that funding would be provided for three offices that he would manage and that with Joseph he would have his very own American to parade around as a status symbol. Further details of what the offices were expected to accomplish were dismissed with a wave as not of interest. With the business of the day concluded, time to move on to dinner and get the rounds of vodka toasts started!

Now at dinner, Ivan Ivanovich Ivanov was in his element and relished his role of Master of Ceremonies. He had just met Joseph a few hours before, but was already embracing him and slapping him on the back as a long-term member of his inner circle. Toast after toast were to Joseph:

"To our business adviser, who will help direct American investments to southern Russia."

"To our single American man – may you fall in love with a beautiful local Russian girl and stay forever."

"To Joseph – may you learn to drink vodka like a local. You will need much practice."

The toasts were endless and the theme was ominous. The Russians were thrilled to have an American presence in southern Russia, but saw Joseph simply as a beacon for bringing in foreign dollars. His expertise in assisting with company restructuring and process improvement was not even mentioned once.

Joseph was smiling and flushed and accepted a top-up of his champagne glass from a thin hostile waitress with blood-red lips imposing over his right shoulder. Meanwhile on his left, Ivan Ivanovich was pouring yet another vodka shot.

What if anything would we be able to accomplish the next day? It was already evident that the schedule would be entirely dictated by Ivan Ivanovich. The whole routine of Russian hosts tormenting their guests with vodka shots upon arrival started to make a bit more sense to me. Joseph had arrived as the business advisor to the privatisation centre where Ivan Ivanovich was the government-appointed director. From the start Ivan Ivanovich had to stamp how the relationship would go forward. He would be in charge. He would dictate the agenda. From the beginning he would be the master of ceremonies, determine who we would dine with, what we would drink and even what we would eat. He had ordered meals for the table. No one else had even seen a menu. His domination of the scene was complete. And therefore he had started the relationship with Joseph with exactly the tone he wanted. He, Ivan Ivanovich, would dictate exactly what would happen at any moment from this point forward.

"*Devushki!*" Ivan Ivanovich exclaimed with despair to the waitresses, "Why is the restaurant so quiet? Some entertainment for our American guests!" Even though the term was plural, he gestured to Joseph only. The American man must be entertained. And at the discretion of the Russian host, of course.

The lights dimmed, the fog machine was switched on and the disco ball started rotating on the ceiling. Sparkling white flecks of light spun around and around and around the room. I was having a difficult enough time maintaining a state of balance and composure after ten or so shots of vodka, the spinning disco lights eliminated all residual connections I still may have had with solid earth. The ground was moving uncontrollably beneath me. Spinning with the lights, around and around. I was vaguely aware of Russian girls dancing vigorously in starched Cossak dresses. The spinning continued and at some point the dresses disappeared and only sequined G-strings remained. The music shifted from traditional Cossack to pulsing modern techno.

Here I was yet again at a business function with strippers – a repeat of prior scenes in Kazakhstan. The men were now pounding the table to the beat. Joseph was clapping in time. He was vaguely aware of the fact that the women were now mostly naked, but I could tell that his eyes were not capable of focusing clearly on the scene. The Russian women at my table were now pushed back from the dinner table and smoking cigarettes silently. They flicked ash onto the floor with a minimum of movement and glared at the scene unfolding in front of them. Not a word, however. The host for the evening had indicated that conversation was now over. Now we would be entertained. Conversation therefore had ceased.

Ivan Ivanovich clapped his hands with enthusiasm. He had asked for the entertainment and here it was. Somehow he had acquired a tamborine and was pounding this in time to the beat. Incongruent with the techno music, but Ivan Ivanovich could clearly do what he pleased. He had controlled all aspects of the evening. In his view the relationship was off to a solid start and going exactly the way he wanted. All was well in the world.

The following morning, I was attempting to determine how disasterous it would be to our relationship with our Russian partners if I vomited in the back seat of their car. Not good, I quickly concluded. I was being punished for my sins from the night before.

Oh the agony. A few months before I had updated my vision of hell with the image of three gnarled Kazakh women sorting rotten potatoes in an earthen underground cavern – lit by a small flickering lantern and shivering from the Siberian winter. Now I was compelled to add another possibility to the nature of hell – perhaps it would be an endless road trip through the southern Russian countryside, terribly hungover and immobilised in the middle of the tiny back seat of a Lada between two massive men. It was the peak of summer and the outside temperature was closing in on 30C. Inside the car, the air barely moved.

I stole a glance at Joseph on my right and wondered if he was as hungover as I. Private conversation in English was impossible as Ivan Ivanovich had brought along his interpreter, Sergei – the hulking man to my left. Joseph gripped the armrest on the door and grimaced silently.

Nerves were on edge. Joseph barked sharply to the driver that we had to turn on the fan inside the car and open the windows. (No air conditioning in Soviet-era Ladas, of course.) Ivan Ivanovich said no – without offering an explanation. Joseph attempted to argue with logical points for how much the movement of air would cool down the interior of the vehicle. Ivan Ivanovich refused to engage in discussion – simply repeating that the windows would remain closed.

The sun beat mercilessly through the car windows onto the trapped inhabitants of the Lada. At least the windows were filthy. I reasoned that the layer of dirt must provide at least some bit of protection from the intense sun. I shifted my arms, seeking a more comfortable position. My bare arm brushed against Sergei's and I recoiled from the slimy contact of two sweating bodies. The air was heavy and stale from five breathing adults struggling to cope with the heat. The walls of the car closed in on me. I needed to be released immediately.

Please let me out now! I pleaded to the driver. The driver turned to Ivan Ivanovich for consent.

"Why do you want to stop?" Ivan Ivanovich asked. Clearly any request would have to pass his evaluation of whether I offered a legitimate purpose.

I could not bring myself to blurt out the truth – that I was about to degenerate into a screaming fit from severe claustrophobia, heatstroke, dehydration, and a hangover. The Russians must display an outward show of strength at all times. Ivan Ivanovich was already attempting to dominate every aspect of our relationship. I could not allow myself to show any sign of weakness. All remaining vestiges of cooperation could be swept away if Joseph or I were to offer a signal that we were weaker physically or psychologically than him. So I whispered that I needed to use the restroom – please.

Well, this was not a satisfactory answer for Ivan Ivanovich. We were driving through the countryside of southern Russia. Two lane roads – mostly asphalt, sometimes dirt roads. Farms with tired dusty crops as far as the horizon. In my mind it would be easy to jump out of the car and attend to nature. But Ivan Ivanovich refused. Women just did not jump out of cars on the side of the road to take care of business. Simply not done.

I pleaded my case, but Ivan Ivanovich turned his eyes forward and abruptly showed me the back of his hand. He was done with the subject. Sergei – the interpreter to my left – offered another explanation – the Chechens. We were within a hundred miles of the civil war that was ravaging Chechnya. "The Chechens," Sergei whispered to me conspiratorially, pointing to the tall fields of wheat. "The Chechens could be anywhere." One more thing the Russians now had decided to blame the Chechens for – the inability to take a nature stop anywhere between Stavropol and Krasnodar.

At least this distracted me from the heat and claustrophobia. My interest was now piqued and I attempted to see through Joseph's body to get a glimpse of the fields that were so alarming to our Russian hosts. No obvious signs of any rebel activity that day, I must report. In fact no obvious signs that we were in the twentieth century at all – with the exception of the car itself and the crusty asphalt.

A well-worn cart track ran paralel to the narrow strip of asphalt. Not exactly the result of Soviet engineering, but rather the imprint from thousands of horse carts over decades, if not centuries. We passed a horse and cart plodding slowly along the track and I craned my neck with curiosity. A grizzled man perched on the wagon and hunched over the reins to his work horses. His clothing blended perfectly with the earth, wooden cart, parched fields, muddy track. He had become one with his surroundings. Perhaps his clothing had never been washed properly. Or perhaps he washed meticulously every day – but the shirt, pants and boots had just absorbed the colors of the earth over time. Or perhaps his clothing had started off that dull shade of brown to begin with.

In the field near the road a group of women were harvesting wheat with scythes. Yes, the big unweildy manual tools that are found in the United States only in museums and as decoration for trendy "rustic" bed and breakfast lodges. No real farmers actually use scythes any more, do they? But here they were. They swung the mediveal tools with a graceful practiced motion. The parched fields of wheat rippled with breeze in the background.

The Moscow subway's images of the proud peasant woman striding forward into the bright Soviet future sprung to mind. Here she was in the flesh. Dressed exactly as the images that portrayed the October Revolution in 1917. Same dusty brown scarf restraining the hair. Same earth colored shirt billowing in the wind. Only the women's faces portrayed a different story than the ideal image offered by the official Soviet artists. These women turned their faces down to the earth, backs permanently bent to the motion of the scythe. Their skin was a thick leather, hardened from years toiling in the fields. Their mouths were fixed, clenched in silent resignation.

"They are using equipment that is at least five centuries old." Joseph voiced the thoughts that were echoing through my mind. "They could harvest twice as much if they even had lighter scythes from more modern materials." He was ready to provide advice to anyone within earshot, even if they were powerless to impact the scene unfolding before us.

I finally gasped in disbelief as we passed another field and another group of women working with medieval farming implements. "What about all those massive harvesting combines that are the classic image of Soviet collective farming?" I asked.

Ivan Ivanovich gave the collective farmworkers a dismissive wave as he continued to look straight ahead at the road. "The collective farms have not had enough budget in recent years to buy and maintain the harvesting combines. So they are now using the scythes. It is only temporary until the economy improves."

In Ivan Ivanovich's mind the use of medieval technology was an unfortunate and temporary necessity. I took another look at another group of women in the fields – they certainly did not give the impression that they had only recently turned in their giant Super-Sov Harvesting Combine 2000 for a scythe. We passed another horse cart trudging slowly through the dirt on the side of the road. The horse stared blankly at a point in the distance and did not give the car a second glance. How much of the great industrial strength of the Soviet Union was actually a myth? Which was closer to the truth – the image of the giant harvesting combine devouring the fields of wheat or a line of women hunched over with agonising back-breaking work?

I searched for other clues that might support Ivan Ivanovich's claim. Was there any evidence that modern technology had been in use in Southern Russia – ever? Not that I could tell. Details of the drive started to register in the slow-moving parts of my dreadfully confused and hungover mind. What had we seen so far? Actually that was not the best question. The real question should have been – what had we *not* seen that would be expected in a modern country.

The road was simply a poured river of crystallised, broken asphalt. Not exactly recognisable to American motorists as a modern highway. No carefully groomed shoulder on the side of the road. No safety barriers around turns. No reflectors embedded into the middle of the road. Not even yellow and white stripes delineating the lanes or indicating safe areas to pass. If I had queried Ivan Ivanovich on this he certainly would have responded: "Why would yellow stripes be necessary? The drivers know where the centre of the road is!" Good point, but still surprising to American motorists.

Then I started to realise that there was a complete absence of signage or any other support for motorists of any sort. No road signs at intersections. No route markers. No indication of how far to the next town or even what direction to take. No shops or petrol stations or even a road-side diner with greasy meat of any sort. Not even any power lines keeping pace with the side of the road.

And, now that I was really paying attention, almost no cars either. We were out-numbered by horse carts about three to one. And the horse carts did not appear very often either.

We were truly on our own out in the wilds of Southern Russia. I started to appreci-ate the insistence of the driver that we clear room in the trunk of the car for an extra tank of gas and his maintenance kit. It went without saying that no roadside assistance would be available. Even if it were, I was increasingly convinced that the Russian men in the car would wave aside any assistance with disdain. "We are strong Russian men! We can solve any problem on our own! No assistance required. Do not insult my pride!"

The little filthy Lada did pull through and carry our sorry team all the way from Stavropol to Krasnodar. Upon arrival in the city, the first order of business was to visit the offices leased by the Local Privatization Center. Anton, the Director for the Krasnodar LPC, enthusiastically showed us the space, narrating all the improve-ments that he had planned – new electrical wiring, a steel door to ensure the promised computer equipment would be secure, new furniture, working telephone lines. The required work just to make the space functional was daunting. Joseph added the valid recommendation that the telephone lines needed to be rewired to allow for modem connections rather than single pieces of wiring from the wall to the telephone handset. All eyes then turned to me to ask when the computer equipment would be delivered.

No, I did not have a valid answer for them. I really did not know what I was doing yet with computer procurement and was just getting this going with the Washington DC home office. I promised everyone that I would keep them in the loop and this sat-isfied everyone momentarily. I was starting to face the reality that my life of remont and purchasing dramas would not end with just my own apartment and our office space in Moscow, but would extend on indefinitely as we worked to establish twelve Local Privatization Centers throughout regional Russia. Anton was excited by every-thing planned for his offices in Krasnodar. I, however, was unnerved and found myself inexplicably looking forward to the first round of vodka shots that would certainly be coming later in the day.

As expected, that night was filled with another dinner in another tawdry Russian hotel restaurant with too many rounds of vodka and another lot of dancers/singers/ strippers entertaining the table. Toasts were made by Anton to Joseph, and the future of Krasnodar, but clearly Ivan Ivanovich's thoughts were already in Rostov – our final port of call. Rostov was Ivan Ivanovich's home town. It would be the centre of attention for Joseph, if Ivan Ivanovich had anything to say about it. And he certainly would. No business meetings would be happen without the express support/intervention of Ivan Ivanovich. Rostov would be the focus of Joseph's efforts. All industry that mattered in Southern Russia had its headquarters in Rostov. Therefore all investment and consulting should be in Rostov as well. The offices in Krasnodar and Stavropol were there to appease the Moscow-based Russian Privatization Center. Ivan Ivanovich's gestures and indifference to Anton made the relationship clear in our minds – Anton served the purpose of allowing Ivan Ivanovich to claim that there was an office in Krasnodar. He had fulfilled his obligation to have a presence in Krasnodar. He made the obligatory initial visit to Krasnodar with the new American advisor. But that was all that was really measurable, so that was all he intended to do here. So now he would be released from any further obligations in Krasnodar in the foreseeable future and could focus on the real target of his interests – Rostov.

And then suddenly on Saturday night I found myself walking arm in arm with an American friend from my days in Kazakhstan, Craig, on the shore of the Black Sea in Sochi. No I had not planned to be in Sochi. No, I had not expected to see Craig. And I was certainly amazed that my Russian hosts had given me the night off from the mandatory social circuit.

From Krasnodar the original plan had been to go north – to Rostov – Ivan Ivanovich's hometown and the focus of all his political energy. But no. Instead the little Lada turned abruptly south – towards Sochi, the Russian resort town on the Black Sea. Ivan Ivanovich offered the thinnest of explanations for the visit – the mayor of Sochi wanted to meet the new American advisor. No other order of business. No companies to visit. No Local Privatization Center offices to be established here.

Conveniently the meeting with the mayor would be over a long lunch on Friday – meaning that we would all have to stay in Sochi for the weekend. Per the plans created by Ivan Ivanovich it would be ridiculous to send Joseph and I back to Moscow for the weekend only to return to Rostov on Monday. Ivan Ivanovich was a good host and therefore would have to stay in Sochi with us. Protests were silenced with a wave of his hand. The plans were made and we had an important lunch with the mayor. Resistance was futile.

The mayor was quick to come to his point. The Olympic Games. He wanted Sochi to host the Winter Olympic games. We were American consultants so obviously we would have the right connections to help him. Joseph was enthusiastic. No, he had no idea how to go about structuring a bid for the Olympic Games, but here was his first Russian in a position of authority actually asking for his assistance. I was a bit more dubious. We were supposed to be supporting recently privatized Russian enterprises, not city governments. I quietly voiced my doubts that we would be able to do anything for the Mayor of Sochi, but was quickly silenced by Ivan Ivanovich and Joseph. While over lunch with the Mayor we must keep the discussion light and positive – yes, we would do anything in our power to support him!

From that point onwards, the lunch with the mayor fit the standard routine – with round after round of vodka toasts. The local variant was the fish that was pulled from the water thrown in a frying pan and placed in front of me without as much as an effort to remove the head and eyeballs. A few glasses of cognac helped me move beyond the penetrating glare of the dead fish and focus on the obligatory socialising at hand. I was pleasantly numb when I spotted Craig in the restaurant – whose presence I cannot explain to this day. The last time I saw him was several months earlier in Kazakhstan and now he was in Sochi.

But no explanations were needed. Life was random in the former Soviet Union in those years. You just went with the flow. People appeared and disappeared. I was supposed to be in Rostov today. But instead now I'm in Sochi. And Craig is here.

Don't question things just act. Seize the moment.

So the next evening I found myself walking arm in arm with Craig on the shore of the Black Sea.

My liver was thrilled to have a reprieve for one evening. And my mental state was lifted by the chance encounter with an old friend. Someone with whom I could relay the events of the past weeks, months, and gain a bit of healthy perspective – from someone who understood my world but was not deeply involved in the present moment.

A walk arm in arm on the shore of the Black Sea on a Saturday night. Laughing and sharing adventures and memories of nights in Kazakhstan. It sounds like a perfect romantic setting. And if you were ready for the context of 1990s Russian reality then it certainly was.

The stretch of shore behind my hotel could only be described as post-apocalypse. Rubble from demolished buildings, shipwrecks, and half-finished structures lay silently awaiting analysis by a future archeologist. Where the water met lan lay a thick barrier of seaweed or mossy sludge and dead fish. Real open water was inaccessible. As if to prove the point several carcasses of shipwrecks lay trapped just a few meters offshore. Immobilized betweeen land and sea. I laughed to Craig that the Mayor of Sochi was determined to rally a bid to host the Winter Olympics. He replied that the venue would certainly require the list of Olympic sports to be modified to include events from futuristic dystopian films like Running Man.

Craig and I had been in the black snow of Karaganda and ventured on the life-threatening ski lifts of Shimbulak in the Tien Shan range of the Himalayas. We had danced under the disco ball to techno beat in the noxious fog of the Otrar dining hall and played "guess the date on the beer can" at Dr Bang's. He was one of the few people I knew who had actually been to Uralsk. Somehow it was totally in context that we would now be walking together through concrete rubble on the shore of Russia's premiere resort town. The more things change, the more they stay the same.

And then suddenly a pause in our conversation. The rubble had abruptly ended and we were standing on black fine pebbles. The stench of the rotting fish and stagnant moss was fading. In front of us lay the mirage of a peaceful moonlit black pebble beach, waves of (relatively clean) water lapping gently against the shore. There was only one problem – blocking our progress was a severe chain link fence.

The beach was deserted, forbidden, and inviting. About 20 meters or so back from the shore was a ramshackle club building of sorts. Muffled noises of a racous dinner party drifted through closed windows. The rightful occupants of the beach were distracted and otherwise engaged indoors. So of course we could not resist. A few pesky rules and one little fence would not stop us.

We removed our shoes and entered the water, working our way around the fence. In hindsight this was probably the most dangerous thing we did that night – given the amount of rubble and the high probability of impaling our feet on some hidden hazard. The water was on our feet, to the ankles, and suddenly plunged to our knees. We laughed silently and paused for any clues to determine whether our presence had been noticed.

We reached the private beach and I was energised by a rush of adrenaline. "No rules – only suggestions!" I repeated the words of wisdom given to me by the experienced American expat on my arrival to Moscow. Once we put our nerves aside, anything was possible.

With the adrenaline surge, all my senses were now on high alert and my body pulsed with sensory overload. Grains of coarse sand oozed between my toes and gentle waves lapped my ankles. The happy sounds of voices and dishes in the clubhouse rose and fell with the breeze. The salty air was delicious and I drunk it in deeply. I restrained myself from squealing with excitement. Craig smiled and impulsively gave me a quick kiss on the cheek – as one would acknowledge an exhuberant small child.

Craig was happy as well, but clearly not feeling the same level of adrenaline-induced ecstasy as I was. He had survived a vicious stabbing and many more months in the more rugged corners of the former Soviet Union than me. His threshhold for adventure was higher than mine. He was not yet feeling challenged.

"Let's go for a swim," he said more as a statement than a question. He was already peeling off his wet trousers and shirt and in a moment stood before me totally bold and naked and smiling.

I needed no further encouragement and rapidly stripped as well. We tucked our bundle of clothes and shoes into the shadows. Then Craig took me by the hand, leading me into the inviting black depths of the unknown.

Skinny dipping at night is a wonderful source of emotional release. It is the triumph of free will over society's rules. Added to my moment of freedom was the intense delight at the unexpected turn of the day. I had expected to be with Ivan Ivanovich and Joseph and yet another round of government officials for yet more fish and vodka and cognac. But now this wonderful turn of events and to be reunited with an old colleague. An old friend. A new lover. No rules – only suggestions! We were free and released into the blackness of the waters. No visible limits to the horizons or the skies. What lay beneath us, or out to sea? We did not know and did not care. All that mattered was the present moment.

Craig's hands found my body, held me, and then gently pushed me away, setting me adrift. I floated through the black expanse of the sea. Momentarily alone – craving the next touch that would ground me back to the present moment. Fingers brushed by body then pulled me into a strong embrace. Here, where I should have felt the most vulnerable – naked and trespassing – I instead relaxed. I was protected and safe. I closed my eyes and felt the warmth of his body envelop us both.

Then suddenly a shout on the shore. The rest of the world came rushing back now into sharp focus. The rush of the breeze, the slap of the waves and sting from the salt-water in my eyes. Every sound, every movement was registered as prey listens for predators. Craig and I instinctively lowered in the water to be just four lurking quiet crocodile eyes monitoring the events on the shore.

Two Russian men staggered together in spontaneous frivolity – drunk, laughing, arms around each other in camaraderie and mutual support. Totally absorbed in their own moment and oblivious to everything except for the ground two steps ahead of their uncertain feet. The light on the back door to the resort was flicked on, flooding the beach with a harsh beam. The staggering Russians were blinded in a pool of light and barked insults back at those in the club house.

Craig and I took advantage of their momentary blindness and slipped quietly through the black water to the protective shadows under a small boating dock. We rested against a mossy slimy support beam and breathlessly watched the scene on the shore. The back wall of the club house was now illuminated and bold lettering was now clear above the back entrance: "Sanitarium of the Navy of the Russian Federation." I suppressed an alarmed gasp and silently gestured to Craig. His grim smile acknowledged that he had also seen the sign and now was simply curious for what would happen next.

Two American consultants found naked and arrested after breaking and entering the exclusive Black Sea resort of the Russian Navy. My mind spun as I started to imagine the headlines and consequences if we were found. What if the reverse were to happen?

Two Russians found naked under a dock of the US Navy in Virginia? And I was explicitly the guest of the Mayor of Sochi. I could barely breathe. Certainly the Russians on the shore could hear the pounding of my heart. Craig quietly pressed his chest against my back and protectively encircled my body with his right arm while holding onto the dock with his left.

The two men were Russian Navy personnel on leave (I assume) and very drunk (quite obviously). First two then four then a dozen men spilled out of the resort onto the beach – laughing and sharing a bottle among themselves. I nervously eyed our pile of clothing, just a few steps away from the growing crowd. The Russians stumbled and supported each other and the bottle passed around to the newcomers. A huddle of focused activity and then a shriek followed by a bright flame. A flare whooshed overhead and cracked with iridescent brilliant light. The Russians on the shore whooped and applauded with approval then huddled to find another flare to launch. The next flare spluttered to life, launched and then quickly fizzled out. A few shouts on shore. Body language and shouts – arguing that the vodka bottle was now empty and there were no more flares. Much better to go back indoors where there was food and more alcohol. Someone from inside opened the back door and beckoned people back indoors – waving a fresh bottle of vodka as inducement. The crowd milled around with uncertain steps, checking pockets for another flare or some other bit of momentary entertainment.

Someone paused to attempt to light a cigarette – with his back to the sea breeze. The stiff wind was a challenge to get the cigarette burning. The Russian waved his cigarette in frustration, still unlit, and gestured to his friends that he was done with the outdoor frivolity. Better to go back indoors where it would be easier to light up a smoke. After a few moments and hesitant shouts, the others followed slowly but deliberately. The door closed as the last of the revelers retreated indoors. The light was switched off.

Craig and I were again alone on the Black Sea. A moment of silence, then Craig laughed and summarised the evening in one short phrase: "*Carpe diem.*"

I laughed triumphantly (and quietly) and planted a kiss on Craig's lips. How true. Live for today, as tomorrow may never come.

5 PARADISE LOST

August 1994 — Rostov, Russia

Ah yes. Where were we? Back to our regularly scheduled program. The next day I rejoined my colleagues and we were back in the little Lada onwards to Rostov. Rostov was the centre of civilised society in Southern Russia. Rostov was Russia's gateway to the Black Sea. Rostov was a critical strategic port for Russia for military, shipping, as well as for fishing industries. Rostov was the source of the brightest industrial talent in Russia and the home of the most significant industry. Without Rostov, Russia would be paralysed. At least this was the view that Ivan Ivanovich pressed on us.

Our agenda would resume at 6:00am on Monday morning. No, Ivan Ivanovich did not share the plan of where we would be going or what we would be doing. Joseph's and my attempts to direct the agenda in any way had been met with a quick display of Ivan Ivanovich's hand and a sharp retort that he had everything under control. No, it was not necessary for us to worry about anything – he deflected the questions – he was taking care of all arrangements. We were to be the honored guests. Or hostages, whatever your mental state was towards the whole situation.

In any case, Ivan Ivanovich did hold true to his word. He did have the car and driver at the hotel to retrieve us at 6:00am and we were whisked away to our morning's destination – which turned out to be the fishing port.

The boats were already returning with the morning's catch. The air was thick with sea brine and the stench of freshly killed fish. Fish in baskets, in buckets, on tables, hanging from ropes by tails. Fish flipping hysterically in their final frantic death throes on mountains of their fallen relatives. Men deftly shifting boxes of fish onto scales and barking out prices calculated with a flick of fingers on an abacus. Stubs of charred cigarettes struggled to stay alight against the splashes of salt water from all directions in the frenzy of activity. Fish and money trading hands with wet weatherbeaten fingers.

Wads of rubles being crammed into pockets and slipped into boxes. Cash cash cash everywhere.

Ivan Ivanovich took me by the arm and led us purposefully through the melee. Of course I was wearing a cute fashionable business suit that was completely inappropriate for the occasion. I attempted to tiptoe around buckets of fish, ducked under fishnets hung up to be mended or for sale. Ivan Ivanovich marched onwards pulling me forward full speed. The heel of my shoe was mangled in the gaps of the docks and the stench of fish enveloped us in a wet blanket. Seagulls circled and screeched – ever vigilant for an opportunity to swipe a tasty morsel. Finally we came upon a man engrossed in his work as he expertly slit the body of a massive prehistoric fish.

The fish gave a final death gasp as the man plunged his knife deep into the belly of the animal. The creature took up the entire surface area of the enormous wet slimy table. I had never seen any sea creature so big outside of an aquarium. The wide unblinking eyes were fixed in a permanent stare. I then became engrossed by the man's knife, slitting cleanly up the belly.

With a flourish of bravado, Ivan Ivanovich produced a jar from inside his coat pocket and placed it on the table. The man dissecting the fish glanced at the container from the corner of his eye, but continued working on the fish. The belly of the creature was now completely sliced, like a neat zipper from top to tail. He put the knife to a side and reached through the opening with bare, gnarled paws and pulled out a handful of black grainy sloppy mash. Oh cripes.

Caviar. My brain finally registered what was going on here. In a single flash of recognition, the scene changed from one of stinking filth and chaos to one of exotic rare pleasure. We were at the fish market in Rostov – the primary source of high grade caviar in Russia. Here we were at the docks just minutes after the sturgeon had been brought to shore and were offered caviar directly from the belly of the animal to our own plates. Caviar would not, could not, ever be fresher or more spectacular than this.

I was stunned however at the reality of watching the animal being killed and its insides being harvested. I had not previously registered the fact that the sturgeon were killed in the quest for caviar. This was in 1994 and the depletion of sturgeon in the Black Sea was only the vaguest of environmental issues in the west. In Russia the environment was a non-issue. Here the animals existed to serve man's desires. But couldn't the caviar be obtained an a bit more environmentally friendly manner? You would never consider slicing open a chicken to obtain the eggs from her. Was it really necessary to slice open the sturgeon? This question met a dark glare from Ivan Ivanovich. Ignorant American. Of course you have to kill the fish to harvest the caviar.

My attention drifted back to the mountain of black gold glistening in the early morning sun. The fish monger filled the jar with the glossy black jewels and accepted a few small notes from Ivan Ivanovich. Pennies really for what we were receiving. Pennies for the life of this ancient creature.

Ivan Ivanovich firmly screwed on a lid then wrapped the container in a plastic bag before stashing the treasure inside his coat pocket. Okay. The fish was dead now. There was no way to bring her back to life. Therefore we should make the most of it and enjoy the caviar. I was nearly frantic with anticipation – when would we be able to taste it? It was so fresh now. Each minute we delayed would torment me slowly and painfully.

"We should eat that before it is spoiled," Joseph was always ready to offer advice at any moment. "Either that or we need to refridgerate the caviar."

Ivan Ivanovich chose to ignore this comment and strode off purposefully in the direction of the car. The schedule would be determined by Ivan Ivanovich. We would eat the caviar only when he said so. He controlled the car and driver. He had the caviar in his coat pocket. He controlled our agenda for the day. We would eat when he said we could eat. The advisor could provide advice, but it would not necessarily make a difference.

The caviar was brought out from Ivan Ivanovich's coat pocket later that morning. We were visiting the director of the Ros-Sov-Kombin-Zavod-Khos or something like that – the largest harvesting combine factory in the former Soviet Union. At its peak the factory employed nearly 50,000 people inside a massive complex. Ivan Ivanovich strove to impress on us the glorious nature of this enterprise. He instructed the driver to circle the compound before we drove through the front security gate. The loop around the perimeter required nearly half an hour. The fortress walls were topped with barbed wire and were more akin to a prison complex than a farm machinery factory.

Ivan Ivanovich lectured us on the great accomplishments of the factory – the harvesting combines could each thresh hundreds of acres of land per day when operating at capacity. This was the factory that provided all the harvesting combines to all the collective farms across the country – and exported to eastern Europe as well. The compound featured schools and housing and medical clinics on site – provided by the factory, of course. It was the achievement of the industrial ideal. The Soviet industrial ideal.

Inside the gates, however, we were met with the modern Russian reality. Listless workers stood in packs without purpose, hands in pockets with bottles of vodka or home made spirits barely concealed from view. Eyes turned slowly towards our Lada and then looked away with disinterest. No purpose really to the visitors. No purpose to today or yesterday or tomorrow. Just another drink and a social chat with the other factory workers. We'll pretend to work and they'll pretend to pay us.

The employees of the factory watched us with only mild interest as we were escorted to the director's office. Foreign visitors were probably the most exciting thing to have happened at the factory that month, I surmised. Inside the office building, Ivan Ivanovich placed the jar of caviar on the desk of the receptionist. A woman with shocking fire red lipstick glanced up from her half-finished manicure with an aggressive pout. How dare we interrupt her morning ritual for some trivial request. Reluctantly she showed us towards the Director's office, which was equipped with the standard corporate boardroom size conference table. The conference table had to be in the director's office. This ensured that no major meetings occurred without his involvement. Control control control at every step of the way, even down to the placement of furniture.

The director pulled us over the entry threshhold before formally shaking our hands and greeting us in the expanse of his office. Very bad to shake hands over a threshhold or a desk or a barrier of any sort – as it poses a symbolic barrier to a relationship. With the director now included in his audience, Ivan Ivanovich continued to sing the praises of the harvesting combine factory. This was the pinnacle of Soviet engineering achievement. At the peak of the production in the 1970s this factory was exporting even as far as Africa and South America. It was *the* major harvesting combine factory in Russia. Certainly this would be a fantastic opportunity for a foreign investor. Joseph should make this his first project – to identify a foreign investor who would be able to provide a cash injection into the factory.

So what would the injection of capital actually be used for? Joseph asked the director.

To pay the salaries of the employees who have gone unpaid for months, was the immediate reply. This is a respectable factory. The employees must be paid.

How many people are employed by the factory?

I already told you – 50,000 people, interrupted Ivan Ivanovich forcefully. Clearly his American guests were not paying attention. Plus the enterprise provided housing for all the employees, medical clinics, and schools for their children.

What was going through my mind was the question – was the great Soviet paradise or the great Soviet prison? Something powerful enough to give you everything is also powerful enough to take it all away. Every aspect of the workers' lives was dependent upon their employment with the factory. If the workers left, or were laid off, they truly would have nothing – no housing, no schools, no medical clinics. They almost certainly did not have their own cars and were therefore dependent on the factory's busses to take them anywhere outside the compound's walls. And once they had left the compound, then what? Obtaining employment or housing in a new city was effectively impossible without a local government official sponsoring the move. Although serfdom had nominally ended over a century earlier, the Soviet system served the same purpose by ensuring a captive labor force. Standing around with a bottle of vodka was a much more attractive option to the bleak prospect of unemployment – without even a roof over your head.

The pouting receptionist appeared with a tray filled with a plate of fresh bread, creamy butter, and a bowl of caviar. Despite the fact that it was only 9:00 am, the tray also featured the requisite bottles of vodka and champagne. The receptionist silently slammed the tray on the conference table and glared at me meaningfully before turning to the exit.

"Yes," agreed Joseph, "Ivan Ivanovich informed us that 50,000 people were employed by the factory when it was at its peak. What about now? Now that the orders have fallen and production has dropped, how many people are needed now? And has the management attempted to find any efficiencies since privatisation?"

The director could barely contain his outrage at the American's questions. No, not one person had been laid off. All of the workers were necessary. These workers made the complex one of the largest and most prestigious in the former Soviet Union. They had the essential know-how of how to build the combines and they were necessary to maintain the prestige of the factory.

Joseph persisted with a new line of questionning – what about the products of the factory? How had the products changed to accommodate the massive changes in the post-Soviet economy?

This factory produces major world-class harvesting combines for the collective farms. That is our product. The director looked at Joseph as if he were an idiot. Hadn't Joseph been paying attention to the discussion so far? Didn't he realise that the factory produced harvesting combines?

"Yes, I realise that your factory produces the massive harvesting combines," Joseph agreed. "But the collective farms no longer can afford to buy these combines. Have you thought of building smaller harvesting machines that can be sold more cheaply?"

The director glared at Joseph. Clearly the American did not understand the situation. "We produce major harvesting combines – the biggest and the most prestigious in the entire former Soviet Union. Right now we do not have very many orders due to the financial situation of the farms. But when the economy improves we will have orders again and production will increase. You will see. This factory is a cornerstone of Russian economic strength. Western companies will be priviliged to be able to invest in such a factory."

With that the director opened the bottle of vodka, indicating that the business part of the discussion was over. He rapidly poured shots all around and held up a toast to Joseph:

"To our American advisor who will help identify foreign investors for Rostov."

Ivan Ivanovich cheered and seconded the toast. Joseph rolled his eyes towards me with despair. The Russians were excited to have the American in Rostov, although their agendas were completely different from our own. There was so much opportunity for Joseph to provide consulting to these companies – if they would only let him. Vodka and caviar could provide a nice friendly veneer to the proceedings at first, but it would only be a matter of time before the clashes would erupt to the surface.

At least the caviar was spectacular. I was quietly sedated. The bubbles of salty gel popping in my mouth were set off perfectly by rich soft butter on fresh bread. The Russians understood how to entertain a visitor. The question remained of whether they would be able to listen to a visitor as well.

That night Joseph and I were exempted from joining Ivan Ivanovich in the never-ending vodka dinner circuit. I do not know the reason, but was just pleased by a reprieve from the forced hospitality. We retreated to the relative sanctuary of the Intourist Hotel restaurant. The forks and knives were twisted and tortured from extended service beyond the call of duty. The cracked vases, dusty fabric daisies and plastic table cloth also wore battle scars and fatigue. The paper napkins were carefully separated to be a single ply and snipped into quarters. Joseph's wooden chair creaked and crunched ominously. He hastily jumped up and swapped to a different chair.

Joseph called over a waitress and pointed out the faulty chair to her. The hazard should be addressed! The waitress shrugged and said to Joseph that if he didn't like the chair, then he shouldn't sit in it. She handed us menus and then wandered off. Joseph was about to enter another round of protest with her – "if this restaurant were interested in improving its service, it would..." But the waitress had already turned away, and the latest volley of advice fell to the gritty carpeted floor without acknowledgement.

Joseph stared intently at the retreating figure of the waitress. Another opportunity for improvement had been missed. I gestured to my colleague to let it drop. We had a relaxing evening ahead of us, I smiled. An evening without vodka when we could decide what we would eat, what we would talk about, and when we would call it a night. The simple pleasure of having these small choices lifted our spirits immensely.

We studied our menus for dinner. For nearly every meal over the past ten days Ivan Ivanovich had ordered every item of food for us. This was a novel concept to be in charge of our own dinner. We could actually determine what we wanted or did not want. The choices and opportunity was tantalising.

"Eggs. Cheese. Mushrooms. Tomatoes. Onions." Joseph read the menu slowly. "Look they serve each item separately."

Well, yes, I knew that already. In every post-Soviet restaurant I had ever been to, every item was ordered separately – order beef, get a slab of boiled beef – period. Want some potatoes with that? Then order some potatoes. If you want butter or salt or pepper or sauce, then of course you must order and pay for that as well.

"I'm going to have an omelette," Joseph decided, looking at the menu.

"Omelettes aren't on the menu," I corrected him.

"But all the ingredients are here," Joseph read down the list again. "The kitchen should be able to make an omelette for me."

Ah yes. There is Joseph attempting to offer his own solution again. I was tired of arguing and did not attempt to dispute him. The waitress would soon set him straight.

And sure enough she did. Omelettes were not on the menu. No he could not have an omelette.

Joseph protested – but all the ingredients were there – eggs, onions, mushrooms, tomatoes, cheese. Couldn't he offer a 20% surcharge for the chef to mix them all together?

"No it is impossible," the waitress glared at this difficult patron. "You must order from the menu."

"Would you ask the chef if he would do this?" Joseph persisted. He was determined to press for customer service and represent the voice of reason and improvement at every opportunity.

"No, I will not ask the chef. We do not serve omelettes," The waitress stood her ground.

But this was not satisfactory for Joseph. He was determined to pry open the minds of Russians by brute force if necessary. He declared then, okay, he would ask the chef directly. So in a few quick steps he outpaced the surprised waitress and charged back into the kitchen himself.

Suddenly a round of vodka shots seemed like an exceptionally good idea. Our days were filled with argument and confrontation – now spilling into the evening. A tranquilizer was needed to take the edge off and unclench the teeth just a bit. I called back the waitress with a sharp bark of "*devushka*" while bits of a heated argument escaped through the doors of the kitchen.

Eventually Joseph stormed back to the table, outraged.

"They absolutely refuse to cook the eggs together with the onions, mushrooms, tomatoes, and cheese. They say it is not on the menu and it is not up to them to make such decisions. All I want is a fucking omelette. Why does this have to be so difficult?"

I was done arguing for the day and could only nod and grimace in sympathy. Joseph, however, was bristling ready for another round of combat – or consultation. If there really was a difference between the two concepts.

The shots arrived and I lifted my glass in the classic style of the host.

"To Russia's future and our dear advisor's efforts to improve it." I tossed my head back and took the shot whole in one practiced motion. The vodka was chilled, but instantly went to work sending a warm pulsing glow through my veins.

Joseph hesitated for only a moment before lifting his own glass. "To Russia's future – whether they are ready for it or not."

6 NASHI

September 1994 — Moscow, Russia

True to the explanation of Andrei in Almaty, *remont* had become a phase of my life. I had been living as a four-star refugee in the Hotel Aerostar with all my worldly possessions in an increasing state of disarray and makeshift clotheslines entangling the room. A simple search for a pair of shoes would soon have me barking insults and curses and questioning my own sanity. My dear kitty would attempt to hide as I dug through the rubble. She was visibly stressed and depressed — certainly partly from the one-room captivity, but then also she was undoubtedly feeding off my anxiety as well.

The makeshift offices in the conference rooms of the Hotel Aerostar had seemed so luxurious when I first arrived. Now, months into the experience, tempers were running short with the whole team. The projects were expanding and more Russians recruited and American expats arriving every week. We were packed onto folding tables, tripping over extension cords, and the Americans were extremely unhappy with the substandard facilities. I was mainly distressed to be in a holding pattern, caught in a continuous loop between my hotel room and the conference rooms.

Everything about our daily lives reinforced a state of continuous chaos and transition. Our work was entirely at the discretion of the whims of USAID and the Russian government. One project with the Ministry of Finance was cancelled by USAID after some political pressure from the Russian government. (The explanation was that the Russians know what they are doing in regards to development of a functional stock market. It is insulting to send American "experts".) Another project for real estate title registration was suddenly expanded to encompass four new cities. No, change that to, three new cities. And then Moscow was cancelled. So the headquarters for that project will go to St Petersburg. Russian staff were traded with related Russian ministries. Americans were brought over as expatriate experts and then released immediately. Or temporary assignments were suddenly expanded to three years. Expats speaking no Russian whatsoever were sent on long term assignment to Ekaterinburg, Pskov, Tver, and other points of exile.

The Americans would arrive in Moscow with either the faces of the adventurous or the condemned. The younger set had signed onto a tour of duty in Russia with enthusiasm and a thirst for adventure. The older Americans fell into three categories – those who were nearing retirement and were seeking one great fun hurrah before retreating to a condominium on a golf resort, those who had just been through some personal drama, like a divorce, and were seeking to reinvent themselves, and those who had been told that the move was "good for their career" and they had reluctantly agreed. The younger set, retirees, and divorcees all plunged into Moscow with a thirst for adventure. Those focused on their careers complained that we sat in conference rooms crushed elbow to elbow and were frustrated that none of us really understood how to fix a misbehaving printer. Tech support was back in Washington DC. The Russian staff were just getting the hang of how to use a mouse (on a mouse pad rather than slamming it against the monitor). Here on the frontier we had to fend for ourselves – and beat the rogue printers into submission ourselves.

Our client nominally was the Russian Privatization Center – a brilliantly misnamed wing of the Russian government that actually was fully funded by foreign aid. Or perhaps our client was USAID, as they were the ones in fact signing the cheques and the work orders. But wait, we were working with the Local Privatization Centers in each major regional city. We were the nominal employers of the Directors and Staff of the Local Privatization Centers, yet these individuals were all actually political nominees from Moscow. We had no direct authority over our own so-called employees, yet were held accountable for their results. All of these entities, however, are government bureaucracies. If our goal is to be supporting the growth of Russian private business, aren't the privatized companies actually our end clients?

In short, there was a never-ending list of demands on our team, with ever-changing priorities from various sources. Consultants were sent to the Local Privatization Centers and recalled. Expats racked up astonishing bills for weeks (or months) on end in the Hotel Aerostar awaiting final signature the work orders – without which we could not procure long term apartments. Then those who obtained long term apartments in Moscow were suddenly redirected to St Petersburg.

We would outline our proposed project plan and it would be rejected by the Russian Privatization Center. Did they actually have authority to reject our plan? Perhaps yes, perhaps no. Raymond was politically savvy enough to understand that if the RPC didn't like our plan it would go nowhere, regardless of whether they had authority to approve it or not. The original work order was only two pages long. We were now attempting to agree the details with all parties for what we would do over the next year and how we would spend $9 million of US taxpayer money. And of course everyone we encountered had different views regarding the priorities and details. Despite this, Raymond was the eternal optimist and always believed that the next round of proposals would satisfy everyone. Rita would float into the office and delight the office staff with demonstrating a new flyswatter that she had found in a Swedish emporium. Then with a stylish flick of her scarf she would signal that Raymond's working day was over and she would whisk him off to the ballet or a dinner engagement at the Embassy.

If we took the path of least resistance, the Hotel Aerostar could engulf our entire existence. Breakfast, lunch, dinner. Sleeping, working, more working until we finally collapsed into bed. Not even escaping outside for a dose of Moscow air during the day.

I was now travelling for a few days each week to various regional cities and at least was aware that the outside world existed. When back in Moscow, at lunch I made a point of trying to extract myself from my desk and venture out of the hotel to eat something – but what? The choice of food in the area was the eternal *shashlik* – meat of dubious origin charred over a fire in an oil drum – or dried fish and Snickers bars found in the precarious shacks of kiosks (amidst a range of random other objects like car batteries, cigarettes, vodka, pirated videos, and ball point pens). The Russian employees were provided lunch in the hotel staff dining area of the Aerostar. The Americans were left to fend for ourselves (although of course we had the salaries to do so). A small wedge between the Americans and Russians, which we tried not to talk about too much.

After once again determining that I did not have the stomach for dried fish, I would return to the hotel and order a club sandwich or soup from room service to be delivered to the conference room. I would try to be grateful for the club sandwich. Wheat bread (per my request) toasted and then cut neatly into quarters. A little toothpick holding the sandwich together and a linen napkin folded just so.

I chided myself that I should be grateful that such things were available and that I could afford them. When travelling I would usually be taken to a government building canteen with the rest of the Russian team. Tin trays would be semi washed and the canteen would smell of cold oily meat and wet dogs. The selection would generally be a piece of boiled meat with cooked cabbage or a watery indistinct soup and a piece of dry bread. Hot over-sugared tea in a glass would help to wash it down. The Russians would laugh and enjoy their meals – quite likely they had been eating at the same cafeteria for the past 15 years, with the same white-capped matrons ladling out the same watery soup. They would give me a side glance to see how I would react to the lunch. I would strive to follow the lead of my Russian host. If they thought the meal was tasty that day, I would eat everything, down to the last crumb of the stale bread. If they complained about the rubbery meat, I found an excuse to poke at it and hope that dinner would make up for the lunch.

It was a risk, of course. I never quite knew what would happen at dinner. Sometimes

I was swept away to a grand banquet with local government officials and business representatives, toasting the future of Russian-American cooperation. At other times I was dropped unceremoniously back at my hotel and left for an evening of scavenging. More than once dinner was comprised only of boiled eggs, mystery pickled vegetables, and hot tea. A local beer (room temperature with the label falling off) usually helped to wash down the meal. Another beer or two would lull me into a state of pleasant ambivalence for the inevitable battle ahead. What would it be this evening – an argument with the *dezhurnaya* for towels, or lack of hot water, or television that only emitted shrieking static? Pounding of random Russian men on my door demanding to "*poznakomitsa*" – the line used for "I want to get to know you" for both casual affairs and prostitutes alike. And all of that would just be a prelude to the adventure of attempting to send email from a scratchy landline.

Back in Moscow for the weekend I would do whatever I could to be away from the sterile confines of the Hotel Aerostar. During the day Sarah would introduce me to her approach to city exploration. Her favorite weekend activity was to take the Metro to the end of a line and then figure out a way to walk to the station at the end of the *next* line – without using a map.

"Where is the adventure of exploration if you actually use a map?" Sarah responded when we first stepped out from the station into a jungle of identical crumbling concrete apartment blocks.

And she was right. The labyrinth of twisting streets, open manhole covers, and dusty storefronts was a raw canvas for adventure. Yes, the endless scenes of deteriorating infrastructure, garbage rotting in alleys, and toothless shuffling *babushki* could be depressing if that is all you focused on. But with Sarah we found fresh bowls of homemade *pelmeni* in hot broth behind a door with a hand-printed sign simply stating "*pelmeni*". We saw fresh flowers being sold next to a burned out shell of a kiosk. And we came across an open-air pet market where everything from kittens to pythons were being sold. Sarah opened my eyes to the real thrill of raw travel – unexpected discoveries in unchartered territory. Uncertain risks. Uncertain rewards. The adrenaline rush of the adventures into the unknown was addictive.

The American guys I worked with, however, had a completely different opinion for what they wanted for adventure. Try as I might, I could not convince them that it was exciting to find delicious bowls of *pelmeni* behind crudely marked doors. The story of the pet market did mildly intrigue them. But what the American men really wanted, however, was young Russian women – *devushki*.

And this is what would inevitably drive us to the heart of the Moscow nightclub scene.

In Almaty, the nightclub "scene" (if you could call it that) was exclusively Dr Bang's – a business academy by day and a dance club by night. Raw and bizarre and relatively harmless (if you stayed away from the expired beer). In Moscow, however, the night-clubs served as the battleground for the power struggles of the new Russians and their musclemen – battleground both in a figurative and sometimes literal sense. The new Russians would use the club as their forum to parade evidence of their new found power – in the form of obscene displays of wealth, with silent thin *devushki* on their arms and muscle men wearing bottle green jackets hovering nearby. Of course, the clubs that we could afford were only for the middle and lower-tier new Russians. Their position in the new social ladder was not secure, therefore they were even more aggressive with their displays of wealth and posturing.

A favorite joke circulating in the expat circles described two New Russians who encounter each other by chance on the streets of Paris. One proudly shows his new silk tie, explaining that he paid over $200 for it. The other says "you idiot, at the shop across the street you could have paid $400."

It was the sort of joke that made sense entirely within the context of Russia in the mid-1990s, but elsewhere people will find to be baffling.

As fascinating as the New Russians were from a social anthropology perspective, the American guys were entirely drawn to the nightclubs by their raw fixation with Russian women. They were thin, severe, and unapproachable – yet wore black miniskirts and metal stilettos that underscored that they weren't *entirely* unapproachable. Paul puffed up his chest and assured the newcomer American and British guys that Russian girls would do anything *anything* you wanted in bed. Would Russian girls go for a *ménage a trois*? Everett immediately had to ask. Paul paused and then said that he was sure they would. (But he had not yet had the opportunity to prove this theory himself.)

The clubs would open at midnight, but the fashionable set wouldn't show until 2:30 or 3am. The guys made their first ventures to the clubs without Gloria and me – but soon discovered that they were more likely to make their way past the bouncers if they had a few American women in tow. Single American men obviously would be on the prowl for single Russian women. Bringing a few American women as collateral would even out the numbers and make the bouncers marginally more accepting of the American men, and their money. The inevitable Big Boris would give all of us an inspection and demand random amounts of rubles (or dollars) from the guys as an entrance fee (us girls would usually be waved in for free). We later concluded that the door fee was roughly based on how well the guys spoke Russian. Alex, the bilingual American expat, would always be charged the least while those being the most obviously American were charged the most. (Stephen, a Brit, of course resented being continuously mistaken for being American.) Sometimes Big Boris wouldn't like the look of one of the Americans and block him from entering – after the rest of us were inside. We had an unspoken pact that if someone was thrown out, then it was their own problem for how to get back in – or hitchhike home. The rest of us could not jeopardize our already tenuous relationship with the bouncer.

Nightclubs are a place for adventure, dropping inhibitions, experimenting with emotions. What are you capable of? What new experience will we have tonight? Dim lights, swirling smoke, a kaleidoscope of sounds. The continuous heartbeat of the Euro house music pulsed through the walls and floors. Bodies, sweat, hot breath, alcohol, smoke moved in rivers and whirlpools, mixing and separating. Recombining in new patterns. The pulsing entered our bodies, our hearts. We were all part of the single living organism of the club. The posturing of the New Russians added a level of tension and intrigue. Violence was just below the surface. For the young expats this was excitement and living and we were part of it.

The faces of strangers would blend together as we fell deeper into the rhythm on the dance floor. A common goal – enjoy the energy of our bodies while we are young and healthy. Who knows what tomorrow may bring. Just live for today, tonight. This moment. We were thousands of miles and an alternate dimension away from the predictable sterile world of Washington DC, and loving it.

As the energy of the club flowed, little clots would appear of the expats that did not quite blend into the mix. We smiled too much. Our haircuts and clothes were out of synch. The American women tried to blend in. We wore the right red lipstick and body skimming spandex skirts, but we never mastered the disinterested pout of the *devushki* and did not quite look the same in black miniskirts as they did. We would eventually spot another group of expats and laugh. Yes, here we all are out for a night on the Moscow scene.

Gloria and I would be happy to meet the other new expats – great to grow our social circle a bit more. The guys, however, would need to keep moving. Their objective had not yet been met – a Russian *devushka* for the night. It was always possible to find some *devushka* willing to go home with you, Paul and Alex stated with confidence, just a matter of continuing to play the odds. And, paying attention that you weren't chatting up the favorite of some thug wearing a bottle green jacket and gold chains.

Anything could happen. Sometimes Everett or Paul would disappear and we would catch a glimpse of them entwined with a *devushka*. "If she accepts a drink, she will be yours for the night," Paul promised. Or Alex would brush by quickly and say that he is leaving *now*. He had just aggravated some Russian with a bad haircut. Or the guys would simply vanish and we had no idea what happened to them. Alliances were short. The American women were useful to help get the expat guys into the club. They would circle the dance floor looking for targets of opportunity. Come back to our sides to re-boost their confidence, then off again.

If we were left alone for a moment, inevitably a Russian man would push himself up against us. *Davaite poznakomitsa*. "Let's get to know each other." The standard opening line to pick up girls for the night. Heavy alcohol on the breath, eyes not quite focusing. Once both of us had told him *nyet* he could rejoin the school of sharks circling around the Russian *devushki* — or he could stay and insult us for a bit. "Do we think that we are so much better than him? What is wrong with American women that they do not want to be with Russian men?" A reply of any sort would certainly aggravate the situation. If we accepted a drink or even a moment of socializing, the assumption would be quickly made that we would be theirs for the night. So we remained silent. No, we do not speak Russian.

If an expat man saw a Russian pushing himself on Gloria and me then he might step in and escort us safely away. As the night wore on, however, the American men would more likely be distracted with their own efforts to pick up Russian girls using the same line, *davaite poznakomitsa*. Gloria and I would be left to fend for ourselves. At the clubs the American men were kids in a candy store — too many tasty options all within reach. The American women, however, were pieces of meat thrown into a cage of hungry animals. And for better or for worse, we were often viewed as rotting meat in comparison to the fresher, more enticing Russian options. We were sniffed and ignored and left to find our own ways home.

The next morning at the office would feature Paul, Everett, and Stephen recounting their adventures with the *devushki*, misadventures with Russians with bad haircuts and bottle green jackets, and random events at the club.

"The live band was supposed to start at 3am, but only started at 4:30am. Good thing you didn't stay, Phaedra."

"Some thugs dragged away one of the Russians near me. No, it didn't even cause a ripple in the room. Of course no one tried to stop them."

"You would not believe who took the stage after you left. David Byrne! Yes, *the* David Byrne just randomly joined the band on stage. Oh my god. I can't believe you had left already!"

"Really scary hitching a lift home after the club. We agreed 10,000 rubles. But then the driver would not stop talking about how Americans are made of money and I really should pay him 100,000 rubles. I was sure he was going to pull a gun on me. But I only paid him 10,000 because that is what we agreed!"

"*Davaite poznakomitsa*! What a great line! Isn't this country great! Just say that and give her a drink and she is yours for the night!"

The guys would then smile with giddy astonishment. Russian women had *none* of the hang-ups that American women did, they were pleased to report. The opportunities with Russian *devushki* were only limited to their ambitions. This would then trigger several escalating rounds of comparing their various conquests. How long did it take to get a girl to agree to go home with you? Who had the record? What would it take to break that? Everett listed off the number of Natashas he had met the previous evening and suddenly decided that he was going to start a whole new "Natasha score card." Just bringing any woman home for the night was no longer a challenge. Now he was going to focus on just finding *devushki* named "Natasha".

"Where do the Russian *devushki* learn how to do such amazing things with their bodies?" Everett continued his monologue. "I thought I was fairly sexually experienced, but then learned a few new uses for a sofa over the weekend. And, can you believe it, she was actually *demanding* that I should be *rougher*."

This was now a bit more than I really needed to know about other people's private lives. At this point Robert would interject. "You really should not bring home the Russian girls. You don't know who these girls are. What if all they are doing is casing your house? Next week they may bring their boyfriend back and break in."

Stephen, Everett, and Paul would tell Robert that he really needed to put down the slide rule from time to time and get out and experience Moscow. There is more to life than the Hotel Aerostar.

And then the conversation would turn invariably to the status of the *remont* and our ongoing office pool. The official dates of early August had long since passed. My wager of 10 September was now considered to be laughable as well. The finalists were all Russians who were more cynical (and obviously realistic) than the Americans. There was always one more reason why the move in date was delayed.

Andrew said that his preferred painter was not available this week. Next week everything would be complete. A different painter would be at least $200 more. I tried to explain that the project was paying over $200 per night for my hotel room. It would be logical for us to just pay the extra $200 to the other painter so I could move in earlier. Andrew was silent on the other end of the phone for a moment and then replied. "Two hundred dollars every night at the Hotel Aerostar? That is stupid. You are working on an aid project, true? Why is this money not given to Russian companies?" But nevertheless, he continued with his original plan of delaying the painting phase by a week so he could contract the cheaper painter.

So the pattern continued.

But then again, one thing that was certain in Russia was that nothing was certain. As soon as we had established one pattern of existence, something would disrupt the pattern. A favorite club would have a locked door at 2am and no one there. Closed without explanation. An expat friend re-deployed by his company to Bishkek. The latest round of inflation would result in a cash shortage of large ruble notes, so everyone was carrying mountains of small notes. Or better yet, dollars. We all carried thousands of dollars of cash. No cards accepted anywhere outside the Western hotels in Moscow. Occasionally we would find one of our hundred dollar bills to have an ink smudge – a sure sign of counterfeit. After the initial thrill of exposure to the dark underbelly of Moscow, then the question became how to unload the bill on its next unsuspecting victim. I found a kiosk that sold Friskies cat food. And then the next time I visited the kiosk it was burned to the ground – only a mountain of ashes remained.

And then one day in late September it really happened. I actually moved into my flat. The paint had barely dried, the hinges on cupboard doors were not totally adjusted properly, and I had not yet found curtains to shield my apartment from the prying eyes from the neighboring building, but my patience had been brought to a breaking point. As soon as my contraband Ikea furniture arrived (taking advantage of Alex's diplomatic privileges to circumvent the 65% import duty) I declared the apartment to be fit for occupation and moved in. Word spread quickly through the office. The Americans lobbied for a grand opening housewarming party. The Russians all offered recommendations of friends or relatives who would be eager housecleaners or cooks or whatever other services I could possibly need.

At first I resisted the idea of a housekeeper. Kazakhstan had been my first experience ever with a "housekeeper" – but this had been thrust upon me rather than a deliberate choice. The Russians stressed that it was practically my *duty* as an American expat to take on a Russian housekeeper. The Americans were paid radically more than the Russians. Per official statistics unemployment was still relatively low. But the reality was that many "employed" in state or recently privatized enterprises had not been paid for months. Plus, in this time of hyperinflation, an American could offer the most coveted term of engagement – hard currency. If I were serious about doing what I could to help Russians then I must do my part and employ one as a housekeeper. Vanya, my driver, eagerly offered the services of his wife. Robert got wind of the proposal and quickly urged me to decline. He emphatically reminded me - No entangling relationships in the office. Clearly, the most diplomatic answer would be to take on a housekeeper – but someone totally unrelated to the Russian staff. I could not be perceived to be playing favorites – or have my home life entangled with office politics.

Sarah enthusiastically introduced Valya – who quickly became a key symbol of the new Russia for me. Valya was my age, or possibly a few years older, and a young single mother of a four-year old girl. Until recently she had been employed as a physicist at a nuclear weapons factory, but she had recently quit that role – as she had concluded that being a housekeeper for expatriates was more satisfying and more lucrative.

Yes, I now had a nuclear physicist as a housekeeper. At first I was mortified. How could a strong educated woman possibly find this to be a satisfying career change? But Valya radiated optimism and lifted my spirits immediately. She had always held philosophical issues with working in a nuclear weapons factory, she explained. The fact that the factory (like most state-owned enterprises at the time) had not paid her in months made the decision to leave a non-event. Even better, when cleaning apartments she could bring her daughter along to work with her – something that would be impossible at the factory.

But didn't she miss the intellectual stimulation of "real" work, I asked.

Not at all, Valya laughed. At the nuclear weapons factory she did what she was told. Other people's ideas. Other people's projects. All centrally directed with no room for real initiative. As a housekeeper she was far more independent. She could figure out for herself what was needed and solve real problems and achieve real results. She believed that foreign investment would pave the road to a brighter future and wanted to do her part by making Russia inviting to the expatriates. Just seeing the way we lived gave her hope that she and her daughter could also improve their standard of living. And everyone was happy. Real job satisfaction.

Valya chomped into the role of housekeeper with a passion I had not previously believed was possible. From the first week I was astonished at the projects she devised for herself – dusting the inside of ceiling lamps, scrubbing the cat litter tray spotless, ironing and folding all my underwear (which honestly left me a bit disturbed), and holding the first line of defense against the continuous invading armies of cockroaches. Valya introduced me to "Chinese chalk" – a substance illegal in the United States but widely available in Russia. Essentially it was nearly pure acid in the form of chalk – just draw a line on the wall or floor and *voila*, the little critters' feet will disintegrate if they cross. I had to question the safety of doing this around her four year old daughter and my cat, but Valya assured me that she had everything under control and that I worried too much.

Valya took pride and initiative in a role that others could have dismissed as being a symbol of a total failure. Her enthusiasm was infectious. Yes, life is good. She was making my fantasy of having a cozy sanctuary retreat a reality.

And so I joined the ranks of young expatriates who had a housekeeper, a driver, and a personal assistant at the tender age of 27.

As pleased as I was that my apartment *remont* had come to an end, the real shock came a few short weeks later with the move out of the Hotel Aerostar conference rooms into our real office space at Chistiye Prudi.

The transformation from neglected classic Russian imperial building to modern American office was complete. The grand façade of the building had been restored to its glorious elegance with a fresh coat of paint and meticulous patching of the decorative exterior details. A small bronze plaque revealed the identity of the occupants – "Arthur Andersen." Anyone unfamiliar with the name would only have to look at the new solid steel fortress doors to understand that the occupants represented the latest beachhead by corporate America onto the Russian frontier.

Inside the building, the domination of modern America over classical Russian style was complete. Yes, the arched doorways remained between grand rooms in the structure, but that was one of the few vestiges of the building's history. Where there once had been chandeliers and painted ceiling medallions now were acoustic tiles and florescent lighting. The main hall was filled with a rabbit warren of sea foam colored cubicles and ergonomically correct rolling chairs.

Most of the Russian staff had never seen an office cubicle before, or, needless to say, had worked in one. The obvious similarities between cubicles and public restroom stalls were quickly noted. Some of the Russians took the desecration of the centuries old building personally as an act of aggression by the Americans against Russian history and culture. One more sign that the Americans do not really understand the Russian people. But most were delighted to be working in a modern western-style office. How prestigious! Some escorted their friends through the office space so they could testify to their extended family and social networks how Vadim or Dmitri were moving up in the world.

With a squeal of excitement petite blonde Oksana realized that she had won the office pool – and the 25,000 ruble jackpot that went with it. Of course rampant inflation had reduced the actual value of the prize by over 50% since the wagers were collected nearly three months prior. That realization curbed her enthusiasm only momentarily – The real prize, she soon appreciated, was to be able to bask in the moment of having proven to all the Russian men in the office that a girl *could* be right and win this game.

No event in Russia is complete without a round of celebratory vodka shots (or three). The office move and Oksana's victory in the office pool were no exception. Robert, the American office manager, frowned on the idea of vodka in the office. Raymond, however, (who himself did not drink at all) understood the importance of letting the Russians be Russian and not crushing every ounce of local tradition out of our team. Besides, concepts like "liability" were quite irrelevant in the context of Russia in 1994. There were probably Firm policies formally against vodka in the office. But then again, there were probably civil code requirements for a standard number of office parties required each year in the name of upholding the morale of the workers' collective. Which rules would be enforced and which could be casually ignored would be entirely a reflection of the Americans' relationships with a web of local government officials – extending often into the families of our team.

Raymond was too gracious to ever argue with Robert in public. But the fact that the office relocation party featured copious amounts of vodka and Robert was looking more tense than usual meant that obviously Raymond had won his point.

The toasts began with Nadya offering the requisite elaborate congratulations to Robert for successful completion of the transformation of this historic landmark (delivered with an acid undertone hinting she really meant "desecration" rather than "transformation"). I followed up with the obvious toast to the glorious future of Russia (spoken with requisite humorous and sarcastic drama, with an elaborate list of future accomplishments by our team, including stabilizing the banking sector, improving the city of Moscow by renovating one apartment at a time, and promoting the cause of

Freedom and Liberty). Kolya led the traditional third toast, which (as always) was dedicated to the women at the party. Kolya gave resounding praise to Oksana for her clever forecast of the office move date. His monologue then expanded to praise all the women in the office, noting especially all the women's exceptional beauty which was a terrible distraction in the office. If this team did not manage to achieve all the possible accomplishments outlined in the second toast, he said it would have to be attributed to the unfortunate distractions in the office.

Paul, Stephen, and Everett loudly seconded Kolya's toast (the vodka was flowing freely now). Oksana, Tatiana, and some of the other women smiled shyly and mumbled some thanks. Nastya responded by jumping onto a chair and pulling her black mini-skirt up a few extra inches – showing the spectators a bit more of her shapely legs than would generally be accepted in an office environment. Nadya offered a quiet retort that "of course the men will always figure out a way to blame the women for their own failures." Quite daring for a Russian girl. Robert was silent, biting his lip and giving a meaningful stare at Raymond that carried the subtitle: "See? I said we shouldn't allow vodka in the office. Look at where this is going!"

I, of course, was totally conflicted. I had endorsed the standard Russian approach to celebrations and socializing to Robert. But now this was at odds with my deep impulse to protect the women on my team from improper advances and to educate the men a bit about civil conduct in the modern world. To make matters worse Paul, Stephen, and Everett had applauded Kolya's toast loudly and were now egging on Nastya (now stepping from the chair to a desktop) to show how distracting she really could be. Everyone was now laughing and enjoying the moment. Now was not the time for a lecture on treating women with more respect.

I did, however, quietly coax Nastya to please come down from the desk. One small step towards having the girls in the office at least treat themselves with respect.

A bit of fresh air was in order. Or, at least what passed for fresh air in Moscow near the oily and garbage strewn ponds of "Chistiye Prudi". I stood outside for a few moments to collect my thoughts. Certainly the Russians must have an expression to help me think through the situation and next steps. "*Otbrosi pervuyu blinichku*" suddenly came to mind. "Throw out the first pancake." It is a simple philosophy. The first time you try something it is bound to fail, but keep trying. The vodka was starting to blur the edges of my thoughts. I would make another attempt at paving the way forward to the glorious future of Russia, but it probably would not be today.

I re-entered the building and bounced up the stairs to our offices. The stairwell smelled of fresh paint – a symbol of renewal and a fresh start. And almost completely foreign to modern Russian reality.

In the stairwell Kolya was quietly smoking a cigarette, leaning against the wall near the "no smoking" sign. Although we had been in the offices less than a day, the floor was already smudged with evidence that the team had made the concession not to smoke at their desks (as was standard in typical Russian offices) but were not ready to take their habit outdoors. One small step forward at least, right?

I pointed playfully at the no smoking sign and asked Kolya in Russian if he needed help with understanding what it meant. Kolya gave the sign a dismissive wave and laughed.

"Too many rules. Too little time," he responded. "I am building the New Russia. Did you not say we are to be promoting Freedom and Independence? I am supporting the cause of Freedom and Independence from oppressive rules. How can you criticize me?"

I laughed and said that at least he was smoking American cigarettes. As much as I dislike stale cigarette smoke, the American brands left a distinctly better smell than the rancid Russian ones.

With this Kolya smiled and stubbed out the butt under his heel. He reached out and held me with both hands by the shoulders.

"Once you have tasted an American you cannot go back," he whispered.

With that, he spun me around and slammed my body against the concrete wall in a playful show of aggression and then planted a firm kiss on my mouth. I drew a sharp breath with the quick realization that Kolya's taste for Americans did not just refer to cigarettes. His body now pinned me and my head cracked against the cold wall under the force of his demanding kisses. The biting scent of latex paint mixed with the last wisps of cigarette smoke. For a moment I let myself enjoy the warmth of his breath on my neck and the abandon of being held by the arms of a man much stronger than me. (Later I tried to attribute that lapse to the vodka taking hold over my brain.)

Then my brain clicked back into gear. I am at the office. Kolya is one of our Russian employees. There were so many things wrong with this scene. I just needed to end this and move on quickly. Instinctively, I pushed him off with a light laugh. "I recommend you limit your taste in Americans to cigarettes," I scolded playfully.

Kolya held me for a moment longer and then relented. "You have escaped today, but someday revenge will be mine," Kolya called over my shoulder as I continued up the stairs. I returned to the confines of my new cubicle – with the wheels in my head trying to figure out exactly what had just happened.

The scene with Kolya sent me deeper into my conflict regarding how to best deal with the relations between the men and women in the office. We had stepped beyond Kolya just making suggestive remarks to now acting on his impulses. And an outside observer could argue that I had been almost been cooperative with his advances.

I had fiercely instructed the Russian girls on my team to alert me to any misconduct by the men. Tales from the interviewees and my own observations left me to conclude that it would only be a matter of time before one of the American men would start to impose themselves on the Russian women. Given their young primal hunting instincts,

I had mentally prepared myself to be one day defending Oksana or Nastya from Paul, Everett, and Stephen. We had a strong ethical standard that I was prepared to enforce in defense of the Russian women. I had not expected the first move to be made by one of the Russian men on myself.

So now what? If I were to follow what I preached I would be walking directly into Robert's office. We were in Russia, but as an American company Arthur Andersen required the American standard of professional behavior. Random advances in the stairwells were not to be tolerated per the firm statements in the employee handbook.

What exactly would happen if I were to raise this as a formal issue? I could hear the conversation clearly in my mind. Robert was the office manager for a reason – he would assess the situation and apply the rules, without any personal favoritism or consideration. The outcomes would be very correct, very clinical, and very foreign to the entire Russian business culture. Kolya's career with the firm, and probably with any western company in Moscow, would have a black mark against it. Did I really want to do that? He was behaving exactly as his culture had raised him. Actually, he deserved even a bit more credit – he actually respected my wishes when I declined and moved on. There were others who would just take what they wanted.

And then what about my relations with the Russian team? Kolya was well-liked by everyone. There were enough strains on a daily basis with the Russian team, did I really need to add one more? In Russia, working effectively was entirely dependent on personal relationships, not formal rules and agreements. If I were to turn Kolya over to the American disciplinary machine I would be choosing to take a giant leap backwards in my ability to achieve real support from the team.

The American rules clashed with the Russian culture. Sea foam-colored cubicles placed in the grand expanse of the classic Russian building. Somehow they would have to coexist.

On Monday morning everyone found a copy of an intra-office memo placed in the center of their desks. The message was printed on company letterhead and formatted according to the classical stylebooks and contained a stern general warning that night-club attire was not appropriate in the work place. A recent increase in the number of women wearing black spandex miniskirts and stiletto heels in the office had been noted. The men were reminded to wear business shirts with a tie – and preferably an undershirt. If women choose to wear skirts, they must be "professional" in appearance and cover the knees, with heels of an "appropriate" height. The memo was signed with regards from Robert, the office manager.

The memo led to a ripple of giggles throughout the office. The following day every one of the women, including normally demure Tatiana, wore black spandex miniskirts with spirited pride. I smiled as sat at my desk wearing my own miniskirt and blood red lipstick in solidarity with their silent protest. Nadya had led the plot and had tipped me off in advance. "Robert is all about rules. He doesn't understand us," she whispered with mischievous conspiracy.

Upon seeing me that day, Kolya looked me up and down with a discerning eye and whispered over my shoulder. "Just as I said last week – the women in this office are terribly distracting. We will never get any work done today." He then added with a laugh. "You are truly *nashi*."

Nashi. Literally "one of us." But the expression means so much more. In a culture where neighbor had been turned against neighbor for so many centuries, *nashi* is the ultimate compliment that you have been accepted into an inner circle and are to be trusted. Your friends will support you. You will succeed. It is us against them.

From his desk in a glass office, Robert looked out at the women in the office and scowled. The rules were being ignored. He re-aligned the stapler, tape dispenser, and pencil cup on his desk in frustration.

I sat at my desk and smiled. In Russia we have no rules. Therefore no rules have been broken.

No, I would not say anything to Robert about Kolya's advance in the stairwell. I would learn to work on Russian terms. I was *nashi* now.

7 HISTORY LESSONS

October 1994 – Ekaterinburg

Two *remont* projects were now complete. But elsewhere others were just starting. Andrei's warning continued to ring true. *Remont* had become a phase of my life.

I was dispatched to Ekaterinburg to check in on the launch of the new Local Privatization Center there. The American advisor, Nathan, had just arrived himself the previous week. The director, Sergei Glebovich, was eager to show us a property that had been recently leased for the LPC's new offices. He was extremely proud of the fact that renovations were already underway.

We travelled comfortably in a large black Volga – the car of choice for the government elite, complete with curtains in the windows. I complimented Sergei Glebovich and his driver on the beautiful Volga. He beamed with pride and gestured meaningfully around the vehicle.

"This is the car of those with real connections and political status!" Sergei Glebovich explained the obvious to me, but this was all new to Nathan. "Of course we must have a Volga (at a minimum) if we are to be entertaining American *biznismen* here in Ekaterinburg!"

We approached a GAI checkpoint and with a flick of the officer's baton, we were waved on. Sergei Glebovich was thrilled. "See this is one of the benefits of the Volga! We are not stopped by the GAI!" Nathan did not understand what was happening and I attempted to play cultural translator. The nice foreign cars and the Volgas are waved around the checkpoint. Everyone else is stopped and assessed a "fine" for a traffic violation. The fine must be paid immediately in cash to the officer.

"What sorts of violations?" Nathan asked.

"Could be anything. Breaking the speed limit. A crack in the windscreen. A headlight not working. But the GAI will always find something."

Nathan nodded approval. Good to see that the transport police was enforcing the rules and keeping the streets safe.

"No Nathan, you don't understand. The GAI will find something wrong for everyone who they stop. And they will *only* stop those who look like they do not have any political status. In the traffic stops they ask for your documents straight away. They will hold the documents until you pay the fine. The GAI is accuser, judge, jury and executioner. The fine is all cash. Must be paid on the spot. No receipt or documentation provided from the GAI. Doesn't this all seem unjust to you?" I started to elaborate on these thoughts and was ready to start a monologue on the whole absence of rule of law and its implications, but soon stopped. It was simply rude to keep up an English-language conversation in front of our Russian host. Nathan would have to learn these lessons on his own. Hopefully.

The Volga was only the first thing on Sergei Glebovich's list of major accomplishments in the name of privatization. His excitement was infectious. He was overjoyed with the project of establishing the Local Privatization Center in Ekaterinburg and he was so pleased that Moscow has selected *him* to be the Director. He was eager to demonstrate that he was the right person for the job and would not disappoint anyone in Moscow. He gushed that through his connections he had obtained the ideal building for the project. It was next door *next door* to Boris Yeltsin's offices. Of course Yeltsin was President of Russia at this time and not often in his home city of Ekaterinburg. But that was irrelevant to Sergei Glebovich's main point – what a prestigious location!

To prove his argument further, Sergei Glebovich drew our attention to the road. The best road in Ekaterinburg led directly to our offices. (Actually, the road led to Yeltsin's offices, but Sergei Glebovich was all too happy to bask in the reflected glory.) Perfect smooth asphalt. Creamy black and flawless. Smooth surface. Perfect texture. It could have just been laid the previous day. I had never seen anything quite like it in Russia or Kazakhstan. No marked lines or reflectors, of course. The shoulder broke away into an uneven shred. Nevertheless, it was the single best road I had seen in the former Soviet Union to date. I had to agree that I was impressed.

Yes, this location is prestigious and the road proves it, Sergei Glebovich confirmed. Yeltsin did not like the quality of the road leading to his private offices, therefore it had been resurfaced. Special request from the President himself! What further evidence did we need to prove that this particular LPC would be the shining star for the rest of the country?

Nathan nodded and smiled and (with me playing the role of interpreter for the day) congratulated Sergei Glebovich on his political connections and excellent choice for a location. Sergei Glebovich beamed at the compliment and stated with confidence that this center was going to be a model for American-Russian cooperation and he was pleased to be working with Nathan.

We arrived at the future offices. I saw a building that should have been condemned. Sergei Glebovich saw the future of Russia.

The Director leaped out of the car with excitement and pride. With a flourish he waved his arms towards a corpse of a building that appeared to be held together solely by the exoskeleton of scaffolding that crept up its exterior. Bricks, metal beams, wires, and pipes were all scattered and mounded in the general area of the building. The structure was either undergoing demolition or construction, but based upon the general disarray of the site, it was not clear which.

In the United States the site would have been a hard-hat only zone – surrounded by a fence to keep civilians at bay. I stood beside the Volga looking at the two Russians climbing on the scaffolding. They shouted insults at each other which were echoed by two other Russians on the ground. No hard hats, or gloves, or steel tipped boots or anything else one comes to expect as basic safety equipment in the West. Watching the general arguments between the construction workers, I was not convinced there was a designated site foreman – or even a plan they were working from.

Sergei Glebovich bounced with enthusiasm from the car through the scrap heap to the cavernous black opening of the building. At the doorway, he turned and smiled and beckoned us to follow. Nathan followed without hesitation – Sergei Glebovich's wish was his command. Once again I was wearing shoes that were completely impractical for the occasion and picked my way more slowly through protruding shards of metal towards the entrance. I ducked under the scaffolding and leaped forward into the dark void beyond – just as an avalanche of bricks fell behind me over the entrance.

I stood on the earth floor inside the shell of the building looking blankly back at a pile of rubble and a cloud of dust where I had passed just a moment before. The implications were obvious. I had been spared by a fraction of a second from a total stoning of biblical proportions.

Sergei Glebovich had seen the cascade of bricks and smiled: "You have to pay attention! This is a construction site!"

Sergei Glebovich was right. In the United States there would be safety warnings, hard hats. Actually we probably would have been banned from the construction site altogether. Many Americans would be mortified by the lack of safety precautions and restrictions. I found it to be liberating and exhilarating. Here in Russia no one was going to stop you from doing something stupid – like wandering around a construction site. You could do what you wanted. But you also had to be ready for the consequences. This, in a bizarre way, was real freedom – and with it came real personal responsibility.

The cascade of bricks was already forgotten by Sergei Glebovich. Our host had moved on and turned his attention to the real point of the visit – explaining the grand vision for this space. My eyes were slowly adjusting to the darkness inside the cavern. To Sergei Glebovich, however, the darkness was irrelevant. The image for the future Local Privatization Center was clearly etched in his mind. Here is the reception area. Very professional, with a desk and a phone for the receptionist, plus around the corner an area to make tea of course. To the right of the entrance is a large hall which can be used to host delegations of foreign investors coming to meet Russian business partners. Sergei Glebovich used the present tense to describe his plans – although all that existed today was a dirt floor and exterior walls.

To the left is a room that is the training facility. We keep the computers in here. Our American advisor uses this room to train our Russian consultants. Nathan replied that he would put the room to good use. Sergei Glebovich turned to me and asked the inevitable question of how long until the computer shipment would arrive.

I sighed while attempting to determine how best to answer him. True to Sarah's warning, the computer procurement was rapidly becoming the bane of my existence.

As promised, Arthur Andersen did have a dedicated team back in Washington DC working on computer procurement. The challenge, I discovered, was that the DC-based team saw their role as ensuring USAID procurement rules were adhered to, placing the orders, and (hopefully, eventually) shipping the order to Russia. Nowhere in that list was actual specification of the equipment.

After my original trip to South Russia I had sketched out the computer equipment requirements for the first LPC and sent the list by email to the team in DC. Based on my understanding of the breakdown of planned administrative staff vs consultants across the three locations, I had requested the following for the region as a whole (to be distributed among the three offices):

5 desktop computers

9 laptop computers

3 printers

3 fax machines

10 telephones

All computers should have the standard configuration required for standard office use in Russia, dial up modem capabilities, network connection, floppy drives, surge suppressors. Russian language required for all software and keyboards. Power supplies and surge suppressors must be European standard.

When I sent the email I was concerned that the DC office might think I was being

condescending by calling out the Russian language and European power supply requirements. But given my prior experience in Kazakhstan I just wanted to do my part to
reduce the risk of unpleasant surprises.

I had received a crisp email the next day from someone named Annabel in the DC
office noting that they would not be able to action my request until I provided detail
specifications of the equipment required. I was baffled. Wasn't there a standard definition in place for what would be purchased if I asked for a "laptop computer" or a "fax
machine"? Apparently not.

I called Annabel for an explanation (at the end of my business day, beginning of
DC's morning, therefore another day of work was lost here). She explained, in an
exasperated tone, that I needed to be *specific*. For example – what processor speed was
required. How much hard drive space was required. An internal or external modem
to connect to the internet. Size and display quality of the monitors. And, look, I didn't
even note that I needed mice for the computers. All mice, cables, etc. needed to be
itemized separately. Once I had the specifications clear *then* she would be able to order
the equipment.

Now what? Raymond, my 65+ year old manager, had never used a computer.
Clearly he would not be able to provide much guidance here. My growing team of
Russians in the office were just learning that mice could be steered by hand on a table
top rather than pressed against the computer monitor as a pointing device. The other
Americans in the office had their own separate projects (none of which involved computer procurement) and besides, in 1994 very few people had ever been through the
process of buying a computer themselves.

With the knowledge base in the office exhausted, I had started to scour the streets of
Moscow for copies of PC Magazine. With any luck I would be able to find some articles
or advertisements with appropriate terminology to give me clues for what to write in
my next draft to Annabel. And of course, to find a copy of PC Magazine in Moscow would
require a bit more resourcefulness than just going down to the neighborhood bookstore.

Sergei Glebovich's expectant look brought me back to the present.

"We are working on placing the order for your computer shipment now. It will be
here in about three months," I said to Sergei Glebovich as optimistically as possible.

He looked stunned momentarily, but then smiled again. "We will make some
arrangement to expedite this!" he said with confidence. There was nothing that his
political connections would not be able to help resolve. Or so he thought.

Sergei Glebovich beamed with pride. His LPC would be at the epicenter of the
economic rebirth of Russia. Ekaterinburg had always been at the heart of the *real*
Russia. (Not the foreign cities of Moscow and St Petersburg that were more focused
on the outside world than on their homeland!) Ekaterinburg was the gateway to

Russian industry and agriculture. Russian royalty and Soviet leaders for centuries had called Ekaterinburg their real Russian home. Outside Moscow and St Petersburg, Ekatcrinburg was the only city that offered direct flights from Western Europe and hosted consulates from most major countries, including the United States. The city was home to prestigious universities, impressive large enterprises, a strong political elite. The city was the obvious focal point for foreign companies seeking to invest in Russian industry.

But enough talk about the local prestigious enterprises. We had to see them for ourselves! Sergei Glebovich escorted Nathan and I back to the Volga and we were whisked away to the headquarters of Samotsveti – a centuries-old artisan factory in the center of the city.

En route Evgeni explained with pride how Samotsveti was at the core of Russian history and culture. The factory produced bespoke pieces of art and fine crafted housewares from malachite and other semi-precious stones. The handiwork of the artisans from Samotsveti was highly prized and often commissioned by the Russian government as gifts of state to foreign dignitaries.

The lecture on the cultural significance of the factory was continued by the director of the enterprise himself. We were warmly greeted by an ox of a man with the firm grip and the standard vodka-and-potato complexion of those well accustomed to hosting political visitors from Moscow.

The director walked us through the factory floor recounting the origins of the factory since the early 18th Century. Here on this very spot, the factory artisans crafted made-to-order pieces for the royal family that could be still seen at Petrodvorets or the Hermitage today. He gestured to a large empty hall with numerous basic workbenches in various states of disarray. A few scraps of broken malachite were abandoned on a nearby workbench, too small and damaged to be possibly destined to be turned into a dramatic piece suitable for a royal palace. Midway across the floor, a number of people congregated around a tea kettle, sipping steaming tea and chatting casually.

"Business is slow these days?" Nathan stated the obvious as a question to the director.

"The Moscow government continues to send us orders, but they do not pay. It is good for our prestige to continue to provide the official diplomatic gifts," the director explained. "Our best customers now are the Russian *biznismen*. Some of them are creating art galleries in their private apartments and dachas. For example, here is one of our special orders that we are working on now."

The director now waved to a dramatic four-foot tall urn that was in the final stages of being crafted from a single block of dark green malachite. The piece had classical detailing that was more expected for a centuries-old museum art object than a modern creation. Nathan spoke my mind when he commented that the piece looked strangely familiar although it clearly was being freshly made.

"Ah yes," the director's eyes lit up with pleasure at the recognition. "This piece is being modeled on the original pair of urns that were made by this factory in the 19th century. The original urns are on display near the Council Staircase in the Hermitage."

I had to suppress a laugh. How totally stereotypical of the new Russian elite. They surrounded themselves with symbols of wealth and power to reinforce their self-appointed status as the new ruling class. The urn was worth tens of thousands of dollars (or hundreds of thousands, I really didn't know) and was a true replica of the original commissioned by the Russian monarchs themselves. What more fitting piece of art could there possible be to have prominently placed in the apartment of a modern Russian *biznisman*?

I looked closer at the detailing and asked how the artisan could be sure that this was a true replica of the urn that was in the Hermitage – thousands of miles away. Did the factory keep the original drawings of their pieces?

The director smiled and winked and said that he would show us the factory's secret. He led us through a maze of corridors and into a basement vault. He pulled a janitor's size key ring from his pocket and deftly selected the correct key for the antique steel vault door. The door creaked open and a light was flicked on to reveal what could have been the forgotten warehouse for a world-class art gallery.

Nathan and I gasped involuntarily as we took in the scene around us. Statues, urns, ornate boxes, and elaborate chess sets were covered in dust and packed unceremoniously into the room. The director weaved his way through the clutter to indicate a pristine version of the old malachite urn I had previously seen at the Hermitage. When the factory completes a special order for the government, he explained, it always creates an exact replica as a spare – just in case the original is ever damaged. The spare could be pulled and substituted, or another replica created. Here he was showing us the fine detailing of the urn – created about 150 years ago by the very same artisan who crafted the urns now on display at the Hermitage.

My eyes wandered over the hundreds of other pieces stashed in the room. The director followed our gaze and was quick to provide a guided tour. Here is a set of goblets presented by Catherine the Great to Louis XVI. Here is a chess set of Peter the Great. This is a gift from given by Brezhnev to Indira Gandhi on her visit to Moscow in 1971. And this, (the director paused for dramatic effect), this one the Americans should recognize!

An eagle and a bear were positioned side by side looking upward and forward in strong camaraderie. Each feather on the eagle and each hair on the bear were individually sculpted. I did not recognize the statue but agreed that it looked familiar.

"This is the official gift from Gorbachev to Reagan at their summit in Reykjavik!" the director beamed with pride. "This is a real piece of modern world history – a first gesture from the Russian people that we were entering a new era of mutual cooperation with the Americans."

I brushed some dust off the feathers of the eagle, feeling the delicacy of the sculpture with my fingertips. This is what made the meals of boiled cabbage and watery soup all worthwhile. Where else but Russia could a young recent graduate have a spontaneous personal guided tour of one of the most amazing private sculpture collections in the world? Many classmates from my graduate school were undoubtedly sitting in comfortable offices in Manhattan with dramatic views, devising investment strategies for their clients. I, however, was thrilled to be witness to the heart of Russia — past, present, and future.

"So will Samotsveti be seeking to attract foreign investors through the Local Privatization Center?" Nathan was ready to start introductions in his role as American advisor.

"Oh no," the director's smile disappeared and he looked mortified at the suggestion. "Samotsveti is the pride of Russia. It is united with our history and culture. Samotsveti is not for sale."

"This enterprise is hundreds of years old and has always been owned by Russians," Sergei Glebovich jumped in to support the director. "Nathan will bring us American clients who will pay in US Dollars.

At this point Joseph would have launched into a monologue regarding the advantages of foreign investment and a review of the product lines against market realities. Nathan, however, clearly had a very different style. He looked at the director and Sergei Glebovich and smiled and simply agreed. Yes, he would do everything in his power to bring American clients to Samotsveti.

The director and Sergei Glebovich praised Nathan for his support — and we were escorted onwards to the director's office for the requisite celebratory rounds of vodka toasts to the future of Russian-American cooperation.

8 ROBERT'S RULES

October 1994 — Ekaterinburg

We left the offices of Samotsveti in high spirits. Sergei Glebovich's optimism for the future of Ekaterinburg was infectious. Everything was on a positive trajectory. Great roads, historically significant companies, flight connections to the west, educated local staff. But the real advantage of the new Local Privatization Center was its political connections with the local political elite. Look at the offices Sergei Glebovich had managed to secure! And the fact that the renovation was well underway already.

"And we have access to a fax machine any time we need it!" Sergei Glebovich shared this last tidbit with Nathan and me in a conspiratorial tone. A senior official in the local state government had recently obtained a fax machine. Sergei Glebovich was one of the privileged circle of insiders who had the favored side of this government official and therefore access to the fax machine at any time.

Then Sergei Glebovich brightened further. He suddenly realized that he actually had a document that he could send today by fax to Moscow! The latest round of invoices for payment for the renovations of the new offices needed to be sent to the Moscow office. I pointed out that I would be returning to Moscow the following day, so of course I could take the documents back with me. In any case the originals would be needed to process payment.

But Sergei Glebovich would not be dissuaded from his decision. The day was all about showing Nathan and I the progress made to date with establishing the Local Privatization Center operations. We had to see for ourselves the wonders of the fax machine.

The obvious subplot to the mission to send the fax was that Sergei Glebovich could parade two Americans into this senior government official's office. With great flourish Sergei Glebovich escorted us into the expansive office of the Minister of Industrial Development (or some similar title). The Minister beamed with delight that Nathan

— a real American businessman — was visiting him in his office. Better yet, this was a consultant who would be making introductions to other Americans who would bring money into the Ekaterinburg region. Of course the Minister would be delighted to work with Nathan to help to identify the most appropriate companies for partnership. "Appropriate" in his mind was defined as companies that were in the greatest amount of strife and clearly needed the most financial assistance. The better performing companies were the pride of Russia and must continue to be Russian owned and operated.

I turned to Nathan to see how he would react to this advice. Joseph would have started a lecture about how an investor must see some redeeming qualities in the company they are investing in. Or he might have noted that some Russian enterprises would be better off being liquidated so that the capital would be used more productively elsewhere. Nathan, however, ever the tolerant peace-maker, just smiled and said that he was looking forward to helping with introductions to potential American partners.

The Minister smiled and slapped Nathan affectionately on the back. Of course we were welcome to use his fax machine. This fax machine had been provided to his office by some prior US government project to support investment in Russian companies. And now a real American businessman was here to use the fax machine! Isn't it wonderful that the Minister has a fax machine now!

The Minister's office was laid out per the traditional plan of the Soviet government style. To get to his office we passed through a receptionist area where a slender attractive *devushka* was writing with a leaky ball point pen on a piece of paper. A typewriter sat on a shelf behind her desk in a battered brown box. She escorted us into the Minister's office and then set about the standard task of preparing tea and biscuits for the visitors. The Minister's office itself featured a large desk in the center of the room, with a conference table positioned in a T-formation off the desk. The fax machine was placed prominently on the Minister's desk next to his telephone. The cords for power and telephone connections were neatly coiled and wrapped in plastic. A large photograph of the Minister shaking Boris Yeltsin's hand was positioned strategically on the desk where all visitors were certain to nod and acknowledge that this was a man of certain connections.

With a grand display of showmanship, the Minister unplugged his desk telephone from the wall, unwrapped the plastic covering from the cables for the fax machine and then plugged the fax machine into the telephone connection. He then uncoiled the power cord, pulled an extension cord from somewhere in his desk and then plugged the fax machine into the wall. He switched the power to "on" and Sergei Glebovich clapped with delight as the green power light sprung to life.

"And now for my next trick I will actually *send* a fax!" Of course the Minister did not actually say this himself, but the wink at Sergei Glebovich and the flick of the document required no words. He not only was privileged to *have* a fax machine. He also was highly skilled in how to *use* it as well!

And then the interstate dialing process began. I was familiar with the routine – so gratefully accepted the tea and biscuits offered by the *devushka* and settled into a chair for what I expected would be the next hour. First no dial tone. Then all lines busy. Then again all lines busy. No connection. Failed connection. Party line now – with multiple chattering voices. All lines busy. No dial tone. And then the recipient phone back at our Moscow office rang. And then finally the familiar tone of a fax machine picking up and awaiting a handshake. The Minister at first looked baffled. No person answering the phone line? But he quickly realized that he needed to hit the "send" button and the fax was on its way.

"Bravo!" Sergei Glebovich applauded the magnificent performance of the Minister. I also was impressed. This was the first operating fax machine I had seen outside of Moscow and St Petersburg save for an adventure sending a fax back in Petropavlovsk a year earlier. But more so, I was impressed that this Minister had made the effort to learn how to operate the machine. In Kazakhstan I had seen computers sitting on government officials' desks akin to a decorative new designer handbag – something to be admired, but not necessarily to be used. This Minister understood that the fax machine had a certain utility if *he* mastered its complexities.

Sergei Glebovich thanked the Minister profusely for his generosity for helping us with sending the fax to Moscow. The Minister shook his hand and said it was his pleasure. He was always striving to assist the local companies and he was looking forward to working with Nathan and coordinating introductions for foreign investors.

Nathan smiled and shook his hand and agreed that the Minister's support was appreciated. I looked at Nathan's radiant smile and realized that Nathan actually believed what the minister was saying. Yes, of course the Minister would be all too happy to make introductions to local company directors, but did Nathan really understand how "appropriate partners" would be identified? Did he understand fully why the fax machine was placed in the Minister's office rather than with his receptionist? The fax machine may carry the label of "enabling foreign investment" but clearly the Minister had placed himself as a gatekeeper for access. In the name of fostering foreign investment, the foreign aid served to entrench the local political elite just a little deeper. Of course, the Minister would support Nathan and Sergei Glebovich's efforts to introduce foreign investors to Ekaterinburg – but on his terms.

"Just one more person you must meet today!" Sergei Glebovich cheerfully gave new instructions to the driver. Sergei Glebovich's exuberance was infectious, but it barely masked the fact that he was controlling our day's agenda as effectively as Ivan Ivanovich had done in South Russia.

With great excitement Sergei Glebovich introduced us to Viktor Mikhailovich, owner of a small but growing company that provided computer equipment and services. The offices were immaculate and freshly refurbished with the latest in German-designed office furniture. The carpeting smelled new. The German language sales tags were still proudly attached to all the new chairs in the office – a deliberate display of the wealth and ambitions of the company ownership.

I involuntarily sighed and turned to Nathan. He too could see where this conversation would be going.

"If you are having difficulty with your procurement through your American channels, we should work with local Russian partners!" Sergei Glebovich declared, quite logically.

I attempted to protest that we really did not have a choice in the matter. We were providing equipment to the LPC with USAID funding. Therefore all equipment would have to be sourced through the United States to comply with US government procurement requirements.

Viktor Mikhailovich furrowed his eyebrows in contemplation. He then launched into his explanation of why it would be far better to purchase all equipment locally in Ekaterinburg. More confidence that the office will get exactly what they need. We will work closely with the office to specify and purchase exactly to their requirements! We will provide personal service for all equipment configuration in the office. If anything is not right we can get new equipment quickly. We can provide initial training services. If there are problems that require service or warranty replacement, we can do that too. We are a full service company!

Of course he was right. With the equipment shipped from the United States, what if one mouse was missing, or if the wrong set of cables was sent? What would we do then? And if everything was purchased from the United States, then how would we ever get warranty work performed if necessary? Ship the faulty hard drive from Ekaterinburg back to Washington, DC?

And, most of all, wasn't the nominal purpose of USAID projects to help cultivate local businesses? Here was a genuine Russian entrepreneur who understood key concepts about customer service and was eager to help. Shouldn't we be promoting working with people exactly like Viktor Mikhailovich? To my first impression, he was doing everything right. I was in physical pain knowing that the rules of procurement for USAID projects would prevent us from purchasing equipment through him. And worse, how can you possibly explain that in the name of aid to Russia we needed to purchase all our equipment through American companies?

So I had to deflect the question. I congratulated Viktor Mikhailovich on his growing business and beautiful offices. His service offering was compelling, but I was not the one who was in a position to make decisions about such things. I would be sure to convey my endorsement back to those making the procurement decisions.

Viktor Mikhailovich gave me a warm genuine smile and a handshake with the grip of a Siberian bear.

And then out of the corner of my eye I saw a copy of *PC Magazine* sitting on his desk.

In English. Here in Ekaterinburg. I barely concealed my excitement and astonishment that he had a copy of *PC Magazine*. They are so hard to come by in Russia!

Without a moment's hesitation Viktor Mikhailovich swept the magazine from his desk and pressed it into my hands. A gift for you! We are looking forward to having you as a customer!

I was nearly speechless with gratitude – as well as disappointment that we would not be able to work together going forward.

Evidence that the fax did in fact go through successfully to the Moscow office was waiting for me upon our arrival back at the Local Privatization Center's temporary offices. Katya, the receptionist, gave me a very professionally hand scribed note simply stating that Robert had seen the invoice and that it could not be paid. For details I must read an electronic letter that he would send me separately on the computer. Oh and Robert said he would be in meetings the rest of the day and would not be able to discuss this further. In Katya's words, I would need to check my "electronic letters".

Such casual remarks made by Americans in the comfort of the Moscow office. Just call me. Just check your email. Just send a fax. Did they have any idea what we actually experienced in regional Russia to perform these mundane tasks? To Sergei Glebovich sending a fax was still a novelty – the fact it required a visit across town to a government office and about thirty minutes of dialing before a connection was considered to be a minor inconvenience. Or (depending upon your perspective) an opportunity to reinforce the political network. A fax was an *event* in Ekaterinburg – not a daily routine task to be delegated to an administrative assistant.

The easy answer would be for me to simply shrug and put the "check your email" request in the "too difficult" column with an array of excuses. I would be flying back to Moscow the following afternoon and be back in the Moscow office the day after that. To the Americans back in Moscow or Washington DC, not retrieving emails for 48 hours would be negligent (the circumstances would not be relevant). Robert had never ventured out of the city. He was blissfully unaware of the conditions that were a reality outside the mecca of modernity. One incoming email with a silly overuse of graphics or attachments would exacerbate the download issues further. Attempts to pound reality into Robert to date had been futile. But Sergei Glebovich's enthusiasm was infectious. I wanted to do everything in my power to help launch his new Local Privatization Center. A delay of 48 hours with processing his invoices would be letting him down.

Also, I was at the point in my tour of duty in Russia where I just simply could not accept "no" for an answer. For every problem there is a solution. The entire question is how much pain and suffering would have to be endured to achieve the small moral victory of maintaining "forward progress" in the face of yet another obstacle.

"Quite a bit," turned out to be the answer for the evening.

Internet connectivity through a dial up connection was a physical impossibility from the office, as the phone line was one continuous cable from the telephone to the wall. I therefore had to wait until after the obligatory festive dinner (complete with the requisite rounds of vodka and entertainment ranging from traditional folk music to scantily clad dancers) before attempting the exercise back at my hotel room.

I staggered back to my hotel room and requested the room key from the *dezhurnaya*. (In these sorts of *respectable* hotels, the guests do not carry around keys themselves. The *dezhurnaya* had to maintain order by controlling who came and went at all times.) She gave me a scowl with pursed lips upon assessing my very toxic condition and handed over the key with a mini-anvil attached. (Just so I wouldn't get the notion in my head to actually take the room key with me anywhere.)

Back in the room I started to run through my standard routine to establish internet connectivity. If there ever was such a thing that could be called a "standard routine" in Russia in the mid-1990s.

I would resist the urge to break out of my business suit into my soothing fluffy pajamas. In my intoxicated state any additional level of comfort would undoubtedly cause me to pass out momentarily rather than focus on the work at hand. I would pound the television to life, struggle with the "bunny ears" to receive something – anything. Sometimes it would just be a predictable weather report. "Siberia – cold, Ekaterinburg – cold, Krasnoyarsk – cold." (No discussion of low pressure systems moving in from the Northwest, or the chance of precipitation.) Sometimes I would find a Mexican soap opera dubbed in Russian – with a bored monotone reading all the lines. "Yes, Rosa, I do love you, but now is not the time." Then the same tired voice responding, "What, Juan, are you afraid that Miguel will be jealous? I do not care what he thinks." Sometimes miraculously the bunny ears would allow a choice in channels, if I could be tolerant of the static. And then a surge of joy with the delight of something totally unexpected – like Speed Racer. In true Russian style, you could still hear the English sound (dubbed over the original Japanese), then a dusty monotone Russian voice reading the script loudly over all the action. No inflection or emotion, just reading the words. "Do you think we'll make it to the start of the race in time, Speedy?" The male voice read Trixie's line without the slightest bit of irony. "We'll have to hurry. I hope the bridge has been repaired by now." The same male voice replied to himself without pause.

Anyway – time to focus! The phone (predictably) was hard wired to the wall. One continuous wire from wall to the phone itself. Defeat, however, was never an option. Necessity is the mother of invention. I had therefore learned to carry a Swiss Army knife and electrical tape with me as an essential part of my travel gear. (And yes, for those who are paying attention, this meant that I was carrying the knife on board with me with all my travels throughout Russia.)

Back in the hotel room, with Speed Racer going in the background, I quickly moved into action. Every moment wasted with the internet connection was a moment stolen from much-needed-sleep. The available electrical outlet was of course across the room from the phone – therefore I sat on the gritty carpet midway with my laptop, stretching out the cables to their maximum length. With quick practiced moves I peeled back the protective plastic covering of the phone cable to expose the metal wires. A few snips from my Swiss Army knife scissors would give me enough wiring to be able to twist a connection together with my modem cable (which had matching peeled back protective casing and exposed wires). A few twists and then sealed in place with a bit of tape established what would allow for a connection – most of the time.

Occasionally I would discover an existing scar on the telephone cable, covered with a bit of electrical tape, or other evidence that another western businessman had fought a similar battle in the room before me. I would smile wryly. We were part of a secret society – so secret that we didn't even know who each other were.

Once the physical connection was established, I moved on to phase two – the internet dial up connection. The same familiar scene again and again. No dial tone. Too much static. All lines busy. Hit a party line. Redial and a phone rings, the handshake starts – then disconnected. No dial tone. It was a battle to keep going as the pleasant fog of the vodka enveloped my body and pulled me towards unconsciousness. It was a battle I had to fight out of fierce pride and determination. I was not a pampered western consultant who lived in five star hotels with a smiling concierge to attend to my every need and who would simply find it unacceptable if the white fluffy bathrobe were missing from its assigned location in the cedar-scented closet. I was a survivor. A battlefield veteran of travel in Russia. Nothing would defeat me.

The dial tone was scratchy and I was disconnected a few times while attempting to receive the emails, but in the end I was victorious. In a strangely poetic parallel, Trixie and Speedy were celebrating their own victory, albeit in sterile Russian monotone voices, while the figures danced around on the screen. Yes, Speed Racer always figures out how to get to his race, even when the bridge is out! What a hero! I was deliriously happy now (in addition to being deliriously drunk). I had achieved success when all the signs had pointed towards defeat. I had successfully received email from a hotel room in Ekaterinburg! I had completely mutilated my modem cable and the telephone in the process, but such was the price of victory.

The email from Robert slapped my mood down from a state of euphoria. Yes, he had received the fax of the invoices for the renovations of the Ekaterinburg office. No, they would not be paid. The reason? Per the USAID procurement requirements, no VAT would be paid on invoices. USAID maintained that there was an agreement in place between the US government and the Russian Government that all US government projects would be VAT exempt. Of course any legitimate Russian business was required to state VAT on its invoices. The letter from USAID would be meaningless

— as the Russian businesses were subject to the rules (and discretion) of the Russian government, not the protests of USAID. I (as usual) would be stuck in the middle between the convictions of American bureaucracy and Russian reality. I braced myself for an inevitable day of arguments with the local Russian team. Best just to roll into bed and let the alcohol take hold and let me have a few hours of peace.

But then again, just when I thought I knew what to expect in Russia, a new twist takes things in a different direction. The following evening I was safely at home in Moscow, contemplating the day's events from the pleasant comfort of my own balcony with a soothing vodka-tonic in hand. A distinct nip was in the air as the bitter fingers of winter attempted to take hold. I ignored this reality, wrapped in a snug coat with my cat purring on my lap, while contemplating the amazing contrast between the white spires of the Kremlin bell tower in the distance against the labyrinth of crumbling apartment blocks. Somewhere in the maze nearby was Krizis Zhanra, the club with no address, no advertising, but a growing loyal clientele. The white symbol of ancient Russia, although far away, was easy to distinguish through the forest of crumbling buildings. The underground club, a symbol of new Russia, was close by, but I still did not know exactly where.

The vodka left me contemplating whether there was a deeper philosophical lesson to derive from the scene. We are all just passing through history. But exactly how will history remember us?

First thing in the morning I had shared with Sergei Glebovich the bad news. The invoices for renovation were rejected. We would have to obtain new invoices from the contractors — this time without VAT stated. Previous such discussions in Rostov with Ivan Ivanovich had left me bracing myself for a heated discussion of "Americans are always criticizing Russians for doing business in underhanded ways. Now here you are asking me to fabricate documentation to satisfy the requirements of the US Government. How can you explain that?" And of course I couldn't explain it. It was just simply reality. After the string of insults and posturing, however, Ivan Ivanovich would say "I will take care of it." And then I would receive updated invoices the next day.

Sergei Glebovich had taken the news quite differently than Ivan Ivanovich. He simply shrugged and said "Okay, if the invoices need to be written without VAT, I will have them written without VAT." He made a phone call. The driver was dispatched. And in an hour or so we had a fresh set of invoices. The bottom line amount was the same, but VAT had mysteriously disappeared.

Sipping my vodka and tonic and watching the evening dramas unfold in dozens of lighted apartment windows I was trying to figure out which scenario was more difficult. Was it better to be in heated arguments with Ivan Ivanovich, who relished in the irony that the American government was asking him to request a forged document? Or did I prefer working with Sergei Glebovich who just smiled and accepted the request and quickly took care of the necessary updates. Such were the choices I was facing. Of course when I raised this point to Robert he simply stated that we were in the right. There was a US to Russian government agreement in place that upheld this approach. (The fact that no one could produce a valid document that confirmed this was inconsequential.)

Robert in Moscow and Annabel in Washington DC would insist that we had to comply with the rules required by USAID. But did they understand that here in Russia, the American way of doing things was completely foreign? You had to improvise and adapt just to get through the day intact.

Arthur Andersen corporate expense policy was to always use your Corporate American Express card for business expenses. But outside of foreign hotels in Moscow, Russia was still an all cash society. And with the extra dimension of hyperinflation I now found myself travelling with shoe boxes full of rubles. Just to check out from the hotel could require twenty minutes of counting and recounting small bills. So no, I would not be using my Corporate Amex card for my business expenses.

And how would Robert, who always had his stapler, tape dispenser and pencil holder in a nice straight row, cope on a domestic Aeroflot flight? Yes, my ticket nominally had a seat assignment, but in reality once the stairs were in place and the doors thrust open the throng of passengers would charge onto the plane in a frenzied struggle to seize and defend territory. Bundles were crammed into every available corner. I even saw live goats tucked into a restroom. The flight attendants gave the scene a bored look and then might carry a bottle of vodka up to the captain and co-pilot. Crush or be crushed. Robert and his need for order certainly would not survive the experience.

Vanya, my diligent driver, somehow located me in the pandemonium of the Domodedovo airport. Vanya would take care of me from here to my apartment and now I could finally relax. But no, en route we were flagged over by the GAI and a handful of rubles was extracted from Vanya for some invented infraction. Like always, I remained silent throughout the ordeal. An American accent would undoubtedly increase the "fine" by tenfold. I mused that Sergei Glebovich was correct – the black Volgas, Mercedes, and other high end cars were quickly waved through the check point with a nod. The actual "fines" were reserved for those driving vehicles that suggested that they did not have any real political clout.

Would Arthur Andersen reimburse Vanya for the fine? My driver laughed at the idea. No, of course not. *Vzyatki* are a necessary part of doing business in Russia, but no they would not be reimbursed. Vanya deliberately used the term *vzyatki* for "bribe" rather than the term *shtrav* for "fee".

Ah yes Robert and his rules. I laughed. Yes, I agreed that there was no way that Robert would approve the *vzyatki* – even though it was a standard part of daily life in

Russia. Fines levied at the whim of GAI were not acceptable. Requesting documents to be forged in the name of US Government requirements were. It was all about following the rules – whether the rules actually made sense or not was another matter.

Nadya, my lead accountant, especially took perverse pleasure in pointing out the illogical rules of the Americans. Her latest round of rants to me had come immediately after she learned the details of how our USAID contract was budgeted and paid. Our project was structured as "cost plus" – which simply meant that everything we spent on the project would be reimbursed by USAID, plus an additional percentage to cover our overhead and profit. The obvious implication here is that the firm was paid based on how much we spent, not what we actually delivered. She understood immediately that senior management back in Washington DC would therefore focus simply on spending money in the budget, not on quality of results. How could such an approach possibly provide the foundation to teach the Russians good business practices? I could only listen to her rant and agree. I had no logical response.

"Did you know that the phones have been turned off in the office?" Vanya brought me back from my contemplations.

No, I was not aware that the phones had been turned off. Everything had been working fine the day before, I knew. What had happened? Vanya looked at me conspiratorially and smiled – "Robert."

We had just finished our first month in the new office. The phones had suddenly stopped working that morning. The rumor in the office was that Robert had refused to pay the phone bill. The reason? I should have known. The invoice had VAT stated explicitly. Robert had demanded that the Russian phone company (a state-owned enterprise) change its invoice for him. Of course the company had totally ignored his protests and simply turned off the connection. Sergei Glebovich or Ivan Ivanovich or someone of better political standing would have been able to make the necessary arrangements without a hitch. Robert, however, was simply an American demanding to have things his way. I had to laugh.

Vanya then proceeded to fill me in on all the related gossip. Raymond, being the practical business leader, had immediately turned to Robert and demanded that he do whatever necessary to get the phones turned back on. Robert had insisted that we had to follow the procurement guidelines of USAID or the phone bill would never be reimbursed. Raymond was outraged that Robert lacked the business sense to realize that having the phones disconnected was a far worse consequence than the phone bill not being reimbursed.

Of course Raymond had attempted to have these conversations discretely with Robert. But the walls have ears in Moscow. Everyone knew everything immediately. At least everyone who had a few friends in the office willing to share what they knew.

Vanya spoke nearly no English. Robert and Raymond spoke no Russian. One of the Russians had obviously filled in Vanya within hours of the event. I smiled with satisfaction that I was *nashi* and therefore in the Russian loop with the latest office gossip. Also I relished in the perverse pleasure I would gain by returning to the office with neatly written up replacement invoices for the renovations in Ekaterinburg. Exactly as requested, on time, with no hassles. The VAT is not that difficult to remove, Robert — you just need to know the right people!

Now home in my apartment, sitting on my balcony I contemplated the lives of those in the lighted windows of the adjacent apartment block. A man sat still in a chair wearing a t-shirt watching a flickering television. A woman washed dishes bent intently over her work. Shadows moved behind drawn curtains. On the surface their lives looked just like mine, but what was novel to me were every day experiences for these Russians.

And my daily life was cause for astonishment for them. What woman travelled alone for business to remote cities throughout Russia? How truly astonishing to be able to take crisp $100 bills out of a machine! (Vanya's first visit with me to the one and only ATM in the country at the American Express office was still a cause for discussion weeks later.) And what single woman lived in the decadent luxury of their own two bedroom apartment?

Yes, I had an amazing life. Yes, my work week was far rougher than if I had taken a sterile desk job in Washington DC. But I was young and needed to live and experience the world. And now my dream of a cozy sanctuary had become a reality. (Thank you dear Valya.) Of course there were cockroaches running for the dark corners of the kitchen, but if I closed my eyes before turning on the lights and counted to ten before opening them, I would not see the little horrible creatures. The floors were immaculate, although they of course were battered as a result of the rough *remont* process. All electronics were nicely dusted and the power cables unplugged from the walls and neatly coiled. Valya had left me a note reprimanding me that yet *again* she had found all the electronics left plugged in throughout the apartment. For my own safety I really needed to ensure that the electronics were disarmed when not in use!

Dear Valya. She was right. I did not fully understand all the hazards that were around me in Russia. I had a lot to learn about how to navigate through life here. And what exactly were the Russians learning in the process from us? What had Sergei Glebovich and Vanya learned in the last few days from their interactions with the rules of our program and our team leadership? What was Nadya learning about American business practices? "We are from the US Government and we are here to help you."

There are reasons why that line is always used for comic relief.

9 PLEASURE AND PAIN

November 1994 — Moscow

I seem to remember reading a magazine article about a scientific experiment where laboratory mice were somehow altered to associate pain with pleasure. I can't remember how it was done — whether some critical connection was severed in their tiny little brains or if somehow through torment or training they arrived at the behavioral association on their own. But somehow the confused creatures came to actually seek out torture like pin pricks and cold water. To the objective observer this behavior was insane. Why would a creature intentionally subject itself to torture? Couldn't it take a step back to appreciate the misery it was actually inflicting on itself? Apparently not. The conditioning had been complete.

I believe that I read that magazine article in the hazy heated comfort of the Metro in Washington DC, going from my color-coordinated office with fluorescent lighting in the city to my sterile high rise apartment in Arlington, Virginia. Shuttling from one featureless space to the other in the modern convenience of the subway, I was sitting on the train in the Metro surrounded by thousands of other suburban yuppies identical to myself. We all wore the same haggard expressions that belonged to people twenty years older and we dressed the way the magazines told us to dress.

I glanced up from my magazine article and looked around. What sort of sick social experiment were we all participating in? The only people that looked vaguely happy were clearly in an alcohol-induced moment of frivolity. The rest were like me, simply going about the motions of what was expected of them. This is what young urban professionals do. This is how we work. This is where we live. If you accomplish everything on the list, then you are supposed to be happy. It was tempting to turn to the person seated next to me and ask "are you happy?" But I'm not the sort of person to start those sorts of discussions with strangers. In any case, I believe I can safely assume what the response would have been. He would have first given me a sideways look to determine if I were simply mad or perhaps a dangerous lunatic as well. Then he would have given a very static answer like "Yes, of course I'm happy." And the discussion would have ended there.

Do people really think about happiness when all the basic comforts of life are taken care of? I mean true happiness, which comes from the overwhelming joy of discovery of some very pure basic appreciation of life or sensual pleasure. If you know that the electricity is going to work and the house will be warm and your clothes will be clean and there will be food in the fridge, then these basic pleasures in life start to fade into the background. The focus tends to remain on items that are more uncertain. As one's standard of living improves then the uncertain items become more and more trivial – Why wasn't I invited to that client meeting, is my colleague playing power games behind my back? Where will I find the data needed for that presentation on Tuesday? What should I wear for that cocktail party on Friday – it is at 6pm, so will people be wearing work attire, or should I change into a cocktail dress?

The yuppies on the train home were all scowling and lost in thought about the petty arguments of the day. The frowning worn faces were matched by mussed up hair and disheveled suits. Life's miseries grow if that is all that you're paying attention to. Go go go. Achieve achieve achieve. But never pause and appreciate the wonderful basic joys of life.

Are we all laboratory mice in some twisted manner? Do we actually have decent lives and not fully appreciate it, then subject ourselves to torment each day with the illusion that it will make us happier? To the young professionals on the train who know no other life, it is impossible to believe that the pursuit of happiness may not require a designer handbag.

This is all a circuitous introduction to the joys of the traditional Russian *bannya* experience. When I first attempted to explain the pleasures of the Russian *bannya* to my American friends and family, I was nearly universally confronted with interrogations into my sanity. Why would a sane human being voluntarily put themselves in an over-heated sauna with thirty naked strangers until you are nearly unconscious and then leap into an ice cold pool? I was warned repeatedly that this was a recipe for heart attacks or other serious health risk. Lunacy was the only rationale the Americans could agree upon. To the Russians, however, it is pleasure. This explanation only served to confirm the opinions of my American friends – if you are confusing pleasure with pain then definitely there are a few screws loose. A bit too much vodka had altered my senses, they were sure.

I replied by asking them if they really enjoyed the yuppie commuter lifestyle in suburban America. A few saw my point and became quiet. It is all a matter of perspective and conditioning.

So how do Russians associate the raw pain of the scalding sauna and ice cold pools with pleasure? And what about the bizarre custom of bringing birch branches into the sauna to beat each other with? How could these acts of torture be undertaken totally voluntarily and under the guise of "relaxation" and "health"? And, even more perplexing, how did the expatriates come to deeply appreciate these traditions and follow them ourselves?

The *bannya* is such the Russian experience. In Moscow I craved the *bannya* during the relentless cold winter. But afterwards, once I was living back in San Francisco, some of my returned expatriate friends and I talked occasionally about going to a Russian *bannya* in the city, but we never got around to it. It would not have been the same. There was not the deep physical and emotional need for a violent release of pressure. When life is going along okay, why subject yourself deliberately to something unpleasant like a dunk in a cold pool? On a cold winter day, isn't a cup of hot chocolate or a hot bath a nice pick me up?

The context of the Russian winter is essential to understand the sensual pleasures of the *bannya*.

Winter in America is fashionably portrayed as a season of white and innocence. Warm woolen socks and cozy sweaters. Hot chocolate with fluffy marshmallows. A white blanket of snow gives the world a fresh glow. Winter is a time of bringing friends and family close. Tables loaded with comfort food. Inviting, crackling fires. Young children's eyes sparkling with anticipation of Christmas. Cheeks glowing from a session of sledding or skiing.

At least that is how we remembered American winters when in Moscow. The expatriate mind is an excellent editor. We remember what we want to remember. We forget what we want to forget.

Winter in Russia is an entirely different reality. The color of the season is a dull grey. As the sun struggled to rise above the buildings each day, what shreds of color that existed in the urban landscape were drained into a bleak lifeless pallor. Fresh produce disappeared from the open air markets – replaced by jars of pickled mystery vegetables laid out on blankets by the Metro stations. Snowflakes descended through the toxic Moscow air and were churned into a thick icy sludge in the streets. Pasty white faces grimaced as the grey descended.

By mid-November, the Russian winter had already grasped the city with its bony grey fingers. The warm summer evening on the shore of the Black Sea was an impossible delusional fantasy from a prior lifetime – an alternate plane of existence. Mid November is (in my opinion) the worst point of winter in Russia. The days are still getting shorter. Months of bleakness lie ahead. And the cold has not yet fully settled in for the long haul.

As bad as the cold is at the heart of the Russian winter, the warm interludes in November and then in the spring are worse. In the heart of winter, the ground would be a solid protected armor plate of ice. The city would be a sleeping giant. Fierce and impenetrable. Dangerous, yes, but predictable cold, quiet, and stable. But an unexpected warm day in November or spring would shake the city violently awake from its slumber. Moscow would grumble and shift before settling back down to sleep.

A sudden thaw would melt the urban snow banks into a thick brown sludge, filling the streets like a trough with nowhere to go. Icicles would warm and drop, impaling unsuspecting passersby. The electric bus, which already was the slowest form of mass transport ever conceived, would wallow through the muck – lurching and jerking uncertainly towards its destination.

A slight warmth on a winter day would result in an unbearable stench on the bus. Muck dragged in on people's boots would melt into dribbling oily puddles. Bundles of leather, fur, and other animal hide clothing would suddenly become intolerably warm in the confines of the bus and the odors that were frozen throughout the winter were released with renewed vigor. The windows on the bus would steam up with the rancid breath of toothless women. Men would stare vacantly into space, clutching the remains of the vodka bottle started the previous night – or that morning. By Sunday morning the older men would usually have a fresh open head wound from some drunken injury or would be clutching desperately onto the bus seat to maintain balance as the bus lunged on its uncertain course.

The other bus passengers showed no outward acknowledgement of my presence. Eye contact with strangers is studiously avoided. If somehow I did manage to catch someone's eye, I would be met with a blank stare or hostile gaze, then they would abruptly turn away. Absolutely no casual smiles in public to strangers.

Sometimes a gypsy woman with a herd of small filthy children would board the bus. The stoic Russians would recoil perceptibly as she started her inevitable speech: "Dear passengers, my family is burdened with a difficult life. I am unable to work. I cannot feed and clothe my children. For the grace of god, please give a ruble for my children."

This plea would often be met with a sharp retort from one of the *babushkas*: "We all have hard lives and no one is helping us!"

The children would be motionless behind their mother, clutching to rags of her skirts and staring darkly at the passengers. My Russian friends were convinced the gypsies muddied the faces and clothes of their children for these expeditions. Looking at them I would have to agree. A responsible parent would not possibly take a child out in public looking like that. Right?

I stole another glance at the gypsy woman. Her face was battered from weather and daily existence. Her age was indeterminate. She could have been in her twenties or in her forties. Had she ever been a young vibrant *devushka* walking with poise and pouty red lips? What had happened? Her back sagged as she carried a ragged bundle containing yet another small child. Her voice drifted through the bus. Maybe someone would give her a coin. Maybe not. Daily existence would trudge onwards. Someone pulled a worthless coin from their pockets and scolded the gypsy to move on.

Why was I even on the bus at all? The air was thick with heavy moist breath and coughing. Ripe breeding ground for disease. Despite this I had boarded the bus voluntarily. I could have easily hitched a ride to the *bannya* for the price of a few dollars, yet had selected the public bus and all that came with that option. The decision was not about money – the decisions of expatriates were rarely about money. Rather the choice to take the bus that day was a reflection of my current emotional state.

Hitchhiking had become second nature. I stepped out to the street and hailed down random cars effortlessly. In the early months I had been nervous (good girls from the Midwest certainly do *not* hitchhike), but as I settled into expatriate life the experience of hitchhiking shifted from nervous semi-concealed terror, to an adrenaline rush of adventure, to a mundane practical daily activity. Never far from my mind was the knowledge that nearly a year earlier, back in Kazakhstan, Craig had been attacked with a screwdriver to the chest while hitchhiking. But the near universal expatriate response to his incident was that he should have known better. There are certain rules one must follow in order to stay safe and he had pushed the limits. Never get in a car if there are multiple people. Trust your instincts with a driver – be prepared to say "no". Don't aggravate the driver by attempting to fasten the seatbelt (usually met with a sharp rebuke of "Don't you trust my driving?") And never ever carry a laptop when hitchhiking. Just be sensible. There are a lot of very decent people out there willing to take a handful of rubles for a trip. Just a few bad ones. Keep your eyes open and you will be fine.

That week I had been traveling again in Southern Russia and returned to Moscow through Vnukovo airport. The airport in Stavropol and then in Moscow were filled with refugees from the escalating conflict in Chechnya. Battered people sat on shapeless mounds of all their worldly possessions wrapped in plastic or burlap and tied with string. Men spoke in hushed voices in huddles and looked over their shoulders. Militsia wearing sturdy boots carrying Kalashnikovs prodded some of the bundles of the refugees and ignored others. Arguments at security checkpoints, then a few *biznismen* wearing polyester green jackets and gold chains ushered around the screening without explanation or a glance backwards at those standing in line. Amidst all of this, I stood in the main hall of Vnukovo looking for my driver, Vanya, while attempting not to appear to be too desperate. Although I had hitchhiked many times from Sheremyetovo and Domodedovo airports, Vnukovo was not a good place to be an American businesswoman carrying a laptop, modern luggage, and looking very alone. I tried my best to dress and act Russian – with my red lipstick and firm stoic stare, carrying my laptop in a nondescript battered leather satchel. But I knew that the minute I opened my mouth to negotiate a ride, I would be clearly viewed to be an American – with cash.

I spotted an American businessman with his interpreter. With his polished shoes, brushed woolen coat, plaid scarf and Tumi laptop bag he might as well have drawn a bull's-eye on his forehead. I could not find Vanya and would have to catch a lift from Vnukovo, so hopefully this American could help. Of course this was well before mobile phones were omnipresent. And Russian airports had nothing resembling a paging system. If an airport connection was missed, then you had to be innovative and sort out an alternate solution.

The American turned out to be incoherently drunk, staggering, and mostly supported by his faithful interpreter. The interpreter smiled at me with a show of camaraderie and explained to me (in Russian) that this was the American's first week in Russia and he had just been in Stavropol meeting his Russian business partners. He had been sent fresh from a vodka-packed lunch (celebrating mutual cooperation and partnership, of course) to the flight. The American was in high spirits and the Russian was trying to subdue him. More attention would not be welcome here. I looked at the semi-conscious American and smiled – He has so much to learn. This is only week one for him.

My hope for a lift, however, was short-lived. The driver for the American businessman also was MIA. The interpreter and I quickly agreed that our best option would be for the three of us to hitch a ride together back into Moscow. The interpreter handled the selection and negotiations with a driver. Several were rejected before we settled on a man with a large Volga. With an unspoken understanding, the interpreter and I slid into the spacious backseat with the drunk American between us and all our luggage packed on our laps. Never ever put luggage in the trunk when hitchhiking.

The driver adjusted his rearview mirror, glanced at us and stubbed out his cigarette before pulling away from the airport terminal. The American was mercifully quiet and now possibly unconscious. I did not say a word – with the hope I could just keep a low profile in the back seat for the long drive back to the city center.

As the car approached the exit from the airport grounds, the driver slowed down and in a quick practiced motion a second man jumped into the front seat. No word from the driver or the second man. The interpreter protested. We did not agree to anyone else being in the car with us.

No response from the driver, other than a push on the accelerator.

I looked at the interpreter with wide eyes and he sharply barked in English exactly what I was thinking: "Get out now."

This was one of those moments where time just stopped and everything seemed to move in slow motion. I saw myself open the door and without glancing at the moving road below, in a single motion I flung myself and my luggage out – pulling the comatose American with me. The interpreter pushed out the American and the three of us rolled in a jumble of coats, luggage, and snow. We tumbled into a snow bank and suddenly the world was silent except for the spluttering of the retreating engine and the pounding of our own hearts. At least my heart and the interpreter's. I don't think the American really understood what was happening.

There were a few bruises and some torn clothing, but miraculously none of us sustained real injuries. After a pause to catch our breath, we stood up, brushed ourselves off and found another lift.

What would have happened if we had stayed in the Volga with the two men? The interpreter refused to discuss the possibilities. It would be tempting Fate. We should just be satisfied to be alive and speak no more of it. I understood and we rode silently into the city.

I gave the interpreter my business card and asked for his details. I wanted to thank him and take him and his American colleague out for dinner. He shook his head. "No. You do not need to know who we are."

When the car finally dropped me off at my flat, the interpreter patted me affectionately on the shoulder. "You are truly *nashi*" he said with a smile.

Nashi. I had beamed at the compliment and thanked the interpreter, wishing him well.

Now, sitting on the bus I doubted whether the compliment was justified.

I was thrilled with the compliment, of course, but lacked confidence that I really lived up to the interpreter's expectations. I had learned to dress and act Russian in public – mainly as an act of self-preservation. Too many acts of violence and insults were directed at Americans and it was better to keep a low profile. For both camouflage as well as practicality, Kolya had helped me buy a *dublunka* – a proper Russian ankle-length winter coat – at an open air market in the Moscow suburbs. During my trips outside Moscow I rarely spoke a word of English – except to other Americans. I navigated and survived an existence in regional Russian hotels and offices that few Americans in Moscow would ever experience. But in Moscow I definitely picked and chose my life. I thrived on the open air markets, the random encounters on the Metro, the hidden gems of local restaurants and clubs not yet over-run with the masses, the deep cultural scene – far beyond just the Bolshoi. But at a certain point I pulled back. If the open markets had a poor selection of vegetables, I turned to *Sedmoe Kontinent* or one of the other extravagant western supermarkets opening each week. My life during the week when traveling was so intense that on the weekend I needed to be able to regroup with friends who would understand my frustrations. Almost by definition, this meant American friends. Friends who appreciated and enjoyed the challenges of life in Russia, and had a common frame of reference.

So this is how I found myself riding the bus wearing my ankle-length *dublunka* and hot red lipstick and attempting to blend in as a young *devushka* on her way to some

Sunday errand. But, of course, it was just an illusion. Who was I fooling? I attempted to blend in, but despite the interpreter's compliment of *"nashi"* I clearly was not of the Russian world. They knew it. It would have been perfectly obvious to all the other passengers on the bus. But they could not have guessed the full story: I was an American – pretending to be Russian on my way to a Russian *bannya*. On my way to immerse myself in a classic Russian cultural experience – with a group of American girlfriends – to escape for a moment my life in Russia. What wonderful games we play in our own minds to attempt to create the illusion of sanity.

And people wonder why a good portion of expatriates are alcoholics or mentally unstable or both.

I jumped out of the bus into a swamp of muck. The hem of my coat splashed into the mud and a cold slime oozed in through the seams of my boots. Black melting snow results in black sloppy sludge. The dirt and mud finds its way into and onto everything. Original colors of vehicles are a complete mystery under the thick disguise. Rubbish and small dead animals and all horrendous forms of animal and human waste start to be revealed as the snow slowly melts away. The refuse is revealed as from an archeological dig, peeled away layer by layer. And as everything is defrosted, it starts to decay. I attempted to maintain the illusion of poise and indifference walking on the street, but my insides are assaulted by the stench. The *babushkas* on their way home from the market shuffled along a trench through the sludge in front of me. If the smell bothered them, they too managed to maintain a perfect exterior shell of indifference.

The world can be a nasty place is so many ways. Your only haven is such a small circle of close friends and a retreat inside yourself. In Karaganda, a year earlier, Natasha had first tried to explain this to me. Russian women take such care with their hair and makeup and clothing, because it is one of the few things they have control over in their lives. Their husbands are alcoholics and most likely abuse them. The effort to live on their pitiful incomes requires a daily struggle for survival. The streets can be visually disgusting and the air unbearable. The American Medical Center had published a health warning in the *Moscow Times* that the air quality on the average street corner in Moscow was equivalent to smoking two packs of cigarettes per day. The air scarred your lungs with every breath. Compared to this cruel outside world, the public bath house was a blissful island of tranquility. Here the women could indulge themselves and seek basic pleasures away from the grim reality of their daily lives.

With great relief my friends Sarah, Gloria, Heather, and I would find each other in the changing area of the women's *bannya*. This was by no means a sure thing. The women at the front desk were surly and had occasionally decided to turn one or more of us away. Sometimes they said that we were not on the members list (attempts to find out more about the members list went nowhere), sometimes we needed to have a reservation, sometimes reservations were irrelevant. Like everywhere else, the rules were in motion – with stern women arguing that "this is the way it has always been" – while providing a different story than the previous week. Offers of an additional "surcharge" we were willing to pay would have no impact on these stern women. They were the keepers of order and decency. They were not to be bribed. No *vzyatki* for them!

Once we successfully gained entry, we would stake our claim to a corner of the changing area and scatter our belongings on a picnic table. As we organized our things, someone would kick off a rant – about the alcoholics with head injuries on the bus, about rumors of a shooting at favorite night club, or about how she nearly fell through an open manhole cover the night before. On this particular Sunday, I shared my latest misadventures of hitchhiking with my girlfriends.

Gloria replied with an even more horrifying story. The name was familiar – Stephen, the British manager in our office, had suffered an even worse misadventure on Friday night.

Stephen hitched a ride home from a club in the early hours Saturday morning. The driver pulled a gun on him and took him to a flat as a hostage. The driver was screaming anti-American insults – saying that it was time Russia got its revenge. Americans were responsible for the pillaging of Russia and keeping the country in poverty. (Needless to say, as bad as the situation was already, as a Brit, Stephen would also have been horrified that he was being mistaken for an American.) At the apartment, a dozen or so Russians were drinking vodka. Stephen was tied to a chair and then a round of beating and Russian roulette began. The chamber of the gun was spun and the trigger pulled at the Brit's head. Again and again. More drinking, more beating. Until the Russians all passed out. Stephen then managed to free himself and flee the apartment building. He had won at Russian roulette – this time. Stephen had managed to get on a flight Saturday to London and was now there seeking medical attention and was recuperating.

We were suitably horrified. And agreed that violence was everywhere. Everyone was impacted. Yes, I did the right thing by leaping out of a moving vehicle earlier in the week. We were agitated by everything around us. Life was a battle and far more vicious than any of us had ever expected. Had we heard about the apartment building that was gutted in a bomb blast this week? Another of our colleagues was living in the apartment above the Russian who had been targeted. The American and his family survived the incident. The Russian was not so fortunate. Life is short. Seize the day – for tomorrow may never come.

We needed to relax and knew it. Focus now. It is time to drop all our outside agitations.

The changing area was warm and humid and inviting. An incredibly refreshing change to outside. There was a desperate frenzy to get undressed and start relaxing immediately. A wonderful contradictory thought – hurry up, we must relax! We frantically peeled off layers of cold muddy clothing and released our feet from the slimy boots. We cast aside these artifacts from the outside world and hung them on hooks on the wall.

I took a deep breath and sighed at the soothing smell of warm wet birch branches and soap. Was it possible that only minutes before I had been choking as the thick air from the street singed the insides of my lungs? Was that truly just on the other side of the door? It could have been a million miles away. I opened my mouth and tasted the fragrant droplets of water in the humid air. Gentle waves of women's laughter and the happy sounds of splashing water enveloped me. I closed my eyes and felt a rush of the sensual experience enveloping my body. I breathed deeply and appreciated for a moment the delicious comforting sanctuary for women.

Like any sensual experience, the *bannya* is best enjoyed naked. I dropped my towel over my arm and felt the air swirl around me. The warm air from the bath area kissed my skin and curled invitingly along my arms. But then abruptly a door opened to the outside and a searing knife of cold stabbed me in the shoulder blades. A harsh reminder that this was only a temporary reprieve from the outside. I had to enjoy it while I could.

The *bannya* experience, like the vodka drinking experience, is a Russian tradition governed by a list of unwritten rules. The Russian women around us were adamant about following the *bannya* rules with others in their own social groups. This was one reason we did not invite our Russian friends along with us. We came here to the *bannya* to relax. Please do not then impose a set of rules for how I am to behave while I am relaxing. Americans are all individualists at heart. We do what we want — and as long as we are not violating anyone else's personal space then it is considered to be socially acceptable. But when Russians relax at the *bannya* or go out drinking with colleagues, all behavior is governed by the unwritten rules.

(Side note here: An entire sociological study into the Russian psyche needs to be done to study this question. Why do Russians find following rules to be a form of relaxation but Americans find it to be confining?)

The first rule was that we had to quickly bathe before going into the sauna. Well, that rule actually makes sense for health reasons. Of course you are supposed to take showers before entering public swimming pools in the United States as well. Enforcement of this rule is usually left up to the discretion of parents monitoring their children. Signs may be up in the changing room, but they can be easily ignored. In the Russian *bannya*, however, if you are at the door into the sauna appearing a bit too dry, a large formidable naked woman will loudly denounce this offense. "A health hazard! You must go and bathe properly, young lady. Don't come back until you are clean!" The Russian sauna matron puts her hands on her hips and guards the entrance to the sauna with a fierce glare. She is the keeper of civility and standards. Order and rules must be upheld. The rule was total nudity, scrubbed down completely. You were, however required to wear footwear of some sort. The Americans plodded in with our beach flip flops. Sarah, of course, had *tapochki* – the Russian-style shower slippers.

Every fifteen minutes or so the large guardian woman (I say large here because almost invariably she was well over 200 pounds of meaty flesh), would announce at the top of her lungs that the sauna doors were about to close. No, you could not come and go from the sauna as you pleased, rather you would submit yourself to being sealed in the small room with thirty or so naked strangers.

Yes, I mean sealed in. We quite literally would agree to being herded into the sauna room and would take our seats on the tiered benches surrounding the hot coals in the center of the floor. Once the room was packed, the "sauna matron" would close the door and barricade it on the inside. No one was going in or out of that door until she permitted it. The matron would sternly survey the motley assortment of women seated on the benches and bark sternly "Silence! We are going to relax now!"

I just about burst out laughing the first time I heard that. Gloria gave me a sharp elbow in the ribs to subdue me, but I stole a glance at her face and could tell she was just about ready to crack up herself. We have been instructed to relax, therefore we must now relax! I choked my laugh into a few quick coughs.

The four of us were quite conscious of the fact that we were the only foreigners at the *bannya*. Although we talked in English among ourselves, we tried not to be the stereotypical Americans. We were deep in Russian native territory here. We would never pass as being Russian, but at least we were determined not to be whining Americans. Therefore we suppressed all our basic instincts to ridicule or ignore someone who was imposing silly rules on us and cooperated. If we are told to shut up and relax, then we would do so – if only to prove the point that we did not want to be perceived to be obnoxious Americans.

Once the sauna matron was satisfied that everyone in the room was quiet, she would start to turn up the heat. The coals glowed red and heat began to pulse slowly throughout the room. She stirred a bucket of water with a birch branch and poured a vial of scented oils into the water. Once the oils were mixed, she dipped a ladle into a bucket and tossed water on the coals a spoonful at a time. The water hissed as it instantly turned to fragrant steam.

Visions of birch trees and forests and clear streams far away from Moscow began to form. Scent is a wonderful escape. A trigger of memory and of longing. The air was delicious and dense. Another spoonful of water and a cloud of steam erupted from the coals. My breathing slowed as I concentrated on the rhythm of the water being swept from the bucket then the harsh sizzle of steam. Sanctuary and escape.

The women sat motionless and breathed deeply. The humid air became warm, then hot, then seared every inch of our naked flesh. My eyeballs burned so I closed my eyes. Pulses of steam boiling from the coals lashed at my face and I covered my face with a towel. I made the mistake of resting my hand for a moment on the wooden bench beside me. The exposed wood violently burned my fingers. And still the sauna matron put on yet more water. "*Khvatit!*" - Enough! One Russian woman finally pleaded bravely from the huddled crowd.

"*Tikho!*" - Quiet! The sauna matron was displeased that one of her subjects had broken the vow of silence. She deliberately poured another large spoonful of water onto the coals, just to prove the point that she was in charge of the proceedings and would not take orders from the masses. Then she dipped her ladle in the bucket again and began to flick water over the huddled women. Droplets of water touched upon my skin, then boiled and evaporated. Gasps and sighs involuntarily escaped throughout the room.

Finally she was done with the water. The sauna matron took a seat on the bench and covered her face with her hands. The air was on fire. I no longer could breathe through my nose as my sinuses burned from the boiling air. I took shallow breaths through my mouth, protected by the thin towel across my face.

This was the cruelest aspect of the *bannya* – the game of chicken played by the women in the sauna. The heat continued to sear our flesh. But we were barricaded in the sauna and ordered to be motionless and silent. Eventually someone would break and beat on the door and demand to be let out. Who would it be? That would obviously be the weakest woman in the room. But it would not be one of the four of us. My friends and I had a pact that would rather have our brains fried from heat exhaustion than give the Russians the pleasure to see the American girls as being weak.

Pride leads us to do rather stupid things at times. I clenched my teeth and held my face firmly in my hands. I was having a hard time maintaining my balance. The room was starting to spin slowly. I had sat down in the sauna wet after a full shower. My skin had quickly dried in the heat. The small hairs on my arms stood individually on end as they were traumatized by the dramatic environmental change around them. I was perfectly motionless. Even breathing seemed to be too much of an effort. The skin around my ribs stretched and contracted unwillingly with each breath.

Gloria, on my left, also had her face buried in her towel. She was obviously becoming faint as she dropped her head to her knees and gave a little moan. Heather, on the other side of me, was a vision of poise and grace. She had been practicing this ritual all fall and had mastered the ability to ignore the pain – or enjoy it. At some point it actually became pleasurable.

Sarah, however, was in a completely different league. She had been living in Moscow several years longer than the rest of us. She had secured a spot on the bench at the highest level in the sauna, thus guaranteeing that she would be subjected to the full impact of the heat. If this were not enough, she also took the very Russian approach of wearing a wool knitted cap in the sauna as well. Yes, hats are what you wear when you are trying to stay warm. Your head is a wonderful regulator of temperature and heat escapes through your head. But Russians into the full sauna experience will wear a wool cap – to ensure they maximize the heat to the highest level possible. I was in awe of Sarah. As much as I enjoyed the *bannya*, I knew I would never be able to take the experience to the same elite level.

The game of chicken continued. There were a few whimpers and gasps from women within the room, but still no one made a move to the door. How much longer would this continue? I could feel my flesh slowly cooking. A droplet of sweat started under my ear and slowly edged down my neck. Then another. And suddenly all fluid in my body had to get out through the pores in my skin. Some switch internally had been thrown and the temperature had to go down immediately. The sweat glistened on my arms and my elbows slid across my thighs as I supported my face in my hands. A delicious release.

Finally, to my relief, one young Russian woman could bear the agony no longer. She jumped up from the bench and ran to the door. "Let me out!" She pleaded and beat her fists on the door. The sauna matron paused a moment, again to reinforce her authority in the room. Then she slowly walked to the door and removed the beam that secured the door.

A blast of cold air swept through the sauna as the young woman escaped. A few loud protests from the remaining women – "keep the door closed!" But the game was over. We were all now free to talk and move about and leave if we wanted to.

The sweat was pouring freely down my arms and back now. My friends and I, however, did not leave although we now could do so without bringing shame to all Americans. As the room cleared out and the door opened and closed, the temperature dropped quickly to a more reasonable level. Still extraordinary, but at least I was able to breathe.

Sarah then produced a fistful of birch branches and started lashing at her legs. Elsewhere in the sauna, women started beating their skin with branches, or turned to their friends and started whipping their backs and legs. The branches had been soaked first in water, so they were softened, but still the bark chewed at the skin. The scent of crushed leaves and sweat filled the thick air.

Once she was done with her own legs and arms, Sarah began to vigorously beat her friends with her soggy weapon. The branches slapped my bare back and I felt pinpricks of small welts rising to the surface. The lashes burned my skin, but then the welts blossomed into a soothing warmth in my muscles. The sauna brought heat from the air to my skin, but the lashes from the birch branches brought core energy deep from within my body to the surface. I started to reach a wonderful equilibrium with the world around me.

A good beating with a soggy birch branch is certainly the original approach to a good exfoliation. And just about as organic and natural as you can get. Feel that old skin get peeled off. And several more layers of skin as well. Until all that's left is fresh pink exposed healthy new raw flesh. I felt like a new natural woman now. As I stood I up, the blood drained from my head and I realized that I was about to faint. It was time to rush into the cold pool.

With a squeal and terrified laughter, the four of us rushed from the sauna and sprinted naked down the hallway to the ice cold pool where we plunged in – with a pause only to kick off the flip flops or *tapochki*. It is absolutely essential to sprint from the sauna to the ice cold pool. Any delay would allow the body to cool down, which would then mean that you would actually feel the temperature of the cold pool as you jump in.

When done properly – at the peak of a full sweat – the cold plunge is absolutely delicious. The sweat continues to pour out of the body, even after the shock of the ice cold water. I floated motionless and reveled in the sudden awareness of my heart pounding, sending hot pulses of blood to my fingertips and flushing my face. A strong heartbeat echoed through my head and chest, enforcing a solid message of good health to every bit of my body. The water truly was absolutely frigid, but the fire burning inside me was stronger. The radiant heat from my body was so powerful it formed a small envelope of warmth. I floated in the pool in my self-generated watery warm cocoon and felt alive and invincible.

I then swam slowly, relishing the moment. I always had a moment of intoxicated delight after successfully leaping in the pool from the sauna. I had to laugh and be pleased with myself. This whole exercise is so contrary to every basic instinct. Only strong-willed people are able to go through with it. And you had to be even stronger to truly enjoy it. I was able to withstand inhumane conditions in a locked sauna and then jump into an ice cold pool, and smile. Therefore I could overcome any challenge. I was strong and energized.

My friends slowly drifted around the pool, lost in their own similar sensual revelry. Their faces were glowing and eyes half-closed in a vision of tranquility. The agitations of the day were irrelevant. Inside the oasis of the *bannya* we could find a moment of peace and draw strength from our own health. Isn't good health and the company of friends the most basic source of happiness? Why should I let the hostility of the outside world agitate me? Just let it remain the outside world. Close it off and just focus on this sanctuary of peace. Here in this private retreat we can find happiness and tranquility from deep within ourselves.

But a moment's ecstasy cannot last. Eventually the frigid water would win the battle against the powerful heater inside. The tranquility of the pool was so paralyzing that it would be a few minutes before we started to realize that our teeth were chattering and the invisible warm cocoon had dissolved. Quickly, back to the sauna for a few moments to warm up.

We would rush back to the sauna, but attempt not to be locked in this time. Two full sessions in a row in the sauna would have been more than us fragile American girls could handle. The Russians, of course, just marched back and forth continuously all day with admirable fortitude. But also their daily lives were much harsher than ours, so I guess they needed the adrenaline rush of the plunge into the cold pool much more than we did.

Next on the agenda was our unabashed indulgence in all the frivolous skin and body products that we had collected on various trips back to the United States or Western Europe. Our skin was alive from the sauna and the birch branches and the cold pool, now let's bring it to the highest level of health and radiance possible. Rice scrubs for the legs and arms, mud masques for the face, and protein treatment on the hair. We breathed in the hot humid air of the bathing area – splashing in soapy buckets of water and scrubbing our backs with wooden brushes.

We were living advertisements for the entire product range from the Body Shop and Clinique. We were privileged to be able to afford such luxuries. And even more privileged to be travelling occasionally to the West where we could replenish our stash. A true luxury is something that you can live without, but is a rare treat and a delight to have. We would not be able to run down to the corner shop for any of these delicious supplies, so we savored every moment. The scents of vanilla, cocoa butter, and eucalyptus oil mixed in with the heavy air of steaming birch branches. Our skin was exfoliated, glossy and smooth to the touch. Our hair was thick and shiny and fell in long wet lashes on our backs.

We were young and visions of health and radiance. Yes, the Moscow air seared our lungs with every breath. Yes, the vegetables at the open air markets were confirmed to contain nuclear contaminants. And yes, we were all drinking far more alcohol than we knew was reasonable. But those were all long term issues and of no concern to us. The weathered faces and shapeless bodies of the *babushkas* were the destiny of the women who lived in Russia after age thirty. For us, the fortunate Americans, we were just passing through. We could enjoy this moment and all that Russia had to offer and brush off the negative. I was *nashi* now and understood how to sidestep the sudden traps of open manholes and hitchhiking mishaps. The hazards around us would not have time to take their toll. We were young, strong, and invincible.

The soothing simple pleasure of hot water and soap and a warm fluffy towel sedated me into a meditative trance. I wrapped myself in my towel and sat quietly breathing in the steam around me as a mud masque worked away on my skin. The Hotel Oktyabrskaya, the Hotel Rus, the Rossiya, and all the other miserable places where I had taken cold showers and been given scraps of towels were all drifting far away.

I savored the contrast of this oasis to the grind of my work week. What would the week hold in store for me?

Yes the week ahead would have its challenges. But in the warmth and comfort of the *bannya* I viewed the project with renewed optimism.

Renovations in the Ekaterinburg offices were proceeding at a lightning pace. Phone lines had been activated in a fraction of the standard waiting time. The building had been re-wired to suit modern office requirements for phone jacks and numerous electrical outlets. We had somehow managed to obtain approval to source the office furniture from Poland rather than the United States, which reduced our lead time for furniture to weeks rather than months. The move in date had been scheduled – together with the requisite grand opening celebrations.

Computer equipment procurement was moving forward. The *PC Magazine* gift from Viktor Mikhailovich had proven to be the godsend I had hoped for. I had managed to copy details for specifications of processor speeds, hard drive capacity, required ports and cables, and produced something that resembled detail computer specifications. And Annabel had not yet rejected my request!

The real work of the Local Privatization Centers was slowly beginning. Nathan was beginning to reach out to his American business contacts to organize an expedition of potential investors to Ekaterinburg. Joseph was identifying the enterprises in South Russia that could gain the most from his expertise.

All of the vodka-soaked evenings with strippers, meals of boiled meat and pickled vegetables, and rank hotel rooms would be worthwhile. We would be making a difference for the future of Russia.

But then I smiled to myself pleasantly. The cold showers with sludgy water would be later in the week. (Tyumen this week.) For the moment I needed to focus on the fleeting piece of heaven that was the *bannya*.

At some point during the day each of us would have a one hour full body massage. What total decadence. Here also the pleasure and pain factor were extraordinary. Honestly I skipped this step several times because I could not get up the nerves to subject myself to the Russian masseuse. The sauna and the cold pool were one thing, but the iron fingers of the Russian masseuse would take me to an entirely different level of excruciating agony. But then again, without pain, how do we truly measure our pleasure? The more violent the pain, the sweeter the pleasure when it stops.

I would lie on the massage table, naked and vulnerable under a thin sheet. The woman working on my body had strength in her fingers I did not know was possible. Her joints surely must be on the verge of collapsing under the pressure she delivered. She pressed and stretched and kneaded deep around my neck and shoulders then down my spine. Her fingers deftly found every major pressure point. As her fingers worked deeper into my flesh, nuclear flashes of pain seared through my network of nerves. Surely she was going to dislodge or sever some critical muscles and I would be debilitated forever with a dislocated back.

The woman ordered me to relax. I was too stressed and my muscles were too tight. She scolded me that I was only making things worse by being tense. This was so painful. I was physically unable to loosen my muscles – the anticipation of pain caused me to recoil unconsciously. I was a tightly wound spring, and she was determined to uncoil every knotted muscle in my body. Using brute force if need be.

She worked her way down my arms. Aren't muscles supposed to remain attached to tendons and bones? Apparently not. She identified groups of muscles that I did not know existed and traced them down to the point they attached and formed. Her fingers ground my flesh into a mushy pulp. I bit deep into my towel to restrain myself from screaming in agony.

The masseuse moved onto my legs, starting on my thighs and working down towards my feet. I held my breath, fearing the inevitable moment when she would pierce the soles of my feet with her dagger-like claws. She bruised and twisted the arches of my feet and blinding white flashes of agony pulsed through my body up to the roots of the hair on my head. Pain ricocheted throughout every living tissue. I was always astonished at the amazing connections of nerves in my feet to each vital organ. I gasped for air then bit down hard on my towel again. Tears welled in the corners of my eyes. Why was I subjecting myself voluntarily to such inhumane treatment at the hands of another woman?

I retreated deep within myself to avoid any conscious acknowledgement of the pain. Or worse, acknowledgement that I had actually paid to have this pain inflicted on me. Actually, like with so many services in Russia at the time, the price I paid was laughable by American standards. This was a one hour full body massage by a woman who clearly knew what she was doing and was determined to ensure her clients got their full value for money. And I had paid the equivalent of only about $20 USD for the massage on top of the $10 or so entry into the *bannya*. An extraordinary amount of money for Russians. This would have been about one-fifth of the average monthly salary at the time. An extravagant waste.

It certainly was a semi-colonial experience we lived. What an astonishing standard of living we could afford on our income. At least in regard to the things that money could buy. Some things like clean air and hot water sometimes cannot be purchased at any price. If I so chose, I could come down to the *bannya* every weekend for this treatment, without a second thought as to the expense. What would be the equivalent for a full day at a health spa in the United States, complete with full body massage? About $200 or so? A rare treat at that price.

I wondered how much of my payment for the massage actually found its way into the pocket of the masseuse. If she was able to keep even a quarter of what her fee was, then she would have been earning a fabulous salary by Russian standards of the day. I did a few mental calculations and determined that if she were working a 40 hour week (which she probably wasn't – her fingers could not possibly withstand the effort), then she would be earning about $800 per month or so. Far higher salary than the average wage of $150 per month and on par with the young professional Russians in my office.

Yes, the expatriate salaries were many multiples of our Russian staff. But our staff were being paid generously as well – many multiples of the equivalent wages with Russian companies. We were providing training and exposure to Western business and the skills they were learning would be shared throughout other businesses in Russia. Tatiana could not use a computer when I hired her. Now she was sending emails, typing and formatting proposals, and answering phones with a pleasant "Hello Arthur Andersen, how may I help you?" Tatiana had taken the executive assistant role to a new level and had taken the initiative to confiscate my suits for dry cleaning and my shoes to be polished. My lead accountant, Nadya, had never used MS Excel before she joined my team. Now she was building models of budget forecasts. We were delivering aid programs on many levels. The official story was assistance to Russian privatized companies. But aid to the struggling country should be viewed through the consideration of our skills transfer and financial rewards to our staff as well.

The hiring and training of local Russian staff was not just limited to my team in Moscow. The full network of Local Privatization Centers was taking shape. Three were now being supported by Arthur Andersen in South Russia, Ekaterinburg, and Chelyabinsk. Five others were supported by other consultancies. Efforts were now underway from Krasnoyarsk to St Petersburg to hire data collectors to help build out the database of Russian companies that were seeking foreign partners. The LPC directors were thrilled to provide a list of well-connected young kids as data collectors. Joseph as well as the advisor in St Petersburg wanted to go through a rigorous interviewing process. Nathan and most of the other American advisors just accepted the candidates as offered by the LPC director. A year ago I would have sided with Joseph. But now I had to agree with Nathan. Nathan just wanted to be amiable with Sergei Glebovich. But I realized that with our young data collectors, their connections would be their most valuable asset. Realistically no one would be starting with American business consulting skills. We could teach them the rest that they needed to know. And we would be making a lasting impact on nearly sixty kids throughout the country.

And beyond the formal project itself, our positive impact extended to others who we touched with our presence. Where would Valya, my dear housekeeper, be today without the American expatriates? She was a trained nuclear physicist who had philosophical issues with her prior profession designing nuclear weapons. Of course, as a single mother her primary concern, however, was income. Nevertheless, the expats were able to offer her a higher standard of living as a housekeeper than she had previously experienced as a nuclear weapons engineer. Some would say that there was something definitely wrong with the world when a trained nuclear physicist was working as a housekeeper. But we all played our roles in this reality to the best of our abilities. Valya was an outstanding housekeeper. She was continuously two steps ahead of anything I could imagine or would even dream of requesting. Dusting the insides of ceiling lamps, adjusting hinges on my cabinets to make them close properly. She was thrilled to have four times the income of her previous role. She was happy to be making a positive impact on people's lives rather than designing weapons of mass destruction. I was delighted to have Valya as my own personal domestic goddess. Just imagine – at age 27 I had a housekeeper extraordinaire, plus my driver, Vanya, and the wonderful executive assistant, Tatiana. What an extravagant life I had.

I closed my eyes and relaxed with the self-satisfied peace of the righteous. Of course I was entitled to enjoy the decadent pleasures of the *bannya* and the massage. I was paid an extraordinary salary because I was willing to work here on aid programs in working conditions that few others would endure. And the money I spent on decadent pleasures would go back to the people who deserved it the most – hard-working and honest people like Valya and this masseuse. We were helping to build the new Russia.

I breathed deeply. The pain was gone. Only a dull throbbing ache remained, pulsing slowly deep within my flesh. Every muscle had been subdued under the masterful fingers of the Russian masseuse. It was futile to resist. I no longer needed to scream and tight. I could not move anyway.

And suddenly the woman was abruptly barking that I get moving off the table, as her next client was expected momentarily. My consciousness returned to my body. Where previously I had ropes and knots of macramé flesh, now I was only aware of soft pliable rubber. Why couldn't someone just provide a wheel chair to transport me back to the changing area? I was sure my knees would buckle under me as I stood up. My legs certainly would not be capable of the strain of carrying my weight and walking, even for two minutes.

I slowly padded back to the changing area. The slightest movement was an enormous effort. The excruciating pain of the massage had faded, but in its place was a deep pulsing calm energy. I was aware of every breath, every bead of sweat, every heartbeat. My arms fell weakly to the side and I strained to stand upright. Just a bit further to our picnic bench.

Back in the changing area I found Sarah and Gloria sedated in a post-massage stupor as well. They were wrapped in towels and moving slowly and speaking quietly. Every motion was an enormous effort. Better to conserve energy and sit still. Heather was being subject to her massage and would join us upon her release.

We were now at the best part of the day – the picnic. Each of us produced our contribution for the day's picnic at our table in the changing room. Coordination of a menu was difficult, as we never knew what we would find at the shops on our way over to the *bannya*. I usually contributed a wonderful fresh loaf or two of bread from my favorite "fresh bread" store, plus I had recently discovered a shop with incredible Dutch cheeses. Everyone provided different delicacies – a fresh cucumber, apples, and of course caviar and champagne.

Gloria deftly cut the apple into wedges. Fresh juice bubbled from the cuts onto the metal blade. I bit cleanly into the apple, savoring the crisp break of the fruit against my teeth. The champagne brought out the sharp sweet taste of the fruit even stronger. I tore apart the fresh loaves of bread with my fingers. A thin crisp crust protected a delicate interior of the bread - crushed in my hands under the sweep of a butter knife. Creamy sweet butter on today's bread, straight from the bakery then topped with glistening juicy caviar. Tender salty beads of salmon roe gently popped in my mouth. What a wonderful life we have. Caviar and champagne lunch after an exhilarating day at the *bannya*.

"Where did you ever find this bread? It is perfect!" Sarah softly moaned with pleasure.

I beamed with the compliment. To be credited with a remarkable discovery in Moscow was one of the highest levels of praise among expats. I was especially pleased to receive such a compliment from Sarah who was usually the first one to unearth new gems. This *bannya* was her discovery. She is the one who finally led me through the labyrinth of Soviet era apartment blocks in my neighborhood to find the cellar door entrance to Krizis Zhanra into the warm secluded nest below. In a world without Yellow Page directories and before the advent of Google searches, knowledge of shops, restaurants, and services was a revered attribute.

I had found the bread store the same way most new discoveries in Moscow were made – by walking the streets of my neighborhood and paying attention to detail. One day I noticed a small hand-painted sign "Fresh bread" posted over a window on an otherwise featureless wall. Out of curiosity I ventured closer and was overwhelmed by the seductive aroma of baking bread. I knocked at the window and a large potato-fed *babushka* took 500 rubles from me (about 25 cents). Wearing oven-mitts she handed me a baton of perfect steaming bread. Although I had to wrap the bread in my coat to keep from burning my fingers, I could not resist shredding off a corner for a nibble. Yes, fresh from the oven. The bread scalded my mouth. Then I relaxed and savored the perfect texture, hint of sweetness, and the morsel melted in my mouth. Pleasure and pain.

Often the best gems were hidden behind unmarked doors. Knock and you never know what you will find. Maybe they will answer and maybe they won't.

Heather had joined us and raved about her latest discovery – Jim's video rental store. Video rental? In Moscow? The only access to American movies we had were the monthly showings at the Radisson Slavyanskaya auditorium (in English, with subtitles in Russian) or poorly pirated video tapes sold next to dried fish at the open air markets (and dubbed badly in Russian). A few tapes of American television shows sent from friends back home were being passed around as well. But a real video rental store? Of course Jim was not Blockbuster. He was a long term expat living with his Russian girlfriend who had somehow amassed an immense video library (the origins of his video library, like so many things, never were explained). He operated out of his apartment and only admitted those who had been introduced through friends. You left a $20 deposit, signed out your video of choice in a register book, and then enjoyed the wonders of American, British, or Australian cinema from the comfort of your own living room.

Yes, we reflected. So much was available in Moscow – you just needed to know where to look and who to call on for assistance. Preparation for Thanksgiving was an adventure in procurement. In a city where most meat was of questionable quality and most chickens appeared to be under-nourished, where would we find a proper American Thanksgiving turkey? But our friend Alex at the American embassy provided the key. Butterball turkeys – real American Butterball turkeys – would circumvent Russian customs via the magic of the diplomatic pouch and were available to those who had friends placed in the American Embassy. We would celebrate a true Thanksgiving in the purest sense – we were so thankful for the opportunities available to us and the friends that we had. Life was good in Russia if you had money and the right contacts – and a bit of imagination and nerves.

Earlier in the summer, the American Fourth of July festivities had also taken on a whole different flavor in the context of expatriate life. The American Embassy had somehow secured the whole of the old inner city Moscow airfield for the day. The Americans picnicked on the airfield, complete with Frisbees, BBQ, and a game of soft-ball – while a fierce wall of motionless black uniformed Russians kept us from venturing too close to a line of MiG fighters parked along the perimeter. Our Russian friends and guests were baffled and amused by the game of softball and terrified of the black uniforms. "OMON", they whispered nervously. The word meant nothing to me.

Vanya, who I had seen settle *vzyatki* with the GAI with ease was visibly shaken by the presence of the OMON. "They are the special forces unit of the *militsia*," Vanya explained in a hushed voice. "Their motto is 'We know no mercy and do not ask for any.'"

I needed no further clarification. We were celebrating our freedoms as Americans, in the shadows of the Russian reality. As the sun set late in the summer evening, an extravagant display of fireworks lit the Moscow sky – no doubt supplied through the wonders of the immunity of the diplomatic pouch service. We had the liberties of Americans, while living in the land of opportunity of Russia.

We enjoyed the thrill of Moscow because we were American. Russia was an adventure, but not our long term reality. We knew that if things ever became too much we could go home. Stephen survived his ordeal with Russian roulette and he was now safely back in London. The bribe-extracting GAI and terrifying OMON were products of the Russian government. The American government, however, provided Butterball turkeys and fireworks.

Our day at the *bannya* was reaching a final satisfying conclusion. We relaxed and socialized and savored the delicacies amassed in front of us. All the agonies and petty complaints of our lives were forgotten. We laughed and shared compliments on the treats procured by each other. We were already moving in a trance-like state. After a glass or two of champagne the environment took on a pleasant dreamy quality. We relished in the simple joys of life that are all too often overshadowed by our petty complaints. We had good friends, fine foods, and excellent health. No need to think about yesterday or tomorrow. Tomorrow all of this will be a distant memory from some far off land. Today is all that matters.

Carpe diem.

10 PRISONER'S DILEMMA

January 1995 — Moscow

As winter descended over Moscow, daylight was devoured by darkness. Of course the days become shorter everywhere in the world in the winter, but in the far north the winters just simply seem endless. This was the cruelest aspect of the Russian winter. Cold was no longer the enemy. My *dublunka* now gave me impenetrable armor when I was outside to battle the elements. But the complete deprivation of sunlight was unavoidable and persistent and deeply disturbing.

And it was not just the fact that the sun sets at the early hour of three or four in the afternoon. During the few hours that could be called "daylight", the winter sky was cast in a dull grey coat. Days would go by without revealing the sun at all. On the rare clear day, the sun would sit so low on the horizon that pale icy shadows suffocated the city. The sun made a feeble effort to peek over the smallest of buildings – and then it was gone.

Life had been drained from all the trees long ago in October. Tortured skeletons remained. Shreds of grass, rare in any case, were covered with snow or perished in the cold. The sounds of birds and other wildlife never really existed at any time of year – unless the squeaks and chirps of rats, cockroaches, and pigeons count. And even they seemed to be hiding through the winter. A dark stillness fell. Blue withdrew from the sky. Colorful clothing of summer eroded and it its place was the dreary drab of the long bleak winter. People's skin took on a pale sickly pallor. The sun retreated and the crisp details of the city were washed over and blurred with a grey watercolor. Grey descended and pushed all other color into hiding for the winter.

Grey worked its way into the minds of the people. The darkness put everyone into a half-sleep. When awoken for moments to interact with others, we jolted into a cranky and fussy state – like children much in need of a long soothing nap. The *babushkas* at the market scolded more harshly. Tempers erupted in the office. The smallest task became an agonizing effort. All anyone wanted to do was to go home and hibernate.

I started to develop a theory of social unrest in Russia based upon fundamentals of sunlight deprivation. The major revolutions and uprisings in Russia's history have typically occurred in November through February. In recent times the Communists and other reactionary groups have fared far better in elections in the winter than in the summer. People are bitter, complaining, and generally dissatisfied with life. Depression sets in and with it comes the urge to sleep until life somehow improves itself. What more fertile ground upon which to build an uprising? Life is miserable and vicious and depressing. Something must be done to improve our miserable lives. An uprising seems like a logical step. Anything to resist the grip of the grey dark depression.

I would force myself to get out for a good walk at midday, no matter how cold the day was. I needed a dose of sunshine to brighten my mood. But the sun was weak and made little impact. The whole experience in Russia seemed a bit pointless now. Why was I here anyway? I was subjecting myself to being a test animal in some sunlight deprivation experiment. And I was doing this voluntarily. Life didn't have to be this way. I could return to the United States at any time. Couldn't I?

On a typical day I would be working until six or seven at night. This meant that I would be at the office for three hours after the sun set – and it would still be early evening. My body would ache and crave sleep. I would try to convince myself to accept an invitation to dinner, but it just all seemed too hard. I was physically and mentally exhausted and would sometimes just crawl into bed minutes after I got home. Dinner would be forgotten in the overwhelming quest for sleep.

The dark cozy nest of Krizis Zhanra became the default destination as I forced myself to interact with humanity – but still could not make the effort to go more than a few steps from my apartment block. The ceiling was so low that I could stand and touch the uneven concrete shell. Lack of ventilation combined with thick cigarette smoke meant that the most comfortable place to be was sitting on the floor with a pint of beer and a bowl of *pelmeni*. (Siberian ravioli in broth and a perfect winter comfort food.)

Sarah served as the listening ear to my laments regarding the ongoing dramas with procuring computer equipment for my Local Privatization Centers. Every time I was certain that I had escaped the inner circle of hell, Sarah would laugh and remind me that I did not yet have the equipment ordered, needless to say delivered to the regional offices. Therefore my troubles were certainly far from over. She had years more experience in Russia than me. I know that she meant to be supportive. Yet each piece of advice from Sarah left me despairing that I had been condemned to some sentence of purgatory from which no exit was clear.

The *PC Magazine* from Viktor Mikhailovich in Ekaterinburg had helped tremendously.

I had meticulously copied out specifications for hard drives, modems, processors and other components into a list that looked (to me at least) that I knew what I was doing. I spelled out things that should have been obvious (if the DC procurement team actually was thinking and adding value rather than just performing clerical functions): European power supplies, Russian language keyboards, Russian language versions of all software, A4 paper trays for the printers. But who to check my work before I sent the list back to Annabel? Raymond had never used a computer. Most of the Russians were still working their way through illicit Russian versions of "Microsoft Word for Dummies".

I decided to give the list of specifications to Joseph as well as Tatiana to review. Joseph would have an opinion on everything, so I might as well as put his energy to good use. (Besides, if I didn't solicit his opinion, then undoubtedly he would be providing commentary later about how everything could have been improved.) With Tatiana she was so eager to expand her knowledge and capabilities that I knew that she would really give it her best – probably including hunting down her own alternate sources of information to verify my findings.

Joseph's first response was outrage. Didn't we have an office in Washington DC that was supposed to provide support for computer procurement? Yes, I sympathized and agreed with him. But their role was apparently defined as "procurement", not "specification". I had fought that battle already and lost. We had to tell them exactly point-for-point what needed to be ordered. Once Joseph calmed down he then provided a thoughtful list of amendments for me, including additional assorted cables, extension cords, boxes of floppy disks, extra boxes of toner cartridges for the printers and fax machines, and other things that would be difficult to find in South Russia.

Tatiana, true to form, came up with her own solutions as well. She arrived in the office the next day with an envelope of stickers to paste on American computer keyboards that would overwrite the Latin letters with combination Cyrillic/Latin labels for the keys.

"Only 18,000 rubles each from the kiosk near the Metro station!" she declared proudly. At about 7 USD each, this would be a huge cost savings over the expected price of $300 for Cyrillic/Latin keyboards to be procured from the United States. Three hundred dollars each for a total of nearly 100 computers that we planned on purchasing, we would be spending nearly $30,000 on keyboards alone. All of the Russians in the office had already purchased stickers for their own computers and Tatiana offered me the new sample packet of stickers as a friendly gift for my own laptop.

Of course, the kiosk by the Metro station is not an approved supplier for USAID and does not provide nice itemized receipts. I knew that Tatiana's idea, although logical, would not comply with USAID procurement rules. I did not have the heart to reject her idea myself, so I enthusiastically thanked her and proposed the solution to Annabel in DC.

Her response was predictable. If we were to purchase two sets of stickers for each computer (assuming that a spare should be on hand for each), this would be approximately $1400. An expense that could draw the attention of the inevitable audit at some later point in the project. No. Everything, down to the last printer cable, would have to be purchased through official channels in the United States.

In the name of saving US taxpayer money we would need to use approved suppliers – resulting in us spending approximately $28,000 more than necessary on computer keyboards. Of course Tatiana was baffled. Aren't we supposed to be using this money to provide assistance to Russian companies? If we save $28,000 with computer keyboards, isn't that some money we can use to actually support the services to the Russian companies?

I really am not good enough with politically correct statements to be able to provide a response to her that made any sense. I could just agree and say that yes, sometimes the rules don't make sense, but we need to follow them.

This left Tatiana lost in thought as she really tried to understand. Nadya, however, had overhead everything. She just laughed that maybe the Russian government should be advising the Americans for how to do things more effectively. If convoluted rules were the goal, then the Americans were just getting started and had a lot more to learn.

I thought that after the specification was reviewed by Joseph (and Tatiana) and submitted to DC that my part in the process was complete. Nadya was right that we were just getting started.

Days went by with no response from Annabel. I would learn that she was off on holiday for a week. Couldn't someone process the request in her absence? No, she was the dedicated procurement support specialist. Now she was in training for a week. Now there was some other project that was taking priority. After what seemed like an eternity Annabel finally responded that further work on the specification was required. I needed to provide *justification* for every item I had listed, together with an explanation of what other alternatives had been explored and why what had been proposed was the best option.

Are you kidding me? She really wanted a written explanation for why each computer needed a floppy drive? Why each one needed internet connectivity? Why a particular modem speed? I protested to Raymond that this was totally unreasonable. Surely this *had* to be beyond what was required for USAID procurement documentation. But in the end neither Raymond nor I were experts. We had to rely on the DC-based office for support. Our designated expert said she needed a written explanation of why we needed a laser printer with a print speed of X pages per minute rather than a dot matrix printer with Y pages per minute.

I sighed and returned to my bible (aka *PC Magazine*) for some nice terminology from the marketing propaganda to help me justify the various processors and other peripherals that I had selected. After the latest round of creative writing, I had hoped that *this* would be the end of my procurement concerns. But, of course, no, the purgatory continued. Weeks went by with no response. Calls went unanswered.

Meanwhile, of course, I was receiving anxious calls from Ivan Ivanovich, Anton, Sergei Glebovich, and others out in regional Russia anxiously awaiting their computers. Ivan Ivanovich and Anton stated that they just could not possibly be *respected* as a modern consultancy without modern equipment. Sergei Glebovich was eager to build the skills of the team in his office and was already trying to plan computer training for his team – but could not move forward without computers. I could not tell them that the equipment had not yet even been ordered, so mumbled some statements that the order was being processed and I would update them as soon as I had any further news.

Finally word back from Annabel. The order was on hold. There was a debate back in Washington regarding the correct scope of the order. The scope of our engagement with USAID was to open four Local Privatization Centers and to support data collection across ten LPCs. To date, however, the central office of the Russian Privatization Center had directed Arthur Andersen only to open three LPCs. The fourth was still theoretical. Therefore should the equipment order be placed for the full documented scope of the project or just for those centers that had already been opened? USAID procurement rules were not clear on the subject and Annabel was attempting to clarify.

Sarah was patient during my monologue. She bought me another beer and quietly laughed that we had not even managed to place the order yet – now five months after the start of the project. The adventures with procurement would continue until we had everything safely configured and operational in the offices.

Another American voice chimed in from nearby. "Oh no. The fun continues long after the equipment has been delivered. What exactly do you think will happen when the first hard drive fails, or a paper tray for the printer breaks? What will you do then? Have you renovated all the offices so that you have proper electrical wiring and phone connections?"

And this is how I met Spencer. He had been eavesdropping on my stories with amusement, but could no longer restrain himself. Another American consultant in Moscow was not a novelty. But very few travelled extensively outside Moscow and St Petersburg. With Spencer I found a shared experience of seedy hotels, vodka soaked dinners, and government ministers protecting the finest assets of Russia from the meddling hands of American investors. We debated whether it was better being a woman in a Russian hotel (where the men would be pounding on the door all night long trying to "*poznakomitsa*") or whether it was better being an American man where the *dezhurnayas* would send prostitutes to the room attempting to sell additional services.

Spencer conceded that women did have a harder time travelling on their own throughout regional Russia. Our friendship was sealed.

Saturday evening a few weeks later I struggled for motivation to extricate myself from my cozy nest and go out into the forbidding winter night. Although it was only eight at night, the sun had set hours ago and I was aching for bed. This was ridiculous, of course. I had spent a good part of the afternoon that day curled up under my fluffy duvet with my cat snuggled by my side. The standard midday walk had sapped away the remaining bits of strength in my body and I was ready for a full winter hibernation. When would this desolate winter ever end? But it was only January. Winter was only reaching the halfway mark. If I were to survive the season mentally intact then I would have to accept social engagements and get out a bit. Hiding at home in bed would be just the next step down the spiral of bleak despair.

I scolded myself that hibernation would be truly succumbing to depression. Despite this, it still was an enormously attractive option. I was so fortunate to have a well-heated apartment –furnished in total luxury by local standards. The goal of my Moscow flat had been to create my own personal sanctuary to recover from the stresses of daily life. Yes, it had been a tough road to actually tame the apartment and procure decadent little luxuries. But now I had achieved my goal to the point where it was now a monumental effort to tear myself away from my cozy urban retreat. Left to my own devices, I could hide in the cocoon of my bed for days (if not weeks). I would burrow under a mountain of soft fluffy pillows. My duvet was made of a thick cozy goose down and I could curl up for hours with my purring cat with a good novel, dozing in and out of consciousness. Outside the bedroom window the flakes of snow would swirl by, reminding me how much more comfortable my bed was than any other place imaginable at that moment.

But no, I had to pull myself away from these thoughts. I was tempted to lock myself away in my apartment for the winter in my quest for peace and comfort. Now that I had access to Jim's video library and my fresh bread store – what more could I possibly want? No, I chided myself – I had to get out and socialize. I needed to keep myself from a trajectory of becoming one of those women who wears plaid and florals and talks to her cat all day. Spencer had just moved to an apartment not far away from me. His house warming party promised to be a good occasion to catch up with everyone who I was neglecting socially as the winter slipped by.

The evening also promised to fuel the major winter vice as well – alcoholism. The Nordic countries and Russia are all notoriously alcoholic. Before moving to Russia I had not appreciated the link between the desolate winters and alcohol. But now, substantially into my second post-Soviet winter, I truly understood. When faced with up to seven months of bleak grey existence, escapism is essential to maintain a bit of balance. As the months drag on and the pallor continues to drain all energy and life from the surrounding environment, it is so easy to slip into a routine to take the edge off the day's frustrations with a nip of vodka. And then just another nip. Why come back to reality when this vodka-induced state is more pleasant?

My contribution to the night's festivities was about eight cans of "Bear beer". This was a brand of beer with a distinct metallic after taste that was the brand on offer this day at the kiosk nearest my flat – alongside dried fish, Snickers bars, L'Oreal shampoo, and cat food. I had briefly contemplated bringing some Black Death Vodka as a joke (complete with skull and crossbones on the packaging). But then realized that if I brought it, inevitably someone would insist that we drink it. Bear beer was not great, but it was palatable and certainly a huge step forward from the out-of-date Tuborg offered at Dr Bang's the winter before. I carried my offering in a plastic bag on my way over to the party.

The walk to Spencer's apartment was pleasant enough. It was a lovely winter night. A fresh glazing of snow brought a breathtaking moment of cleanliness to my neighborhood. Barren trees were decorated with fragile lace of ice. The filth of the streets was momentarily shrouded under a blanket of white powder. Fresh snow crunched crisply under my boots and tiny wisps of icy flakes swirled about and kissed my nose. Street lights were virtually non-existent, so the night was lit only by the low cool reflections of lights from apartments on the crystals of ice and snow.

I wrapped my head and neck in the fine goat hair shawl that had been a gift from the women in the Orenburg office. Apparently Orenburg was known for producing some of the finest quality shawls in the world. One of the women explained that the sign of quality was that the whole shawl could be pulled through her wedding ring. Featherweight to the touch but strong and warm in the cold. After wearing the shawl for the first time in the snow I had to agree entirely. With the amour of the *dublunka* and now this shawl, I was nearly impenetrable to the cold.

I crunched my way through the neighborhood and passed embassy after embassy – Australia, Finland, Vietnam. The embassies all proudly beamed spotlights on their national flags and imposing facades of the buildings, but then ominously illuminated the front gates. On the sides of the gates, sentries kept watch huddled in the shelters of their guardhouses. Beyond these pools of light, the neighborhood disappeared into darkness. The stillness of the night was disrupted only by the occasional movement of the guards in their huts.

Street signage never was a strong point in Russia. Now in the total darkness of the winter night, I realized that it would be trial and error to find Spencer's apartment building. No numbers or signage of any sort were visible from the street. I knew I was in the right area, but the apartment buildings were characterless and without identification or lighting. I would have to trudge up to each one through the snow. Never mind that – it was a beautiful evening and I was pleased to have pulled myself out of hibernation and into society.

Across from the Vietnam Embassy, I passed through a gate into a courtyard leading up to the first apartment block I was going to inspect. I followed a small beaten path through the yard towards the entrance. It would be good to get inside. Although my *dublunka* and shawl were impenetrable to the snow, my boots were not. The thin soles of my American boots were a poor defense against the constant numbing cold of the Russian ice and snow beneath my feet. Only a few more moments and I would be able to see the numbers on the side of the building.

Three men huddled in the courtyard fumbling for cigarettes in their pockets. As I passed, one turned to me and asked for a light. Without pausing I muttered "*nyet*" and continued to the entrance. My feet were definitely in pain now. I needed warmth.

Suddenly the shawl tightened around my neck and I was tugged backwards and stumbled. I fell into the arms of the three men and choked as the shawl was jerked tighter. They had caught me as I stumbled, but why was I choking? I quickly reached to my neck to fight to breathe. But just as quickly, a strong hand gripped my wrist and pulled it down, twisting my arm unnaturally behind my back.

I was now being dragged by my neck, arms, coat, whatever could be grabbed quickly, and propelled to a dark corner of the courtyard behind a small shed. The three men moved quickly and were a blur of strong arms, hands fumbling all over my body, and heavily intoxicated breath pressed against my face. I was gasping for air and coughing, but quickly coming to the realization that I had not just stumbled but was now in a nasty situation. Three on one are never good odds and I had no idea what they intended to do next.

As amazing as it sounds, I was not frightened. Call it adrenaline, or stupidity, or a visit from my guardian angel, or whatever you want – but a wave of anger and determination pulsed through me with a level of intensity that I could feel every inch of my skin on high alert. I must maintain control over the situation and I would not be a victim.

Thug A was now strangling me, jerking the shawl tightly around my neck. His other fist was pushed deep in my mouth. I was gagging and strangling and considered attempting to bite his fingers off. He was hissing at me not to scream or fight and I would not be hurt. I defiantly swung the bag of beer cans (which for some reason I was still clutching) and smacked him in the kneecap. This earned me a rough jerk around the throat and a hiss that he could break my neck if he wanted to.

Behind me Thug B pressed himself aggressively against my body and gripped and twisted my arms into paralysis. I was now immobilized and facing Thug C. He plucked the bag of beer cans from me and then hopped around, demanding my money. Thankfully I had decided to leave my wallet at home and only had a pocketful of rubles and some business cards. With Thug A's fist in my mouth I could not answer Thug C's hysterical questions, which became more insistent. He then tore open my coat and started fumbling around through my pockets. I glared at him over the fist of Thug A as he felt for money and then began to amuse himself feeling elsewhere as well.

Things were going downhill very quickly with Thug A as well. His heavily intoxicated breath stung my face as he pressed his face against mine. His eyes weren't focusing, but his grip on the shawl strangling my neck remained firm. Then the fist was removed from my mouth. I gasped for air. But to my horror he then pulled me against him by the neck and shoulder and started covering my face in wet disgusting kisses, telling me firmly to remain calm and everything would be fine. Fine? What exactly did fine mean? Six hands on me now – four pinning me and two having a sloppy grope. If a few are removed, then I would have a chance for escape.

"Give me your rings!" demanded Thug C in front of me. Thug B obligingly released my arms and Thug A pulled his noxious face away from me so I could remove my gloves. Now down to two hands pinning me – the others had backed off. I was a bit closer to escape. I stood up straight and attempted to burn Thug C with laser vision as I pulled off my gloves. I moved slowly and deliberately and showed him firmly that I was wearing no rings. I was gaining control of the situation.

Suddenly Thug B exclaimed "She's wearing diamond earrings!" Cubic zirconia actually. I probably paid about $6 for those earrings, but unfortunately they had the drunk thugs fooled. "No they're fake. But you can have them if you want." I said firmly to Thug C in front of me. This, however, interested Thug A, who released his grip on my neck so he could have a closer look at my earrings. No one was holding me. All three were attempting to see my earrings through the darkness.

I glared icily at the two thugs in front of me and took a confident stride towards the gate to the courtyard. They did not move. Another step with confidence and determination and I was out of reach. Then I broke into a run, sprinting across the courtyard back to the street beyond.

The gods were certainly smiling on me that night. As I escaped out onto the street I saw a team of *militsia* socializing and sharing a cigarette with the Vietnam Embassy guards. My neck was still recovering from the near strangulation and I coughed for air. I struggled at first to come up with the right words in Russian, then clumsily shouted out that I had just been jumped by three men in the courtyard beyond. "Just now?" They asked, cigarettes poised in mid-air. I nodded breathlessly. To their eternal credit, the police officers and embassy guards leaped into action and charged into the dark courtyard.

Now what? I stood in the middle of the street with two police officers who remained with me as the others disappeared into the night. I had no idea what would happen next. Somehow, I still thought that I was going to be able to continue onwards to Spencer's housewarming. But the wheels of the Russian justice system were now in motion. From this point forward I was simply swept along by the process, like a twig tossed into a torrential river. I would not be able to extricate myself from the situation if I had wanted to. For better or worse, I had turned to the police and now the situation was in the state's hands.

The two remaining police officers leaped into a nearby car and lit a rancid cigarette.

They called for me to jump in the back seat. We were going to cruise the neighborhood and search for the thugs by car, while the others were running around on foot. The police car was a dilapidated old Lada, reeking of stale cigarettes, alcohol, and vomit, and who knows what else in that back seat. I quickly wound down the window for a gasp of air, despite the chill of the winter night.

With admirable intensity the two police officers stared out the cracked windshield into the darkness beyond. They hunched up and pressed their faces closer to the windows, cigarettes clenched tightly in their teeth. They drove slowly, then raced to the next corner, then prowled down an alley. Then we caught sight of a body scrambling over a wall and a chase was on. The little Lada spun out around a corner in pursuit and I fumbled for my seat belt (which, not surprisingly, turned out to be broken).

A real live police chase! The three thugs were now running across courtyards, scrambling over walls, appearing and disappearing from view. About eight police officers and Vietnam Embassy guards were running in all directions around the neighborhood. In the black winter evening it was impossible to tell who was who. I had no reason to believe the criminals would actually be caught – the apartment blocks were arranged in labyrinths of identical buildings, all shrouded in total darkness. One could easily vanish into the night without a trace.

In the movies police chases are always accompanied by appropriate high-powered music. A good sound track is essential to give the mood of the excitement of speeding around corners, glimpsing the criminals, then losing sight, and charging onwards again. A Hollywood movie would ensure that there would be plenty of revving of finely tuned engines and aggressive heavy pulsing rhythms pushing the action onwards towards a climactic moment. In the bizarre world of Moscow, however, I found myself nearly bursting out laughing as the scratchy radio in the Lada played "Yellow Submarine" by the Beatles. This absurdity was accompanied by the puttering of the feeble engine of the Lada, which backfired occasionally.

"We all live in a Yellow Submarine… a Yellow Submarine, a Yellow Submarine!" I found myself singing along to the chorus. This was simply ludicrous. The Beatles were in their drug experimentation phase when they wrote the lyrics. Would they have possibly have imagined that the song could be a background for a police chase scene through a Moscow night in a sputtering old yellow Lada? This scene may have even tested the creative powers of the Beatles.

I was in high spirits – intoxicated on a rush of love for life. I had successfully extricated myself from a horrific situation with three drunken thugs. A team of Russian police officers and embassy guards had leaped to my aid. And now I had entered some alternate reality world of the Beatles. The thugs would disappear into the night certainly, but I felt victorious and I loved the Russian police officers and Vietnam Embassy guards for their valiant display in the quest for justice. I threw my head back and laughed. What a night. That which doesn't kill you makes you stronger. And I felt ready to take on the world. Shots of adrenaline can produce unimaginable highs, once the immediate threat is removed. I was ready to leap out of the car and charge after the thugs myself.

The officers in the front seat glanced at me in the rear view mirror with concern. If I truly had just been attacked in the courtyard, why was I now laughing and singing along with the Beatles? I tried to calm down. I realized that I may not be playing the appropriate role of "victim" in their eyes. And I did not understand the Russian system well enough to know what would happen next. I just knew that I had a role to fulfill and I should do so efficiently in order to minimize any complications with the police.

Finally the driver concluded that we had lost the thugs somewhere in the neighborhoods and we just were not going to find them. I had expected that. Honestly, if the police officers had not been right outside the courtyard, I would never have reported the attack. The Russian legal system was too much of an unknown and the prospect of actually finding nameless attackers is so slim in any case. But I had brought the case to the police attention, therefore I needed to give a statement. They drove me to a nearby station. I looked at my watch and concluded that this would delay me another half hour or so, but I still would be able to get to Spencer's housewarming. The night was still young.

I was laughing and joking with the police officers as we entered the station. My Russian vocabulary to describe the evening's incident was just about non-existent. I explained to the police officers that I would need their assistance to write the statement. I could describe what had happened, but would have to act out words like "strangle" and "drag" and "grope". Nonetheless, I was willing to give it a go. I would write a police statement in Russian if I had to.

At the entrance to the police station, two police officers firmly and severely restrained a blond young man who was staring at me intently. The officers asked me quickly "was this one of the men who attacked you?"

I looked at his sharp angular cheekbones and icy blue eyes. He was not the one who was strangling me or the one who was grabbing me from the front. But honestly I never had a good look at the one who was pinning me from behind. I replied that he could be the one who attacked me from behind, but I just could not be sure.

This was still enough to put the police into motion. With a single swift and practiced motion, the officer slammed the man's face into the concrete wall. No police lineup. No rights being read. No statement of charges. Not even a firm accusation from the victim. A sharp cry from him was echoed by a gasping squeal from me.

"But she didn't..." started the blond man.

"Silence," barked a second officer. He gave the man a swift punch to the stomach. The accused buckled over and fell to his knees. I took a step back silently and wide-eyed. What were the laws here in the criminal justice process? But like every-thing else in Russia, I quickly realized that the laws were quite irrelevant to the matter at hand.

An officer turned to me and instructed me to sit down and start writing my state-ment. Without a word I complied. I sat down as directed to a small battered writing desk and was handed a leaking ball point pen and a few fragile sheets of slippery Russian writing paper. If the officers insisted on me writing a statement, then I would write a statement. No arguments. Total cooperation.

All the police officers from the precinct were now gathering at this station. The room filled with about ten shouting angry men. The blond accused was now seated in a chair a few yards from me. I saw him out of the corner of my eye as I attempted to start writing. He stared at me. This angered the officers further, who then dealt him a swift swipe at his jaw or kick at the ankles. My hand started shaking as I attempted to write.

Then total chaos erupted as two more detainees were dragged into the police sta-tion. Screaming and shouting from the accused was matched by louder yelling and threats from the officers. I looked up and saw the unmistakable faces of Thugs A and C, who I had last seen just a half hour before. Just a few steps away, Thug A glared at me with a piercing stare of pure hatred. He muttered something under his breath, which was lost to me, but prompted all the surrounding officers to throw him to the ground and start kicking him with unreserved animosity.

I scarcely breathed, wishing I could just cause the scene in front of me to melt away. I had never witnessed police brutality first-hand before and I hope never to again. Savage recklessness and street justice drove the officers into a mad frenzy of pummel-ing the three men senseless. The bodies thrashed around in a blur – the three thugs and about ten police officers. Fragile toy Russian furniture was tossed aside to clear room for everyone to get involved. Dull thuds of boots against bodies, heads against concrete. Groans and screams and yelling from all sides. I edged my way to the back corner of the room, to stay clear of the brawl.

I considered simply fleeing the scene. The Russian police system was too scary to get involved in. This was even more alarming than the attack in the courtyard. The actions of the police officers were above the law and no one would be criticized. I had not yet given my name to anyone. I could run and leave this whole situation for good and no one would ever find me. To get to an exit, however, I would have had to run through the mob. I was trapped. Besides, would the police actually let the criminals go if I disappeared and there was no crime reported? I was not sure. Their approach to legal process and morality were so far removed from anything I could comprehend based upon my sheltered American Midwest upbringing.

One of the officers paused and smiled at me. "We take good care of *devushki* here. Anyone who attacks our *devushki* must be punished." In his gnarled paw he held a wad of my business cards – pulled from the pockets of one of the Thugs. "Guilty! Guilty! Guilty!" I screamed in my head. All possible doubts that these were the guys who attacked me were gone. But then immediately years of American civil approach to justice jumped into action and pulled the brakes on my enthusiasm. Yes, the evidence was totally overwhelming. My business cards were found on these thugs. But were the police now writing their own rules? What exactly was going to happen to the accused? Although I was certain about their crime, the police really should not be judge and executioner. I was torn horribly by a deep primal craving to see them punished immediately and a moral need to see justice levied in a fair manner. Morality won in my mind, but not in the officers'. I felt physically ill and started to scream myself as the beatings continued.

And what were the rules governing how they could handle the victim? I have heard that in parts of Mexico victims are held by the police in custody until trial, in an attempt to prevent victims from dropping charges and failing to appear at trials. Was I going to be held indefinitely as well? I looked anxiously around at the thirteen or so angry violent men who were authorized by the state to do whatever necessary to uphold their version of justice. Or actually, perhaps the authority of the state was irrelevant here.

And suddenly a cold chill of panic paralyzed me.

Absolutely no one knew where I was at this moment, except for these police officers. They could do anything they wanted with me and I could vanish forever without a trace. I desperately wanted someone to be there with me. Someone who would be able to look out for my rights but understand the Russian system. I wanted a representative from the American Embassy to be with me.

I have a terrible memory for numbers, but for some reason I remembered the general switchboard number for the American Embassy. I asked one of the officers if I could place a phone call. He consented and I started dialing. The three thugs were now subdued and moaning and the officers had stopped tormenting their captives – for the moment. I surveyed the scene with alarm as the after-hours operator answered the Embassy phone.

"Hello, yes I was hoping you could connect me to someone who can assist American citizens in distress," I asked the switchboard operator hopefully.

"What is the nature of your emergency?" the operator asked in a very bored voice.

Well, this is Moscow in 1995. What exactly is classified as an "emergency" here by the US Embassy? Probably coup attempts and nuclear weapons violations. I attempted to explain to the woman that I was seriously alarmed to be by myself in a police station giving a statement after being assaulted on the street.

"Are you in any immediate danger?" The operator seemed to be reading from some standard checklist.

This was difficult to answer. "I don't think so, but it is difficult to say. This is not exactly a calm situation." To add impact to this thought, one of the officers threatened Thug A with his billy club, but then relaxed again. "I really would appreciate it if an Embassy representative could be here with me."

"You should call back during normal office hours, which are Monday to Friday 10am to 5pm," the operator said brusquely.

"Would you at least take down my name?" I asked quickly. What if I disappeared? I would like at least a formal record of where I was last seen.

But no, she refused to take down my name. She simply re-stated that I should call back during normal office hours and then hung up.

So much for the American Embassy being there to assist citizens in distress. I recounted this story to Alex when I saw him the following week. He asked me if I informed the operator that I was working on USAID projects in Russia. No, I hadn't included this detail in my discussion. Was it relevant? Apparently so. He explained that the Embassy would have leapt into action if someone on a government project was in distress.

I was astonished (and obviously hopelessly naive). So the US Embassy was prepared to assist US government staff and project members, but general distress calls from American citizens were not important? Alex explained to me (with a bit of exasperation in his voice) that the US Embassy is not a general social services center, but is there to support the official business of the US Government. So apparently there are two tiers of Americans abroad – those who work for the government and those who don't. And those who don't should not bother asking the Embassy for assistance when in need.

Yes, I was hopelessly naive. But I was learning slowly. And I was learning to be self-reliant. I was also learning to ask what it really meant to hold a US passport. Yes, I could live and work in the United States any time I wanted. But how welcome was I there? And what does it really mean to be American? What values are the government really promoting?

Without the support of the US Embassy, I would have to rely on my friends to give me strength with the Russian police. But it was now late on Saturday night. And I did not know any of my friends' phone numbers by memory. Even if I did, they certainly would not have been home to take my call. This was well before the days of omnipresent mobile phones. I had to face the police officers alone.

The police station had calmed down. The three thugs had been removed from the main room. I could still hear shouts and slaps occasionally, but the level of intensity had mercifully dropped. One of the officers sat with me and helped me write my statement. At first I attempted to write it myself in Russian, with him correcting my grammar as I went. But quickly it became obvious that the most efficient solution would be for me to explain to him what had happened and he just wrote my statement for me.

This arrangement provided opportunity on his part to provide a bit of editing. When

I tried to explain how Thug A was covering my face in sloppy kisses while Thug C was groping me and fumbling my pockets for cash, he scowled and said that he didn't want to include all that. His version read that Thug A was only strangling me and Thug C was searching my pockets for cash. Whatever. I was too alarmed by the police to start an argument with him. I agreed and signed the statement. The truth was not as important as expediency after a certain point.

I was under the illusion that I would be able to leave once I had signed the statement. But no, things in Russia are always a bit more complex than you initially expect. The police officers explained that this was a highly exceptional case, since an American woman was involved. I did not understand why that mattered, but it was very important to all the officers. Therefore we would all have to be transported over to the regional headquarters and continue discussions there with the Regional Police Chief, who would oversee the case personally.

I was then whisked away to another location, somewhere in central Moscow. The three Thugs were transported separately. At the regional headquarters, Thug A was thrown into a cell by himself and Thugs B and C were put into a cage in the main lobby. Actually to call the area a lobby would imply that it met some form of Western building standards. Like all Russian government buildings, the building construction had stopped shortly after the electrical wiring was underway, but not yet complete. Therefore the interior was unfinished cold concrete with bare light bulbs exposed at odd intervals. Exposed plumbing snaked around the ceiling and through unexpected points in the walls.

The police officers gave me a chair next to the cage by Thugs B and C and told me to wait. Then the left the room and I was alone with my assailants. Just a few feet away, but behind bars. They were battered and bruised and obviously exhausted, but stared at me intently through the bars. I stared back.

How long was I supposed to wait here? What would happen next? Although they were behind bars I did not feel at all reassured. As their eyes penetrated my skin, I felt every inch of my face being scrutinized and memorized. The police records would certainly show where I lived. Would they be seeking some sort of retribution against me? It would be just too easy.

"*Devushka*," Thug C pleaded to me. "Why are you doing this to us?"

"I am not doing anything to you. You are here because of your actions, not mine," I responded quickly.

"*Devushka*," his tone became more urgent. "Have them let us go!"

"It is not my decision," I snapped back. My mind was spinning. Hadn't they suffered enough? But they were not even apologizing to me. If they had shown a tidbit of remorse at this point, I would probably have sided with them over the police. But then again, I wanted to see this through. How many other times had they assaulted other women and not been caught? The police whispered to me that the previous week the body of a Russian woman had been found stuffed in the trunk of a car in the very neighborhood where I was attacked. Could these three have been responsible? The thugs who had played Russian roulette with Stephen had not been caught. Nor had Craig's attackers. Would this trio strike again? I had no way of knowing if I were a random incident or part of a pattern. I concluded that I could not have been the first – their attack on me was far too coordinated an effort. I decided that it would be my contribution to society to get them off the street.

The two men then started hissing a long string of profanities and threats at me, only bits of which I understood. They became more agitated as they realized that I had no intention of retracting my statement. I could not just sit here and let them stare at me and memorize every detail of what I looked like. The adrenaline was finally wearing off and the fear and horror of the night started to swell inside me. Shadows flickered in a bleak light as I sat in that cold concrete room. And then a wave of fear spread a cold chill over my skin. What would these creatures do if they were released and had my address from the police files and knew exactly what I looked like?

I had to move away from the leers and hisses of the two thugs. As the adrenaline rush subsided, the emotional rollercoaster of that night was taking me on a rocky road downwards. I was now shaking and felt nauseous as I invited myself into the office of the team of police officers. They were laughing and joking amongst themselves and totally oblivious to the situation they had left me to with the accused men. I took a seat in the corner and tried to hold myself together a bit longer. My nerves would not be able to take another spin – I was rapidly heading for a total emotional breakdown.

The minutes crept by. No obvious purpose for waiting. Waiting waiting waiting for something. Nothing to read – not even a scrap of newspaper. I needed the night to end so I could go home and collapse. All thoughts of going to the housewarming were gone. After another hour or so of agony the regional police chief arrived at the station. For some reason we had been waiting for him to sign off on the paperwork.

The police chief was quite excited about the case. He confirmed what I had already started to contemplate – Moscow was rife with attacks on expatriates, but to his knowledge none of the attackers had ever been caught and brought to trial. I interjected my objection that I didn't think that the men had attacked me because I was a foreigner. That, however, did not matter to the police chief. He was thrilled that his precinct had accomplished what the others had not – the attackers on the American woman had been caught and would be taken to trial.

The police chief's excitement did not end there. In addition, all three of my attackers were from Chechnya and in Moscow without a *propusk*. The Russians nearly universally viewed Chechens to be dangerous thugs and second class citizens. This view was only reinforced for them by the events of the evening. Under the old Soviet system everyone was registered to live in a particular city and needed to obtain a *propusk* (essentially a "pass") to move to a new city. Without the *propusk* one would not be able to obtain housing or employment, therefore it was an effective tool of government control. I had thought that the *propusk* laws had been discontinued, but for the police chief this was further evidence of the criminal nature of the three thugs. And his precinct would get the credit for removing these undesirables from the streets of Moscow. It was a great night for the police chief.

The police chief asked me to officially identify each of the attackers for him. I thought that finally there would be an American-style police lineup. But no. He simply escorted me back into the room where Thugs B and C were in the cage and asked me if they were involved in my attack. The two men glared at me and muttered hostilities under their breath. This was met with a sharp retort from the police chief who then beat his billy club against the bars of the cage as a warning.

The police chief then opened the door to the cell where Thug A was being held. The room was a tiny cold concrete cell with no windows or conveniences of any sort. Thug A was passed out (either from alcohol or the beating he received or both) and curled up on the concrete floor in one corner. The police chief gave him a few sharp kicks in his back and told him to show his face to us. With a groan, he rolled over and looked at me — mercifully he was too far delirious to recognize me or further exacerbate the situation. I quickly identified him and retreated from the dark gloomy cell.

That's it for tonight. The police chief was in such a festive mood. He clearly was relishing the discussion with his superiors the next day, informing them of the brilliant work of his precinct. He told me, however, that I would have to return to the precinct headquarters and finish off the paperwork for the police report the next day. It was too late tonight and the process would still take a few hours more.

So I was free to go. It was after midnight now. The streets were deserted. The Metro was closed. Taxis don't exist anyway in Russia. I faced the prospect of hitchhiking home or walking. As I stood on the doorstep of the police station looking out into the dark winter night, neither prospect sounded great. My nerves were completely shattered. I was having a difficult time stringing sentences together coherently. The idea of going back out into the back streets of Moscow alone was alarming.

I must have stood on the front step of the police station for a few minutes looking out into the night. The police chief finally saw me there. He kindly offered to walk me home. I breathed an enormous sigh of relief. Yes, of course I wanted someone to escort me home. I just was too ferociously proud to ask for assistance.

It was a wonderful gesture, but also this added even more tangles to my emotional state that night. In true Russian style, he took my arm in his and escorted me arm in arm along the frozen silent streets of my neighborhood. Walking arm in arm is reserved in America for lovers, but I grew attached to the Russian style of taking the arm of any acquaintance when walking. This simple human contact quickly lightens the mood and adds a level of intimacy and friendliness to any situation.

With the police chief I found the intimacy a relief and a shield from the unknown dark corners of the neighborhood. The police chief was flirtatious and kind and carefully pointed out perilous bits of ice and open manholes hidden in the night. Was this the same man who earlier had been kicking an unconscious man like a sack of potatoes? How could both personalities co-exist within the same person? I cooperated and socialized, but found this end to the night to be somehow even more disturbing than if I had walked home alone.

I had seen the dark brutal side of the Russian police. Being exposed immediately then to the kind social side of the same people raised too many questions about human nature and society as a whole. I looked over at his smiling, friendly face and could only think of all my other friends who would have offered to walk me home in the same situation. What would it take to push these same people over the edge where they wouldn't hesitate to kick an unconscious man in the back? Even I had been quietly cheering on the police as they had landed the first few blows on the accused.

What was it that really differentiated the two of us? Why did I recoil at the sight of police brutality, but this man participated without a second thought? How much longer before I would be willing to join into the fray, meting out justice according to my own whims? How close was I to losing my own moral foundation? In this grey dark and cold world, the clear edges of images blurred into the night. Right and wrong no longer are clear concepts.

I felt a rush of affection for American democracy and the principles of due process in the justice system. But then immediately this emotion was retracted as I contemplated the rejection from the US Embassy. The Americans may profess to support the ideal of due process, but what good is that principle if no one is present to see it through? The American Embassy would provide feel good moments of Butterball turkeys and fireworks, but the moment I really needed assistance I had been left on my own at the police station. In the end, this Russian police chief was the one who was looking after me. Which system should I endorse? The one that held to ideals and procedures, but rejected my personal pleas for assistance? Or the people who did things the way they wanted to, and in the end offered support before being asked?

Back in the refuge of my flat I marched on a mission straight from the door to the kitchen, not even pausing to remove my coat or shoes. A bottle of vodka was waiting for me in the freezer. Startled cockroaches scampered to tiny crevices in the kitchen cupboard. I felt my breathing slow down and my stress fall away as I poured the thick clear liquid into a glass and then laughed at myself as I topped off the drink with tonic water. I was now Russian enough to have a bottle of vodka in the freezer at all times, but not localized enough to drink straight shots of vodka voluntarily – yet.

I stood on my balcony — the far left corner where I could catch a glimpse of the illuminated pure white bell tower of the Kremlin. A single beacon of light in the quiet winter night — nearly obscured by the dilapidated tenement block in front of me. Most of the windows of the apartment block were dark. Forms moved around in others. Hundreds of people shared this little part of Moscow with me but we were scarcely aware of each other's existence. What other dramas had occurred on this winter night in others' lives? If I had disappeared, would any of them even notice?

I finished my drink and the chill of the bitter night overpowered the warm glow of the vodka in my veins. I retreated into the sanctuary of my flat and closed the curtains — sealing myself into a safe warm cocoon.

Nothing could touch me in my safe haven. And another drink would help me deny that any outside world existed at all.

11 WALKING WOUNDED

February 1995 – Moscow

"It's always interesting to see how people react after an attack here," Sarah said more to herself than to me the following weekend. "Back in the US I would worry that a friend who has been attacked would retreat from the world in fear. Someone who has been a victim can easily board themself into their apartment and hide away from the unknown. But here.... Here I worry about the opposite for you."

I really did not understand where Sarah was going with her comments and asked her to explain. Conversation, however, was difficult for more than a sentence or two at a time. We were ice skating at the make-shift outdoor rink at Gorky Park. In the summer, the area was an inner city lot filled with trees in shock, trampled dirt, and random bits of metal protruding out of the ground. In the winter the park was flooded (deliberately) and frozen (by Mother Nature). The rough ground, ad hoc hose treatment to create the ice, and lack of ice-grooming equipment resulted in a skating surface that could kindly be called "natural". Tangled metal wires, rocks, and other hazards protruded through the surface at irregular intervals.

Neither Sarah nor I were especially graceful on ice skates. To add to the complications of the day, we had hired skates from the chaotic on-site rental location. Similar to the experience of hiring skis in Kazakhstan the prior winter, I now was just pleased that I had manage to battle my way through the rental experience and now had something resembling ice skates. They didn't fit properly, the blades had not been sharpened in years (if ever), and the laces were broken. But for the equivalent of two dollars or so, Sarah and I were delighted to have a day of Russian entertainment. Whether or not we actually managed any real skating out of the ordeal was secondary.

Sarah emitted a short yelp as she tripped over a protruding rock and then regained her balance. She then continued to explain her theory while keeping her eyes firmly focused a few feet in front of her.

"What I mean is that people who choose this life here in Russia — we are different. In the USA people who are victims often cower and hide…"

"But I'm not a victim," I protested to Sarah. "I fought off my attackers. I helped to put them behind bars. I came out on top."

"That is exactly my point," Sarah continued. "Here in Russia those who survive are defiant. We refuse to be defeated. We continue to fight with an attitude of 'is that the best you can do?' and then we have to prove to ourselves that we are capable of more."

"I'm not sure what you are saying," I still wasn't following Sarah's point. "Are you suggesting that I am not acting properly like a scared victim of a violent assault? You know that I'm not like that."

"I'm worried that you are coming out of this too strong and too confident. Virtually every expat here is a victim of violence at some point. I've been here long enough to have seen everything. Too many people come out of their episode with a sense of invincibility — 'I survived this, now what is my next challenge?' Be careful of that, Phaedra. Over-confidence is what leads to putting yourself in the line of fire for a second — even more violent — incident. Or doing something else that really pushes the bounds of safety far beyond that which is reasonable."

"Like skating in Gorky Park?" I laughed, pointing out a tangle of metal wiring protruding through the ice in front of us. Someone would undoubtedly impale themself on a rock or metal protrusion skating that day — the entire suspense was who and how severe the injury would be. "We are living in a world of survival of the fittest. No one expects an army of ambulance chasing lawyers to be protecting us from our every move here."

"That is exactly my point," Sarah tried to explain further. "The only person looking out for you is you! There are no laws here. Everything is uncertain. You can't rely on anything that would be a given back in the United States. Keep your eyes open. Just because you survived one attack doesn't mean you will be as fortunate next time. Don't go and hide under a rock — but don't be arrogantly over-confident either. This is a dangerous place."

"Yes," I replied. "It is dangerous. We are the survivors. And that is why we are having so much fun here."

I was being flippant. But Sarah was right. I had seen it myself. There were two standard responses to being involved in a violent incident. Flight or defiance. In Kamchatka, the American airport construction manager had fled the country, never to return again after an appendectomy without anesthesia. Craig had thrived after the violent assault with the screwdriver — but pushed things further than most of his friends thought wise, including skiing in avalanche zones of Shimbulak. Plus of course skinny dipping at the Navy resort on the Black Sea. More recently, the day after Stephen's unwilling participation in Russian Roulette, he had left Moscow with no intention of returning. Hazards were a part of daily life. To thrive we had to embrace and accept the chaos. But at a certain point we could be called naive in the face of risk – stepping over the line from confidence to arrogance to stupidity.

Was balance possible? Or were the two paths mutually exclusive – retreat from expatriate life or seek the next level of the adrenaline rush?

I contemplated this further with my friend Adrian later that evening. Adrian was a new addition to the expat community. He was the sort of expat that I instinctually disliked – arriving in Moscow with no background in Russian language. His work experience to date was firmly planted in the ideals of academia and now he was working in an English speaking office writing analyses based upon government data and media reports rather than personal experience. Despite all this, Adrian professed to be eager to learn more about Russia beyond abstract economic analyses and I decided to do my part to try and expose him to a Moscow beyond just the nightclubs and the Bolshoi Theater. So far Adrian had been a willing participant in all the adventures I had proposed. I found myself reluctantly enjoying his company, even if he still retained a naïve academic glow that idealized every positive official report as *the* signal that Russia was now affirming itself as the next major emerging economic power on the global stage.

This evening we were at the Moscow Circus – which I now was seeing with a fresh eye as simply a dramatic rendition of daily life, hoisted up on stage for all to view.

The Moscow Circus is where the Russian Olympic gymnasts all come to retire – or pursue a second rebirth of a career (depending on your perspective). The athletes are superb, each taking their talents to breathtaking levels just simply not possible within the structured confines of gymnastics competition. In world level competitions there are rules, and elements, and standards that must be adhered to. In the Olympics top marks are awarded to those who achieve perfection per the established standards. Here, in the stark contrast of the Moscow Circus, the expectation is to break all the rules – attempt stunts never before conceived. Maybe the athlete will succeed, maybe he will fail. It's not points he is after – but glory.

The performance stage of the Moscow Circus is laid out as a classic ring with seats 360 degrees surrounding the action. The athletes are in the center of the crowd and absorb the energy of the gasping, delighted, and sometimes terrified audience from all sides. With the action in a ring in the center, an element of unpredictability is introduced. It is no longer just us watching them. But rather *they* are a part of *us*. The performance is in our midst. It is among us. We are a part of the action.

On this particular night, the stage was flooded and frozen. The evening's show would be an ice spectacular. I laughed at the parallel with my afternoon adventure with Sarah. She and I had worn battered skates, stumbling over rocks and other obstacles, forever struggling to look poised and graceful (without much success). Here at the Moscow Circus the daredevils on ice had a perfect glossy manicured surface and proper ice skates.

"Now where is the adventure in that?" I laughed to myself. "For some serious daredevil activity, let's see the Moscow circus attempt to perform their show on the ice at Gorky Park wearing the rental skates!"

Of course I had to bite my tongue. The athletes stormed onto the ice with an energy reserved only for the elite few who have chosen the passion of athletics and performance as their life. The skaters soared over obstacles then were caught gracefully in another's arms — with silver blades slashing the air just inches from the faces of their partners. Now a man speeds around the rink and takes hold of a trapeze, lifting into orbit. A woman grasps his ankles and she too is catapulted into space — marking a dramatic arc with her deadly blades menacing the crowds below. Then she deftly intertwines with her partner and reaches down and they clasp a third skater. A second trapeze with additional skaters begins to orbit the stage as well. Soon the skaters are being tossed above the ice in graceful tumbles between the swinging trapezes. Blades, ice, soaring heights, daring tumbling.

"Doesn't look that difficult," Adrian commented quietly, suppressing a yawn. "They don't even have a safety net."

I resisted a sudden urge to hit him upside the head.

"There is no safety net, but do you understand how much practice and planning goes into this?" I hissed back at him. "The contradiction is that they have to work so hard just to make this look effortless." I took Adrian's comment personally. He was dismissing the skills of the acrobats of the Moscow Circus, but somehow I felt slighted and misunderstood as well.

The daring stunts of soaring acrobats wearing ice skates was choreographed carefully and then practiced endlessly to the point where it looked effortless. But when the stunt looks effortless, do we appreciate it more or less? Do we really understand how difficult these tricks are? What if we instead were watching a trapeze act that was hastily compiled and thrust out for performance? The athletes looking terrified, mishaps a virtual certainty. Wouldn't that be much more in line with the illusion of "daredevil" that the circus was attempting to portray?

But no, there is a fine line between "daredevil" and "suicidal maniac".

A daredevil is an adventurer with a clear plan. I will scale this mountain, and this is my plan. This is how I will train for the adventure. This is my equipment. This is my back up team. And here is my Plan B if everything goes awry. There is always a Plan B.

A suicidal maniac has an idea and then just plunges into it. He might succeed. He might not. The outside observer is quick to criticize the suicidal maniac. He didn't know what he was getting himself into. He wasn't wearing the right safety gear. He didn't have the right training. Where was his backup plan?

What an amazing contradiction. The skilled adventurer is the one who actually has limited his risk. He knows the terrain. He has planned for contingency. There is a backup plan – therefore he will be fine if everything goes wrong. When he executes the plan everything looks effortless – due entirely to the amount of effort that he put into the planning.

Would the adventurer feel the same glorious rush of adrenaline as the suicidal maniac – the one who hasn't mitigated his risk? The adventurer understands the risks he is taking. He has spent a lot of time thinking about the risks and planning for this moment. Perhaps the suicidal maniac hasn't thought about the situation at all. If you are blissfully unaware of risk, then would there even be an adrenaline rush at all?

And of course, adrenaline was the ultimate goal.

Awareness of risk is what puts your senses on high alert. Knowing that you have the ability to overcome the risk fills you with strength. And then the prize for overcoming the obstacles - An adrenaline rush – this one more intense than the one before. A surge of pure life. Pure pounding energy. Yes, we are alive, we are young and we are able to achieve anything we set our minds on.

I had emerged from the attack on the street victorious and filled with positive energy that anything was possible. An unexpected bonus from this was the positive lift this gave all the Russian women in my office. Just as every appearance of Raymond's wife, Rita, helped to shatter the image of all older women as toothless hunched shape-less beings, the Russian *devushki* were incredulous that a woman could be assaulted on the street and come away from it feeling stronger and more independent.

March 8 is International Women's Day – a significant holiday in Russia, even cause for a national public holiday. The cynics say that International Women's Day is the one day a year in Russia when it is unacceptable for Russian men to beat their wives. It is a date that traditionally women can get away with a lot more than they do the rest of the year. Push the boundaries just a bit today and we will see what happens tomorrow. With the girls in my office, the date was discussed with subversive giggles – Our Own Holiday. We need to do something to celebrate.

In 1995 the date for International Women's Day fell near *Maslenitsa* – the Russian Orthodox festivities marking the beginning of Lent. One of the interpreters in the office, Marina, lived a few blocks from the office. All of this led to an obvious plot for all the Russian girls to go to Marina's house for an extended lunch in early March – a dual celebration of *Maslenitsa* and International Women's Day. I was the only American invited in the covert escape by the girls from the office.

With various stated reasons for errands each of us had to run over lunch, we disap-peared from the office and then with delight rendezvoused at Marina's apartment. I too had given false pretenses why I had to be out of the office for a few hours. Robert had made it clear to me that he did not approve of how friendly I was becoming with the Russian staff. In his eyes I wasn't maintaining a proper separation between work and social relationships. Not that Robert actually had any management authority over me – but he could be seriously unpleasant when he wanted to. The Russian *devushki* laughed at Robert and his rules and viewed this as even more of a reason to extend the duration of the festivities and bring an extra bottle or two of champagne.

Once we reconvened at Marina's place, a proper *Maslenitsa* luncheon was quickly assembled – blinni batter mixed, fillings of fruit compote, sour cream, and caviar ladled into serving bowls, and the requisite rounds of vodka and champagne poured. They all shrieked with delight as the batter for the first blin was poured into the pan. Then per tradition it was cooked and then immediately discarded. *"Otbrosi pervyu blinichku!"* They squealed with delight. Not just a tradition, but an important philosophy of life. Throw out the first blin! The first attempt is bound to fail – but keep trying!

Tatiana, usually quiet and collect and the foundation of my team was beaming with delight as she held her champagne glass. "Phaedra, I am so happy right now, I cannot even speak!" She said with genuine joy. "Before this project I was a single mother struggling to support my daughter and my mother. Now I can use a computer and work in a prestigious American office. There is so much opportunity now."

The other women gushed similar sentiments – leaving me at a complete loss. They were amazed that at the age of 27 I had moved voluntarily to another country, I was living by myself in a *grand* apartment. (Outrageous actually by Russian standards to have two bedrooms and one bath all to myself.) They were impressed that I did not hesitate to argue with the men in the office, even Raymond the senior partner when warranted. I was in the position of authority to hire people and manage teams of data collectors across ten cities in Russia. They would never have dreamed that a young woman could have such a role until I came along!

And most of all they were inspired how I showed no fear with travelling to new cities. Southern Russia (with all the Chechens!), Ekaterinburg, Tyumen, Krasnoyarsk, Chelyabinsk, Nizhni Novgorod – the list went on. So exciting to be flying around the country. Seeing new places, meeting important directors of state enterprises and American consultants and government officials. So daring and glamorous to be taking the train by myself overnight (in a first class cabin!) to St Petersburg and to Nizhni Novgorod.

I was about to protest that surely any of them could travel and see as much of Russia just as much as I did. But then I realized that no, it really was not possible.

The Soviet Union had held a policy of strict internal passports until very recently. Under the law you could travel to a city only after obtaining a *propusk* – permission to travel to the city. That rule had nominally been removed but barriers still remained to prohibit any meaningful travel by Russians just for the sake of travel. Central control of travel remained in fact, if not in law. Hotels were virtually non-existent in most cities. Where they did exist, a reservation could be obtained only by virtue of an official city request. This was not a country with visitors' bureaus, rental car agencies, tourist maps – or even restaurants. Once you arrived in a city you had to fend for yourself – or be at the mercy of your government host. On many occasions I had found myself unceremoniously deposited back at my hotel and scavenging a dinner of boiled eggs and mystery pickled vegetables, washed down with a warm beer before retreating to my room. The evening would then feature battling hard telephone wiring with a knife and duct tape to establish an internet dial up connection, a fifty percent probability that there would be no hot water, and generally a television stuck on a piercing squeal and/ or random men beating on my door. This was not the travel of elegant matched luggage and cocktail dresses that is featured in the pages of *Cosmopolitan*.

And did they really understand what I did with my role? In the end I had no power whatsoever. I hired who the local government officials told me to hire. My agenda when visiting the regional cities was dictated by what they were willing to do. My ability to accomplish anything on the project was entirely a reflection of whether the local government officials and LPC directors felt inclined to support the project. The statements in the USAID work order could be grand, but we were entirely dependent upon the whims of the local officials to make it a reality.

I opened my mouth to protest the women's glorification of my job and role and everything that I did on the project. But then I looked at them and stopped.

What I was doing was opening a whole new world of opportunity for them. They had previously viewed their destiny as being a typist bound to the corner of some non-descript Soviet office, subject to the whims and desires of the enterprise director. Their fate was to live in a small apartment with multiple generations of family until some man took them in – who hopefully wouldn't mistreat them too badly. In their eyes I was living independently, taking control of my life, taking control over my career. My nature would be to be the realist and resist the idealization they were making of my life – but it was giving them hope that they too could change their lives. Therefore I would let them believe what they needed to believe.

"Anything is possible if you set your mind to it," I said with more conviction than I felt. These women had been dealt a rough hand. Their circumstances were difficult to imagine for most sheltered professional American women like myself. That being said, they were on the leading edge of a new optimistic generation that was grasping at any sign that the future could be – had to be – better than the past.

Nadya spoke boldly of going to an American business school. She did not want to be a bookkeeper reviewing receipts for the rest of her life. There were new opportunities now and she wanted to take advantage of them. I promised to write her a glowing letter of recommendation. The girls squealed with delight. Another round of vodka was poured and we all toasted Nadya's future as a businesswoman — armed with an American MBA.

Like with any round of toasts, eventually we had to toast our hostess Marina and her beautiful apartment. The flat was absolutely stunning — lavish in its rich pre-Soviet detailing and soaring ceilings. The building was one of the very few pre-Soviet grand apartment blocks left in Moscow. Of course she shared the space with a number of relatives. She thanked us for our compliments and then sighed that in the early 20th century the whole building was a single mansion owned by her family in its entirety. After the Communist Revolution, the government seized control over all private property and chopped up the mansion into apartment blocks. Marina's family was crushed into a few rooms and others with political connections were granted the remaining apartments in the building. In the recent wave of privatization Marina had hoped that the building would be restored to her family in its entirety. But no. Residential privatization had essentially been a game of "musical chairs" — whatever apartment you were occupying at the time of privatization was the apartment you were granted title to. Marina had to believe that her future was better than the past — but there was a long way to go.

"At least you still have a few rooms left to live in," Oksana was barely holding back tears in a sudden outburst of emotion. "My family is about to lose everything."

"But Oksana, you just finished renovating your flat — what happened?" Tatiana asked what was on everyone's mind, while Nadya instinctually filled Oksana's glass of champagne to help calm her nerves.

After a shudder and a few tears, Oksana blurted out the story. Her family had just been served notice that their apartment block was condemned and would be demolished. All the residents in the block had to find new accommodation and move out within two months. No compensation for their losses, simply a notice to move out.

"But we were just all at your apartment block for your post-remont party," I was baffled. Yes, the apartment block was a classic crumbling Soviet era tower of poor construction. But so was every other apartment block in the city. Why was this block identified to be condemned? "I wasn't even aware that there were safety reviews of apartment blocks," I mused.

Nadya was quick to correct me. "Don't you understand? This has nothing to do with public safety. It never does. There is someone in the building who has clearly crossed someone in power. This is a form of vengeance."

"But can't the demolition decision be protested?" I said reflexively, but then realized the silliness of the idea even as the words came out of my mouth.

"To whom?" Nadya said simply. "What process do you think exists here? Yes, of course there are formal rules allowing a protest. But nothing will actually happen unless someone in the government endorses the protest. Just as nothing ever happens regarding a demolition – unless it is requested by someone in power."

The apartment blocks had been nominally privatized in Russia. But in the end what did "privatization" really mean if on a whim someone in power could raze the whole building? The life savings of all the residents would be demolished in a single blow. Hyperinflation had already destroyed all monetary savings. The only real assets anyone had at this point were their apartments. Oksana's family was about to lose that last remaining asset without even an apology from the local government.

Yet another reminder that the processes and rights that we take for granted in the United States just simply did not exist. The Russian girls sensed that there was a better way, but had no experience with what that would be. Russian history was just one long chain of people seizing power and using their power to hand out favors and punish those who resisted. The names on the business card had changed from "Communist Party of the Soviet Union' to "Mayor of Moscow", but besides that, what else had changed?

Oksana downed the rest of her champagne and summoned her strength. "It will be okay," she said with a level voice. "I know something will work out. I am still young and healthy. I have a good job. Something will work out for me. I have to believe in Fate."

That statement of strength was echoed reflexively by a toast from all the *devushki*. "To Oksana's future!" We lifted our shots of vodka and smiled with sincere admiration at Oksana. Her family was about to lose everything, with no recourse. This was a world where your Igor with a sledgehammer had to be bigger and more convincing than the other person's Igor with a sledgehammer. In this case the other side was backed by the Mayor of Moscow – therefore Oksana's family had to concede. Yet she had the strength to carry on – and even face the world with a glimmer of optimism. She was the real survivor here and the true inspiration.

I was just doing my job.

Before my next business trip I gave Oksana a key to my flat and invited her to house sit for me while I was away. She had not yet sorted out a long term solution to her housing situation and was grateful to escape from the crush of the extended family for a few nights each week.

"What will Robert say?" giggled Oksana as if we were sharing a mischievous secret.

"I really don't care what he will say," I replied. "You need a place to stay and I have an apartment that is vacant nearly four days each week. It is the right thing to do."

Oksana just smiled and said, "*Spasibo*" – Thank you.

Oksana's first house sitting assignment came the following week while I returned to Ekaterinburg.

In addition to my own luggage and laptop, as a personal favor to Spencer I was transporting a full size fax machine from Moscow to his project office in Ekaterinburg.

Of course I would take everything onto the place as carry-on baggage. No this would not be possible in the United States. But in Russia I was now eagerly taking on new challenges. This one would be relatively simple – just a few extra handfuls of rubles to someone to help carry everything on board for me. Plus potentially I may have to offer a "service fee" to someone at Aeroflot if they started to challenge all the excess luggage

Domodedovo in 1995 shared little resemblance to a modern western airport. Yes, planes arrived and departed and passengers with tickets and boarding passes somehow found their flights, but that was where the resemblance ended. The building design had no relationship to the process flow standard in western airports – check in, receive boarding pass, deposit luggage, clear through security, find departure gate and waiting area, then board plane. The main hall was virtually devoid of signage. Small teller windows lined the walls, with most of the windows solidly closed. Not the open counter that one expects in the west.

The design of the space was an accurate reflection of the airport staff's approach to "customer service." I would battle my way to a check in window. Sometimes the clerks would take my ticket and stamp it. Other times I was told that I needed to go to the "VIP section" reserved for foreign passport holders and others who had paid an extra fee for VIP service. With much exasperation, the woman at the standard ticket window would reluctantly explain to me how to find the VIP service area. (I did ask every time – as the location changed erratically.)

The "VIP section" bore no resemblance to something Americans might expect based on the name. This was not the Red Carpet Lounge or any other elite membership area with comfortable chairs and cocktails. The design of the area (in my opinion) was simply a holding pen where the authorities could keep a closer eye on the foreigners. Sometimes my bags were x-rayed when I entered the holding pen – sometimes they weren't. Entirely depending on the mood of the guy monitoring the entrance. The Russians who were in the VIP area with me were the sort who were used to getting what they wanted – for a price, if necessary. Many bags were waved around the x-ray machine after a few sharp words spoken too quietly for the rest of the room to hear what was being said.

Once inside the main area of the "VIP section," all the Russian men would immediately light cigarettes. The room was filled with the dense haze seen in the smoker aquariums in western airports. No air conditioning, of course, so the smoke just lingered, the air mixing slowly as the men walked around the room. I attempted to sit still with the poise expected of a Russian *devushka*, so as not to draw too much attention to myself and was thankful that these were the sort of men who would only smoke high end western cigarettes. Not a single putrid Russian cigarette among them.

And then, of course, I had to laugh, reflecting on Sarah's and my discussion regarding taking unnecessary risks. The air quality in this room must have been equivalent of smoking four packs of cigarettes at once. Who knew what was in the bags that had skirted security. These were the sort of men who were often at the center of the shoot outs at the clubs that were becoming ever more prevalent.

Upon command from some Aeroflot representative, we would all march together from the VIP room across the tarmac (dodging planes and fuel trucks) to our waiting plane. Although our boarding passes nominally had seat numbers written on them, in reality the boarding process was all about aggressively staking out territory on the plane – the stamped seat assignments were irrelevant. All the passengers would be bringing their luggage on board with them – piled in the aisles, the restrooms, any empty seats. Passengers roamed the plane at will – including during takeoff and landing.

Aeroflot had stopped publishing its safety statistics. The westerners who travelled regularly on Aeroflot had started to refer to ourselves as members of Aeroflot's "frequent survivor" program. Our information for what was happening with Aeroflot came from each other rather than the official media. Spencer had been on a flight recently where clearly the navigation equipment had failed. With a dense cloud cover the pilot kept ducking down below the clouds, (apparently looking for the airport) and then climbing up to a higher altitude. Sarah had been on a flight from Tyumen to Moscow when a Russian *biznisman* had bribed the flight crew to divert the plane to St Petersburg. Once in St Petersburg the flight crew had solicited money from the remaining passengers to raise enough cash to purchase fuel to return to Moscow. We had seen flight attendants carry bottles of vodka with shot glasses into the cockpit. We had colleagues who had bribed their way onto a full flight, desperate to get out of Siberia – and given a space on the jump seat in the cockpit between the pilot and co-pilot. Paul and Alex had witnessed their own variation on chaos while attempting to leave the country for a quick holiday. The standard procedure had been followed to walk everyone out onto the tarmac, but in this case boarding was delayed while the wreckage from an earlier crash was being cleared from the runway. The Americans took the opportunity to pull a Frisbee from their luggage and engaged some of the other passengers in a surreal game of catch on the tarmac with the smoldering ruins of a plane in the background. (None of this was covered in any of the media – we all knew each other's stories had to be true because we had seen so much ourselves first hand.)

And the prior year, back in Kamchatka, I had been on a flight where a passenger had actually flown the plane.

With all of that, did it really matter that I now had a fax machine with me? I took it for granted that I would be able to get the fax machine and all my luggage onto the plane as carry-on items – probably placing the fax machine in the aisle or wedged under my feet. Yes, when I eventually would break down and ask one of these Russian men in a bottle green jacket and gold chains for assistance my accent would immediately identify me as an American. Yes, there was a possibility that this would make me a target as a wealthy American, especially if I missed my connection and needed to hitchhike from the airport in Ekaterinburg. Thoughts of Stephen's horror of Russian roulette and Craig's screwdriver assault, as well as my own near miss at Vnukovo were never far from my mind. But then again, what real marginal risk was I really exposing myself to, in comparison to that which I was already undertaking? If I attempted to avoid all risk then I would be refusing to travel at all in Russia.

The planners in Washington DC clearly did not understand our daily lives. They had certain expectations of what we would achieve and how. Although we all received nice generic notes from time to time regarding "safety in the workplace" – the memos clearly had a different understanding of risk than that which we actually lived. We were on the circulation list of emails that reminded us to use proper task lighting at our desks and to position our chairs and keyboards in an ergonomically correct manner. Always walk up and down stairs holding the handrail. Your safety is our priority! We care about our employees!

But was I being unduly harsh on the planners back in Washington DC? Lack of awareness of the risks and challenges we were facing was not limited to those back on the other side of the Atlantic. Even those who should know better were blissfully ignorant at times. In Nizhni Novgorod, a local American consultant, David, had thoughtfully escorted me from dinner to the train station for my overnight train back to Moscow. When travelling, but especially for the trains, I dressed as Russian as possible – with my red hot lipstick, leather *dublunka* coat, and goat hair shawl. I tried to board discretely and take my first class cabin without anyone noting the location of an American woman travelling solo. As I boarded the train in Nizhni Novgorod, however, David cheerfully waved to me from the platform and shouted in English. "Great seeing you, Phaedra! Enjoy the trip back to Moscow!" His beaming face and eyes were sincere. He really was wishing me well – but his calls to me now guaranteed that my trip would be anything but restful.

On the overnight trains, a *dezhurnaya* is placed on every first class car. Similar to the *dezhurnayas* in the hotels, their role was more to monitor the activity on the train rather than to provide any real services. I would give the *dezhurnaya* a $10 USD note and ask her to please keep people from disturbing me overnight. Sometimes the request worked and sometimes it didn't. With this particular trip from Nizhni Novgorod to Moscow, too many people had witnessed the American board the train. All night long men were pounding on my door, some asking to *poznakomitsa*, but others, more ominously, were working on the latch outside just simply trying to break in.

Inside my cabin I had mastered the art of turning the little two bed cabin into a fortress that I believed to be impenetrable. Yes, the door could nominally latch from the inside, but I learned on one of my first overnight train trips that this could be easily picked and slid from the outside. Plus the *dezhurnaya* held a master key. And if I could bribe her, so could others. On the inside of the door, the latch slid through a metal pocket about the size of a large highlighter pen lid. If I jammed the lid from a highlighter pen into the pocket and secured it with duct tape, the door could not be opened from the outside. If this were somehow not enough, I also brought a metal coat hanger, which could be twisted neatly around the inside door handle and secured against a hook against the wall. One of the many benefits of the Soviet era trains was the standardization. There were variations on this theme, but in general a highlighter pen, some duct tape, and a coat hanger helped me to establish an extra line of defense from the inevitable men attempting to break into my cabin at night.

I don't want to give the impression that I cowered in my cabin with fear. Far from it. I was just simply being practical. Once I had established the necessary lines of defense, I proceeded to enjoy the pleasures of the overnight train trip. The wonderful clickety-clack of the rails. The soothing rocking of the train. I would pile all the blankets onto my one bed in a cozy nest. And of course I would have my fluffy snowflake pajamas and a bottle of champagne to help me sleep soundly through the night. Overnight trains were fabulous if you were prepared and in the right mental state.

Was David totally unaware of the fact that men always attempt to break into women's cabins on the overnight trains? It just didn't seem possible. He had been living in Nizhni Novgorod for nearly a year. The main way in and out of the city was by overnight train. He must just simply have chosen to ignore the risks that surrounded him. I had to explain away his actions. Ignoring the risk had to be a deliberate choice on his part. If you think too much about the dangers that surround us, you can easily become paralyzed.

I would not avoid risk, but would attempt to manage risk and overcome the challenges. Taking a fax machine to Ekaterinburg was a challenge, not an excessive risk. Personal favors are important. We have to help each other out. Only with each other's support we will survive. The adventurous daredevil rather than the suicidal maniac.

The arrival of the fax machine proceeded without incident. The event was cause for celebration with Nathan the evening following my arrival in Ekaterinburg. We were sitting in the restaurant at the Hotel Rus, the only hotel in town and the place where Nathan had taken up permanent residence. Nathan was soaring on an emotional high. He was thrilled that another fax machine had arrived in town. Spencer's project team in Ekaterinburg was grateful for the fax machine and offered the services to Nathan until our own equipment arrived. Nathan was elated. He would no longer be dependent upon the favors of the local Minister of Industrial Development to send and receive faxes.

Even more exciting for Nathan – the shipment of computer equipment destined for Ekaterinburg was now in Moscow awaiting customs clearance. I, however, could not share his enthusiasm. After months in procurement purgatory I had reached a point of total numbness and now held the opinion of "I'll believe it when I see it."

Nathan could not contain his excitement. The arrival of the computer equipment was imminent. In the end we had even concluded a service contract with Viktor Mikhailovich's company to assist with the set up and service of all the equipment. The office would be totally operational soon.

The real work of the Local Privatization Center in Ekaterinburg could really begin now! Nathan and Sergei Glebovich were starting to make real progress with the goal of introducing American foreign investors to Russian enterprises. It had been so slow working through the US Consulate and the Minister for Industrial Development, but despite this their plans for an "investors' tour" of the Ekaterinburg area was coming together. Real potential American investors would be meeting with real privatized Russian companies! The list of American visitors was being finalized. The Arthur Andersen office in Moscow would assist with all visa arrangements. Sergei Glebovich was sorting out the agenda of Russian enterprises to visit. Dates were being marked on the calendar for early August.

The long term goal was to establish the centers to be self-funding through offering for-fee consulting services. Nathan, ever optimistic, visualized the Ekaterinburg center to be a growing hub of consulting activity.

"Maybe we can send some of the more promising consultants to Arthur Andersen's training camp in St Charles!" He glowed at the idea.

I tried to temper Nathan's enthusiasm by pointing out that his consultants had not yet used a piece of equipment more sophisticated than a pocket calculator. Arthur Andersen consulting training camp certainly would have a starting premise that everyone was proficient with basic computer skills.

"Then we can do a two stage training plan!" He modified his proposal. "First we will build their computer literacy. Then we will send them to St Charles for consulting training!"

To Nathan's eternal credit, he was always enthusiastic and positive. Yes, it was fantastic that Ekaterinburg appeared to be the first LPC to be on the verge of executing a meaningful project despite all the challenges and obstacles they had to overcome. I, however, had been subject to his excitement for the whole day and was now only half listening to Nathan's animated ramblings. I was completely distracted by the view out the window of the restaurant. Something did not look right and now I had figured it out.

"Nathan," I rudely interrupted him. "Last time I was in Ekaterinburg there was the marvelous street going through the center of town. That beautiful fresh asphalt that had been requested specifically by Yeltsin himself. What happened?"

Where just months earlier had been a fresh perfect river of blacktop surface, now was a post-apocalyptic landscape. The road had been shattered into pieces and the broken blocks of asphalt hastily shoveled into small mountains at assorted points along the roadway. Of course there were no orange cones or other safety barriers around the rubble. Cars and busses continued on their way, averting the new obstacles and crunching through the pocketed remains of the road. As strange as it had been to see a shining new road, it was now stranger to see it suddenly disassembled and discarded.

Nathan followed my gaze and looked at the mountains of broken asphalt.

"The rumor is that the road was discovered to be radioactive, therefore it is being removed."

Rumor of course. Never confirmed. These things would not actually be reported in the news. I looked at the mountains of debris and laughed. With the hazards that surround us, somehow this one was viewed to merit being addressed. Oh yes, of course. This is the road that had been specially requested by President Yeltsin – therefore undoubtedly there were people worried about what might be noticed by people in positions of power. This one hazard was singled out to be remediated, not because it was more dangerous than any of the others, but because it had a higher probability of being noticed.

I laughed at the scene. Issues of risk and public safety were most likely being determined based on the how the road would be perceived by people back in Moscow. If the radioactive road were laid in Southern Russia – near the Chechen border – would the reaction be the same? Somehow I doubted it. The local officials made decisions based on how their actions would be perceived in Moscow. We made our decisions based on how our actions would be perceived in Washington DC. Whether our decision-making process was relevant to achieving any longer term goals, beyond pleasing those in power, was an entirely secondary question.

"How does a road become radioactive in the first place?" Nathan's thoughts had gone in a completely different direction than mine. I was amazed that the road was being removed as a hazard. Nathan was astonished that it was radioactive to begin with. He started musing about the lack of proper safety standards and need for stronger regulations. I was certain that there were all kinds of nominal safety standards on the books. The entire question was which ones were enforced and why.

"This isn't a country entirely without rules," I said. I reflected on the lessons from my initial arrival in Moscow. The American businessman knew that he was in violation of Russia's immigration policy, but he charged ahead anyway. I was now concluding that there are rules everywhere, but to get anything done you just have to keep going. You never know what is going to be enforced and what isn't going to be. Actually, if you are politically savvy, you know exactly which rules will be enforced – or you can ensure they are enforced at opportune moments to your advantage, or to your adversary's disadvantage. Oksana's apartment block was being demolished in the name of public safety. The street in Ekaterinburg was demolished in the name of public safety. Meanwhile dozens or hundreds of similar violations would go unchecked. Everyone at some time would be breaking the rules. It was just a matter of staying with the right political allies to prevent being crushed. Easier to say, much more difficult to do.

"You have to be joking," It was Nathan's turn now to be distracted. His attention was riveted outside the window. "Are those really Mormon kids? They really are everywhere!"

Nathan was right. Two fresh faced teenagers wearing suits and name tags and backpacks were valiantly riding their bicycles through the detonated minefield that until recently was a real road. They dodged potholes, evaded Ladas honking at them, and circled around the mountains of radioactive waste. I had only rarely seen a bicycle in Russia. Two kids on bicycles wearing white dress shirts with nametags and neckties could only be explained if they were Mormon missionaries. We were stunned speechless momentarily watching them.

"I wonder how you are chosen for a tour of duty in Ekaterinburg vs Costa Rica?" Nathan said more to himself than to me. "Do you think that they volunteered for this or if they were just assigned here?"

"I would wonder if the people handing out the assignments really know the difference between what life is like in Ekaterinburg vs Costa Rica," I mused. "Or, perhaps it was sold to them as an extra challenging opportunity and therefore extra-rewarding for completing this mission. Do you think their parents know that their kids are cycling through radioactive hazardous waste?"

"Who knows. Perhaps it is all in the course of the Mission," Nathan replied.

I watched the Mormon missionaries and suspected they were going through similar experiences to us. What challenges did they have to overcome on a daily basis? Did the home office back in Salt Lake City have any idea what daily life was like for these kids? Did the home office even really care? And what would await them when they eventually returned to Utah? Would anyone appreciate everything that they had endured – all for the cause of "the Mission"?

"Is it even possible for the Mormons to be successful in Russia?" Paul asked the following weekend. I was at a classic Soviet-era apartment Paul had recently rented together with Alex and Everett. In true US consultant style, Paul had agreed to rent the apartment together with Alex and Everett, but then immediately had been transferred to a different project in St Petersburg. We had found multiple reasons to celebrate the occasion and now were in the midst of dinner and a few drinks before inevitably moving onto the clubs later in the evening.

I asked Paul what he meant by his comment. Why would the Mormon kids face more challenges than us? The Mormons were young and sincere. Besides the obvious harsh living conditions and the difficult business and climate realities that we all endured, what else would be problematic for them?

Paul just sighed and then gestured silently and dramatically to the bottle of vodka that he was holding. He was in the midst of pouring yet another round of shots for the four of us.

Vodka. Yes. That would be a problem for the Mormons. Vodka was the great social lubricant of Russia. Vodka shots were a necessary rite of passage for the beginning of any relationship. How would the Mormon kids possibly gain the respect of anyone they were trying to convert if they weren't willing to undertake the requisite rounds of vodka shots? And what Russian would give up alcohol in the name of salvation?

I noted that Raymond never drank, but was still held in extremely high regard by all the Russians. He had a natural level of leadership and authority that helped him, but also he firmly stuck to a line that said that his doctor prohibited him from any alcohol. He had no choice in the matter. It was his doctor's decision. Whether or not that was actually true, I have no idea. I just know that his statement actually served its purpose – Raymond was able to maintain the respect of all the Russians he met. He *wanted* to have shots with them, but his overbearing doctor had prohibited it.

Well yes, it is one thing to say that when you are over sixty, but quite another thing when you are twenty something years old.

The guys concluded that between the no-alcohol rule and the prohibition from dating Russian *devushki*, the Mormon kids really had it far rougher than anyone else doing a tour of duty in Russia. Really, without the vodka and the Russian girls, what would be the upside of living in Ekaterinburg, Russia? We all had rough lives here, but at least there had to be a few simple pleasures, right?

With that, the discussion of the Mormons cleanly shifted to become (yet another) discussion about Russian *devushki*. Everett reported progress on his "Natasha scorecard" – yes, he really decided that just picking up any girl was no longer a challenge and was now focusing exclusively on finding "Natashas". Alex filed a report on which restaurants now offered a "*devushka*" menu – a version of the menu that was printed without prices. The guys compared notes and agreed that definitely "*devushka*" menus were key to selection of a date restaurant. Russian *devushki* were notorious for simply looking at a menu and selecting the most expensive item – just as a point of status and bragging rights to their friends for how much they had their date pay for dinner. Paul was looking forward to St Petersburg – a whole new city of *devushki* awaited him. Obviously by now he had worked his way through most of the population of Moscow's young women.

The vodka shots were kicking in and the guys were getting fired up over imagining the *devushki* they would encounter that night and an animated debate of which club we were going to start with. The evening was still young, only 10pm or so (the clubs would only open around midnight). To kill time, another round of vodka was poured and then suddenly Paul said that we all needed to explore the apartment.

Yes, explore the apartment. Paul, Alex, and Everett had just rented the apartment a week or so earlier. True to the general standard of the time, the apartment was left not just fully furnished, but full of all the owner's junk. Most of it was packed onto the enclosed balcony off the kitchen. Balconies were always a bit perplexing in Moscow anyway. Weather conditions meant that they were only really useful a few short months each year. Enclosed balconies, therefore became a magnet for junk storage. Too cold of a space for people, but large enough for general accumulation of stuff – just in case you needed it sometime in the next fifteen years. And in Russia, almost everyone became pack rats. If you saw something interesting for sale you bought it – never knowing if it would be available tomorrow, or ever again.

The balcony of the apartment was a hoarder's delight. The bottom layer was furniture in various stages of disrepair – chairs, desks, a mattress. The guys climbed on the furniture, inspecting items on the next layer of sediment – car tires, bits of electrical wiring, car stereo components, grout for tiles, pieces of disassembled cabinets. Each item was identified and then debated for how long it had been there and whether the final project would eventually be realized. We all concluded that the owner was obviously stuck in his own cycle of *remont* for an indeterminate amount of time. Perhaps serving purgatory. Vodka, ever the social lubricant, made everything that much more hilarious and entertaining. Alex poured a round of vodka shots saluting the mysterious apartment owner and wishing him success in his endeavors.

Then suddenly a shriek and a crash and a yelp and another crash. Then the tinkling of broken glass. Through blurred vision we all realized the same horror in one moment. While exploring the mountain of junk, Everett had slipped and plunged both arms through the glass window in the enclosed balcony. Fortunately his head and body had remained inside the apartment – eight stories up. Everett stood dazed and silently held out his two arms, gushing blood from all main arteries. He was pale and looked like he was going to pass out momentarily – either from the shock, the vodka, loss of blood, or all three.

Our minds were not moving as fast as they should have in such a situation. Five shots of vodka now? Or were we at six? Somehow, however, we managed to get Everett to hold his arms over his head and some clean socks were found to bind his wounds. Blood covered the rats' nest of the balcony and was splattered now over each of us. Our dazed state kept us from being in a high panic, which was probably a good thing.

We quickly realized that we had to get Everett to the American Medical Center – the 24 hour medical clinic that served the expat community for such emergencies. None of us had been there before, but we all carried the emergency details in our wallets. This was one of the benefits of being American – we had access to the expatriate clinic. God help us if we had to go to a Russian hospital for treatment. The four of us staggered out onto the street, drunk, dazed, covered in blood and trying to make our way to the American Medical Center.

And of course we had to hitchhike. No taxis in Moscow in 1995, so our only option was to attempt to flag down a passing car. At this point it was about eleven o'clock at night. We were four very drunk 20-something Americans covered in blood. In an effort to hold back the bleeding, Everett was holding his arms over his head with bloody socks wound around his wrists and forearms. To this day I am still astonished that someone pulled over and was willing to give us a ride.

The driver was properly incentivized with $40 USD in hard currency to drive as fast as possible through the streets of Moscow, ignoring all traffic signals. Then again, most cars that I hitchhiked with in Moscow did not really need any extra reason to ignore the traffic rules.

At the AMC the doctor on duty gave us compliments for how well we bound Everett's injuries with the socks. I have no idea if he was sincere, or if he was just trying to humor us. Either was possible. Everett was immediately escorted into a room for sterilization of his injuries and stitches and, of course, Alex and Paul had to follow in morbid fascination. At various intervals Alex and Paul would appear back in the waiting room wearing surgical masks and gloves and declaring in a serious tone that a) "congratulations, it is a boy!" or b) "sorry but we must amputate his left foot" or c) "the procedure was a success but unfortunately we lost the patient". They would then congratulate each other on their witticisms and then disappear back to the examining room.

While the guys were playing ER, I attempted to wash the blood off myself – but dark stains remained in my clothing. I returned to the reception area, content to be drinking as much water as I could in a vain attempt to sober up. I turned to the Russian receptionist and asked if this was a typical Saturday night for her. She smiled and sighed and said yes. As much as the Americans love to criticize the Russians for their drinking, the majority of the incidents for the expats on weekends involved vodka. And yes, usually it would be some incident at a party that would relocate the entire group over to the AMC. Alcohol or falling into open manhole covers – or a combination of the two – were the most common reasons for a visit to the American Medical Center. She was only surprised that there were just four of us. Usually the injured person had an entourage of at least a dozen drunk expats in their wake.

Eventually Everett emerged from minor surgery, flying high on a combination of pain killers and vodka plus delighted about his groovy zipper stitches on each arm topped with mesh protective medical gloves. The blood splattered shirt set off the look. I had been drinking water continuously for an hour and felt like I was now the most sober representative of the group. I offered to help Everett find a lift home.

"Are you kidding me? We are going out clubbing now. I am going to be such the chic magnet! Look at these groovy gloves! Who can resist me now?" Everett held out his mesh gloved hands and started to jump around the reception area to some euro techno beat pounding in his head. Paul and Alex whooped a laugh and bounced behind him. They too wore their blood splattered clothes as a badge of honor. I, of course, had to cooperate and go along with them to whatever the next venue held for us.

The American Medical Center was just a few hundred yards from our regular haunt, Pilot. Therefore obviously that was our club of choice for the night. We arrived around 1am, still very early by the standards of the Moscow club scene. The line had barely even begun to form at the door.

We were about to begin the ordeal with the bouncer of negotiating the entry price and hoping our blood-stained clothes wouldn't disqualify us from entry when the door burst open and several dozen people rushed out. Among them were Sarah, Spencer, Adrian, and Heather. The night was just getting started. We weren't shocked to see friends randomly. There were limited places where the young expats went on weekends – so if you chose the club scene inevitably you always ran into people who you knew. But why were they on their way out rather than in?

They looked at us and our blood-stained clothes with disbelief. They were rushing out of the club at the time of night when everyone was queuing to get in. They physically pulled us from the queue and away from the club. We all had questions for each other, but apparently they could be discussed as we were walking elsewhere – anywhere away from Pilot.

Spencer, Adrian, Sarah, and Heather had fled the club as it erupted in general chaos. Their general conclusion was that some execution just happened on the dance floor. A few shots most likely with a silencer – as nothing was heard over the deafening pulsing beat until a restrained surge of screams. No they were too far away from the epicenter to know exactly what happened. This was one of those situations where it is just simply best to move on and not ask questions and not look too closely.

Adrian looked us over before stating the obvious question. "The four of you are covered in blood and you were *not* inside? What then are you doing waiting in line to go *into* the club?"

We stared at each other. Our story would be just as long as their story for what had happened earlier that night.

Sarah gave me a disapproving look. "Phaedra, I thought we discussed this the other weekend. No excessive risk taking. What were you guys doing?"

I protested that I was just sitting at the kitchen table minding my own business. Paul noted that I was doing a very good job of keeping pace with the requisite vodka shots – but then agreed that I was just sitting at the kitchen table. We all put the blame for the misadventure squarely on Everett.

"Sarah," I countered with a laugh. "You are one to talk. You, Spencer, Adrian, and Heather were in the club during a hit. Who's the one taking excessive risks here?"

"Yep, only in Moscow," Paul chimed in. "If you think my dinner parties are danger-ous, you just haven't been to the clubs with me."

Sarah said that she was deciding on behalf of all of us that we needed to continue on to a club that was a confirmed mafia-free zone. And she had just the place in mind.

True to form, Sarah was leading us onwards to a gem of the new Russia that she was among the first to discover. After another round of hitchhiking we found ourselves at "Aquarium" – one of the first clubs in Moscow targeted squarely at the gay erotic market. No signage marked the entrance, but inside the message was clear. From the moment we entered the club we were in full view of floor to ceiling tanks of water – featuring swimming men who were very fit – and very naked.

"Okay, this isn't *exactly* what I had in mind for the evening's entertainment," said Paul averting his eyes from the spectacle on the walls.

"Welcome to one of the few 100% thug free zones in Moscow," Sarah said with obvious delight. "I can guarantee that none of the guys wearing green jackets and gold chains will bother us here! I can also guarantee that the music will be very good and the drinks will be very potent."

This was my first entry into a gay night club. And Sarah was right. An immediate obvious benefit was that it was one of the first night clubs I had been to where I could just simply smile and not worry that some Russian thug was hovering about. I looked around and concluded that I was one of the late ones to have discovered the delights of the gay club scene in Moscow. Everyone was happy, the music was fabulous. The drinks were poured generously. The disco ball spun on the ceiling and the euro techno pulse pounded on. A few drag queens twirled on the floor in Scarlett O'Hara dresses – a scene I cannot explain to this day. Their partners were dressed immaculately and attentive to every turn. The crowd was mixed with young *devushki* not quite haughty enough to only be seen at Pilot and Hermitage. A good number of expats filled out the crowd. Most notably, this was not exactly the sort of place where the arrogant Russian thugs would want to be seen.

This was a dance floor filled with happy people who were just thrilled to be alive and out living life on a Saturday night. The beat pulsed through the walls, through the aquariums, through our veins. The lights dimmed and Everett noted with delight that his mesh gloves glowed a wonderful fluorescent green in the black light. It was now time for the American men to work the crowd. They were out to impress the *devushki* with the goal of bringing one home for the night. And at *Aquarium* they were pleased to discover that they were among the very few single straight guys in the entire crowd. The *devushki* were open marks for them. And, Paul quickly noted, the *devushki* here were either single or they were lesbian. Time to test his theory that any Russian woman would be willing to do just about anything. There simply wouldn't be a girl in the crowd who was escorted by a Russian man. Real Russian men would not be seen in a gay club.

In a single stroke, the American expat men became fans of the gay nightclub scene.

"This beats the nightclub scene in Uralsk!" Spencer laughed.

"What?" I exclaimed with disbelief. "You've been to Uralsk? *Is* there actually a nightclub there? The most excitement I had in Uralsk was with a random group of Iranian sheep traders out at a dacha in the middle of winter. Oh yes, also partying with the airport staff in the airport control tower."

"Oh yes," Spencer had to yell to be heard above the techno beat. "The *dezhurnayas* from the *Oktyabrskaya* took me to a place where everyone was wearing knitted caps and plaid and dancing to a *balalaika*. And they all weighed at least 200 pounds."

I was about to comment that the more things change the more they stay the same.

"The real news, however, is that I actually managed to get a dial up connection from Uralsk and send an email," Spencer said with real enthusiasm.

I was truly astonished. In a city where obtaining a dial tone was about a 10% probability only a year ago, Spencer had managed to establish an internet connection for long enough to send email.

"Don't get too excited however," he concluded. "Note, I said an email — singular. The connection died after about five minutes."

So few of the Moscow expats actually travelled to the regional cities. It was a pleasure to share a bit of our war stories with someone who appreciated them. I took Spencer's hand and laughed and pulled him onto the dance floor. What a life we had. Our clothes were splattered in blood. We had gay naked men swimming in aquariums behind us and a disco ball spun overhead. I was still intoxicated from far too many rounds of vodka shots earlier in the night. Plus, of course, we were all flying with the extra adrenaline boost that was the side effect of the great Moscow unknown. And for some reason I was exhilarated that Spencer had managed to send an email from Uralsk. We had faced danger this evening and come out victorious. None of this was planned or expected. I had not planned on seeing Spencer, Adrian, or Sarah this evening. Hours ago I had not even heard of *Aquarium*. Such was Moscow.

Carpe diem.

Seize the day. We are alive. We are young. Life is an adventure and we are privileged to be a part of it.

12 RED PILL, BLUE PILL

April 1995

What was it that I was just saying? Life is an adventure and I am privileged to have the opportunity to participate fully in it? Did I really believe that? A few weeks later my mood had changed dramatically and I was attempting to recapture the moment of bliss and excitement of the unknown. What had been drama and adventure now was annoyance and aggravation. The wave of Russian daily life has wonderful crests and then crashes deep, churning the unwary into despair. Every incident could be a shot of adrenaline and excitement and the thrill of the unknown. But then again, taken from the wrong perspective, the same incident could just serve to pull you deep into a quicksand of lament.

I was on a train – my preferred way of travel in Russia when possible. But this experience was decidedly unpleasant, I had already concluded. My previous train trips had all been in the luxury of first class cabins – complete with the romantic film noir setting of midnight departures, vintage rail cars veiled in mystery and fog, and a bottle of champagne tucked in my luggage to be enjoyed as the clickety-clack of the train rocked me into a soothing trance . "Vintage" is just a kind word for "way past their use-by-date" I now acknowledged (in my new and highly agitated state). Those rail cars would barely pass a health and safety review for third class status in the United States. First class was scarcely tolerable to the American eye. To the spoiled rotten American eye. I accept that I am a spoiled rotten American. Of course I have no choice. That is how I was born and raised. As an American it was my birthright to expect more, demand more. My mood had shifted entirely.

I was now subjected to not a second class cabin, but somehow I had ended up in a third class carriage on the train from Tver to Moscow. I was deep in the midst of filth I had previously only witnessed on the Discovery Channel. And I would be stuck here for the next few hours en route to Moscow. Me and my tidy little American business suit and my laptop and my cute rolling Samsonite luggage. We certainly did not fit here in the third class carriage.

Actually, the real problem was the fact that it was a Murmansk to Moscow train, which stopped in Tver as one of the final stations before Moscow. The total journey from Murmansk to Moscow was something like 36 hours. I was in cattle class, in a carriage that was lined with straw (quite literally) on the floor and racks of bunks. The entire area could sleep possibly 80 or more people. The stench of unwashed bodies packed into a small space was overwhelming. The air enveloped me in a suffocating stale blanket.

One small mercy was the fact that I boarded at some ridiculous hour like 6am. Everyone around me was asleep. Actually, based upon the number of empty vodka bottles rolling around on the floor, I should say that everyone was unconscious. The scene was like something from *Doctor Zhivago* or another film where the prisoners are packed forcefully into a train and deported off to Siberia. No "real" luggage by American standards. Every bit of floor space was covered with bundles wrapped in plastic and tied with string. Bodies filled racks of bunks. I spotted an empty bunk on the third level (yes, three racks of bunks) and climbed up the rack with my laptop and green Samsonite rolling overnight bag while wearing my trim suit skirt and high heels. No, I did not blend. At some point the unwashed Russian masses would awaken from their night of vodka-induced debauchery and find an alien American businesswoman in their midst.

It was difficult to believe that this train car could co-exist in the same plane of existence as my oasis of an apartment. Oksana was again house sitting for me. At this hour in the morning she would still be tucked in bed under my glorious down duvet. Could the Russian girls in the office really look up to me as inspiration? Did they want my life? Did they know what they were aspiring to in this wretched place?

Perched high on my third-level bunk I surveyed the scene. I tried to find the situation to be adventurous and amusing but could only fall deeper into a state of horror. I covered my face with my shawl. The air was too thick to breathe without protection. The inhabitants of this third class cabin did not bathe frequently in any case. Now they had been in close quarters for the greater part of 30 hours without clean water or exposure to fresh air. The cabin was toxic and hazardous and I hoped that everyone would remain asleep until our arrival in Moscow.

The passenger below me stirred and immediately started convulsing with a racking deep cough. The sort of cough that involved every muscle in his body in the effort to expel the entire contents of his lungs into the surrounding cabin. Although I could not see him, each cough made me cringe and recoil further into my bunk. He was making no effort whatsoever to cover his face and protect the masses around him from whatever horrendous disease he must be carrying. Tuberculosis perhaps? Not too irrational a thought. The country was going through a full epidemic that was being understated by the government but written about with increasingly alarm in some smaller independent newspapers. I had recently heard that Cole, one of my colleagues in Kazakhstan, had left Almaty to return to the United States for analysis and treatment of suspected tuberculosis. The horrors of post-Soviet reality were closing in.

My skin crawled with horror as I took in the scene around me. What was once adventurous was now exposed in its true light. Life in Russia was hazardous. How could one survive such conditions? Why was I living here? Why did we, as Americans, voluntarily live here when the comforts and cleanliness of America was available? I had received word the day before that Adrian had fallen suddenly and horribly ill and had been taken to a Russian clinic. There he had been diagnosed with a critical condition that was so severe that there was no time to evacuate him to a western hospital – he would have to undergo emergency surgery right then and there in Moscow. The American Medical Center was able to handle nothing more serious than a few stitches. More serious emergencies were redirected to – gasp – a Russian hospital.

As I received this news I felt that my world was falling apart around me. An adventure is fun only if the safety wire is secure. The paradox of the daredevil came abruptly to the surface. The Russian adventure was hilarious and light and fun because we had western passports and could leave if we needed to. We never really were part of this Russian world anyway. We were just visitors who could enjoy it for a moment and leave if things became too rough. A daredevil without a safety plan is simply a suicidal idiot.

For Adrian the safety wire had snapped. He had the British passport. He had the med-evac insurance. He had all the plans to be able to escape to safety if things became too rough. But then life does not necessarily operate according to plan – especially in Russia. Somehow his condition was not diagnosed until far too late. He had to be operated on immediately. His body, his life, his essence was thrown at the mercy of the Russian hospital. They had cut him open and done god knows what to him.

I cringed remembering Max who I had met in Kamchatka the year before. His business partner had been through emergency surgery in Russia as well – without anesthesia. He had survived the experience, at least. Although afterwards he had fled Russia never to return. The Russian women in my office were openly envious of my med-evac insurance. A few of them had recounted horror stories to me of giving birth in Russian hospitals – no anesthetics, doctors yelling in the delivery room at first-time mothers that they were "doing it wrong" while the women were writhing in labor pains. Doctors abandoning other women in labor because they were taking too long. They had heard that things were different in the west, but had no experience of it themselves.

Rumors had spread in the expat community of a recent major traffic accident in Moscow where a minivan full of US government employees had all suffered broken bones. The victims all rapidly agreed to extreme measures rather than subject themselves to the horrors of the Russian hospitals. They voluntarily rolled their broken bodies into a second minivan that transported them 15 hours over pot-holed roads from Moscow to Helsinki where they could receive proper medical treatment in a Finnish hospital. The message was clear: get out of Russia if you have a serious medical condition.

The passengers on the train around me provided further alarming evidence of the state of the Russian health care system. The bunk below me continued to shake with a racking cough. Men struggled to stand and walk, tottering uncertainly in the moving train — visibly aged well beyond their American counterparts. And now that I was paying attention I noticed that no one was wearing eye glasses. It is statistically impossible for eighty something people to have perfect vision. They certainly would not have been able to afford or access contact lenses. Among the ragged masses surrounding me there were undoubtedly men who were stumbling through life half-blind. And, come to think of it, they were probably driving as well. Ah, the things we take for granted in America.

I had to see Adrian as quickly as possible. No one I knew had managed to visit him yet in the hospital. I myself had never been to a Russian hospital before. Everything I had read and heard and seen, however, led me to fear the worst. What horrible fate was awaiting him there? Did he have anesthesia at least for the surgery? Was anyone bringing him food? (I knew that Russian hospitals did not actually provide food for their patients and were utterly dependent upon the diligence of friends coming by to visit.) That being said, I recoiled when I thought of my own kitchen. Yes, my apartment had cockroaches, but Valya had been valiantly trying to keep them at bay. Last week, however, I had found maggots squirming in a bag of flour in my pantry. This led, of course to a hysterical purge of every morsel of food in my kitchen. All food I bought afterwards (even rice and spaghetti noodles) was now stored in the refrigerator. If this was what I was experiencing in a high end American apartment, what was the state of squalor that Adrian was experiencing in a Russian hospital? Would he survive the experience without massive complications and infections? I heard a goat bleat weakly somewhere in the train carriage and my heart sank. What sort of place were we living in? Why would we live here voluntarily when the luxuries of the west were within reach?

How long before I would become one of the haggard women staggering around in battered clothing and coughing? My hair was already coming out in handfuls. My clothing was shredded beyond recognition to the western businessman. And the whole of Arthur Andersen had recently relocated to a new office building at Park Kulturi — where my desk was covered with a mysterious green sludge every morning. If this is what I found on my desk, what was happening to my lungs?

I recoiled against the wall on my bunk as the other Russians in my carriage started to stir from the persistent coughing. If this was the true Russian existence then I wanted no part of it. Somewhere a hundred miles away Adrian was in the deepest darkest heart of Russian reality. I was only looking at its surface and I was horrified. The men who occupied my carriage (almost all were men, there were maybe one or two women in the whole lot) eventually woke one by one from their state of advanced coma. In gruff agitation they swore at the coughing passenger and then, with jerking uncertain motions, searched for the vodka bottles that had been discarded the night before. Each bottle was thoroughly examined each for any drops that might remain. This was seven or eight o'clock in the morning.

No hygienic activities of the slightest were even attempted as the men woke and started about their morning. No toothbrushes, no hair brushes, no clean change of clothing. No soap or even water on a towel to splash on the face. As the men started to move about the cabin, the air shifted a bit and wafted up to me in waves of assault. I tried not to breathe too deeply. Soon we would be in Moscow and I would be able to escape this chamber of horrors.

The train came to a pause somewhere on a remote track outside Moscow. I looked out the window and saw an open top train car filled with garbage. As bad as things were here in the third class car, it was a momentary relief to see something worse outside. Then there was a bit of motion in the garbage heap. An arm moved and then another. It took a moment for me to realize that about a dozen grizzled men were *sleeping* in the garbage. My horror deepened as I saw that all of them were wearing tattered Soviet Army uniforms and medals. War veterans. The horrors of my current situation were suddenly irrelevant. What was a passing annoyance for me was the culmination of decades of catastrophe for these battered men.

This was the country where Adrian was being held in a hospital. I could not bring myself to say "treated". Held. Who knew what sort of treatment would actually be available.

Hours later, the source of my agitation had been redirected from anxiety over Adrian's condition and medical treatment to barely-suppressed hostility towards Russian bureaucratic procedures. I was in the visitor registration area of the hospital and was now entering the second hour of negotiations in my quest to visit my friend. Yes, the second *hour* of negotiations. I had passed the point where seeing Adrian was my real objective. Now I just needed to score a victory over the Russian bureaucratic machine. I would not allow myself to be defeated.

Fortunately I have had only limited occasion to visit friends or family in hospitals in America. The process was pretty straight forward – come during visiting hours, sign a visitor log, the nursing station might check in with the patient to see if they are awake and up for seeing a visitor, then you go to their room. This is really the fundamental basics of what is required for a visit to a patient to a hospital. Or so I thought.

The issue was surrounding the requirement that I must have a pass before I could be permitted to visit Adrian. The massive potato-fed woman behind the barricade of a reception window barked at me angrily for my complete lack of knowledge on the subject. What was my pass number? What was the name of the doctor? She waved her arms at a wall of pigeonholes (none of which, incidentally, had any labels whatsoever — how it actually served as a filing system I still do not know). Bits of paper poked out at random angles from the pigeonholes. Every bit of possible countertop space in the enclosure was covered with scraps of paper. No sign of any technology more advanced than a telephone and a ball point pen.

"I don't know," I answered. "I was told that there would be a pass behind the desk here for me. Can you help look up the name of my friend's doctor?

The woman behind the barrier recoiled as if I had reached over and slapped her.

"What pretensions!" she cried in astonishment. "This is not a secretarial office. If you do not know the name of the doctor, then you must find it yourself. Once you know the doctor's name then we can locate the pass for you."

With that, she pulled the screen across her window with a definitive slam, thus ending the conversation and sealing her tightly away from the unwashed and ignorant masses.

What now? I did not have a chance to determine the name of Adrian's doctor without the assistance of the hospital staff. But wait — what about the Russian staff at Adrian's office, who organized the pass in the first place. Certainly they would know.

Miraculously, tucked in a dark corner of the registration area was a dilapidated telephone (hard wired to the wall of course). It appeared to be a relic from the 1950s. To my astonishment the phone was actually operational. Even more amazing, I was able to reach Adrian's executive assistant, Lena, who (after adding her own string of insults that I had not paid sufficient attention to our previous conversation) was able to give me the next tidbit of information for my quest: Fyodorov. The doctor's name is Fyodorov.

Now back to the queue for a second attempt to obtain a pass from the hostile registration clerk. Aggression from the clerk was met by aggression from the visitors. It is the Russian way. From an early age Russians learn to meet each challenge head on. Every interaction is a potential conflict. You must be prepared. You must hold your ground. Any show of weakness and the other side will win. Every interaction will have a winner and a loser. The idea of a discussion resulting in a mutually beneficial outcome is simply a foreign concept. Black-white winner-loser. To prevent the world from taking advantage of you, you must always be on the offensive. Go in for the kill. Be ready for anything that might be an obstacle. Run over the opposition before they know what hit them.

"The doctor's name is Fyodorov." I stared at the registration clerk evenly and with focus. "You will give me the pass now." I said with more confidence than I felt.

As acknowledgement of this request, the woman gave me a dismissive huff then ambled over to the wall of pigeon holes. There she proceeded to pull scraps of paper out of each pigeon hole and examine them one by one. I stared with disbelief. There was no indication of order or structure whatsoever to the papers. She was not even reaching into the pigeonholes with anything approaching methodology. It was simply random searching through the compartments. Her back was to me and she was hunched over, not with concentration, but with complete lack of interest in her task at hand. Whether it took her five minutes to find the pass or twenty, she really would not have cared either way.

After an eternity had passed, the registration clerk finally returned to the window and announced that no there was no pass for me. Next person in line! She turned her attention towards the man behind me. Her responsibility to me was over.

I quickly stopped her before she moved on to the next person. "Why can't we just call Adrian and find out if he wants to see me?"

"The patient has nothing to do with this!" the clerk answered with exasperation. "If you want a pass, then you must arrange a pass."

Still I refused to move away from the window. After a silent moment of glaring at me, the registration clerk gave a sigh and scribbled a phone number on a scrap of paper. With a sigh that implied that she was going far and beyond any reasonable expectations, she explained that I needed to call this number to find out how to contact the floor warden. The floor warden would then need to find the doctor, who (when he had a moment) would be able to issue the pass.

The phone was now in use by an old *babushka* who could not believe her good fortune that she had found a free public telephone. She was now using the opportunity to call all her friends and family that she had apparently had not spoken to for the previous year. Discussions dragged on about how the grandchildren were growing, and how the prices for everything were so impossible these days. I was impatient with agitation and finally convinced the *babushka* to relinquish the precious telephone for a few minutes.

So I placed the call — and a gruff woman's voice picked up the phone. The voice echoed over the telephone line and resounded through the registration area. I looked around. The voice was coming from a surly woman at a desk not three steps away from the registration clerk. The situation was becoming a scene from a dark comic Monty Python-esque view of bureaucracy. Here is this phone number for further information. Go to that telephone and call the next desk over. Why can't I talk to that person directly? Because that desk provides information by telephone, you moron.

And I was the only person, apparently, who viewed this scene to be ludicrous. I suppressed the urge to hurl insults at everyone and managed to complete the required next steps to obtain the floor warden's phone number then contact her. Of course the floor warden was agitated by the request. The doctor had far more important things to do than to prepare a visitor pass! But in the end she conceded to look for the doctor, with no promise for when this may be completed.

I hung up the phone with the reluctant realization that there was nothing more I could now do other than wait.

The clerk at the window was right about one thing – the patient's interests had nothing to do with the process! I laughed at how the comment was an appropriate summary for the events not just of the day but for the past few weeks.

Now that the Local Privatization Center offices were close to being fully operational, I was now focusing more of my attention on the second part of my project – establishing a database of privatized companies. The goals were described in two simple paragraphs and now everyone had a different view for exactly what was intended. Utilizing official government records was dismissed, as it was unclear which government agencies would have information we were seeking and how we would even gain access to it. Data collectors would be hired in thirty cities throughout Russia and request information directly from the company accountants themselves.

Once the data was collected, then what? The promise given to the companies was that the data would be used to facilitate bringing in foreign investment. USAID, however, had no specific plans for how that would happen – our mandate was simply to collect the data, not conduct any promotional or matchmaking campaign with American or foreign investors. The Directors of the Local Privatization Centers argued that the data should remain housed in their regional offices – the LPCs were supposed to evolve into for a fee consulting centers. The data found in this privatized company database would be a valuable service that they could offer! The Moscow headquarters of the Russian Privatization Center argued that the database should be for the exclusive use of the RPC – they were best positioned to have a holistic view of companies in Russia and would make the most efficient matching between investors and companies. Arthur Andersen had engaged a American business information service provider to help me identify what data to collect and how to train the data collectors. In return for their efforts this service provider was now expecting that they would own the distribution rights for the data.

I was the only one asking what approach would be in the best interests of the privatized companies, on whose behalf the project was nominally being conducted. This question was summarily ignored by the senior executives from the warring parties. Central planning may have nominally ended with the collapse of the Soviet Union, but in practice it lived on with the agencies vying for control over my database. If knowledge was power, they were determined to gain control of the knowledge and use it as a vehicle for furthering their own power.

When I had first arrived in Moscow I had been brimming with youthful optimism. This project would make a real difference for the privatized companies. All my efforts would be worthwhile. But now I watched clerk bark hostile retorts at another visitor and began to realize a bitter truth about my project. The clerk at the reception desk was right: the patient had nothing to do with it.

My mood spiraled downwards. Were all our efforts a complete waste of time and taxpayer money? Millions of dollars were being poured into establishing the privatization centers, hiring staff, now hiring data collectors and building this database. And for what? So that the resulting data could be kept behind locked doors and accessed only by a privileged few to offer as favors based on their whims?

Actually "wasting time" would be putting a positive spin on the situation. Were we in fact entrenching the political elite further with our actions rather than offering a way for the newly privatized companies to establish themselves independent of government control? I had come to Russia intending to help promote the lofty ideals of democratization, economic development, and pave a path towards future prosperity. Now I was left with the bitter question of whether my actions in fact were hurting the democratic future of the country rather than helping.

My black musings were interrupted as a door opened at the back of the administration area and a woman walked into the room holding a fluttering bit of paper that looked suspiciously like a pass. My spirits soared for a moment, but then were dashed again as the registration clerk scolded the woman that the paper had the wrong stamp on it. "I have said this before! The circular stamp! Not the triangular stamp!" Both women gave an accusing look in my direction before the woman holding the incorrect pass disappeared without further comment or explanation.

The futility of the situation left me craving a stiff drink to calm my nerves and temper my frustration. This scene would be bad enough in your average bureaucratic government setting, but this was the undisputed top hospital in the country. All the expatriates had explicit instructions with med-evac that if it were necessary to be sent to a Russian hospital, then only this elite facility would do. Russian parliamentarians based in Ekaterinburg would fly out to Moscow for procedures here. It prided itself on the most modern technology and the most advanced medical practices. But again, the term "customer service" was a foreign concept. And, as the registration clerk had pointed out to me, the patient really was not part of this process in any case.

Believe it or not, a valid pass was eventually delivered to the registration desk. Close to two hours after I had started my quest and less than an hour to go before the end of visiting hours. Nevertheless I had succeeded. My emotional state lurched into violent upswing with the victory. I had earned the right to proceed through the front gates into the grounds of the hospital.

The complex was more akin to a military or prison camp than a patient care center. Imposing brick walls surrounded the grounds, topped with ferocious barbed wire. The one set of gates remained closed at the front, with an armed guard scrutinizing each person requesting the right to enter. Once inside the fortress, the grounds were devoid of any greenery – no flowers, no ivy, no trees, no shrubs, not even any real grass. A few brave weeds struggled to press through the packed solid dirt, but they were quickly obliterated by the churning filth of the grounds and the persistent Moscow acid rain.

And yes, I eventually did find Adrian and gained admittance to his room. He shared a room (or a cell, depending upon your perspective) with a member of the Russian parliament who had been admitted a few days earlier with some heart condition. The parliamentarian was semi-conscious after his recovery from surgery the day before. He lay on his bed, groaning occasionally. No heart monitors or technology of any sort in sight for this elite patient. No charts were by his side, no bells, intercom, or telephone where he could call for assistance if needed. The bed was a flimsy metal frame cot, more suited for a summer cabin than a top tier hospital. As I sat with Adrian, I subconsciously kept one eye and ear on the other patient. If he were to deteriorate rapidly, his only chance of survival was for his roommate to alert the appropriate authorities.

Adrian was in astonishingly good spirits. His mood actually far surpassed my own. Given the entire ordeal I had been through to visit him, I was more in the mood for a few shots of vodka than socializing in a hospital ward. He was delighted by my gift of packets of food wrapped in newspaper and impressed that I had remembered to bring knives to cut the cucumbers and cheese. He then pulled up his shirt and showed me an absolutely astonishing fresh gash and stitches that extended nearly twelve inches down the length of his abdomen. To the untrained eye it looked to me that he had just been sawed open without any thought as to the least invasive way possible to address his internal injuries.

Adrian just laughed at the whole ordeal. (Then moaned at the pain of his chest moving.) It was all part of the Russian experience. The doctors here were competent. Probably more so than in America and Britain where they relied heavily on technology. Here the doctors had to have real skill and creativity. At least he had anesthesia. No recollection of the surgery or anything immediate before or after it.

So how was he coping? Very well actually. In fact he pointed out that one of the huge benefits of this whole experience was that he had now been through several days or so of complete Russian language immersion and his competency was improving each day. Adrian was able to see the sunny side of the situation from start to finish. He had zero Russian language skills when he had arrived in the country just a few months earlier. Now he was excited by the opportunity to have a complete Russian language immersion program in a Russian hospital for a week or so. He had to communicate! He was learning! He showed me books and papers strewn across his bed of the various terms and phrases he was learning and working on.

"Maybe I should start dating my assistant, Lena," Adrian only half-joked. "My Russian would improve so much more if I were seeing a Russian girl. This immersion program in the hospital is fantastic."

"Why do Brits have such bad taste in humor?" was all that I could answer. "That is so *not* funny."

His comment was just a little too close to home.

After a recent trip away I had returned to the office to be greeted by an unusually happy Robert. He was making random comments totally out of character like "I had such a great time last weekend at Hermitage!" (The popular club of the moment with the expats) and "Homemade *pelmeni* are really incredible. There is so much to Russian cuisine that the Americans don't appreciate."

There is always a primary explanation for any sudden mood change. After a few more random comments, the reason became clear. "Phaedra, you have such a great view from the balcony of your apartment. The Kremlin Bell Tower! Who has a view of the Kremlin Bell tower from their apartment!"

I had not invited Robert to my apartment, so clearly Oksana had. Robert was clearly besotted with Oksana. What had led to the invitation from Oksana to Robert for dinner I couldn't say, but I was determined to be on the defense for the protection of my girls. Especially Oksana who previously had told me explicitly that she had been pressured into unwelcome relationships at work. I had promised her that I would defend her interests and therefore launched into Robert with a recital of all his proclamations to me about keeping work relationships separate from social relationships.

Robert simply brushed off my lecture with a dismissive wave. His position was simple – Oksana was an adult and could make up her own mind about her relationships.

No, I argued. That is not true. She (like all Russian women) sees the men in power around her as an obligation. It is simply part of the expectation that in order to secure oneself in the workplace that you offer "additional services" to the men in certain political positions in the office.

Of course Robert did not accept that at all. Oksana was interested in *him*, Robert. Not out of some perceived obligation. He defensively declared "No". He had never suggested anything to her!

As further evidence I reminded him of Raymond's trip to Ekaterinburg where he had planned to take Oksana as his personal translator. For Raymond it had been a completely professional request and he was innocently oblivious to the stress it had caused Oksana. It took my intervention to substitute Kolya as the translator.

"Did Oksana ask you to intervene?" Robert asked.

No. But her history was such that I knew that she felt there was a certain obligation. Or at a minimum the Russians with the LPC would make certain assumptions about what would be happening in the evening between her and Raymond.

"She did not ask you to intervene, but you did anyway," Robert stated simply.

True. But Russian women are not exactly conditioned to stand up for their own interests like American women are.

"Phaedra, you really need to stay out of other people's business," Robert scolded me and ended the discussion.

Of course Adrian took Robert's side of the issue. Why was it my concern whether Robert had dinner with Oksana? Did I need to tackle everyone else's issues? Couldn't I just let things run their course?

I suggested to Adrian that perhaps I shouldn't have battled with the hospital front desk for two hours to be allowed to bring him food. Perhaps I was taking the issue that he was being held as a semi-prisoner in a Russian hospital too personally and maybe I should just let things take their natural course.

Adrian waved his hand dismissively and laughed. Time for a new subject.

At this point a nurse marched into the room and roughly shook the member of parliament awake. "Time for your medication," she barked. She glared at the semi-conscious man for a moment, awaiting a response. When he groaned, she considered this to be enough of a sign that he was ready for his medication for her to continue.

The nurse held a tattered plastic baggie with dozens of pills of all shapes and sizes — little blue one, big round red ones, yellow with stripes. All mixed like a bag of assorted candies to be sampled. No labels whatsoever, of course. The nurse peered into the baggie and poked around a moment until she collected a handful of pills that satisfied her. She handed these to the parliamentarian and stood watchfully over him as he dutifully swallowed each pill.

Mission accomplished with the first patient, the nurse now turned her attention to Adrian. She again dipped into the baggie and pulled out an assortment of multicolored pills. She handed them to Adrian and demanded that he take his medication.

"You aren't really going to take those are you?" I was incredulous. "Do you have any idea whatsoever what she is giving you?" (I was counting on the high probability that the nurse understood no English, therefore we could pass casual insults without consequence.)

"No, all she does is hand me pills. They seem to be different colors each time." Adrian said, staring at the handful of red and blue pills.

"She just handed the other patient — the heart patient, mind you — a stack of pills as well. She hasn't looked at either of your charts. I am assuming that you have charts, right? How does she know what to give you?"

Adrian stared doubtfully at the pills in his hand. Could be heart medication. Could be pretty much anything. He was feeling pretty good, so all he really wanted was to socialize with me and then get some rest. He laid the pills on the top of the cabinet by his bed.

"No," the nurse scolded him sharply. "You will take the pills now." She put her hands on her hips and stared severely at Adrian. She would not leave the room until her patient had cooperated with her instructions.

"Let's at least take an inventory of what you are swallowing there," I offered. "So if something kills you, we can figure out later what it was – perhaps. And yes, I am probably meddling too much in your life by your standards."

So I jotted into one of Adrian's notebooks – 3 blue pills (little round ones), 2 red pills (oblong), 2 yellow pills (little round ones). Adrian swallowed them obediently. The nurse turned on her heel and left, satisfied. I continued to watch Adrian carefully for a few moments – perhaps he would start shuddering with mysterious convulsions. We had no idea.

A cockroach climbed up the wall near the foot of Adrian's bed. Not a small little insignificant American cockroach, but the mutant survivors of nuclear wars that bred industriously in Moscow and were certainly planning to overthrow the government in the near future. Just one cockroach. But where there is one there are always thousands more. I recoiled from horror, not at the cockroach (I was now accustomed to seeing them in my apartment), but at the fact that it was in his room in the hospital. Adrian gave it a dismissive wave. It was all part of the Russian experience.

So Adrian survived the experience. He actually did not just survive, he thrived. This was his equivalent to my night of being assaulted in the back streets of Moscow. Neither of us chose our harsh steps into the reality of Russia, but we both chose our attitude of how we would deal with it. You could either choose fear or choose life. We chose to live. We could not let the incidents of daily life get to us. If we worried about everything that could happen, then we would live an isolated existence – if it could be called living at all. If we were to live, not just exist, in Russia then we had to be prepared to face life and everything that came with it.

I left the hospital on a glorious emotional upswing. Adrian was thriving. He loved life. He had faced every expatriate's worst nightmare – surgery in a Russian hospital – and come through it laughing and pumped with the adrenaline rush of the experience. The Russian bureaucracy may not care about the interests of the client – but I did and I would be able to overcome all odds and make a positive difference. We would charge back out into the streets of Moscow looking for the next challenge, the next adrenaline rush. The next rush would have to surpass the last. A new challenge, a new accomplishment that would be more uplifting and more satisfying than before.

Actual dangers in Russia? Don't be silly. Every challenge can be overcome. Complaints are for the weak. You are either victorious or defeated. No one wants to be the conquered. We had to be strong. We were young and invincible.

13 WOULD YOU LIKE FRIES WITH THAT?

May 1995 — Moscow

Spring was fighting its way out from under the frozen earth, but winter never gives up easily in Russia. In Europe and the United States, spring is a time of tulips, and fresh green grass, singing birds, and baby animals. The air is fresh with cleansing rains and the sky is blue. In Moscow, however, by the time March came around, the grey depression had drained the life out of the city so completely that grey seemed certainly to have established itself as the permanent mood and color scheme. The thick armor of ice held its grip on the roads, roofs, and earth. A brief warming spell would create daggers of icicles poised as fierce fangs over the sidewalks. A single drop of water would linger at the tip of an icy shard, the dangerous game of warming had begun. The suspense would build and then the blades would plunge down towards their victims below.

On the streets, the snow throughout the winter would be mounded unceremoniously to the side or packed into a plate of sheer ice on the smaller streets. As spring approached and fresh snow no longer fell, the residual mountains of discard became blacker. Soot and ash continued to be trapped in the crystals of ice — but no new dusting would give the illusion of clean on the surface. As the sun struggled to peer over the buildings into the streets, the slightest bit of warmth would release whatever refuse had been frozen in the mountains of ice. Half-digested garbage and even corpses were vomited from the ice mounds into the streets. Sewer drains were few and far between, so the melting sludge just sat as an oily mushy swamp. Cars and busses wallowed through the muck. Pedestrians wore tall boots, but inevitably the cold slime would work their way in through some hole in the seams.

At night the temperature would drop again as winter reasserted its hold. Puddles transformed back to hostile ice. In defense, pedestrians walked arm in arm. Everyone knew someone who had fallen on the precarious ice and broken a wrist or an arm — and then faced the horror of having the bone set in a Russian hospital. The battleground between winter and spring was ugly and dangerous. After weeks of the struggle it seemed possible that perhaps this would be the year where the winter would win its final battle over spring and establish bleak and dreary as the permanent state of the world.

Finally, at some point in late April, the sun hoisted itself up decisively over the city and declared victory over the winter. The grey retreated to the shadows of doorways and unlit stairwells. Pedestrians paused on the street lifting their faces to the sun and smiling, feeling its warming rays finally regaining strength. The sun warmed the earth and warmed our souls. A pounding rain scrubbed the cars and busses, removing at least the first layer of the dull blackened grime of the spring sludge and returning a bit of color to the street scene. And then one day, as if there were a secret memo circulated, all of the women packed away their winter coats and the vibrant color of spring clothing appeared on the streets. *Babushkas*, who were selling car batteries and toilet seats by the Metro subway entrance last week, now offered fresh flowers wrapped in newspaper. Occasionally they even managed to break into a brief toothless smile.

Light and optimism had won their seasonal battle over the forces of darkness and depression.

The return of the sun and daylight and warmth affected everyone. The surge of optimism was infectious. Signs of hope and resurgence were everywhere. Moscow's future was bright and we were privileged to be witness to the rebirth of a nation.

Sarah and I were walking through central Moscow. The sun was invigorating and delicious, so of course we had to be outdoors. The 40th Anniversary of VE day was the following day, therefore a stroll through Red Square was on the agenda. Red Square never failed to amaze us. The area is smaller than most people imagine, but that only serves to intensify the experience. Here in Red Square you realize that we mere mortals are just passing through history. The Kremlin *is* History. We knew that point already, but this day, on the eve of the VE day celebrations, the point was driven home clearly.

Red Square had been transformed from May 1995 back to May 1945. Enormous banners hung from every wall facing the square proclaiming "Glory!" "Forward!" and "Victory!" Bold figures painted in classical Soviet realist style marched purposefully with determined focus on the glorious future of Russia. The colors were primary, energetic, creating a surge of faith that yes – together we can overcome all obstacles. We turned back the invading armies from the gates of Moscow. We survived the siege of Leningrad. We defeated the Nazi aggressors and have re-established our nation as the Empire it was destined to be.

Standing in Red Square surrounded by such powerful images it was easy to understand how the full force of Russian national pride had been channeled to unite the Soviet Union for so long.

Sarah and I debated what the message was of the scene before us. Was the Russian military attempting to re-live their glory days for just one more celebration? Was Yeltsin trying to re-invigorate a battered nation by turning to the same symbols that had united the country for decades? Was this just a moment of true reflection of the achievements of the Great Patriotic War – or was it perhaps a more ominous sign of the aspirations of some of the top Russian leadership?

The first Russian Presidential elections would be held in one year. First. The first time in the 750 year history of the Russian nation the leader would be elected by democratic means. In the wake of continued economic chaos, Yeltsin's hold on the leadership was viewed to be tenuous at best. Others from within the military elite were already beginning to voice their challenge. What would happen in the course of the elections was far from certain.

"Only time will tell what direction the country will go," Sarah observed. "Red Square will be here to witness what happens next. I won't."

After a moment I realized that Sarah was starting to tell me that she was leaving Russia and going back to the United States.

"Everyone has to go home eventually. But why now?" I protested.

The positive energy in Moscow was palpable. The country had won the annual battle over winter and signs of renewal were everywhere. The windows of the GUM department store were no longer bleak and dusty. The serene face of Estee Lauder smiled with quiet confidence as she gazed out on Red Square. Less than a hundred meters away, Lenin lay silent in his tomb.

Sarah laughed and waved her arm symbolically at the VE day banners and the GUM shop windows. "Isn't this what we came here for? Estee Lauder is smiling at her victory over Lenin! For me it is time to declare victory and go home! Everyone knows when their time has come. You will understand some day. The day will come when you just *know* you have to return back to the United States.

"Besides," she added, "I turn thirty next month. We have all noticed that something happens to *devushki* in this country after they turn thirty. Their hair falls out, their sense of style vanishes. They turn into shapeless, toothless *babushki*. I don't know if it is something in the water or in the gene pool, but I don't want to take a chance. I need to get out while I still look young."

I tried to be happy for Sarah. She was totally at ease with her decision. And she was right about something happening to the women in Russia after the age of thirty. The evidence was everywhere. I, however, was devastated to lose a friend. Clearly nothing I could say would change her mind.

The agenda of the day therefore became a walking tour of Sarah's favorite places in central Moscow. From Red Square we turned southwest along the banks of the Moscow River to the construction site of Xram Xrista Spasitelya – Cathedral of Christ our Savior. We stood in awe of the growing white spires of the Russian Orthodox cathedral that was clearly intended to be an epic presence worthy of its location within view of the Kremlin. The prior cathedral on the site had been violently crushed to the ground under Stalin and now, as a symbol of renewal for the whole of Russia, was being rebuilt anew — grander and bolder than ever. Unlike other construction sites that languished in a state of limbo, the white glowing walls of the Xram reached purposefully upwards.

We marveled that someday this amazing cathedral really would be finished. We could tell already that it was going to be an example of ostentatious excessive use of marble and gold and bronze. But wasn't that in some ways what Moscow needed at this time? A beacon of hope for others. A triumphant show of glorious rebirth onto the world scene. This incredible project can be completed — just wait until you see what else we can do. We are here. Look at us. We are back and bolder, stronger, more magnificent than ever.

"Maybe I should declare victory and go back to the United States too," I commented.

I did have my own victory to celebrate. All of the computer equipment actually had finally cleared customs, was successfully delivered to all the LPCs, and installed. Joseph and Nathan provided testimony that yes, it was all true.

Sarah smiled at me. "No, it is not yet your time to return home. You are still invigorated by the challenges here. You are inspired by the successes and want to see what is next."

She was right. I was awestruck by the changes happening around me. Last week I had called the office in Rostov looking for Joseph. When the receptionist had answered the phone I was no longer greeted by a gruff "Da," but a sweet "Rostov Local Privatization Center, how can I help you?" Clearly Joseph's efforts to improve everyone around him were starting to make an impact. "And then when I asked for Joseph you will never believe what happened next!" I was nearly breathless with the memory.

"So clearly the phone wasn't just dropped on a table while the receptionist wandered off looking for him — per standard practice."

"No, she actually said. 'Just one moment let me *transfer* you.' Can you believe it? They really got the PBX hub working in Rostov! They are receiving calls to a central number and *transferring* calls to desks."

"Next up will be voice mail," Sarah said with a twisted smile. This, of course, sent us both into fits of laughter. Voice mail in Russia! That would be another lifetime away.

Sarah was right. I was enjoying evidence that we were accomplishing something. She pressed me for details for everything that happened to result in the equipment being finally delivered. The last update I had given her had been months ago in the smoky basement of Krizis Zhanra. At that time I was lamenting that the order had *still* not been placed as a result of the debate for whether to order equipment for three or four LPCs.

In the end the decision had been made to order equipment for the full scope of the project – four LPCs plus ten locations for my data collectors. The order had been triumphantly placed with Dell – several months after I had originally written the specifications. Word quickly came back from Dell that the processor model I had requested was discontinued. More delays while the order was respecified with the current model and then further delays while Dell experienced a parts shortage.

Eventually everything was delivered to Virginia and inventoried and then shipped by boat to Hamburg then by truck to Russia. All was going well until the shipment hit the Russian border and a customs duty of 40% was assessed against the equipment. Once again USAID refused to reimburse Arthur Andersen for any taxes or duties, so the shipment sat at the border until someone senior enough in the Russian government was convinced to give a waiver for the collection of import duties.

Once customs was cleared everything moved fairly quickly. To the DC team's credit, the shipment had been pre-packed into separate crates for each destination and everything was actually delivered correctly. The only thing that seemed to be missing were Russian language versions of all software. We had paid for the licenses, but the software simply was not included in the shipment. This left the regional teams with a few options a) wait until the US team actually sent the software that was purchased (another few months?), b) buy additional licenses somehow in Russia (through procurement channels that were not authorized by USAID) or c) obtain pirated Russian language software. No option was actually acceptable. No matter what we did someone would criticize us. Therefore when I learned that pirated versions of all software had been installed within hours on every computer in every office, I did not really protest. What other option did we have? The Russians were excited about learning how to use the computers. They did not speak or read English. Really, were we going to ask them to just ignore their computers for the next three months while we sorted out procurement for Russian language software via official channels?

"And what about the equipment for the fourth LPC that has not yet been authorized?" Sarah asked astutely. "Where is that?"

"Locked in a warehouse somewhere in Virginia," I answered. "It wasn't authorized to be shipped because it did not have a valid destination. So now the equipment is just held in a bureaucratic limbo until a fourth LPC is authorized. If that doesn't happen, it will be just locked away until someone figures out how to sort out the paperwork to re-deploy it to a different project." I paused before my conclusion. "You and I both know that centuries from now, archaeologists will probably discover the computers in their original plastic wrap nicely preserved in the temperature-controlled warehouse."

Sarah laughed at the situation and analyzed the situation further. I was the unfortunate guinea pig for Arthur Andersen's first foray into procurement for a US Government project. The procurement team was inexperienced and determined to follow the rules. Every single last one of the thousands of mysterious rules that governed US

Government procurement practices. It was simply physically impossible to follow all the rules and actually achieve the goals of the project. The challenge is knowing how to keep the goals vs the rules in balance. A more experienced team would understand how to request exemptions. They would understand which rules would be enforced and which ones could be side stepped. Only a team of complete novices would actually attempt to comply with every single regulation.

"We did manage to achieve one exemption!" I offered. "The DC-based team did tell us that the LPCs could source furniture for their offices from Russian suppliers if the origin of manufacture was other 'emerging markets.'"

Sarah laughed that this was a just standard part of the USAID procurement practice. It is quite the statement about both government procurement regulations and our DC-based sourcing team that it took them nearly six months to figure out this rule. With even more experience a team can be bolder, gaining more exemptions and cutting corners on other paperwork. Of course, exemptions are discretionary from those in senior positions. But the net effect is that those that receive exemptions move faster than those that follow the rules. The team that moves fastest will be recognized in the end for being the most successful. Which would be a result of their political influence to get their way, rather than any other significant skills of the team. The favors for exemptions of course are conveniently forgotten with final assessments – all that matters is that Team A completed the project while Team B did not. Of course this means that political influence and exceptions becomes rewarded and even more entrenched. Knowing that you are rewarded for the appearance of completion and violations can be swept aside, then why would you have any respect for the rules at all?

And of course the net result would be that at any given time, any project would have to be violating some part of some rules in order to just move forward. It was a time honored technique of the government to maintain order and control. At the core is maintaining a relationship with senior people in power. Anyone who dared challenge authority would be able to be disposed of quickly by simply thumping the rule book. Of course the challenger had some transgressions that must be punished (everyone did) – it was just a matter of finding them and bringing the issue to judgment. In the name of "justice" those in power held the ability to bring down their opponents with a flick of their fingers. A contradictory and confusing rule book was key.

"Are we still discussing US government procurement or have we moved on to the Russian legal system as well?" I was trying to follow Sarah as she was becoming increasingly more abstract.

"Both really," she answered with a bit of bitterness to her voice. "And more. It is the same for any controlling relationship. Make rules. Make more rules – some which require violation of the first rule. Then look at your challengers, determine who you want to eliminate, and figure out what they are doing that is illegal or inappropriate."

Sarah had not shared with me exactly what had led to her decision to leave Moscow, but it was easy now to guess the generalities. Either control or be the one who is controlled. Crush or be crushed. Peaceful coexistence was not an option.

We continued our walk silently for a few minutes. In front of us a Russian man was walking with a decorative *devushka* on his arm. Her shoes were terribly impractical for a Sunday stroll. She struggled to keep the pace of her partner. He steered her firmly through the growing pedestrian crowd. This was not a lovers' stroll of equals, happy simply to be in each other's company. Control or be controlled.

Sarah took my arm and we turned onto the Old Arbat – the wonderful pedestrian walking street that was a microcosm for all the change happening in Moscow at once. We joined the Old Arbat on the east end of the boulevard, amidst the bustling chaos of the traders near the Arbatskaya Metro entrance. Carrots were held high above a *babushka's* head, showing her prize wares to a wider crowd. Fresh carrots! And L'Oreal shampoo today. Another woman held Barbie dolls in battered boxes, trying to sell them to passersby.

The crowds moved slowly along the Old Arbat. Savoring the first sunny day of spring. Enjoying a walk along one of the few roads that were without cars. Passing under the ornate antique street lamps. Much of the classic architecture of pre-Soviet Moscow had been retained along the Old Arbat. Scaffolding crept up the front of some of the buildings, with a suggestion that restoration was intended, if not entirely yet underway. Like elsewhere in Russia, most of the shops were hidden behind closed doors, or identified with basic signs like "Meat" and "Produce". But every so often a brilliant new spot of color would emerge. An Italian flag was painted on the sign of a new pizzeria. Smells of fresh baking pizza crust, garlic, and sausage drifted onto the street. In front of another shop, a flower box perched precariously in the window. A woman fussed over the stubborn plant, attempting to coax it to life.

We found ourselves walking towards the McDonald's that anchored the western end of the Old Arbat. In the United States we would never view McDonald's to be a destination for a leisurely afternoon stroll. In Moscow, however, as expats we found ourselves frequently drawn to the golden arches. Not because of the food (although the perfect warm fries were quite satisfying on a cold winter day), but because the entire experience never failed to evoke wonder and a strange renewal of optimism.

On the surface, everything at McDonald's in Moscow was exactly the same as back in the United States (or anywhere else in the world). The burgers were exactly the same texture, cooked to exactly the same level of medium well. The fries were cut to the same shape and length of their American cousins. The restaurant featured the familiar fixed tables and rotating fixed chairs and trash bins with handy areas to place the used trays.

A visit to McDonald's in the United States is generally a casual afterthought. A convenience. Or a way to appease a group of children. Given that the monthly salary in 1995 was around 150 USD per month, a visit to McDonald's in Russia, however, was an *event*. *Devushki* sitting with their dates would eat very slowly to draw out the moment as long as possible, sitting properly with a subdued smile – very clearly *pleased* to be lavished such attention. Older couples or groups of friends would be wearing their Sunday finest while patiently waiting in line. Most amazing to me were the parents with younger children. The children were almost universally extremely well behaved and visibly awestruck that they had been granted the privilege of a treat at McDonalds.

A closer look with tell an even deeper story. Occasionally one mother with two children would have a single hamburger and one packet of fries on her tray. She would hold a knife with perfectly manicured hands and carefully slice the burger into three portions then allocate the fries between three napkins. The children would be quiet and taking in the momentous occasion.

The highlight of the trip to McDonald's, however, was the enthusiasm of the Russian staff. The young kids behind the counter wore baseball caps with the traditional "M" emblem and name tags that read "Tatiana", "Viktor", and "Svetlana". They looked positively ecstatic to be working at McDonald's and said amazing things like "Welcome to McDonald's, can I take your order?" and "Would you like fries with that?" and "Thank you, have a nice day!"

The first time I heard those phrases (in Russian mind you) spoken by a radiant girl with the name tag of "Elena" I was stunned into silence. I had always heard about McDonald's obsessive drive to achieve globally standardized processes, but this was the first time I had clearly witnessed its effects. Real Russians offering genuine pleasant customer service – with a smile.

Sarah then shared an urban legend that was circulating in the expat circles regarding the very first squadron of young Russians that was indoctrinated by McDonald's into the American way of customer service. I have no way of knowing if the story is actually true or not, but I have complete confidence that it is entirely possible and quite realistic, given the clash between American and Russian customer service attitudes. The training session was intense and focused on controversial concepts like – be pleasant to the customer, the customer is always right, thank you, and have a nice day. Smile often and make it look genuine and welcoming. This entire concept of service was quite difficult for some of the Russian youth to grasp. Nothing like this had ever been attempted before in Moscow. Despite this, the Russian twenty-somethings were attentive and at the end of the session were ready to ask questions. A hand shot up and a puzzled kid asked: "I don't understand. Why do we have to be so nice to them? We have all the hamburgers!"

"McDonald's really is the evil capitalist aggressor forcing such foreign concepts as pleasant customer service on Russia," I laughed sarcastically – and then had to add.

"McDonald's will probably do more to advance the cause of introducing basic business concepts in Russia than all of our stupid government aid projects combined. At least McDonald's isn't promoting insanity such as US-government style procurement and openly demanding exemptions from VAT and import duties."

"True," Sarah smiled. "But look at what is happening here."

To the right of the Arbatskaya McDonald's was a small alley that led behind the restaurant to the service entrance. A crowd was gathering in amazement watching a full size modern truck attempt to maneuver its way out of the alley, through the pedestrian street and onto the Sadovoyoe Koltso Boulevard beyond. To date all the trucks I had seen in the former Soviet Union appeared to have been designed and built in the 1930s. This Scania truck was shiny and modern and painted with an enormous golden "M". And it was not moving. Blocking the progress of the truck was a dilapidated Lada that had been parked and abandoned in the narrow alley.

Now we were curious for what would happen next. This symbol of all things modern was immobilized by something as trivial as a tiny Lada. Of course there were no such things as tow trucks in Russia that could be called to remove the nuisance. Who knew where the owner of the car went. If the McDonald's truck driver were anywhere as motivated as his colleagues operating the counter, he would not sit idly by just waiting for the owner to return.

We had our answer a moment later as the driver rallied a group of nearby Russian men to simply *pick up and move* the offending vehicle. The Russian men were eager to demonstrate their prowess in front of their dates and in moments the path was cleared. A few quick handshakes from the driver in appreciation of the favor, then the massive engine roared to life and the truck was again on its way.

Sarah and I laughed. We knew that if a Volga had been the offending vehicle then the resolution would have been quite different. A Lada could be safely discarded. The owner would be inconsequential and have no voice to protest. The owner of a Volga, however, would have been a force to be reckoned with. Control or be controlled. For every situation there is a winner and a loser.

"And for our final lesson today, let's watch this gypsy girl for a moment," Sarah said with amusement. She turned her attention from the departing truck to a young gypsy girl sitting in a battered wheelchair in front of the McDonald's.

At first I wasn't sure what Sarah wanted to show me. The gypsy girl was just like hundreds of others in Moscow. She was thin but not obviously malnourished. A blanket covered her legs and she held a shoebox to collect rubles from passersby. Virtually all younger Russian women, regardless of income, were meticulous in their appearance. The notable exceptions were the gypsies who almost seemed to deliberately go to great lengths to exhibit grime and tattered clothing.

We watched as the girl rested the shoebox on her thighs and began to sort her rubles into stacks of notes. She had enormous stacks of paper notes in various colors – but with the exchange rate now passing 3500 rubles to one USD, a stack of 100 ruble bills still could be worth just a bit over one dollar.

A small breeze swept over the gypsy girl, tossing her stacks of money carelessly into the passing pedestrians. Without hesitation she flung aside her blanket and leapt after her day's takings, now scattered with the wind. The girl quickly gathered the bits of paper, elbowing her way through the crowd as necessary. When all was safely back in the box, she returned to her wheelchair and once again pulled her blanket across her lap.

None of the passersby had paused for a curious glance at the disabled girl who had miraculously found the use of her limbs in her moment of need. Sarah and I were apparently the only spectators who were amused by the scene.

"Appearances are more important than reality," I stated the lesson I concluded I was supposed to derive from the situation.

"Yes," Sarah confirmed. "But still you are only seeing part of the story."

Had I or anyone else really believed that the gypsy girl was disabled, even before I saw her chase after her money? No. I had laughed because it just revealed the charade that I had already believed to be there. Similarly the rest of the witnesses had been unmoved.

But then, the next level of question was whether I believed any of the money was going to be kept by the little girl? With the box full of cash she would certainly be taking in more money today than most typical wage-earners. No, I agreed. Obviously she was not directly benefitting from all her collections – otherwise she would be cleaner and better dressed. The little gypsy girl in a wheelchair was a daily fixture on the Old Arbat near the McDonald's. No matter how much money she collected, she was always wearing the same scruffy clothing.

Sarah then told me about how on a prior stroll down the Old Arbat she had seen a Mercedes with tinted windows plow onto the pedestrian street, aggressively parting the crowds like the Red Sea. The car came to a stop in front of the gypsy girl in the wheelchair. The door opened and she obediently stepped inside. The driver folded her wheelchair and placed it in the trunk of the car and they drove away.

The gypsy girl was not keeping any of her collections – the men in the black Mercedes were. This statement of Sarah's did not surprise me, it only confirmed what I had earlier suspected but had not been able to verify.

"Intellectually, deep down everyone knows that the gypsy girls are not benefitting from any of the money they collect. Yet people continue to give them a few rubles anyway? Why?" Sarah was getting to the point of her lesson. "It's because people *want* to believe that they are helping the gypsy girl. The truth – that in fact she is controlled by some group of thugs driving a Mercedes – is too difficult to really focus on. We are powerless to help her in that situation. We want to feel that we can *do* something. Therefore we focus on the illusion rather than the reality. The actual objective of helping the little girl is lost somewhere. In the end, appearances are far more powerful than reality. Even appearances that you know to be false."

Sarah really had reached a point of cynicism far deeper than my own. I battled through my daily challenges because I believed that somehow what we were doing actually mattered. All of the daily frustrations were worthwhile because in the end we were helping to improve the lives of even a few people around us. But clearly Sarah had lost confidence that even any benefit was being derived from our efforts. Or worse, perhaps our efforts were furthering the cause of those seeking to maintain control. Every move we made could be tightening the noose around the neck of the Russian people rather than releasing them.

"Some day you will fully understand," Sarah said cryptically in parting. "When it is your time to leave Russia, you will know."

With that Sarah gave me her parting gift – her *tapochki* for the *bannya*. Sarah's *tapochki!* This was a symbol of how entrenched into Russian life she had become over the past years and now she was putting it all behind her. She said she would not need them back in the United States. She would not be going to the *bannya* again. Back home life would resume some balanced normalcy. There would no longer be the need to find pleasure through pain.

I embraced my friend in a tearful farewell. She then turned and disappeared into the underground labyrinth of the Moscow Metro.

14 VODKA DIPLOMACY

June 1995 – Southern Russia

Of course one American who persisted in his efforts to force change in Russia was Joseph. He had been in Southern Russia for the better part of a year and nerves were now quite frayed on all sides. The true business consulting side of the project was more Raymond's area than mine, but still I heard enough in passing to know that Joseph had protested to Raymond that he was frustrated with the ability and efforts of the Local Privatization Center to deliver real consulting services to the enterprises in South Russia. Ivan Ivanovich, for his part, had lodged complaints against Joseph with the Mothership – the Russian Privatization Center in Moscow. His side of the story was that Joseph was antagonizing the local key enterprise managers and not being cooperative and supporting the LPC efforts as required.

With Joseph being the only English-speaker in Southern Russia and Raymond's Russian communication limited to "*da*" and "*spasibo*", all attempts to resolve the situation thus far had been via interpreters by phone between Raymond and the team in South Russia, with predictable lack of effectiveness. Raymond needed a fresh perspective for what was going on there. With core relationships on the line, the obvious solution was vodka-diplomacy.

This was my first trip to regional Russia where I was deliberately trying to create opportunities to have vodka-soaked evenings with the team. The objective of my trip was to get to the bottom of what was going on between Joseph and Ivan Ivanovich. I was experienced enough now in Russia to know that to achieve these objectives I would have to publicly script an entirely *different* set of goals for the trip. My stated goals would need to have plenty of excuses for excessive amounts of vodka with large amounts of frivolous company so that somewhere in the mix I would be able to derive what was really happening. A standard American manager would attack the objectives head on and set up meetings with Ivan Ivanovich and Joseph jointly and separately with the stated headline of identifying and resolving issues. I knew if I did that, there would be a high probability that Ivan Ivanovich conveniently would apologize that he had some medical emergency or other reason why he couldn't possibly even see me, needless to say share his real thoughts. Only by stating that I would be in South Russia for a completely *different* purpose did I have a chance of talking with him frankly.

Joseph, of course, would be ready to share his opinions with me, no matter what.

The official reasons for the visit were easy enough to compile. The renovations in all the offices were now complete, the computer equipment had finally been delivered and deployed – therefore I would be visiting with Nadya, our lead accountant, who would help to ensure that all the service contracts and documentation were as in place and computers secured per USAID requirements. In addition, my data collection project was now in full swing and I needed to check in on the six data collectors now scattered throughout South Russia working on documenting key facts and figures about recently privatized companies. Finally, I would bring along a fresh young new American manager in tow. Todd would be managing a new totally separate USAID project for Arthur Andersen. He had never been to Russia, nor spoke any Russian. It would be a good introductory experience for him to witness what happens on a Russian business trip before he would actually be expected to accomplish anything himself.

Todd was actually my key "bait" for the deeper agenda. In my experience to date, Russians could not resist an opportunity to parade their accomplishments and celebrate their successes – especially when there would be a fresh new American manager on hand. His presence would help to ensure that the attitude would be kept light and celebratory rather than perceived to be under deeper scrutiny.

On the flight Moscow to Rostov I watched Todd revel in his first Aeroflot flight. Details that had ceased to surprise me had Todd nearly leaping out of his skin with excitement. The labyrinth of Vnukovo airport and militsia patrolling with Kalashnikovs. The complete lack of signage or visible procedure at Vnukovo. Our inflight meal was distributed by three surly flight attendants – served from large plastic garbage bags. One flight attendant slapped down boiled chicken parts (cold), one gave us a can of beer (warm), and one offered a bag of Cheetos (printed in Hebrew).

Todd, being quite the American tourist, had to pull out his camera and take photos of his Aeroflot in flight meal. He was thoroughly entertained. Even the approach and landing into Rostov had him in high spirits. Per standard Russian procedure the plane landed nose first, rather than the Western traditional landing style of rear wheels first. The uninitiated are always certain that the plane is on the verge of crashing head first into the tarmac. Todd, however, was fascinated by the whole experience and punctuated everything with "Wow, did you see that?" I was glad. With the American managers you never knew whether they would recoil in horror when exposed to the raw edge of life in Russia or whether they would embrace it with a sense of adventure.

It was already apparent that Todd would be perfect for the role I assigned to him on this trip. (Although, of course, I did not advise him of my double agenda.)

The day in Rostov followed a pattern that I was all too familiar with, but Todd drank in with enthusiasm. First was the tour of the new office space. I lavished praise on Ivan Ivanovich for the successful completion of the renovations and rapid installation and configuration of all computer equipment. I pointed out details to Todd that he would never have otherwise noticed – Cyrillic keyboards on the computers, real phone jacks, extra phone lines for multiple dial up connections to the internet, surge suppressors, a laser printer, a copy/fax machine, and a PBX phone system – all with European power supplies. Ivan Ivanovich then opened a large wall cabinet and my stomach turned over.

"Look at these things the Americans think we need!" Ivan Ivanovich gestured to the contents of the cabinet. I was pleased, however, that he was referring to "the Americans" in the abstract rather than blaming me or anyone else specifically.

English language keyboards, American power supplies, English language software, letter size paper printer trays. An entire cabinet containing thousands of dollars of doo dads in their original packaging provided testimony to the ridiculous procurement exercise we had just been through. As everything needed to be US-sourced, the US-based suppliers were only able to provide European components as an *add on*, not *instead of* the American components. Nadya thanked Ivan Ivanovich for ensuring that everything was retained and organized. If there were an audit in the future, we would need to show the full inventory of everything that was purchased – including that which we knew we would never actually need.

"Joseph has been teaching the team how to use the computers," Ivan Ivanovich stated proudly.

And it did look like the Rostov office actually was using their computers. Not necessarily with confidence, but certainly a huge step forward from the equipment merely sitting as decorative objects wrapped in plastic.

Ivan Ivanovich then had to excuse himself for the rest of the day. Before his departure, however, he did ensure that my agenda was secured (with Todd in tow, of course). First, my lead data collector, Seryozh, would take us to visit one of the local privatized enterprises, a bicycle factory, so we could witness one of the data collection visits first hand. Then Seryozh would take us to meet with the LPC's service provider for the computer equipment configuration and servicing. Meanwhile, the office manager would show Nadya their filing systems to show how everything was organized and documented per USAID requirements.

"We will look at everything," Nadya smiled wryly. "Including all the documentation I know you have had forged, like the lease agreements without VAT and receipts for 'taxis.'" The office manager laughed. She and Nadya had laughed over the intricacies of USAID documentation requirements by phone for months. Now they were enjoying meeting each other in person.

Per the plan outlined by Ivan Ivanovich, we would all convene for the requisite vodka and dinner later. Ivan Ivanovich beamed at Seryozh. "Seryozh's contribution to the Rostov Local Privatization Center has been invaluable," he said with pride.

To my side I could see Joseph silently fuming. I would hear his side of the story later.

The rest of the day passed predictably enough. Seryozh was at ease with the chief accountant of the bicycle factory. They bantered as old friends, while the chief accountant flicked beads across her abacus and scribbled numbers on a piece of paper for us. Once we were handed over to the computer service provider, we did not set foot in an office, rather Todd and I were shuttled around Rostov for an impromptu tour of the various monuments of the City - to the Agrarian Heroes of the South, for the 25th Anniversary of the Tractor Combine Factory, and of course the mandatory Lenin statue striding purposefully to the great Soviet future.

The day was concluded with a dinner hosted by Ivan Ivanovich. Singers cooed in a minor key to a melancholy accordion. Rounds of vodka were poured. Toasts were made. Todd was totally enthusiastic (which I was counting on), keeping the mood light and festive. Nadya showed impressive fortitude with her ability to match the men round for round with the vodka shots. I noticed that Ivan Ivanovich and Joseph had placed themselves apart from each other at the table. Ivan Ivanovich's main attention was directed to Seryozh – who was seated strategically between Ivan Ivanovich and myself.

Joseph had brought a guest to the dinner to introduce to Todd and me – Noah, an American Peace Corps volunteer who was posted in South Russia. Noah was introduced by Joseph as having established great connections throughout the Rostov business community during his two years in Rostov. He was clearly at ease and happily chattering away in Russian with the Rostov office team. I casually asked Ivan Ivanovich who Noah was and his response was that "he, like all these Peace Corps people, are just in Rostov on holiday. They are not interested in actual work."

Todd's eyes were no longer focusing as he struggled to keep up the pace of vodka toasts at the table. And even if his eyes were focusing, I doubted that the newcomer would have really registered the various dynamics at the table. To the American this was just a novel dinner. But to me things were now clear. Russian dinners were much more than simply entertaining guests. This was where alliances were solidified and battle lines drawn.

In the morning Todd was visibly a little worse for wear. Nadya had pulled herself together immaculately, of course. I lacked the Russian *devushka* gene, therefore it definitely took effort on my part to appear to be presentable and functioning. Joseph was totally unaffected by the prior night's frivolities.

Todd, Nadya, Joseph, and I were now driving to Stavropol, with Krasnodar as a detour on the way. Ivan Ivanovich had protested that Krasnodar was a waste of our time. There was no reason for us to visit. I, however, did want to ensure that the nominal purpose of the visit was upheld. We would swing through Krasnodar just for a quick visit – long enough to just confirm the computer equipment and related files were all in order.

With Ivan Ivanovich back in Rostov and the driver unable to understand a word of English, the road trip offered ample opportunity for Joseph to deliver his rant to a captive audience. I sat back and listened, knowing that a free form rant would be the best way to hear exactly what was at the heart of his thoughts.

Joseph was incensed – *furious* – that I had been off to visit the bicycle factory the previous day. He had been struggling to get an appointment there for months but without success. And now, I just come to town and say I'd like to see what my data collectors have been doing and *whoosh* off to the factory the same day. Both Ivan Ivanovich and Seryozh had the connections in the city to make such appointments. Of course Seryozh had connections – he was the Mayor's nephew after all. They used their connections for my data collection project – which somehow had now achieved the purpose of a holy crusade for Ivan Ivanovich. But when Joseph would request an introduction to the very same enterprises for the purpose of introducing a consulting relationship *no* that was not possible.

He had tried then to spend more time in Krasnodar and Stavropol. But Ivan Ivanovich had complained bitterly when Joseph was out of the office. Why? It's not like he was able to visit any companies in Rostov! Might as well be useful in Krasnodar or Stavropol. Did I know that Joseph had only been to Krasnodar *once* in the past year since our visit last summer? That visit had raised such a fury with Ivan Ivanovich that Joseph had felt compelled to return to Rostov the following day.

"So what is it that Ivan Ivanovich expects you to do?" I could no longer contain my questions.

"Oh the usual," sighed Joseph. "Drink vodka and put on a happy face when delegations from Moscow come through. Make appearances at key events with the title of 'American Advisor to South Russia.' But heaven forbid I actually want to *do* anything. I am actually reprimanded when I make a connection on my own to an enterprise director – not following correct protocol! But now that the computer equipment has arrived, Ivan Ivanovich expects me to provide all the training to the office staff for how to use MS Word and Excel and how to replace the toner in the printer. *Me.* A senior paid expatriate advisor providing training to the team here for how to use a mouse properly."

And Ivan Ivanovich's comments about the Peace Corps volunteers being on "holiday"? This question set Joseph's rant off to a new level – it was another example of how Ivan Ivanovich wanted to control everyone's actions in the region. Noah's projects were not directly controlled by the LPC, therefore his efforts were simply dismissed by Ivan Ivanovich as being irrelevant and frivolous. Russians know what is best for Russian companies! Consultants are not needed, just give us American money! Joseph's rant continued unabated for the next several hours until we reached the Krasnodar offices.

Although Ivan Ivanovich was averse to Krasnodar, our local host, Anton, was thrilled to escort our team through his offices. The same skanky concrete office building that I had visited a year before – a building that could have existed in any Russian city. Concrete walls, erratic lighting, thin hollow doors with handles that did not quite work properly. Anton led us down the gritty corridor and our shoes made soft sandpaper noises. With a grand sweep of his arms he indicated his door – an impenetrable steel fortress of a door. My eyes darted from the dozens of identical dilapidated Soviet-era plywood doors to the imposing steel barrier. What was going on here.

"I take my responsibilities very seriously," Anton advised us. "We have been entrusted with computers. If we do not take security measures, they will be stolen. The Chechens, you know, are everywhere in Southern Russia."

Inside the office we entered a different world. Not exactly a western modern office, but more a Russian bureaucrat's vision of a modern office. The floor plan followed the standard Soviet era plan of three rooms – a small reception and secretarial area in the middle, then an executive office to one side and a large common staff office to the other. Anton gestured for us to enter the large staff office space.

The room was dominated by a massive conference table – which could have seated twenty people or so. Black lacquer with gold trim and set off by a matching aircraft-carrier sized desk at the head of the table. The classic Soviet plan for an executive office – the only conference tables were in executive offices, therefore no substantial meetings could take place without the knowledge of the manager. The walls were plastered and painted white – in a poor chalky paint that was already disintegrating into dust. Dust that was falling onto a red pile carpet that extended wall to wall. The overall effect was nothing short of garish. Despite this, the fit out and furnishings would have cost an absolute fortune – funded by US taxpayers in the name of privatization.

The computer equipment was all neatly organized in the empty room, presented meticulously in the original plastic wrap. Placed next to each mummified computer was a small cactus plant. Every computer, even the laptops, was bolted with massive steel cables to the conference table. The scene would have made a sensational still life art exhibition by some disturbed modern artist.

Anton beamed with pride at our astonished faces. "Yes, aren't the offices wonderful?" He stood a bit taller and swept his arms across the room. "These offices are without a doubt the best offices in Krasnodar. The furniture was shipped in from Hungary and the carpeting came from Turkey. We have such a great reputation in Krasnodar now that we have these renovations complete."

Reputation. Yes. So what work has this office accomplished to give it such a reputation? The Americans were curious.

Anton shook his head and corrected us. No, actually the project work is only now just starting. You see, with the expense of the renovations Anton was unable to afford to hire any staff consultants to work with him. Therefore the office staff consisted just of himself and his secretary and his driver. But with these fantastic offices and this wonderful computer equipment he now has a great reputation and will be able to host all of the luminary executives in town!

Anton was so pleased with his accomplishments and fished for compliments. Look at these fabulous offices! He had a fantastic reputation in Krasnodar. And he managed to come at his budget for total expenses for the year. Wasn't it smart to hold back from hiring staff consultants? That surely would have put him over budget. The three Americans exchanged anxious glances in bewilderment. Mercifully our mandate was simply to channel funding and provide a foreign advisor for the region. The head office for the Russian Privatization Center in Moscow vigorously argued against any involvement from us in operational management. Our duty was simply to ensure that expenditures were made according to proper USAID sourcing practices, not whether the operations of the LPC were actually effective. Coming in under budget for the year by virtue of having no operational staff may be exemplary management performance in the alternate reality of Soviet practices, but we would have difficulty justifying the situation to any American observer. As ridiculous as the scene was, it still complied with what USAID expected us to do in the region. However, if we had interfered with Anton's plans, that would have been outside of our mandate – and would have certainly provoked the wrath of the Russian Privatization Center to complain to USAID that the American consultants were acting outside their authority.

Just another day working on our aid project. The frustration to American sensibilities left us speechless. Joseph so vigorously wanted to support the cause of bringing in foreign investment to Southern Russia, but he had no control over the management of the privatization center's operations. This was the sort of team he was forced to work with – a manager that values office renovations over operational staff and who does not see even the slightest paradox in the decision.

Early the next morning, with a smile and a wave and a kiss on the cheek for Nadya and myself, Anton bid farewell to us and we continued onwards to Stavropol. "Be careful of the Chechens!" Anton warned us with a smile. A standard farewell in the area, it seemed. The conflict was several hundred miles away, but the Russian loathing of the Chechen people permeated the air in Krasnodar. The Chechens could not be trusted. They were all criminals. They must be kept under control so that civilized society could continue in peace.

We motored across the countryside from Krasnodar towards Stavropol and our driver ranted on about the Chechens as well. The theme continued that the Chechens were essentially untrustworthy people and must be kept in their place. This entire conflict was unnecessary – as soon as the Chechens recognized the authority of the Russian government, everything would return to normal. Nadya joined the conversation and told the driver about my attack in the streets of Moscow a few months earlier – attacked by a group of Chechens. Yes, they were Chechens, I confirmed upon cross-examination from the driver. But just because the men who attacked me were Chechen did not indict an entire nation, I protested.

To the driver, however, it was yet more evidence that the Chechens must be controlled. And look at what happens when they get out of Chechnya! What were they doing in Moscow anyway? They should stay in Chechnya.

A moment later more irrefutable evidence presented itself that Chechens were nothing but savages. (Irrefutable to the Russians at least.) A news broadcast came on the radio that a group of Chechens had invaded the town of Budyonnovsk and had taken an entire hospital and its 1,800 plus occupants hostage. Budyonnovsk? The driver turned up the volume of the radio and the passengers fell silent. Todd, the only non-Russian speaker in the car, begged us to explain what was going on in the news that had silenced the whole car.

Budyonnovsk was about 200 kilometers away from our destination, Stavropol – and represented a significant shift north for the action. For the first time the front line of military conflict had moved from the Chechen territory into another state – the Stavropol Krai, where we were now going. Russian military were being dispatched to the region and gunfire was heard in the background of the news report. A hostage situation on a grand scale. The driver was outraged and gestured violently at the radio in protest. One man's terrorist is the next man's freedom fighter, I attempted to argue. But the driver and Nadya would hear nothing of it. The Chechens must be exterminated. They were evil. Here was more proof.

Upon our arrival in Stavropol we were greeted by a formidable barrier of Russian tanks. A team of gruff soldiers inspected our vehicle and waved us on after pausing with interest to note that three of us carried American passports.

At our hotel we were greeted by Viktor, the director of the Stavropol office of the Local Privatization Center, and the rest of the privatization center staff. We were also "greeted" (if that is the right word for it) by a formidable squadron of men dressed in black uniforms and carrying Kalashnikovs. Nadya visibly recoiled at seeing the men in black and took a defensive position shielded by Viktor. "OMON," she whispered. Slowly I recalled Vanya's visible nerves at seeing the OMON at the Fourth of July Picnic the previous year. Nadya gave me a meaningful look.

It took me a few moments to really fully registered Nadya's angst. In this land where the elite could write their own rules, the OMON were the elite of the military special forces. They were well armed, well-trained and accountable to – just about no one. The afternoon of the attack in Budyonnovsk the OMON had decided that their mission was to protect the main hotel in Stavropol. Today they were on our side, at least. We hoped.

Todd, the American tourist, fortunately was wise enough to realize that it would not be a good idea to photograph the OMON guarding the hotel.

Viktor made an effort to laugh and casually brush aside the OMON and the tanks rumbling through the streets. The afternoon was still young, but he had decided that all business appointments for the day were cancelled. And certainly it was unwise for three Americans to stay at the main hotel in Stavropol. Just imagine if the Chechens advanced and attempted to take hostages at the hotel here in Stavropol. Yes, the OMON were there, but their main concern would be eradication of the Chechens, not protection of any hotel residents. The situation was bad enough with 1,800 Russians held hostage in Budyonnovsk. But if Americans were held hostage by the terrorists – or worse, killed in cross-fire with the OMON – this whole situation would rapidly escalate into becoming an international catastrophe.

Viktor had resolved the situation in true Russian style. The best solution would be for all of us to retreat to a dacha out in the woods – with enough food and vodka to keep all of us occupied until the threat had been reduced. There was no chance to argue with Viktor. He had decided and everything was arranged. The dacha was apparently provided by the mayor's office to our team. It was owned by some government agency, so the mayor allocated the use of it according to political favors that needed repayment. At least that was my conclusion. The Russians always kept the details deliberately vague regarding how the logistics worked for these sorts of arrangements.

In any case, we did make the most of it. The first bottle of vodka was opened around three pm. A fish soup was produced. And fish pie. Plus meat salads with overwhelming amounts of mayonnaise. And cucumbers, tomatoes and yet more bits of meat. Wonderful salty cheese bread – xachapuri – which was my favorite part of South Russian and Georgian cuisine. Plus of course glistening caviar – with fresh creamy butter and bread freshly baked that morning. The vodka flowed freely and someone brought a portable tape player with somewhat damaged speakers. The sound system blared to the best of its abilities and the group danced and sang and celebrated perhaps our last night on earth before the Chechens overran Stavropol and shot all the residents.

I have read in social history books how people in war zones tend to celebrate with a fervor that can never be equaled in peaceful times. The raw abandon that accompanies a sudden awareness of our own mortality and a question of whether we really have lived life to the fullest. Then suddenly a desire to see everything, do everything, experience everything now. Now is all that matters. The present moment. For tomorrow may never come.

Bottle after bottle of vodka were drained. The carcasses piled up on the ground. Bad luck to leave bottles on a table. The dancing continued. The party was partly to celebrate the 50th birthdays of two of the team — Ekaterina and Viktor. Joseph vigorously raised toasts to their health. Additional toasts and shots of vodka were volleyed in return. I sought refuge by slipping under a picnic table and passing out for a few blissful moments (or hours). It seemed to be a sensible choice of location at the time, as the table protected me from the stomping dancing feet.

A champagne cork popped — accompanied by a delighted scream from the crowd. Viktor and Ekaterina decided to switch clothing. Viktor's polyester blend green coat and wide striped tie somehow looked okay on Ekaterina. But Ekaterina's brown floral dress could not button up over the round Buddha bulge of Viktor's belly. Ekaterina offered to switch back to her own clothing, but Viktor was content in just his Speedo-style undies. The night was clear and warm and I drifted in and out of consciousness, vaguely aware of an over-sized 50 year old Russian government official dancing nearby wearing nothing but shocking red bikini underwear.

The night was spectacular. A nearby pond beckoned and people stripped in a frenzy and ran into the pond with squeals and shrieks. Todd found me under the picnic table and poured a bowl of the frigid pond water on my face. What was I doing under the table passed out? I should be swimming in the pond with everyone else!

How delicious. I floated on my back at attempted to focus my eyes on the stars and the moon. Our revelry echoed through the nearby forest. What a wonderful release. We were stressed, tightly wound, and now we were letting it all out in one decadent night. Nadya swam slowly to my side. Her smile beamed through the night.

"So this is what happens on business trips," she was breathless. "I definitely need to go to business school so that I can do more business trips." She rolled onto her back and gently splashed the surface of the pond, contemplating the night sky and the years ahead of her.

Joseph overheard Nadya's comments and laughed bitterly. "Oh if Nadya thinks that this is a normal business trip, then I have even more work to do in Russia than I had anticipated!" He then turned and swam away from us with a few powerful strokes into the black night.

This was Nadya's first business trip. This was her idea of what business trips were like. I opened my mouth to try to explain that Joseph was right - no, this was not normal. But then I paused. Normal. What was normal anyway? All the objectives of my trip had been achieved without a single set of photocopied and stapled handouts. A city patrolled by tanks and a vodka-infused evening at a dacha made a lot more sense at this moment than the prospect of sitting under florescent lighting sternly pointing at a chart of sales forecasts.

I looked at Nadya's face, smiling and peaceful while Joseph muttered to himself somewhere out in the darkness. Joseph was frustrated that he was being asked to provide training on basic computer skills while his American insights of operational efficiency and budget management were ignored. Nadya, however, was an intelligent, insightful accountant who was amused rather than furious as she calmly did her part to comply with the madness of USAID procurement and documentation requirements and Anton's crazy operational decisions. Why get worked up over that which is beyond our control? The Russian reality did not have monthly sales targets, rigorous uptight HR policies, or formal meeting agendas. But who really wants such things anyway? Russians were going about progress in their own way. And normal would have to be redefined.

"I have to agree," I finally responded as I floated alongside Nadya. "This is a typical Russian business trip. Isn't it fantastic?"

15 HEAT WAVE

June 1995 — Moscow

Just when I thought that nothing else could possibly surprise me, a heat wave hit Moscow. Yes, a real stretch of weather that could be categorized not as warm, but *hot*. In the land of the seemingly endless winter I never would have believed such a thing to be possible. Yet sweltering amidst evidence to the contrary in my office in Moscow, it very clearly was.

In the spring, our project had outgrown the offices in Chistiye Prudi and we relocated near Park Kulturi. From the outside, our new building looked like it had just barely survived an intense air raid. Most of the windows were broken and a whole section of the exterior walls were missing around the eighth through tenth floors. Our offices were higher — on the eleventh floor. You could tell from the outside of the building where our offices were because it was the only floor where all of the windows were intact.

Every morning when I reached my desk I was greeted by a thick film of green sludgy dust. My morning routine now began with a brief wipe down of all surfaces on my desk and computer. I tried not to think of the green slime. If this amount of gunk accumulated on the desk each night, what exactly was filling my lungs each day?

The floor plan followed the modern western tradition of the 1950s — one long corridor down the middle, with rooms behind closed doors to each side. Renovations to prepare for our arrival had included modernization of the electrical and phone wiring, but the budget had not allowed for removal of interior walls to create a larger open space. Mercifully the exterior wall was mostly glass, so the closed in space was lightened by what natural light that was able to penetrate the green slime on the windows.

Well, there was natural light until the new cubicles arrived. The offices at Chistiye Prudi at least had a large interior space with high ceilings. The cubicles, while foreign, were grudgingly accepted. Here at Park Kulturi the team referred to the cubicles as "chicken coops," and they had a point. The six foot high burgundy fabric walls barricaded each of the girls into dark cells of solitary confinement.

The lack of natural light was already making the team edgy. The heat wave threatened to make them surly. Of course the building did not have air conditioning – who would ever need air conditioning in Moscow? The sludge covered wall of glass faced south, so predictably the interior space heated up like a greenhouse. The situation was rapidly deteriorating from unpleasant to tortuous. The only things that enjoyed the heat were the cacti. Each of the Russian girls had placed cacti on their desks near their computer monitors. They were convinced that this would counterbalance dangerous radiation that was rumored to be emitted from the computer monitors. At least the cacti brightened up the sterile office space a bit – and they actually thrived in the heat of the office.

As the heat wave continued, we did what we could to survive and continue functioning in the office. Raymond handed Vanya an envelope full of cash and instructed him to find some fans – or anything else that would help to keep the office cool. I tossed aside formal business attire and pulled sundresses out from the back of my closet. Even sandals were too confining and I started to go barefoot in the office. I encouraged my team to dress for comfort as well.

Nadya, the unofficial ringleader of the office *devushki*, arrived at the office one day wearing a beach holiday dress. After a brief "good morning" she pulled a number of tools from her handbag and began to quietly disassemble her cubicle with focus and determination. The intensity with which she worked told me that that it would be pointless to argue with her. If disassembling the cubicles would help to keep peace in the office while we lived in a pressure-cooker, so be it. Oksana and Marina also appeared wearing flowing breezy summer dresses. They seemed to have been tipped off about the cubicle revolt and pulled out their own tools to assist with the demolition. Tatiana arrived next, carrying a large bundle of dry cleaning that she had organized for me. In one of her moments of Tatiana-style initiative, she had decided to remove all the buttons from my clothing before it was sent to the cleaners (as a precaution, so that the cleaners wouldn't have a chance to lose the buttons themselves). Now she sat with focus sewing each button back into its proper place.

A new girl, Natasha, had recently joined the team. She now bounced into the office, wearing a Raggedy Ann costume – a blue starched skirt with petticoats and held up by blue suspenders. The costume was complete with red yarn braided throughout her hair and stage paint freckles and rosy cheeks. Natasha paused for a moment frozen by the stares of disbelief from her senior colleagues.

"Oh," she gasped timidly. "I thought you said today was a *costume* day."

Of course I had said *casual* day. How she interpreted that as *costume* day, I have no idea. Oh well. Raggedy Ann slid meekly into her chicken coop, probably pleased that the six foot high burgundy walls were shielding her from further scrutiny.

Vanya returned from his shopping expedition armed with a collection of fans and extension cords. He watched Nadya, Oksana, and Marina struggling to dismember their cubicles and provided commentary that the reason why Russian women don't drive is that they don't know how to use tools properly. What would any of them do if their car broke down somewhere? Clearly none of them knew how to use a wrench. How would they ever repair an engine?

Nadya hissed some profanities at Vanya that were beyond my level of Russian comprehension. He then backed off from the girls' mission and started his own project — building a cobweb of extension cords, cubicle parts, and fans.

The girls were now buzzing with energy and purpose and motion as they disassembled the cubicles, mended my jackets, and organized the office. Then suddenly, as if on cue, they all came to a stop and their gaze latched onto an unfamiliar young man who stood in our doorway. The newcomer had the body and structured cheekbones of an Armani model. He wore a simple white cotton business shirt - unbuttoned just a bit too far for what would be appropriate in the office. He stood quietly and scanned the room with pale blue eyes. Siberian Husky eyes. Siberia.

Oh. He really was Siberian. It took me minute to recognize Alyosha, the team leader for my group of data collectors in Krasnoyarsk. What was he doing here in my office rather than back home in Krasnoyarsk, thousands of miles away?

Alyosha's eyes lit up with recognition. He quickly moved to embrace me and plant firm kisses on each cheek. He then recoiled involuntarily and fluttered his shirt against his chest to cool off. The heat of the body contact was just too much for such a steamy day. After the necessary round of introductions, six pairs of eyes followed us intensely as I pulled a chair to my desk and gestured to Alyosha to sit down.

In a serious conversation, Russians remove all physical barriers that may be perceived to inhibit communication. Alyosha purposefully slid his chair around my desk to be close at my side. He leaned forward in an effort to have a private conversation in this very public place. His glassy blue eyes were riveting.

Alyosha had taken a few days holiday to visit the big city of Moscow. On impulse he had decided to come to our offices. He was perhaps the most intense and dedicated of my data collectors. The fact that he was taking time out from his holiday to come into the office just served to reinforce this view with me further.

I had first met Alyosha in Krasnoyarsk about a month prior. As per standard practice that I had come to accept, when we were ready to begin the data collection effort in Krasnoyarsk, the Director of the Local Privatization Center had simply presented me with a list of names of who I should hire — with an asterisk by Alyosha as the proposed team leader. The primary dependency for success with the team was always good local political connections. The Directors of the LPCs understood this implicitly and never failed to round up an impressive assortment of relatives of the local political and business elite. My role in the hiring process was reduced to simply ensuring that the paperwork showed that we had considered a valid list of candidates. To maintain a shred of the illusion that it was my team, I still interviewed all the candidates. I would then cast a veto vote against the nominee in each region that seemed most likely to treat the role as a Right rather than as an Opportunity.

At first I worried that hiring a team of sixty young kids across five time zones, whose main qualification was their parents' pedigree, would be a cause for endless strife – verging on babysitting rather than managing. (I say young kids, although realistically they were probably my age or, at most, a year or two younger than me. I just was starting to feel a bit battle worn – therefore everyone looked like young kids to me.) Then, it rapidly became clear that almost without exception every one of these young kids was acutely aware that they were being given an astonishing opportunity – and they were not going to waste it.

Alyosha was even more intense than most with his gratitude and dedication to his new role. Opportunities abounded in Moscow, but in Krasnoyarsk change was coming more slowly. Now here was an opportunity to gain experience working with a real American company, learning how to use a computer, and helping to lay the foundation for future foreign investment to his capital-starved home town. When I hired Alyosha (or, more accurately, confirmed his nomination), he swore with sincere devotion that he would do "Anything, absolutely anything" that I asked.

He had also witnessed in Krasnoyarsk as I told a young *devushka* that she would not be confirmed for the role of data collector. She wailed and sobbed that her young life was over. Never again could she possibly dream of earning so much money on her own. The position would have paid 300 USD per month for a fixed contract of six months.

I bit my lip and reflected that back in the USA there were people protesting that these USAID contracts were paying the Russians less than 5% what their American counterparts were earning. Exploitation to pay so little, some would say. If this was exploitation, then why was the daughter of a local politician in tears that she was *denied* such a role?

Alyosha's approach to his work was definitely from the angle of deep commitment rather than resigned exploitation. The first order of business in Krasnoyarsk (like in each region) was to ensure that the word was spread quickly about the data collection project and the local enterprises were all rallied to participate. The regions I had worked in to date all had close ties to Moscow, therefore if the Director of the Local Privatization Center was unable to generate sufficient support himself, the full weight of the Russian Privatization Center from Moscow would step in. It is a directive from Moscow – therefore it will be followed. Old ways die hard.

Krasnoyarsk, however, was in the peripheral vision of the Russian Privatization Center, if within view at all. A lot could go on in Siberia with very few people in Moscow knowing what was happening out there. And vice versa. The LPC in Krasnoyarsk was funded by USAID through a different consultancy, therefore the western advisor there, Carl, had no formal ties to Arthur Andersen. He took my calls as a professional courtesy, but clearly he had no reason to go out of his way to support my project. The Director of the LPC, having secured jobs for the children of his various friends, had no further real interest either.

As a result of all these factors, interest from the local enterprises to participate in the data collection project was virtually non-existent. The Director of the LPC was going through the motions of organizing a kickoff event to formally launch the data collection (it was part of what had been formally agreed with the RPC for the project), but Alyosha was concerned that the upcoming event did not have the level of buzz necessary to really invigorate the enterprises to participate. He wanted to take the promotion of the launch event beyond the standard word of mouth between political connections. He wanted the local media involved as well.

Oh no, not the media. After an encounter with the media in Kazakhstan over a year earlier I had hoped that I never would have to turn to them again. Engaging the local journalists would not be a matter of just providing a press release and a compelling interview. There would undoubtedly be an expectation that we would provide funding as well.

A moment later Alyosha confirmed my fears.

He had already taken the initiative to reach out to the local newspaper in Krasnoyarsk. A journalist there had agreed to run a story promoting the data collection and kickoff event – *if* he received payment for his efforts. It wasn't clear whether the payment was requested for the newspaper or to the journalist directly. In any case, the answer was still the same.

"Sorry, but no." I had to tell Alyosha. "The limit of what we are authorized to fund for this project are the salaries of the data collectors and their immediate expenses for computers, travel, etc. Promotional expenses are out of scope."

Alyosha was melting in the heat. His white shirt was now clinging to his body. Despite this, he took my hand in his sweaty palm and pleaded with me. Oh, how I wanted to say yes to those gorgeous blue eyes. But there just was no way that I could provide funding for the newspaper article.

Alyosha paused for a moment in reflection. "But you could come out to Krasnoyarsk to be at our launch?" he noted.

Yes, I could. In fact, I was due for a return visit, as the data collectors had been hired about a month ago and I needed to go back and see how everyone was going. The timing could be arranged to coincide with the launch event.

"Excellent!" Alyosha was delighted and impulsively leaned closer and placed an affectionate kiss on my cheek.

I was suddenly aware of a new pair of eyes scrutinizing the scene.

A tall man wearing an immaculate pressed blue suit and perfectly shined shoes stood in the doorway to the room that housed my team. He had neatly trimmed hair and a crisp knotted tie. I had never met him, but it was easy to figure out who he was – a Senior Partner from the Washington DC office of Arthur Andersen. An American from the Mothership. Now here in Moscow to check in on us.

Time stood still as the Senior Partner took in the scene. The sundresses. The bare feet. Cacti placed throughout the room. The red yarn braided through Natasha's hair. Tatiana sewing buttons on my jacket. Vanya still creating a cobweb of extension cords and fans across semi-demolished cubicles. He had no doubt also noticed Alyosha's exposed sweaty chest and the kiss that would never have been appropriate in the DC office. The Senior Partner ran one finger along a dismembered cubicle part and looked at the resulting green slime on his finger with a barely concealed grimace.

I leaped from my chair to introduce myself and my team, but I could tell from the look on his face that it was too late. He had already reached his conclusions about our team. We were obviously running wild.

Just when I thought the situation could not deteriorate further, Todd passed by in the corridor. He beamed with delight when he saw me standing with the Senior Partner.

"James!" Todd exclaimed. "Hey, glad you made it to the office okay. Have you met Phaedra? She's the one I was telling you about over dinner last night. She led the trip a few weeks ago where we all were drinking vodka shots and skinny dipping in South Russia during the hostage crisis."

Todd's enthusiasm was genuine and innocent. James paused and looked at me again – and obviously still aware of the slime on his finger. He muttered some pleasantries to the team and then turned to Todd and asked where he could find Raymond.

I watched the retreating figures with despair and then quickly wrapped up my discussion with Alyosha. Yes, I will see you soon. Now get back to your holiday! Aren't you supposed to be in Moscow on vacation?

Raymond's total unwavering confidence in me was the only thing that kept me from being fired on the spot by James – or at least that was my impression of how the day was going.

I had returned from South Russia with exactly the information he was looking for.

It was very simple really. Ivan Ivanovich was appointed to his role as Director of the South Russia LPC by the Russian Privatization Center in Moscow. He was a political appointee. As such, his allegiances were with the RPC in Moscow. Nothing else mattered other than his political position and how to maintain it. Ivan Ivanovich supported the data collection project because it had been mandated by Moscow. Whether or not he believed in it was irrelevant. Moscow had decreed the project. Therefore Ivan Ivanovich would show that he would support the requests of the center.

Joseph, however, had no such allegiance. He very purely and sincerely wanted to provide consulting services to the local privatized enterprises. The stated long term goal of the USAID engagement was to create self-sustaining consulting centers throughout Russia. Real consulting centers with real clients. Joseph earnestly wanted to make that vision a reality. To do so, however, required real clients.

This was outside the scope of specific instructions that had been delivered to date from Moscow to Ivan Ivanovich. Therefore why would he do anything to support Joseph's outreach to build a real client base? If such consulting engagements were successful, then this would be perceived to be a threat to the authority in Moscow — actions had been taken without their express directive. If such consulting engagements were negatively received, then this would be even worse — negatively impacting the reputation of the LPC to the enterprises in the surrounding region and weakening the ability of the RPC to implement further centrally mandated projects.

The best course of action for Ivan Ivanovich was to smile and take delegations out for dinner. Upon request from Moscow he would act, but until then it was all about maintaining pleasant relationships.

After watching the dynamics in South Russia, the situation there was totally obvious (to me at least). Joseph would be tolerated as long as he remained useful for Ivan Ivanovich. This meant smiling on command at dinners and providing MS Word training to the staff. If he did anything to challenge Ivan Ivanovich's authority or aggravate his reputation with the local enterprise directors, his days would be numbered. My perspective was scconded (unsolicited) by Nadya. Todd's version of the trip to Southern Russia was that we had some absolutely fantastic dinner parties.

Raymond had trusted my judgment and said he would provide guidance to ask Joseph to back down (if that were possible) until a central mandate for consulting services could be channeled more clearly.

And now I anxiously stared at Raymond's closed door as he was in conference with James. Hopefully he was prepared to stand to my defense against whatever charges the Senior Partner would certainly file.

I received my answer later that day. After James had left, Raymond called me down to his office and closed the door. No, James was not impressed by the level of professionalism he saw in the office. In fact, he was concerned that the Arthur Andersen brand name was even associated with our operations at all.

Raymond had spent considerable effort attempting to explain that our situation was not exactly like typical Arthur Andersen offices. He should know — he had been made partner in 1967 and therefore could claim more experience than pretty much any other living member of the firm. Although Raymond was now retired and nominally a contractor for the engagement, he still commanded significant respect within the organization. As such, he was able to negotiate an agreeable truce with James.

The general terms were disarmingly simple. A team of internal auditors from the Arthur Andersen offices in Washington DC would be sent to Moscow to comb through our operations. And I would be sent to St Charles — to Arthur Andersen manager training camp.

Although I told myself that I should be elated by this outcome, I had a premonition that the worst was yet to come.

16 GLORY TO THE HEROES OF OUR INDUSTRIAL FUTURE

July 1995

Rumors travelled fast. Within a day, Paul had called me from his office in St Petersburg and chanted in a robotic voice "You-will-be-as-sim-il-at-ed."

Oh, Paul. Just shut up. Yes, the Arthur Andersen training camp in St Charles had that reputation. You come in as individuals – you leave as Arthur Androids. But still, I wanted my career with Arthur Andersen to extend beyond an expatriate assignment in Russia. I *wanted* to be accepted some day in a US-based office. The St Charles training session was one step in that direction. The question plagued me, however, whether they would want me.

And then there was the not-so-small matter of the auditors. I have always been one to take my work just a bit too personally. From my hyper-sensitive perspective, the looming invasion of the auditors would be not just a routine check of the Russian operations for Arthur Andersen's USAID projects, but would call into question all the accomplishments and efforts of my team over the past year.

So now the agenda for the next month was set. First to Krasnoyarsk to support Alyosha and the launch of the data collection efforts in Central Siberia. Then to Chicago for a week of Arthur Andersen indoctrination/training – together with a few of the Russian managers from the main accounting practice in Moscow. I would return back to Moscow just prior to the arrival of the auditors – and then… Who could possibly predict what would happen once the auditors landed.

A crash of cultures was about to happen. I feared that I was about to be crushed in the middle.

Internal audit, by definition, are people who live for the rules. The rules are not options. They are, after all, rules not suggestions. The rules are set out in the United States by Americans for Americans, following standards that are generally accepted by Americans. Principles of integrity and clarity and documentation are quite sensible and the basic premise of these rules is certainly widely accepted.

Internal audit's activities are based upon the assumption of an orderly business environment. You get coherent quotes for services in writing, you sign contracts, you make payments based upon receipt of goods and an invoice. Staff are paid directly into their bank accounts and petty cash is wired to remote office accounts. Business is quite structured and is conducted in a predictable manner.

By now anyone paying attention to my rambling diatribe must start to become vaguely aware of a few points. A) Russia and Russians did not exactly follow standard western business practices, but yet B) We were working on US government contracts which mandate compliance with basic western business practices. Nearly all of the companies working on US government contracts in Russia were awarded additional contracts periodically (my company included). Therefore from the perspective of the US government we must have complied with the basic points of western business practices, right? Certainly the government would review the performance of its contractors before awarding additional multi-million dollar contracts. Being awarded additional contracts over the years must therefore be a proxy for a stamp of approval from the US government that we were complying with their purchasing and contract management guidelines.

But really, how was that even possible? Take a look at the last trip to southern Russia. The funds of US taxpayers had covered a glorious fit out of an office in Krasnodar, but no staff. We had to pay an additional handful of cash to our driver to take us from Krasnodar to Stavropol in the midst of a civil war. We stopped for petrol along the way at a tanker truck on the side of the road and handed over another handful of cash. The hotel was perceived to be too dangerous and therefore we spent the night at a government dacha on the outskirts of town. Exactly how do we appropriately document these expenses for the purpose of US government procurement compliance?

In the absence of taxis, I would hitchhike to the airport – negotiating a price with the random guy who stopped on the street to pick me up. On a train, if I received too many direct stares while boarding, then I would slip $10 to the *dezhurnaya* and ask her to ensure that no one disturbed me. A "service fee" I would note on my expense claim. No receipt, of course. It was simply the way Russia worked. If we were to actually get anything done, then we would turn to Volodya, our "fixer" on staff to take care of the unsavory errands – he would ensure that I had a seat on a flight when absolutely necessary – despite the fact that Aeroflot had said that the flight is full. Just an "administrative charge."

Ah yes. Those "service fees" and "administrative charges". How many things did I note to that category on my expense claims? There really was no other way, unfortunately. And really, where did the line end between legitimate service fees and bribes? Don't Americans on business in the United States tip taxi drivers and waiters and porters? To ensure service. To ensure your bags are delivered to your room at all. And what is the difference between a tip and a bribe anyway? The term "tip" just sounds more legitimate.

How would internal audit possibly understand that we were not operating in a western business environment and therefore western documentation and business practices were not possible? How would they cope if a massive tax penalty was imposed on every wire transfer so that petty cash funds in regional offices were virtually impossible? What if employee expenses for travel were taxed as income? What if there was hyperinflation, so the value of the petty cash fund vanished overnight? What if employees had to be hired on a permanent basis and there were no legal options for hiring contractors? What if you had to provide a computer to a particular non-employee just to ensure that you received the necessary level of government cooperation to continue your business? The list was virtually endless. Just to manage to operate, the edges of clean business practices started to get a bit frayed. Then you started to realize that certain activities would be even easier if you just frayed the edges a bit more. Full legal compliance was never an option, but at what point down the slippery slope of the grey area were you able to put on the brakes and try to reclaim some state of business normalcy.

On my trip to Krasnoyarsk, I contemplated my every action through a new perspective. No driver was available to take me to the airport, so I hitchhiked and paid $20 cash to some stranger. No receipt, of course. En route to Domodedovo airport we were stopped randomly by the GAI – just to extract a few thousand rubles as a "fine" with some "safety hazard" on the car cited as the nominal reason. How would I record that on my expense claim? The process changed yet again at Domodedovo that week and I had to get a stamp on my ticket for a few dollars fee, for no obvious reason. Was this a legitimate expense or yet another bribe? Difficult to differentiate at times.

Alyosha met me at the Krasnoyarsk airport with a formal embrace and proper kiss on the cheek as a greeting. His reserved manner here compared to our last encounter took me by surprise. I didn't have to wait long, however, for my answer. While still in the concrete shell of the terminal, he thrust a newspaper into my hands with great agitation and excitement. Look here, you must read this immediately.

There, on page one of the local paper, was the fantastic headline "American spy arrives in Krasnoyarsk." I glanced at the headline and turned back to Alyosha with bewilderment. "Who is the American spy and why are you so agitated about it?"

"Keep reading," Alyosha gestured to me urgently.

The article stated in severe alarmist tones that an American spy, under the auspices of a so-called "foreign assistance" program, was collecting strategically sensitive information about Russian business and the military-industrial complex on behalf of the American government. Okay. Yes, it was starting to sink in. The article did have the basics of my project correct – I was leading a data collection effort on Russian privatized companies. The stated purpose of the project was to make more information available to potential foreign investors. Of course, since the US government was behind the effort, any number of assumptions could be made about the project's unstated objectives.

So this is what the local newspaper decided to publish in regards to our project. They had asked Alyosha to provide "funding" for the article. The funding had been refused. This is the article that ensued. Would the article have been different if we had agreed to provide the requested payment? I could only speculate. And I laughed at the Catch-22 situation I was now in – Option 1: make a payment to the newspaper and then need to justify myself to the auditors, or Option 2: don't make a payment to the newspaper and be labeled as an "American Spy" and need to justify myself to my own project team and everyone else who we attempted to work with as well.

I turned from the newspaper to Alyosha – who was now looking at me with a combination of fear and excitement. "So, are you really an American spy?"

Of course, the conversation had to continue over dinner and alcohol. (Mercifully the choice that night was local beer rather than vodka.) Alyosha was the most passionate of my data collection team leads. He had accepted the job offer based upon my explanation that this data collection exercise would help to bring foreign investment and economic opportunity to his home town of Krasnoyarsk. Alyosha was young and educated and idealistic and he was a joy to work with. But now his world had been thrown into disarray. He thought he was working for the bright Russian future, but now perhaps he had been duped into providing unwitting assistance to American espionage operations.

Alyosha ordered us another round of beer. His black polyester-blend suit jacket sat badly on his shoulders – rumpled up and shiny, visually reinforcing his distress. He chose his words gingerly. It was no longer clear to him whether he was working for or against the greater good of his country. Perhaps if he turned his back on the project now I would bring the full force of the American underworld to his home and force him to complete the task he had started. "So," he asked. "Are you really an American spy?"

What sort of a question is that? The answer is no. But then again, if I were a spy, would I actually answer "yes"? I restated my role on the project and the goals of the data collection exercise. Alyosha was unconvinced.

"Why are we asking Russian enterprises to simply hand over information for nothing in return? Isn't the capitalist way that everything must be paid for? Shouldn't we pay companies for the information they are providing?"

I explained that the basic financial data we were attempting to collect from Russian companies was already publicly available for every major American company. Besides, it was a voluntary exercise. If a Russian company did not want to provide information, then no one could compel them to.

This statement did not make any sense to Alyosha. "America is a rich country. If American companies want this information on Russian enterprises, they should be willing to pay for it," he argued. "Why should Russian companies provide valuable information to American companies for free? Americans are wealthy. They should pay for this information."

I countered this by pointing out that if Russian enterprises really wanted foreign investment, then they should make it as easy as possible for foreign companies to investigate them and conduct due diligence. An open business partner would be far more attractive to an investor than one that withholds information.

"Why do the Russian companies have to be the ones that give out information?" Alyosha still was not certain the project was structured to the advantage of the Russians. And, (given that in the Russian mindset every transaction has a winner and a loser) if it was not to the Russians' advantage, then it must be to their disadvantage. "Why don't you bring American companies here and we determine which ones we want as investors? Besides, what will looking at financial information of a company tell a foreigner other than the fact that Russian companies need money? The managers here know what they are doing. They have been running these companies for decades. They just have run out of money to keep operating. That is why they need foreign investment."

Ah yes, that was the bottom line always, wasn't it. The Russian managers know what they are doing, they just need additional money. Foreign investors are welcome for their cheque books, but any management ideas are strictly rejected as irrelevant. The American side expects that foreign companies will happily reveal their true financial state and then welcome all suggestions for improvement from the incoming MBA-trained American management teams. The Russian side knows that they have a long-standing enterprise that holds a monopolistic cornerstone of the post-Soviet economy. A foreign company should feel privileged at the opportunity to invest money with an enterprise that is poised on the verge of greatness.

Alyosha was engaged and passionate throughout the dinner. Alcohol, of course, helped to raise the emotional level higher. He loved his country and wanted to be on the forefront of building Russia's future. I could only match his energy with my own. Yes, I too wanted to help build Russia's future. And I sincerely believed that opening Russia's struggling privatized enterprises to foreign investment would only help with a much needed infusion of western management practices, capital, and global trade connections.

I believed in the core principle of the project. My main question was regarding the execution. A full year after my arrival in Russia, the issue of how access to the data would be provided (or controlled) was still locked in a power struggle between the

Russian Privatization Center, the LPCs, USAID, and the third party consultancy we had engaged. I also had raised the obvious point that data starts aging the minute it is collected. My project was simply funded for initial collection, not ongoing engagement with foreign investors and Russian partners. If there wasn't a plan for ongoing renewal, then the data would soon be worthless to everyone – including the US taxpayers who had footed the bill.

Despite all this I did my best to continue to be a positive champion for the project. At a minimum I was hoping that our efforts would help more Russians understand the value of greater openness and transparency – even if the actual results were unsatisfactory. In the end, Alyosha believed me. But I could tell that he was now torn – he would continue to dedicate his energy on the project out of faith and loyalty to me, but perhaps the US government was simply using both of us for its own purposes that had nothing to do with building the future of Krasnoyarsk.

As we wrapped up dinner, I expected Alyosha to instruct the driver to take me onwards to my hotel. But then another twist to the evening. The hotel had advised the LPC that my reservation was cancelled. Was this related to the newspaper article? Had someone in the local government decided that I was not welcome in Krasnoyarsk? All hotel reservations still had to be made through local government connections. One could not simply call a hotel as an outsider and get a room on your own. The hotel had offered no explanation. I was just amazed that they had bothered to advise the LPC at all that the reservation was cancelled, rather than me showing up late at night and being turned out to the cold Siberian night.

Alyosha took my hand and kissed it and explained that although the hotel room was cancelled, he was looking after my interests. At this point I simply expected that he would announce that I was to be staying at his place (with everything that implied). I reveled in the electricity of his touch. Oh, how I wanted to say yes to those beautiful blue eyes. But as much as I wanted Alyosha, he was my employee. And in the wild world of Russia without rules, there still were some lines I would not cross.

Then, Alyosha advised me that Carl, the American business advisor to the Krasnoyarsk LPC, had offered a room for me.

This tumbled my emotions further. Alyosha stood holding my hands in a clear gesture of invitation but had organized for me to stay elsewhere. Yes, that was all for the best, but what was it that I wanted? And it is always the forbidden fruit that makes you long even more.

Alyosha slowly smiled as he studied my face and held my hands a bit tighter. I could feel his passion for life through my fingertips.

"Of course, you are welcome to stay with me if you prefer," he added quietly.

Something in my expression must have offered a bit of invitation. He encircled my body with strong but gentle arms and met me with a curious kiss. It took all my strength to breathlessly tell Alyosha that I was flattered, but please ask the driver to take me to Carl's apartment.

By the time I arrived at Carl's apartment I was a highly emotional bundle of alcohol-infused nerves. The public accusation of being an American spy. The seeds of doubt were growing that perhaps all our efforts were simply part of a larger scheme of the US government, or unwittingly feeding the Russian power structures further, or simply a complete waste of time and money as the results would just rot on a deteriorating hard drive in the dark. The simmering underlying stress that the American audit team would soon be scrutinizing my every move. And then of course, the tantalizing illicit kiss — with the unspoken suggestion there would be more if I wanted it.

Although at first I had been irritated that my hotel reservation had been cancelled, I was now actually looking forward to staying with Carl. All of the positive aspects of the arrangement were clear. The last time I stayed at the Hotel Krasnoyarsk I had been firmly advised that "my kind was not welcome." (As I was a single woman taking a hotel room alone, I was obviously viewed to be a prostitute.) The deep penetrating stares from all the men in the hotel restaurant had reinforced the assumption that the only women who were in hotels alone were obviously working in the world's oldest profession. The food would certainly be better at Carl's apartment. And, most importantly, I would be able to discuss all the dramas in my life with another American — in English.

Okay, maybe not *all* the dramas in my life. I would keep the kiss from Alyosha to myself.

Carl welcomed me to his flat with a vodka — and then realizing that I may not be quite as Russian-ized as he was, he added the offer of some tonic. I really did not need anything else to drink that night, but gratefully accepted the tranquilizer — and then launched into a monologue that wandered through the various themes of the day. What was it that we were accomplishing out here in Russia anyway? Did any of it actually matter? Was Alyosha right — were we all just being used by the US Government to do their fieldwork for them and in fact this whole economic assistance statement was just a front? After all, nothing in our project goals actually measured *delivering* any services to Russian companies. All we were engaged to do were basic tasks required by the US government for funding offices, performing data collection, and placing an American advisor on site. Although the stated headline purpose was the establishment of self-sustaining consulting centers and bringing in foreign investment to the region, we could complete all tasks in the work order but the higher objectives could remain unachieved.

And even completing all the tasks in the work order in their most basic form was challenging enough. Would the US-based auditors have even the slightest degree of understanding of what we were up against in Russia just trying to get our work accomplished and delivered? I was an emotional wreck and the vodka helped to exacerbate my excitement.

I was sure that the internal auditors would leave my charred remains as a warning sign to others. Did they understand what we had to go through just to get computer shipments into the country through customs? To get a ticket on a flight? To organize phone lines in the regional offices? To arrange for every receipt to bury the 23% VAT just so that the paperwork would pass USAID scrutiny for reimbursement? Every office had "fixers" who were well connected and helped to expedite the necessary paperwork required for the most routine of tasks. Without a "fixer" quite likely our office would be left without electricity or we would be at risk for having the office invaded by Russians stating that they were representatives of the tax authority in to collect "back taxes."

Carl listened quietly to my passionate rant and topped off my vodka and tonic. I then turned to start questioning him. How was he so calm in the midst of such a clash of cultures? Like Joseph and Nathan he was the American consultant designated to be the onsite ambassador to promote foreign investment and advisory services for the local Russian enterprises. Joseph was frustrated by the lack of true partnership with Ivan Ivanovich, his LPC Director. In Ekaterinburg, however, Nathan had established a good working relationship with Sergei Glebovich. They were moving forward with organizing a tour through the Ekaterinburg region for prospective American foreign investors. Their frustrations were shared as a team – jointly directed at the lack of support from the Moscow head office of the Russian Privatization Center.

Carl smiled and said that it should be obvious why he was so calm while Joseph and Nathan were stressed. Carl took the definition of his role quite literally. He was in Krasnoyarsk to *support* the Local Privatization Center as the American advisor. He would simply perform tasks as requested by the LPC or from the Moscow offices of the RPC – but he was certainly *not* going to drive his own agenda. He would show up at meetings when required, speak at dinners when asked, meet delegations from Moscow when instructed. But he was not initiating anything on his own. And as a result, Carl was calm and satisfied with his life in Central Siberia. No, this work was not challenging at all, and yes, he certainly could be doing a lot more to promote the advancement of foreign investment and economic development in Krasnoyarsk. But Carl was savvy enough to know that without the backing of the local government or the RPC that his efforts would be futile. Therefore, it was best just to sit back and be pleasant and act upon requests only.

Carl's approach went completely against my nature. We are here on a USAID project with the explicit objective to promote self-sustaining consulting offices and to build the foundation for foreign investment and economic growth! You are here in Krasnoyarsk as a highly paid consultant and the front lines of this multi-million dollar project. Of course you must do everything in your power to promote these objectives!

Carl was American, but had been living in Russia long enough to deflect my questions with questions of his own.

"So if Joseph and Nathan are deeply committed to the cause of Russian economic development, what have they managed to accomplish to date?"

With great pleasure I recounted Nathan and Sergei Glebovich's plans that were coming to fruition to bring prospective American investors to Ekaterinburg. Nathan and Sergei Glebovich were working extremely effectively together. Using Nathan and Raymond's business connections in the United States, they had amassed a delegation of several dozen businessmen who would be visiting the region within the month.

"Who from the Russian Privatization Center in Moscow is sponsoring this?" Carl asked.

"No one," I replied. "Nathan and Sergei Glebovich were not getting any support from the Russian Privatization Center for their efforts, so they plunged ahead with their own connections back to the USA. All the visas are being organized with Arthur Andersen as the sponsor rather than the RPC."

Carl shook his head like the old master scolding some unruly but adorable school-children. "It is a very dangerous thing to have ideas of your own in Russia. The future is uncertain. All that matters is the present moment."

I disagreed with Carl. "Sergei Glebovich is politically savvy and connected in Ekaterinburg. He knows what he is doing."

Carl waved his hand in casual dismissal of the conversation. It was not worth debating further this evening. The American delegation was scheduled to arrive within the month. Carl simply stated that nothing was actually certain until the delegation actually had come and left. This was Russia. Anything could change at any time. Only time would tell who would be right.

I thought about Carl's perspective and relative state of calm later that night as I curled up in his bed. Alone — I might clarify. Carl loaned me his bed for the night. He moved into one of the other smaller rooms. I protested that I did not want to displace him, but there was no use arguing. He had decided that I would have his bed and that was the way things would be. I could protest, but my opinion was not valid. How Russian. Hopefully he would not be pounding on my door at night.

On paper Carl, Nathan, and Joseph all had exactly the same role - American advisor to the Local Privatization Center. But their approaches could not be more different. Without a doubt, Carl was the most calm and content of the three of them. He had immersed himself into life in Krasnoyarsk and chose to just go with the flow. His guiding philosophy resonated with me. "It is a very dangerous thing to have ideas of your own in Russia." These principles guided Carl's approach to work in Krasnoyarsk. But these principles apparently also guided how he operated in his personal life as well — his apartment was 100% vintage Soviet furnishings and décor. A ghastly chandelier struggled to illuminate the corners of the brown, orange, and green bedroom. Tired flocked wallpaper absorbed all the light and the aged mattress groaned as I crawled into bed. He had not even attempted to exert his own opinions with the taming of the Soviet-era apartment.

Then I noticed another small clue to his demeanor. A strand of long blonde hair on a blanket on my bed – Carl's bed. I do not have long blonde hair. Neither did Carl. So who did it belong to? Who was the guest in his bedroom just a night or so before? "All that matters is the present moment. The future is uncertain." This was Carl's advice, which he apparently followed. My curiosity was piqued – with whom? Apparently there was a part of his personal life when Carl was willing to pursue his own opinions and agenda.

Carl lived a life of exile in Central Siberia. The only American I met while in Krasnoyarsk. He was content and at peace with his situation and treating the role as some glorified holiday where occasionally he was summoned to business functions. He spoke Russian well enough to order soup at a restaurant, but that was about all. He was truly alone in Siberia, but decided to go with the flow for the whims and requests (or lack of action) by the local government. Another expatriate, such as Joseph, would probably have leaped out of his skin with frustration – agitating everyone around him in the process. Once again I was amazed at how differently two American professionals could respond to virtually the identical situation. Expatriate life was certainly quite the deep personality test.

And I was worried that this was a personality test that I could fail.

Tragically I have lost my copy of the newspaper with the headline "American Spy Arrives in Krasnoyarsk." Today I would love to have this framed and hanging in a position of honor in my flat. The day after my arrival in Krasnoyarsk, however, the headline was a source of anxiety for everyone.

The main purpose of my visit to Krasnoyarsk was to support the formal launch of the data collection effort in the region. Alyosha, together with the minimal token assistance of the LPC, had organized an event where a number of speakers would talk about economic development projects and foreign investment prospects in the region. The main point would be to encourage all the local enterprises to participate in the data collection exercise and I was scheduled as a key speaker for this event.

The newspaper headline had changed everything for Valerei Nikolayevich, Director of the LPC. The Director summoned Alyosha and me to his office first thing in the morning. Given Alyosha's reaction to the newspaper headline, I assumed that Valerei Nikolayevich would want to cancel the session. No promotion of American spies in Krasnoyarsk. But then, to my surprise, he offered a completely different solution: The conference would go on, but I would only sit in the audience as a quiet spectator. The data collection effort must be firmly promoted by himself as Director of the LPC

— showing that this is a Russian program, run by Russians, for Russians, in the Russian best interest. He was definitively *not* pleased by the impression given in the newspaper that his office was being manipulated by the American government.

The Russian man's pride had been insulted and now he was in full offense mode to prove to everyone that he was truly in control of the operations of his Local Privatization Center and the data collection project. Valerei Nikolayevich thumped his desk with his fist in his emotional monologue. He did not ask for my opinion or point of view. He stated what would happen at the afternoon conference as a *fait accompli*, not as a consultation. One newspaper headline had changed his interest in the data collection exercise from giving just minimal token lip service to now full ownership and engagement.

Later that afternoon I sat in the audience of the conference hall, trying to be as inconspicuous and Russian as possible. I wore a grey dress that was showing the ravages of the Moscow acid rain together with the requisite blue eye shadow and fire engine red lipstick. I sat quietly and no one gave me a second look. The auditorium filled with several hundred Russian men dressed in polyester brown and black suits and battered shoes. The few women in the crowd were matrons rather than *devushki* and wore brown floral house dresses and stern expressions. Their complexions belied diets of potatoes and vodka and endless winters devoid of sun.

The directors and chief accountants of the local privatized enterprises had all come to the conference hall with the same questions — "Why do the Americans want information about our businesses?" and "How do we get some of the promised American foreign investment?" "If the purpose of data collection was to attract foreign investors, then show us the foreign investors. Where are they? Otherwise the data collection request is being made under false pretenses."

Valerei Nikolayevich pounded the speaker's podium with emotional fervor and declared that a new day was rising in Krasnoyarsk. Economic opportunity and the rebirth of Russian businesses, by Russians and for Russians. He spoke passionately that the Directors of the local enterprises had an opportunity to be a part of this rebirth of Russia. To lead the rebirth of the country — from its geographic center here in Krasnoyarsk. Behind Valerei Nikolayevich, a vintage Soviet era mural portrayed the rise of industry — young determined men and women carried anvils and marched forward to a new dawn — led by Lenin and his cloak billowing in the wind.

Valerei Nikolayevich's speech resonated with the practiced delivery of a long-term politician. He was rallying people to action. Now — let's work together for the future of Russia! His speech was full of emotion but short on specifics. Perhaps just a few short years earlier he had stood in this very location in the Soviet regime before these very same enterprise directors making the very same speech about the great Soviet future. By just changing a few key words it could have been a speech by just about any political leader trying to rally support for the cause of the day.

I laughed that if, in fact, the whole data collection exercise were in fact part of some covert American plot, that in fact Valerei Nikolayevich was unwittingly playing his part superbly.

I looked around the room to see if I could read the reactions from Alyosha and Carl. Alyosha was easy enough to spot. He was seated prominently on the edge of the stage, as Valerei Nikolayevich would be introducing him shortly as the lead for the data collection exercise. Alyosha was visibly pleased by the turn of events. Prior to today he had struggled to get the smallest token of support from the LPC for his efforts. Now clearly the Director of the LPC was engaged. This project was to be led by Russians for the benefit of Russians!

Carl was seated discretely in the auditorium with his interpreter at his side. Long blonde hair, I quickly noted. Her attention was focused on Valerei Nikolayevich as she was softly simultaneously translating the highlights of the speech. Carl leaned towards the blonde woman, obviously pleased that this beautiful woman was whispering in his ear. He leaned a bit closer and his hand now rested lightly on her arm. The blonde woman flinched and pulled her arm away, never turning her gaze from the speaker at the podium.

And was I surprised? Not really. Disappointed, yes, but not surprised. The more things change the more they stay the same. Valerei Nikolayevich's speech could have been recycled from a speech he gave under the Soviet era. The blonde interpreter was clearly accustomed to (though not necessarily welcoming) the advances of her employer – as undoubtedly she had been in the same position previously.

I left Krasnoyarsk having nominally achieved a great success for everything that I had set out to do for this trip. We had formally launched the data collection effort. We now had the full engagement of the Local Privatization Center. Alyosha had proclaimed his total devotion to me and the project.

But yet, despite all of this, I was left with a nagging feeling that in fact actually nothing had changed.

17 LOW FAT OREOS

July 1995

From Krasonoyarsk I returned to Moscow for a few brief days. I would then fly onwards to Chicago for the promised Arthur Android assimilation session.

Oksana greeted me in the morning with two pieces of information that were superficially simple, but in reality were quite significant. First, the American auditors had arrived – ahead of their original stated date. Second, she advised me that she would no longer be staying at my apartment when I was out of town.

Both pieces of news required full discussions on their own. I started with the personal announcement first. I was pleased for Oksana that she had resolved her long term housing situation. Where was she living now? How had she found a flat that met her budget and requirements?

Oksana lowered her eyes to avert my direct questions. She gave a quiet general answer that she had found satisfactory accommodation. I paused and studied her face. She clearly was not comfortable telling me the whole story. Perhaps she had greeted me with the statement about the auditors in order to deflect my attention from her personal situation. I would not pry, but still I felt a personal protective responsibility for the girls on my team. Yes, I am referring to them as "my girls" although realistically we were all about the same age. I just instinctively felt that if anyone was going to stand up for their interests, it would have to be me.

A moment later the answer to my question became perfectly obvious, although not answered explicitly. Robert, who rarely had cause to speak to me in the office, appeared in my team's room with the superfluous announcement that the auditors had arrived and I should go and introduce myself. But then after delivering his message, Robert paused to smile at Oksana and took a step towards her. Clearly the message about the auditors was just a basic front to give him a reason to visit my team's room.

The real objective was to see Oksana. Oksana said some generic pleasantries to Robert (in English) and then quickly sat at her desk and pretended to be absorbed in her typing.

I looked in amazement from Oksana (who blushed slightly but otherwise studiously ignored Robert) to Robert who was visibly enamored with Oksana's perfectly manicured nails tapping rhythmically on the keyboard. Robert! How could you! Here he was the self-proclaimed defender of decency – leading his own battles to remove spandex mini-skirts, vodka, and inappropriate relationships from the workplace. He was the front line of order and rules – ensuring that every receipt was precisely accurate and every stapler was in working order throughout the office. And now – here he was not just having a relationship with Oksana, but was plotting to live with her as well.

I pierced Robert with an angry glare. I caught his eye and silently made it clear that I completely disapproved of the whole situation. Robert gave me a self-satisfied smirk then turned and strolled back to his office. I stalked closely behind him.

Moments later Robert and I were alone in his perfectly-organized office. I closed the door behind us. We both had our speeches prepared.

I launched into a tirade about how *dare* he take advantage of the girls in the office. Did he know what all these women went through regarding harassment and abuse? The least we could do would be to offer a work environment where they could have a sanctuary from such intrusions and where they could develop and flourish professionally.

Robert asked if I was representing Oksana's opinion or my own. She was an adult and could make her own decisions. She had decided to live with him. Why was this any of my business? I really should not be meddling in other people's affairs.

I tried to quote what I could about Arthur Andersen's sexual harassment policies. Robert just laughed and waved this aside. "That is in regards to *unwelcome* advances. She has accepted my invitations. Therefore the concept of 'sexual harassment' does not apply."

"But Oksana feels compelled to say yes to you," I argued. I had seen enough of young *devushki* interacting with men in positions of authority to believe firmly that her decision to say "yes" to Robert's advances would have little to do with romantic interest.

"Do you really think that lowly of your team to say that you do not believe she is capable of making her own decisions?" Robert retorted to put the blame back on me for the viewing situation in a negative light.

In the mind of the American man, this beautiful Russian woman wanted him. And all I was doing was stirring up anxiety in the workplace unnecessarily. I fumed silently for a moment – and then (in a moment of black malicious humor) I turned the stapler on his desk a few degrees. Just enough so that it was no longer in a perfect parallel to his tape dispenser.

I turned and left Robert's office with a victorious smirk. Robert sputtered some incoherent words of outrage at my back, while scurrying to set his stapler and tape dispenser back in alignment.

Although I had reached a temporary cease-fire with Robert, I could not just let the issue rest. I pulled Oksana into a corner of the kitchen area where we could hopefully have a few moments to speak alone.

"I knew you wouldn't be happy," she said simply.

I tried to explain that my happiness was not the issue here – hers was. I just wanted to be absolutely confident that she was moving in with Robert entirely because of her own decision. When I had interviewed Oksana a year earlier she had asked simply at the time of the interview "who was she expected to sleep with around here." I had replied at the time "no one" with the definitive statement that our office did not work that way. I had to be sure that this was what she really wanted.

"Yes, this is what I want," she said quietly.

I studied her face. I was not at all convinced that Oksana was happy about the arrangement. But if she said she wanted this situation (I could not bring myself to say "relationship") with Robert, then I would not interfere.

I would, however, jump to her defense in a moment if she asked for it.

I reminded her.

"Yes, I know. Thank you," Oksana smiled quietly and returned to her desk.

Nadya was next in the line of people who wanted to talk to me that morning. As the lead accountant on my project, I assumed that she would want to talk about the audit that was now underway. She, however, led off with the subject of the morning – Robert and Oksana.

Nadya was the unofficial ringleader of the Russian girls in the office. She had led the movement to dismantle the cubicles, the black spandex mini-skirt day, the Women's Day escapade from the office, and many other minor subversive statements to prove her independent spirit. She had openly declared her intention to attend an American business school and if any woman in the office were to break free of the standard *devushka* role, I was convinced it would be her. I was certain that Nadya would appreciate my determination to defend Oksana from the advances of Robert.

I was wrong.

Nadya calmly but firmly told me to back off from trying to disrupt the Robert-Oksana relationship. Her reasoning was simple. Yes, she understood where I was coming from. Yes, in the American world, relationships between management and staff were not condoned. But I needed to really understand Oksana's situation. Robert's offer for her to live with him represented a significant opportunity – far more than most Russian girls would dare to dream of. Here was an American man of staggering financial means offering to take her in. Even if this only lasted a few months, Oksana would be able to consolidate her savings and enjoy time in surroundings of relative incredible luxury. If all went well she could even potentially get that most elusive of offers – an opportunity to move to the United States and the possibility of a Green Card.

No this was not a romantic vision by any means. None of the girls in the office actually even liked Robert. But put that all aside – he was offering opportunities that they all aspired to: a bit closer to financial security, a bit closer to an American Green Card.

The message was clear. I was to back off and leave Robert and Oksana alone. As much as the situation appalled me, in its own way, their "relationship" actually inspired the other girls in the office.

And as much as it went against my entire nature, I would respect their wishes.

Nadya then turned the conversation to the American auditors. On this point, I knew that she and I would be in total alignment.

"These auditors are going to demolish our relationship with the regional LPC offices," she said in despair. "Is there anything we can do to stop them?"

She quickly relayed that the auditors intended not just to go through the documentation on site with our project office here in Moscow, but in addition they intended to visit every single location of our LPCs and review the procurement and inventory, down to the last mouse and keyboard.

"Is this really necessary?" Nadya protested. "We were just in Southern Russia a few weeks ago and I performed the inventory myself. Now we are sending a whole second team of accountants down there to look at everything again."

I had not yet met the auditors, so I agreed that I would talk with them and see what we could possibly do to simplify their plans. I could already hear the voice of Ivan Ivanovich calling in protest: "What? You do not trust our team? You have already seen all our equipment yourself. Why do we need to continue to prove ourselves!"

The American auditor, Denise, was easy enough to locate. I found her in an office she had confiscated. The regular occupant of the office, a Russian senior manager, had been ousted to one of the team rooms for the duration of her stay. How very American of her. Her work was obviously so much more important, therefore the local client-serving staff should be able to understand a minor inconvenience. She had piles of paperwork already all over the desk and she was busily typing away at her laptop.

And there, atop a stack of documents, was a package of low fat Oreos.

I was dumbfounded. I actually had no idea that low fat Oreos even existed. They certainly were not available in Moscow. She must have decided that they were part of her essential gear to bring on her trip to Russia. I can understand a fixation with Oreos. Chocolate is a necessary part of any balanced diet in my mind. But low fat Oreos? What sort of a mad person would even think of such an oxymoronic product? And what sort of a confused woman would buy them? Are you trying to eat healthy? If so, I don't recommend Oreos. If you want to indulge, then at least do so properly. Good grief. Make up your mind and lead a consistent life.

I was at a loss for how to communicate with this woman. She had no qualms to simply stroll in and uproot one of the Russian senior managers from his office. Would she have done so if he were American? I doubted it. Then if that were not enough, the low fat Oreos already convinced me that she had a way of thinking that I could not possibly begin to comprehend. And I had not even introduced myself yet.

I started our conversation with a few pleasantries that I hoped would be innocuous enough to at least allow us to have a civilized start to our relationship. The evidence so far was indicating that it was going to be a challenge to work with this woman, so I should therefore make an attempt to get off to the right start. I asked about her flight and whether her hotel was satisfactory.

Of course, Denise had been traumatized by the experience of arriving at Sheremyetovo. Fair enough – the passport control area was more akin to a battleground than an orderly area for paperwork processing. The worst instance I had experienced was nearly four hours of pushing and arguing before finally successfully clearing immigration – although more typical was about ninety minutes. The hostility of the arrivals area at Sheremyetovo had caused more than one arriving American businessman to simply turn around and take the next departing flight. If this is the entrance to the country, what is the rest of Russia like?

Denise, however, never seriously had to contemplate this question. She apparently had a miraculous arrival in Sheremyetovo and cleared immigration in under an hour. I was quite impressed, but she was still writhing from the experience. Our driver, Vanya, had met her efficiently and whisked her off to the Hotel Aerostar – my old haunt before I had moved into my apartment. She was clearly disappointed that there was no gym or pool at the Aerostar and rated the hotel as barely passable due to its depressing décor and small rooms. She had not ventured outside the hotel before being picked up by the driver this morning and deposited here at the office.

So Denise's total Russian experience so far was Sheremyetovo airport and the Hotel Aerostar. If she was going to have any comprehension of what we actually had to deal with on a daily basis to accomplish basic business activities, then she would have to get out a bit more than that. I asked what she was planning to do outside of business hours when she was in Moscow. Denise was all excited about shopping for "those cute painted wooden nesting dolls". Oh yes, *matryoshkas*. Every American tourist needs a *matryoshka*. To Americans they symbolize Russia just as much as vodka and Red Square. But are they an accurate symbol of what life is really like? I thought of bringing her a dried fish, with the suggestion that it would make a more meaningful souvenir.

I wanted Denise to get out for a walk, to see the open manhole covers, the street traders at the metro stop. She needed to go into the neighborhoods on the outskirts of town, away from the thriving hub of Moscow, to see the crumbling rows of apartment blocks and bleak shops and dirt – endless dirt – in a city without street cleaning equipment or storm drains. She needed so see the throngs of refugees from Chechnya desperate at Vnukovo airport. She needed to be with our drivers when they were attempting to find petrol for their cars, driving down back alleys trying to find a hidden place where someone could provide a few liters of gas. She needed to go into the staff cafeterias in government buildings where a watery stew of boiled meat and gristle would simmer with glistening oil and then be dished out onto small tin trays.

"The concierge at the hotel is organizing tickets to the Bolshoi ballet for me," Denise announced. "I can't believe how expensive that is – about $120 per ticket. But I'll only be in Moscow once, so I really should go."

I could scream. Yes, she should go to the Bolshoi. It truly is a national treasure. But if you are looking for the total Russian experience, the way to buy tickets is to argue with the scalpers on the front steps of the Bolshoi itself. No tickets were even available from the Bolshoi directly, they were always consumed by the various scalper channels and hotels. I had fortunately found a rather reliable scalper who seemed to be on the south side of the Bolshoi Theater around noon every day. He would wink and nod and claim I was getting a great deal as a regular customer and his favorite American *devushka* (although in true Russian style, I was still sure that he was taking me for a ride). And then I would have a pair of box seats for *Swan Lake* for $30.

Denise came from a different world. And here in Russia she was going to live on an alternate plane. But she probably was not even slightly conscious of this fact. She would go home to America with her stash of *matryoshkas* and other souvenirs, her photos of the Kremlin, and ticket stubs from the Bolshoi and believe that she had seen Russia.

And she was here in Moscow to pass judgment on how we performed our daily activities.

"I hear that you are planning to visit each of our regional offices. That will be quite the adventure!" I was already pitying the interpreter that would be selected for the tour, suspecting that there would be a great deal of babysitting activities required for her to function How to democratically decide which interpreter would get this assignment?

"Oh no, I'm not travelling to all the regional offices," Denise was shocked by the suggestion. "I am the *lead* auditor. I am working with the headquarters and project management. There is a junior auditor arriving in a few days. Zeke is actually really looking forward to the grand tour of Russia. He is quite the adventurous type. After college he went to Israel to live on a kibbutz for a year. Sitting behind a desk is a bit tame for him I think. How many locations does your project have now – twelve?"

Outside of Moscow there were nine LPCs – I corrected her. Three regional central offices, each with two satellite offices, for a total of nine locations. The procurement of computers had been for twelve locations – three of which were still unspecified and therefore the equipment was in a holding pattern somewhere in a Virginia warehouse. There were also an additional ten cities where I had data collection efforts underway – at LPCs that were supported by other consultancies. I voiced my genuine disappointment that she would not have the opportunity to experience for herself the challenges we have travelling and working in regional Russia.

"Oh, we appreciate the difficulties you have working out here!" Denise smiled with the self-satisfied confidence that she was establishing herself as a true champion of the team. "We know how difficult it is to stay in contact – therefore Zeke will be bringing cell phones with him for the whole team."

I paused for a moment to contemplate this latest bit of advice. The idea of having a mobile phone had never even occurred to me. Why would I want a mobile? In Russia, mobile technology was the exclusive domain of the elite new Russians. And even with them, the mobile phone was more a status symbol to be placed on the center of a restaurant dining table, rather than a business tool. I was still focused on trying to determine a reliable way to establish a dial up connection to the internet when travelling.

After a moment of reflection, I realized that there were a few critical flaws to the idea of Zeke bringing mobile phones from the US to Russia. First, the wireless technology standards were different in the US from Europe. Cell phones purchased in the United States would simply not work in Russia. Second, clearing immigration and customs at Sheremyetovo was never easy under the best of circumstances. If Customs discovered twenty plus mobile phones in Zeke's luggage, he certainly would have additional unwanted scrutiny. And wait, Zeke spent a year on a kibbutz. Was he Jewish? If so, this could trigger the worst of Russian prejudices for even harsher treatment at the border.

True to the politically correct sensitivities of any Arthur Andersen manager who has been through indoctrination training, Denise was mortified by my question of whether Zeke was Jewish. I should be more sensitive than to pass judgment based on his religion and ethnicity. I explained that I was asking in order to help protect Zeke himself. Russian border guards were not known for their cultural sensitivity – especially as the country was in the thick of a civil war and the recent Budyonnovsk hostage crisis was still a hot subject of conversation.

Denise dismissed my concerns with statements that the DC-based procurement specialists were experienced professionals. They knew what they were doing. I did not need to worry about things that were out of my area of responsibility. Denise gave me a condescending smile, similar to that which Robert had given me just an hour earlier. The message was clear – I was to just mind my own business. Let the DC-based Program Leadership team take care of important decisions like how to procure equipment and coordination with the auditors.

Of course, my attempts were in vain to work an approach to the audit that would be less invasive than an on-site inspection of every office. The auditors had a plan. My role was simply to ensure that the local Russian team in each city was available to support the execution of the plan. The discussion was over. Denise had the situation under control. She would let me know if she required anything further from my team.

After retreating from my conversation with Denise, I needed a quiet moment to reflect on the lessons of the morning and contemplate my next steps. Quiet time at my desk was never a possibility. Out of desperation for a moment alone some months earlier I had discovered the stairs leading from our floor down towards the tenth floor of the office building.

Note that I stated the tenth floor "of" the office building, not the tenth floor "in" the office building. There is a difference. The term "in" implies a closed space with walls. As I pointed out in an earlier chapter, the exterior of the building looked like it had just barely survived an intense air raid. Descending from the eleventh floor via the stairs you entered a space that was more rubble and exposed metal beams than recognizable as an office building. The exterior walls were mostly missing, creating a wind tunnel which churned up the layer of green slimy dust. Black smudges on the raw concrete gave evidence that this was where the Russians from our office slipped out to have a quick smoke break. The cigarette butts themselves had been swept away with the relentless wind.

The uninhabited post-apocalyptic space offered a temporary safe haven away from the continuous drone of the office. I swept a bit of the green slime clear of the bottom step and sat down to collect my thoughts.

The lesson of the day was clear. Everyone wanted me to simply just focus on managing the data collection effort. My opinions on other subjects were not welcome.

Of course I had a problem with this. I have a hard time keeping my opinions to myself under the best of circumstances. With the events that I saw unfolding in front of me now I knew that the longer term implications were not good for my team.

A year earlier I had failed to act when I recognized the signs of domestic abuse on Ingrid – our temporary typist. Today I had no knowledge of her status or condition. She had disappeared forever and I was haunted that I could have – should have – done *something* to help her. Now I was watching Oksana being pulled into a relationship with an American manager – the same woman who had been open in her interview with me that she was resigned to the fact that sleeping with the management was part of her job description. At the time I had told her that I would defend her interests. Now I was failing here as well.

And then look at the calamity that was about to happen with Zeke attempting to enter the country with twenty mobile phones. (Which would not work anyway when they finally got here.) Yes, on the surface Denise was right – I could just sit back and let events take their course. The decisions were made by the Washington DC team. Zeke would suffer the consequences. If only it were that simple then I could possibly let it rest. I knew, however, that if Zeke were detained by immigration that the driver dispatched to Sheremyetovo to retrieve him would inevitably have to get involved.

Vanya was the driver who was generally assigned to such tasks. He was incredibly patient and diligent and was prepared to wait one hour or four hours or however long it took for the inbound American to clear immigration and customs. The airport pick up for Zeke, however, would likely be anything but routine. More likely than not the driver would have to be ready to intervene or negotiate or support the inevitable ordeal with customs in some way. It would be unfair to put Vanya in such a position. Although the life of a driver always meant operating on a grey line with the law – continuous payoffs to the GAI, questionable sources for supply of petrol. No auto insurance meant that any accident would result in a resolution of a dispute via street-justice rather than formal legal proceedings. Vanya did everything in his power to distance himself from provoking the police and the military. He had confided in me that he had dodged the military draft – his years of required service would have been at the peak of the Soviet-Afghan conflict. As such, he knew that he was always just one encounter with the police away from some severe form of punishment or retribution.

If I let the decision of the Washington DC based procurement specialists take their course, Vanya could easily become an innocent victim if he were pulled in to the inevitable conflict with customs and immigration. Yes, I was being overly protective. But if I did not act and something happened to Vanya... I would never forgive myself. I would not be able to stand on the sidelines again when I knew the risks to my team.

And I had not yet begun to seriously contemplate how much agitation the audit would cause with the local Russian team in each city. Yes, it was necessary for compliance purposes, but as the sole American on the core team who spoke Russian, it would fall to me to spend the hours on the phone necessary to ensure that this exercise would not adversely impact our already tenuous working relationships with the regional teams.

At this point the skin on the back of my neck pricked with the sensation that I was not alone. Someone was watching me.

I turned to see Kolya standing at the top of the stairs, leaning casually against the closed door. He would have come out here for a smoke break, but his hands were empty and relaxed. He then did the most un-Russian of actions – he *smiled* at me. A genuine smile that simply said that he was happy to see me and somehow we were co-conspirators.

"Difficult morning?" he finally said in English. All of the Russians in the office generally spoke in their own language with me. But something in my face must have tipped him off that I needed to relax and express myself in English.

I stood up and attempted to brush off the persistent green slime from my clothing. Belatedly I realized that I must have been resting my hands on the steps, as I managed to simply spread the gunk around on my battered skirt. The wind tossed my hair in front of my face. As I pulled the hair from my eyes I realized that now I must be spreading green slime on my face too. All I could do now was laugh and look at the mess I had made of myself.

"It is good to see that you can still laugh. You do not need to take everything quite so seriously."

I returned his smile as I started up the stairs back to the offices – and towards Kolya. "Of course I have to take everything seriously! If I don't, who will? Certainly not you – out here just lounging around on a smoke break!"

"Oh, I'm not out here for a smoke break. I am here to enjoy the beautiful view."

"The beautiful view?" I repeated with a mocking smile as I gestured to the crumbled slime-covered ruins of the 10th floor.

With this, Kolya pulled me firmly by the wrists up to the 11th floor landing and spun me around, with my back to the wall. "Yes, the beautiful view," he answered quietly. "That is why I came out here onto the stairs. To enjoy the view."

Before I could reply, he had planted his mouth on my own and pinned me firmly by the forearms against the cold concrete. My hands were left flailing weakly in protest. No, this wasn't right. This was exactly what I had been fighting.

In previous encounters with Kolya (and there had been a few) he had always relented when I protested. But this time... my protests did not even convince me. After a moment I stopped resisting. Then I succumbed. And then I melted completely under the force of his persistent kisses and the full pressure of his body against my own.

After a few moments of bliss I could feel the strains of the day fading away. Why was I holding firm to the rules of not dating in the office when our Chief Rules Enforcement Officer – Robert – was openly doing it himself? Why were the American guys offered an open season for all their exploits and adventures with the Russian *devushki* while the American women were sidelined as frustrated observers?

All that mattered was this moment. The future is uncertain. Live for today. We all said the expression *carpe diem*. Was I the only one who had yet to learn how to live it? Under Kolya's strong embrace I was protected from everything. I could let go and relax and let the wind just carry all my troubles away.

"You don't have to take everything so seriously," Kolya repeated lightly when he finally released me.

"Thanks for helping me realize that," I replied sincerely.

We eventually did have to leave this post-apocalyptic paradise and return to the next round of torment in our office. I ran my fingers through Kolya's thick black hair – nominally to remove some of the green slimy dust, but of course I just enjoyed the sensation of touching his hair as well. Kolya turned me around and patted me down under the pretext of removing the toxic dust that was certainly covering every inch of my backside.

I tried to slip back into the office quietly. But this gesture was futile. The walls had curious eyes everywhere. Kolya, however, had no qualms about being a bit too close at my side as we re-entered our floor.

Nadya's gaze passed over Kolya, to me, and our green-slime covered clothing and gave me a silent knowing smile. There were no secrets among our team. Within minutes Kolya's and my encounter on the stairs would certainly be public knowledge.

And a mischievous spirit within me whispered that this was a good thing.

18   CONSULTING GAMES

August 1995 — St Charles, Illinois, USA

Finally I arrived at the much-anticipated training session in St Charles. Through various friends in the Big Six consulting circles I had heard many stories about Arthur Andersen and Andersen Consulting's training program. Entry-level consultants were subjected to six weeks of a rigorous curriculum of core consulting skills. You arrive as individuals – you leave as Arthur Androids.

I was actually looking forward to it.

Although I was now managing a team of nearly sixty to deliver the data collection project, to date I had never received any formal training in the area of client consulting or project management. My undergraduate degree was in Political Science and my graduate degree in International Economics. I operated entirely based on instincts, guided occasionally by general senior level advice from Raymond. Base business instincts had taken me this far to date – I knew that there was much more I could learn. I had heard abstract terms thrown around like "methodology" and "best practices" but really had no idea what this meant.

I had heard that students in the Andersen consultant training program often pulled all-nighters working on group projects and homework assignments. This gave me flashbacks to the intensity of my final months in my graduate program at Johns Hopkins University in the grueling lead up to the final ordeal of oral exams. The normal new consultant training program was six weeks. The session I was enrolled in was an abbreviated session of just one week – specially designed for managers within the firm that had started their careers elsewhere and were now being brought into the Andersen fold. I braced myself to be capable of another intense period of academic immersion. I was ready to throw every ounce of energy I had into absorbing the training that was made available to me. I had to. This was as a matter of professional survival and advancement. As James had made perfectly clear, Arthur Andersen was a firm dedicated to certain standards and practices. This course would be the next step in my journey to establish myself as a core member of the firm's consulting practice – and eventual transition back to the United States.

Or so I believed.

Ever the compulsive honors student, I arrived early the morning of the opening session. The primary room for the course was a stunning State of the Art kiva. Cascading rows of comfortable chairs and continuous writing surfaces of solid oak curved around a central stage. Evidence of high end technology was everywhere – from microphones built into the desk at each seat – to elaborate stage lighting and retractable large projector screens. Two young men worked industriously in an enclosed control room to ready all the technology in the room for a seamless operation of the day's events. All the rumors were true. This was a firm of incredible resources that was prepared to invest in their employees.

I took a central desk where I could have a good view of the speaker as well as my fellow colleagues and began to finger through the folder of course materials that had been beautifully prepared and arranged at every seat. An Arthur Andersen pen, an Arthur Andersen notebook, a list of participants printed on creamy rich paper. All standard practice. Then I found a few dried flowers pressed into a pocket of the folder, a packet of seeds, and a slim notebook with a lavender colored cover titled "Transitions". Baffling in the context of corporate training, but all would be made clear soon, I was sure.

The room quickly filled with professionals in fresh blue suits, sharp haircuts, clear skin, and bright intelligent eyes. Here we all were – the company's future senior management! And I was part of it!

Then the day began. The opening featured a monologue about the *Transition* that each of us was going through in our lives. Changing between companies is difficult. New corporate culture, new role, new expectations. But it is *okay* – we are here to help you with this *transition*. (She said the word very slowly and deliberately with emphasis on each syllable.) Then a big self-satisfied sigh from the presenter as she smiled at us all. The poor lost souls that were left in her care.

"How do we *feeeeeel?*" She cooed to us. "Are we stressed and anxious about the decision we have made to join Arthur Andersen? Let's pull out the *transitions* notebook and write our feelings down. We will get through this together."

On this cue, Pachelbel's Canon began to play softly through the hidden sound system and the lighting was dimmed. We were forced into a few minutes of reflection. Around the room, heads obediently bent forward as everyone quietly clasped their Arthur Andersen pens and began to write in their *transitions* notebooks. I was dumbfounded and continued to stare ahead at the facilitator who was smiling to herself as everyone in the room followed her instructions.

Then I noticed that I was not the only one who was not adhering to the plan. In the back row, where disruptive students of all ages tend to gravitate, two young men were struggling to contain their laughter at the scene. The lighting had been dimmed and it took me a bit to recognize them – Dmitri and Slava – two managers from the Moscow audit practice who had also been sent to this session. As bizarre as this session was for me, to the two of them, it was undoubtedly an out of body experience. The Soviet education system was known for its formality, structure, and rigorous focus on the rules of mathematics and science. *Povtoreniye mat' ucheniye* is the classic Russian saying for education – Repetition is the Mother of Learning. And now as the opening exercise for their first American training course, the Russians were being asked to write about their *feeeeelings* while Pachelbel's Canon plodded along slowly in the background.

Only a week or so (or was it a lifetime?) earlier I had been at a general session in Central Siberia in a 1950s era auditorium with a dodgy sound system and a giant mural of Lenin striding purposefully into the Great Soviet Industrial Future. I became lost in thought imagining the scene if this woman were speaking in front of a group of Russians who were directors of recently privatized state enterprises. What would their reaction be if she were cooing to them "We know you are going through a difficult change in your lives. Let's write about your *feeeeeelings.*"

The next segment was to be an introduction to Arthur Andersen corporate culture. I perked up, hoping to gain some insight to what held the company together across dozens of cities and countries. A team of comedic actors took the stage accompanied by circus tent music. A hilarious but frivolous skit then demonstrated a litany of "career limiting moves". A desk was over decorated with lava lamps and movie posters, people wore beach attire in the office, a consultant returned from a client lunch blind drunk, office romances blossomed, gossip ran amok, and key information was withheld from the senior partner. The audience roared with laughter. I noted with bitter amusement that, with the exception of withholding information from the senior partner, every other activity was standard procedure in our office. Yes, I already knew that our office was on the fringe of acceptable society for Arthur Andersen – but what could we do to fit in? The session provided amusement, but no answers.

During the first break I hunted down the lead facilitator and turned to him with desperation – is there anything in the agenda that would help to further my professional skills and career with the firm? Or is this going to be a series of comedic sketches with intervals of pop psychology? He smiled at me and said simply that we were just getting warmed up. Yes there would be more to come on core consulting skills, such as client communications. I was relieved.

That afternoon was the promised session on client communication skills. For this everyone was paired off and given Lego sets and a screen to place between you and your partner. Each pair had to agree an object to build and then design and build identical objects. You could not show your partner what you were doing – you had to communicate everything orally. "Let's build an airplane. Okay, let's start with using a long orange rectangle as the wing." I listened to the coaching from my partner hidden behind the screen, staring at the pieces of Lego in front of me, and very nearly broke into tears. I felt terribly cheated. I had come all the way from Moscow to Chicago to build my competencies with consulting and project management. And now I was playing with Lego.

During the next break I went on a mission to find Dmitri and Slava. I was seething with fury at the direction the course was going. We needed a *real* education about Arthur Andersen's business practices, not some corporate psycho-babble games. I wanted a real future with the firm. Did they?

It was easy enough to find the Russians. They had stepped outside for a cigarette break, of course. They were casually talking together and standing apart from the rest of our colleagues. I switched to Russian language to join their conversation and so that others nearby wouldn't overhear us. What did they think of the session so far? Is this what they had expected when they were sent across the Atlantic Ocean to a manager training course? Did they share my frustration? What could we do together to overcome this?

Dmitri just laughed and said "*Detskii sad*" – Kindergarten. This wasn't a training course, it was Kindergarten where we were playing children's games and were entertained and fed. He gave a dismissive wave with his cigarette towards the entrance to the building. Dmitri saw how stressed I was and gently chided me for it. What was going on here was amusing but completely irrelevant. I should just relax and enjoy this week as entertainment.

Slava's response was a tone darker. To him this session was reinforcing all images he had held about American business practices and how foreign they were to Russia. This was why Americans should not attempt to provide consulting advice in Russia. What were we expected to do with this – take Lego into our next meeting with a government official and say that we needed to work on our communication? Dmitri and Slava broke into quiet laughter – but then quickly paused and added a footnote. "We don't mean you, Phaedra. You are *nashi*. You understand us. It's them that we worry about," he gestured with his cigarette in a sweeping abstract stroke to the identical Arthur Androids in blue suits all earnestly engaged in a few moments of networking with their colleagues.

The rest of the week followed the same pattern. I looked with excitement at the agenda, hoping that maybe this *next* session would have some bits of content that would help to build my consulting skills and knowledge of the firm. But then my hopes would be dashed. Dmitri was right. The week was thoroughly amusing, but irrelevant.

The company motto of "Think Straight, Talk Straight" was thrown in at regular inter-vals – amidst moments of raucous frivolity. The introduction of different knowledge resources available within the firm was delivered as a comedic sketch emphasizing the absurdity of the alphabet soup of acronyms and jargon that the firm used in its com-munications. The Americans in the audience laughed knowingly – they actually under-stood the silly strings of acronyms being spouted. I, who had actually come seeking knowledge, was left no more enlightened then when the session began. To learn about the other service areas in the firm we were broken into teams and given the assignment to create a three minute info-mercial for a selected service area. Planning and prepara-tion occupied our team into the wee hours of the morning – with way too much alco-hol as a lubricant to keep the creative juices flowing. The end results were shared with the whole group the next day. Each skit was terribly amusing and clever – featuring props and music and costumes cobbled together overnight somehow. But altogether devoid of meaningful content.

As the course concluded, the facilitator smiled that with every end there is a new beginning. She urged each of us to take our packet of seeds back to our homes and plant the seeds. Nurture the plant. Watch it grow and blossom. And remember that this is a new life. I stared at the packet of seeds trying to remember if I had ever seen a flowering plant anywhere inside the Moscow city limits. With the exception of a win-dow box on the old Arbat, I had to answer "*nyet.*" My seeds were destined to rot – or perhaps attract cockroaches and rats.

The facilitator continued with her cooing. Back in our home offices we would continue our *transition* from our old life to our new life at Arthur Andersen. But we would no longer be alone. We had each other! With this, all the participants were issued a photo-booklet as a commemoration of the week. The booklet featured photos and contact information of all the participants. It was a nice effort by the organizers (and another demonstration of the amazing resources at the disposal of the firm) but I was doubtful that I would be in contact with any of my colleagues again. When I had attempted to socialize with the Americans, I learned that we had virtually nothing in common. They were auditors or tax consultants and lived a life of structured account-ing procedures, American television comedy, and sending their kids to soccer practice. Page after page of the photo book showed big American smiles and genuine commit-ment to the firm. Russians always comment that American portrait photos look ridicu-lous with toothy silly smiles. (Russian portraits are always serious and poised.) I had to laugh and agree and then quickly flicked to my photo. There I saw the model of a stern Russian woman glaring back at me. I knew Dmitri and Slava's photos would be the same.

There was an important lesson here somewhere. To the Russians I was truly *nashi.*

But what was I to the Americans now? And what did all of this mean in regards to ever returning back to the United States?

The week in Chicago was, in many ways, a short holiday from the reality of my life back in Moscow. Although my team all had computers now, in 1995 email was still extraordinary rather than a common day occurrence for us. Our senior partner, Raymond, still did not know how to send an email and the Russians on my team saw communication by email and phone to be an *event* rather than a constant chatter. Really, while I was in the United States, what could I possibly do to help them resolve anything in Russia anyway? Only Robert was linked to email regularly and even he had rare reason to send me anything. Even less since the development of his affair with Oksana. Mobile phones were non-existent for us. Therefore my week in Chicago had proved to be a week of blissful ignorance from whatever was going on back in Moscow.

My reprieve from the chaos and stresses of the project was short-lived. Vanya filled me in on all the news during the drive from Sheremyetovo back to my apartment. Like always, I was amazed at how although Vanya was nominally "just" a driver, he was totally linked into all the latest events and sub-plots going on with the project. And clearly he was understanding far more of the English language conversations going on the back seat of his car than many people realized.

Vanya opened by thanking me profusely for intervening with the arrival of Zeke, the junior auditor. Yes, the twenty mobile phones had been found in his luggage and yes, he had been detained for questioning. Fortunately, thanks to my tip, Volodya, our fixer, had gone to the airport to retrieve Zeke, rather than one of the standard drivers. Volodya's role was simply to make these sorts of everyday problems go away using his various connections and mysterious tactics. After a few hours Zeke had been released and was safely deposited at the Hotel Aerostar.

And of course the mobile phones didn't work. This started a rant by Vanya that went on for some time. Any of the Russians could have told the Americans that the American mobile phones would not work in Russia. But did they listen to the Russians? No! The Americans coming from Washington are all idiots. Yet again the views of the Russians are irrelevant. Why do the Americans think that they know what is best for Russia?

I tried to calm down Vanya. Look, the Americans didn't listen to me either! I tried to warn them as well that the American mobile phones wouldn't work in Russia, but no one listened to me. The DC office thought knew what was best for all of us.

Vanya muttered for a moment and then offered the next piece of news. The delegation of American investors to visit Ekaterinburg had been cancelled. The visas for all the participants had been suddenly revoked. Yes, the visas were organized through the Arthur Andersen main office, which was proficient in such things. No, no explanation was given for why the visas were cancelled – they just were. No, there was no form of recourse. No, Volodya, our fixer, would not be able to do anything. Volodya was a low level fixer — he could obtain a plane ticket for a flight that was sold out, or learn where petrol was for sale, or extract a person who was detained by customs. But he did not have the level of influence needed to sort out visas for twenty-something Americans — especially if there was someone in a higher power of authority who had already made known their opposition known to such an exercise.

Vanya's advice was simple. If some mysterious person in the Russian government had decided to cancel these visas, then our project should not challenge this. We had clearly crossed someone the wrong way. If they had the influence to cancel business visas suddenly, then who knows what else this person would be capable of.

So who was behind this? I knew that Vanya would have a theory. He sighed with frustration and looked at me. He had figured things out already based on snippets of overheard conversations. He tried to remain separated from political entanglements but it was not easy. But then, Vanya was always keen to demonstrate his insider knowledge to me. I knew I would get the answer out of him.

The same day that the visas of the American delegation were withdrawn, the auditors were summoned to meet with senior management of the Russian Privatization Center. This immediately caused me to pause. How did the RPC even know that our internal auditors were in town? Why did it matter to them?

Vanya replied to my questions with exasperation. The RPC knows *everything* of what is going on around here. And knowledge is power. It is all a matter of deciding what pieces of knowledge to use for what purposes.

Anyway, it was just the American auditors that were summoned, not the American management. Raymond was not even made aware of the meeting. In any case, the auditors were alerted to the "fact" that the Russian Privatization Center was "concerned about allegations of corruption" at the Ekaterinburg LPC. The RPC was doing its duty to alert the American auditors. The auditors would have an obligation to investigate.

There was silence while I digested this news. My heart sank. First the visas for the delegation to Ekaterinburg were revoked and then the auditors were called in. This was no coincidence. We were being churned in a classic Soviet era tactic that was now recycled in the bright new age of Russian power politics. Accuse your political enemy of breaking the law and then bring them down very publicly using some forum that could be called beyond reproach.

"So who did Nathan and Sergei Glebovich cross in Ekaterinburg?" Vanya asked the question that was already forming in my mind.

The answer was obvious. Carl had already seen it coming and had tried to warn me. The delegation of the visiting American investors had been organized by Nathan and Sergei Glebovich independently of the Russian Privatization Center. They had used Nathan and Raymond's own connections back in the United States to drum up interest in the event. Ever since I had delivered the fax machine to Ekaterinburg, they no longer had to rely on the Minister for Industrial Development for assistance with sending and receiving faxes. Sergei Glebovich was too independent, too willful. The Russian Privatization Center and its contacts were at risk of losing a power base in the region if Sergei Glebovich's plan to introduce American investors independently went ahead. Therefore it had to be stopped.

Upon my return to the office I found my team in an advanced state of uproar.

The directors from the Local Privatization Centers had been calling for me (and instead talking to Nadya, my lead accountant) in protest. They had been *notified* (not advised or consulted) that an American auditor would be coming by their offices at an appointed time to do a control check on the equipment and other accounting at their local offices. Some of the visits were being scheduled over weekends – as the auditors wanted the tour to be completed as quickly as possible. The calls came in to me all day from Rostov, Krasnodar, Stavropol, Chelyabinsk, Ekaterinburg, Tyumen, etc. I had been to their offices. I had seen the equipment myself. I had helped to place the orders. Nadya had already reviewed all of their records and inventoried their equipment against our purchase orders. Why was it necessary to send in American auditors? Did we distrust the Russians that much that we needed so many layers of review? How much were we paying the American auditors? Was this money paid for American auditors considered to be "aid"? If so, this was a very funny definition of aid – as all that the Russians saw was yet more reasons to bring in American consultants to pay ourselves. And why was it necessary to perform the audit on a Sunday? Did they understand how difficult it was to obtain building access on a weekend to these government facilities?

In addition, the "concern" from the Russian Privatization Center that there was "corruption" in the Ekaterinburg Local Privatization Center had resulted in predictable consequences. Denise had returned from her meeting at the RPC invigorated that she was going to do her part to expose and end corruption in Russia. Anyone who would be found to engage in corrupt practices would be publicly flogged and then cut off. No exceptions.

Zeke, the American junior accountant who had been tasked with the project of auditing the inventory and accounts of the LPCs, had already been dispatched for South Russia. Time was of the essence to review the books now for Ekaterinburg. More importantly, it had to be an accountant who spoke and read Russian – to get to the heart of what was happening in Ekaterinburg. As a result, Nadya was nominated somehow to be the unfortunate accountant to go out and review the activities in Ekaterinburg. If necessary, a formal independent enquiry would be rallied. But first, we had to send our own team out there for a first line investigation.

I found Nadya at her desk spouting a stream of profanities that I had only previously heard from the drivers when swearing about the GAI under their breath. She turned to me in a state of despair. She had worked hard for the past year to build her reputation and trust with the senior accountants at the LPCs. She was probably at least 20 years younger than them and therefore had a lot to prove in her own mind as well as in the credibility of the LPCs. And now.... She was asked to go and find evidence of corruption in Ekaterinburg. Sergei Glebovich was a favorite among the team. He was really trying to promote foreign investment. He truly believed in the future of Russia. And now Nadya was being directed to dredge up evidence against him! Just when she was starting to believe in the future of Russia and had started to hope that our project would produce something useful, it was all coming crashing back down on her that although the names were new on the business cards, nothing really had changed. Those in power would determine who would live and who would be exiled.

I pulled a chair up next to Nadya and tried to calm her down. If Sergei Glebovich has done nothing wrong, then she could just quickly return to Moscow and give Sergei Glebovich the stamp of approval. Everything would be fine. I said these words as encouragement, but then also realized how hollow they were.

Nadya immediately filled in what I had left unstated. "Phaedra, I'm sure you understand by now — I have no choice. I *have* to return from Ekaterinburg with some evidence of corruption."

Although she really did not need to remind me, Nadya then launched into a monologue of Oksana's recent troubles. Her family had been unceremoniously evicted from their apartment. Why? Because her apartment block had been condemned. Why had the apartment been condemned? Well, the written record said due to "safety hazards" — although everyone knew that in fact some unnamed occupant had obviously irritated people of higher authority.

Nadya continued with her rant. "Do you know the proverb? *Altinnova vora veshayut, a politnnovo chestvuyut.* 'One hangs the thief who stole 3 kopeks but honors the one who stole 50.' The little thief is the one who will be punished. The real criminal continues to operate as per usual. This is the way things are in Russia. The way they have always been."

She then fell into a meaningful pause, leaving her obvious conclusion unstated: "The way things will always be."

Nadya was right. Her options were simple — go out to Ekaterinburg and dig up something that would convict Sergei Glebovich of corruption, or otherwise she and her family would be drawn into the line of fire next from the higher authorities. A martyr would make a valiant statement in the face of such injustice. Martyrs exist in mythology and in documentary films. But in the real world of 1990s Russia, Nadya knew that if she exonerated Sergei Glebovich that she would be next in line for public retribution in the name of a higher cause — without anyone of substance to back her up. Nadya had dreams of an American MBA and a brighter future for herself. If she defended Sergei Glebovich, her whole professional reputation and future would be at risk. So of course she would go to Ekaterinburg. And of course she would dig up something that would provide evidence of corruption. This was the Russian tradition of the past 750 years or more and she would carry it on.

My reaction to Nadya's point of view was predictable — I started fuming and storming around the office, determined to solve the problems of the universe. Kolya's reaction upon seeing me in such a state was equally predictable. He pulled me into the stairwell for a few moments of alternate universe bliss and told me to calm down. There was really nothing I could do to change the situation. All my storming around and being frustrated about how Russia operated would be of no use. I would just be beating the wall with a dead fish. I had might as well realize it now and focus on what I could accomplish — and enjoy.

I emerged from the 11th floor stairwell in a much more positive frame of mind — with a bit more green slime on my clothing and in my hair and an agreement to go to Kolya's apartment for dinner on Friday evening.

19 TWICE SAVED

August 1995

Why did I accept that invitation from Kolya for dinner at his apartment? I was build-ing a list of justifications and rationalizations in my mind. (One obvious sign that I was getting involved with him for reasons that had little to do with romantic interest.)

At the top of the list was the simple observation that my cultural experience in Russia would be incomplete without actually dating a Russian. Yes, I had been out on weekend adventures with the girls from the office and my work weeks were a full immersion in Russian work experience. The Russians called me "*nashi*" but I won-dered if I really deserved that recognition. I was increasingly envious of the American guys and their never-ending stories of their adventures and escapades with the Russian *devushki*. Yes, they were focused on building a reputation for themselves and their sexual exploits – but I was envious to be hearing about a side of life in Russia and not participating fully in it.

And to be honest, I had become increasingly frustrated to be sidelined on the dat-ing scene in Russia. It was a fate that all the expat women had more or less resigned ourselves to – the expat men were almost universally focused on the delights of the Russian *devushki* that were limited only by their own imagination. The expat women had the option to abandon the dating scene altogether, be silently seething on the side-lines, or to concede and date the Russian man who seemed to be least likely to be overly controlling and dominating. None were satisfactory options and the young single expat women found ourselves to be the subject of scandal and gossip no matter which course we took. We were labeled as alternatively frigid or desperate by the expat men, who meanwhile were in competitions with each other regarding how fast they could walk into a nightclub and get a girl to agree to go home with them for the night.

Yes, it was a double standard. And yes, I was becoming extremely tired of it.

So finally I had concluded that if Kolya was going to offer me attention, then I was willing to take it.

So I wanted to step into the Russian dating scene and I got it – starting with dinner at Kolya's apartment. Of course by this point I knew the basics of what to expect over dinner and was braced for round after round of vodka shots and fish and potato pie. The best glasses were brought out for the occasion, with the price tags still stuck on. In my early days I would have picked at the labels and pulled them off (much to the horror of my hosts). Now I knew better – I paused to admire the price tag and commented on the fact that the glasses were from Stockmann's – one of the more expensive Swedish emporiums. The price tag on the glass was left as a declaration to all that Kolya was doing quite well for himself and could now afford such luxuries.

But this evening included an extra dimension that I had not fully anticipated – Kolya was living at home with his parents.

Of course, I should have realized this in advance. I knew that most Russians lived with multiple generations in a two or three room apartment. To the typical 28-year old American this idea is truly shocking. No matter how penniless we are, most American twenty-somethings would far prefer the abject depravity of a group house in some skanky neighborhood over continuing to live at home – under the watchful and judging eyes of the parents. Young Russians in the mid-1990s, however, did not have such options available.

So this leads up to dinner with Kolya's parents. There were four of us at the dinner table. This meant a mandatory minimum of four vodka shots – and we blasted by this threshold and kept going. Vodka is the great social lubricant and we were all quite festive and happy and talkative. But at some point the parents decided that they should cut their participation in the evening short and give Kolya and me a bit of space. So the classical music was turned up full volume in the living room and Kolya pulled me into his bedroom and closed the door. This was clearly a pre-organized arrangement. Whatever went on in Kolya's bedroom would not be overheard by the parents. Kolya looked at me and smiled and pulled me down onto his twin bed.

Just too strange of a situation. I instinctively recoiled from his touch. The opera belted out of the stereo in the living room and reverberated through the walls. His parents had encouraged us to retreat to his bedroom and now were just steps away. For Kolya the time for talking was over and now he wanted to move on to other activities. For me, this was not exactly the most intimate of environments. And a wave of doubts washed over me. Really, Kolya was an interpreter from my office. What was I doing here? This was going against everything I had attempted to promote with the girls on my team.

But then what did I really expect? I knew the Russian style of dating was that as soon as a girl accepted a drink from a guy that she had essentially consented to be his for the night. I had agreed to come to his house for dinner and was now in an entirely predictable situation. As Kolya had rightly observed on the stairwell at the office, I had a habit of taking everything way too seriously. The American men had, on many occasions, all pointed out the obvious fact of why they preferred Russian *devushki* over American women – the Americans had far too many hang ups. And so far this evening I was proving their point for them.

For some reason my thoughts wandered to the *bannya,* one of my favorite authentic Russian experiences. And then I heard the stern instructions from the sauna matron: "Quiet everyone! Time to relax!" She was right. To truly relax sometimes you just had to force all the other conversations in your mind to the side. I laughed that I was now lying in bed with an attractive Russian man while taking subconscious advice from a fierce naked woman built from 200 plus pounds of potato-fed flesh.

I laughed and pulled Kolya closer. Yes, my various stresses and anxieties would still be there tomorrow. Tonight, however, I should just push that all aside. What good is a moment if you don't seize it and enjoy it?

"*Carpe diem!*" I repeated the motto of all expats and released my tension with another round of laughter.

Kolya needed no further encouragement.

The following weekend Kolya brought me along to the "Twice Saved" exhibition at the Pushkin Museum in Moscow (together with a number of his other friends). Now, I must note that this was one of the most incredible gallery exhibitions I have ever seen for many reasons. It was a phenomenal collection of top-tier Impressionist and early Modernist paintings – all art that had been spirited away from Germany into hiding by the Red Army during WWII (known as the "Great Patriotic War" to the Russians). The Germans had proclaimed that the paintings were stolen. The Russians had not even acknowledged the existence of the art prior to this exhibition. Therefore for decades speculation had mounted for the art's whereabouts and many assumed the pieces to have been destroyed in war. With this as background, you must recognize that the exhibition was an extraordinary affair. Absolutely world-class pieces of art on display for the first time in over 50 years. Plus the event represented a major landmark in Russian history in that the government was actually acknowledging it had these pieces in its possession – where for the previous half-century the question had been met with only denial or silence.

Of course, although the Russians now acknowledged the existence of the art – the title of the exhibition "Twice Saved" demonstrated that there was still quite a gap between the German view and the Russian view of the situation. The official statement of the exhibition was that the art was rescued from certain destruction by the Red

Army. And now, in the spirit of openness, the art was "saved" a second time – this time rescued from the dark dusty corners wherever it had been held in secrecy for the prior five decades. The German response was that the art should be returned to Germany, not displayed and flaunted in Russia. The European media tagline was "Twice Stolen".

The controversy became a hot subject of discussion with all the Russians and expats. Most expats started with the belief that stolen property should be returned to the rightful owners. The Russians responded then with the question of whether we held the same view regarding the British Museum in London – packed to the ceiling with prizes from various British Imperial conquests. Once you started to argue for repatriation of war prizes, where would those claims end – 100 years, 500 years, 1000 years? And soon it became apparent to everyone that, like many problems in Russia, there was no black and white answer. The truth was somewhere in a zone of grey. And as a result, everyone in Moscow was determined to go visit the exhibition for themselves.

The weekend we visited "Twice Saved", the lines to the Pushkin Museum crushed down the front stairs, the length of the approaching path, then several hundred meters down Ulitsa Volkhonka. The line was not moving forward at anything resembling a reasonable rate. I fully expected that by closing we would still be a hundred meters away from the front entrance.

Kolya rapidly assessed our predicament, gave me a quick kiss and promised that he would sort out the situation. It was unacceptable that we would be waiting in line here with the common public. So off he marched to the front door and slid inside for some negotiations with god-knows-who. The friends compared notes and assured me that they were confident that Kolya would figure out some way for us all to bypass the line.

A few minutes later Kolya appeared by my side and gestured to the group that we would be able to slide into the museum by the side entrance. The security guard there would let us in with no questions and no wait. Kolya planted a kiss firmly on my cheek as ownership more than affection. With a hand on my waist, he steered me towards the side entrance, with a whisper that I was to remain silent and look Russian while we made our way inside. I had already anticipated that. Like with the GAI, if the building security knew that there was an American in the group, the admission price undoubtedly would be raised.

Kolya had a reserved smile. The ability to secure privileges and exemptions was the currency of social prestige. Of course, I was curious how he did it – whether it was raw cash or something else that allowed us to circumvent a queue that would otherwise have meant four plus hours of purgatory. When we reached the side entrance I learned Kolya's little secret – his Ministry of Finance security pass. He had obtained it the prior year through our USAID project with the Ministry of Finance and he had wisely held onto it since then. "A key to all that Moscow has to offer," he assured me. He had a full-fledged Ministry of Finance *propusk*, but no positions were actually stated on the passes. Therefore when Kolya aggressively pushed himself to the front of the line and flashed the pass as a right of special privilege, no one really was the wiser that he was actually just an interpreter for an American consulting team that did a small project at the Ministry over a year earlier.

Kolya smiled with self-satisfaction, took my arm in a classic display of Russian male control, and propelled me through the side entrance of the Pushkin Museum under the watchful eyes of the gallery security. The Ministry of Finance pass served its purpose. Kolya's social status was validated with the audience of his friends. And I, at his side, had quietly followed his instructions, like any obedient *devushka*. Kolya was having a great day.

Saved or Stolen? The debate went to the core of the Russian way of life.

Nadya returned from Ekaterinburg a changed woman. "Loss of Innocence" is not the best description — as she was not exactly a naïve girl to begin with. But it is one thing to be aware of what happens in the political machine that is Russia and another thing to be churned by it. Nadya was no longer a bystander. Sergei Glebovich's future and her own would be determined by what she would do next.

I intercepted Nadya before she had a chance to speak with the American auditors.

"Please tell me that you are going to be able to clear Sergei Glebovich's reputation regarding the accusation of corruption," I begged quietly.

The bright light in Nadya's eyes had gone out and she just returned a stoic stare. "Phaedra, you know that I had to return with something. This is Russia, everyone is breaking some rule at all times just to get through our lives. If I protected Sergei Glebovich, the investigation could easily be expanded to include me and all the others here in this office."

So what was it that she brought back as evidence? I wanted to know the accusations that would be levied against Sergei Glebovich and what evidence Nadya had found. She gave this question a dismissive wave. "I don't want to discuss it. You have seen enough that you should already know."

And yes, it was easy enough to guess where to look if you wanted to find some-thing to unearth as a black mark against Sergei Glebovich. Look no further than the fact that the standard waiting time to install a telephone line was about two years. The Ekaterinburg office, however, had telephone lines within weeks. Undoubtedly this was just the tip of what could be investigated as "evidence of corruption". But what was corruption for the American auditors was essential just to get anything accomplished for the Russians.

Zeke had also returned from his quick tour of Russia with a notebook full of findings.

Top on the list was the fact that every computer he inspected (without exception) had pirated software installed. Although Denise claimed that she was horrified to learn such things, I could see that she was secretly pleased that her trip was turning up such results for her. This was further justification of her existence and evidence to those back in Washington that she was an asset to the team.

I groaned in despair as I tried to explain the situation to Denise. Yes, we had ordered Russian language licenses of all Microsoft Office software. But English language versions had been delivered. (They were still in their original plastic wrapped packaging, nicely organized in every office.) We had attempted to obtain the Russian software through the proper channels, but there was delay after delay. If we had purchased the Russian software legally in Moscow, we would have been violating USAID procurement rules – as the licenses had already been purchased in the USA and we did not have an authorized supplier in Moscow. Therefore if the LPCs had followed all the rules, they would be stuck with English-only software – despite that fact that (with the exception of the interpreters for the American consultants) none of the local staff knew any English at all. And, of course, none of them had used computers before either, so the possibility of them being productive on computers with foreign language software was simply laughable. Our options were to break the rules or to just keep the computers in their boxes for a few more months until the official licenses arrived from the USA. Honestly, she had evidence that we *had paid for* proper Russian language licenses, but English ones had been delivered. How bad was that really?

Bad enough, apparently. Rules were rules. And rules had been broken. So, in the absence of pirated Russian software and no legal licenses, what was the team supposed to do? Denise simply responded that I was the project manager and it was my problem to sort out – but we needed to ensure that we complied with the USAID procurement practices and international laws at the same time.

I would be told what I could not do, but was not offered any solution for the way out of the corner we were in.

Although I was miserable, the real burden of the audit findings fell not on me but on Raymond, as our in country lead partner. I invited myself into his office, intending to commiserate and plan how we could continue to move the project forward in light of such challenges. How could we get the American auditors to understand the situation we were in? Punishing Sergei Glebovich through a public accusation of corruption was simply not fair. We all knew that he was simply being crushed by political forces because he had threatened the power base of unnamed people who were on a higher level in the food chain.

Raymond had said himself that Sergei Glebovich was the only LPC Director he had met who really earnestly wanted to do something meaningful to build Russia's future.

He was sincere with his efforts to bring in prospective foreign investors and promote real restructuring of the newly privatized companies – which was more than what we had seen anywhere else, for the millions of dollars that had been sunk into the project.

Raymond himself had invested enormous personal effort into the project to bring over the delegation of American investors. Was he now just going to let that drop?

"Phaedra, you know already what we have to do next. We have to condemn Sergei Glebovich's actions and then request the RPC to remove him from his role as Director of the Local Privatization Center. We may be on a project in Russia, but in the end we are part of Arthur Andersen. We are part of an international audit practice – where there is nothing more important to the firm than its reputation. We cannot be seen to be protecting or defending accused criminals. Can you imagine the headlines if we attempted to dispute the accusations? 'Arthur Andersen defends corrupt government official.' No. Obviously we cannot do that. We have to be on the side of investigating and removing corruption from Russian practices – no matter how much we may like them personally."

Everyone would play their designated role in the grand game of Russian politics. Raymond had been cornered and he knew it. He liked Sergei Glebovich. He knew that the accusations were hollow and originated from a higher level political grudge. But it would have to be him, the Arthur Andersen partner, to request the removal of Sergei Glebovich from his role as Director of the Ekaterinburg LPC. The unnamed Russians who had felt threatened by Sergei Glebovich's growing direct relationships with the local enterprises and foreign investors would be able to remain safely in the shadows, their power base secured for another day.

And what would be the consequences of the audit findings that we had pirated software on every one of our computers? I knew that this finding, while incidental to the events that were playing out with Sergei Glebovich, could also be potentially manipulated by those influencing the actions of the Russian Privatization Center.

"To be determined," Raymond answered simply. "We will have to do something to look like we are serious about responding. But to be determined exactly what."

Although the auditors would profess that they were only concerned about the facts – at the end of the day, perception was apparently more important than reality. Denise would return to the United States, to glowing praise that she was upholding the integrity of the firm and fighting corruption in Russia. She would be praised, while Raymond and I were barely averting a reprimand from senior management – look at what had been happening just under our noses! Good thing that someone with the keen observational skills of the audit team had been sent in to investigate!

And I was left wondering if our efforts were helping or hurting the cause of private initiative and Russian economic development.

Over the weekend I was absolved from making any further decisions, as I fell into the role of Russian *devushka* on the arm of Kolya en route to whatever he had organized for the evening's entertainment together with his friend, Evgeni, and his girlfriend, Natasha. The four of us plunged into the caverns of the Moscow metro system, taking an obscure line deep into the dim crumbling neighborhoods where real Muscovites lived – a different world entirely from the bright lights of the increasingly affluent city core. I was then led through a labyrinth of identical Soviet era apartment blocks, each as bleak and colorless as the next.

I asked my companions where we were and where we were going. Kolya asked if I was lost yet. I confessed that I had absolutely no idea where we were in Moscow. He smiled and said "good."

We were on the way to what he declared to be the "best restaurant in Moscow." My glance at the neighborhood must have betrayed my skepticism and he continued.

"This is a Russian-only restaurant. No foreigners allowed. I had to get special permission from the owner to bring you tonight. I told him that you are *nashi*, not like the other Americans."

And with that, Kolya pushed open a door into an ordinary apartment block and led us to an unmarked door. After a knock we were admitted by a gruff matronly woman, into what was clearly originally a private apartment. I smiled with a "Good evening." The woman flinched at my American accent, but gave a stern grimace to Kolya that said that she was prepared to concede an exception – just this once. She then added a sharp notice that the bathroom in the apartment was off limits to us. "If in necessity you must go onto the street," she advised.

I was immediately in love with the restaurant. Every square inch of available space had been packed with mismatched tables and chairs. The features of the original Soviet era apartment had been left intact, including the orange, brown, and green flocked wallpaper and hideous chandelier in the center of the room. Not one ruble had been spent on redecorating the flat or furnishings to make it look more attractive to the customers. This was not some corporate interpretation of a Russian family restaurant, it was the real thing. The chairs creaked and bit at my clothing.

"You are a Russian *devushka* now," Kolya whispered in my ear while squeezing my arm gently. "Don't act American or you will get us all thrown out and I will not be able to come back."

I smiled. Yes, I would play the role of *devushka*. I was deep in Russian territory now and would do what I needed to in order to fit in. It was a privilege to be invited here.

And of course what this meant was that for the bulk of the dinner, Natasha and I would be decorative objects at the dinner table while Kolya and Evgeni engaged in animated discussion among themselves. They were quickly on to subjects that would be difficult for me to participate in anyway – the latest Russia v Sweden hockey match, issues they were dealing with for car repairs, reminiscing about friends from college.

The Russian terminology was difficult for me – as this was far outside what I talked about on a daily basis in the office – but besides the terminology, it was clear from their mannerisms and body language that this would be a dinner where Kolya and Evgeni would have a great conversation as two friends and Natasha and I would be parked to the side.

In the United States if two couples are out to dinner and the guys are engaged in their own conversation, instinctively the girls will strike up a conversation of their own. I tried to talk to Natasha, but really knew nothing about her and didn't know where to begin. (And, as I noted before, my general Russian conversational skills were not great anyway on non-business subjects.) Natasha gave me brief one or two word answers to my questions, but quickly made it clear with her body language that she was perfectly satisfied with just sitting quietly on the sidelines.

Now being ignored by Kolya, Evgeni, and Natasha, I turned my attention to the food – which had started to arrive. And yes, Kolya was right – this *was* the best restaurant in Moscow. The couple who ran the restaurant had completely ignored the cosmetic touches of western restaurateurs and focused on what really matters – the food. All the same traditional Russian dishes that I had eaten many times before at countless functions with Russian government officials, but now served up the way they were intended to be made. I was now pleased to be excluded from the conversation so that I could focus my undivided attention on the food.

Blinni were light and delicate and just seconds from the kitchen to our table. Creamy butter melted in moments. Then a spoonful of glistening caviar on top. Devoured greedily and far too quickly, I must admit. Next were mushrooms – fresh picked, earthy and sautéed to an incredible consistency. Just tough enough to give a bit of texture but then the teeth would slice through and give a deep woody warmth to the stomach. A bowl of pelmeni – a Russian-style ravioli in a delicate stock, topped with a splash of fresh sour cream. The pastry shell dissolved in my mouth and the contrast of the light broth and hearty meat was invigorating.

This was the genuine article of a family restaurant, running wild in Russia. Such a place would be crushed from existence in the United States under the burden of health regulations and compliance. Like with Jim's video store and Krizis Zhanra, the best places in Moscow were unmarked and found only via word of mouth – and clearly operating in very grey areas of the economy.

But then again, was there anyone who was operating with clean business practices in Moscow at this time? The drivers told me it was nearly impossible to get a driver's license without bribes to the right people. The same would certainly be true for operating a business of any sort. In the absence of individual rights, there were permissions that could be granted and withdrawn at the discretion of those in authority. Places like the western restaurants, that operated openly – with street signage and even the occasional advertisement in *the Moscow Times* — would certainly have connections and sponsors in much higher places. Under the veneer of respectability, shades of grey were everywhere.

I laughed to think of what Denise's reaction would be to this restaurant. Denise would see the situation in much more simple terms. She would take one look at the lack of a restroom, the cramped tables, lack of ventilation and declare that the place must be operating illegally and a health hazard. Someone must be alerted to these violations! She would be doing her good deed as an upstanding citizen to ensure full compliance of the law — whatever that was.

Never mind, that in the face of such rigor nothing would be left standing in Russia.

Many hours later, Kolya, Evgeni, Natasha, and I left the restaurant with no name and continued on to the next destination of the evening. It was after midnight so the Metro had closed and we hitched a ride from the nearest main street.

The destination? The White Cockroach. In keeping with my role as the subdued, indifferent *devushka*, I tried not to show too much excitement at the prospect. But inside I was absolutely elated. First the hidden gem of a restaurant, now the White Cockroach — the agenda this evening was exactly what I had hoped for when sticking my toe into the cultural experiment of the Russian dating scene.

We were on our way to one of the more exclusive clubs in Moscow — invitation only. I had learned about the White Cockroach mainly through reference in news articles and on television. This was a club of the Russian intelligentsia elite — academics were welcome, New Russians were not. That being said, the club had still been in the news a few times as the scene for assassinations. Apparently even the intelligentsia had their enemies.

A single light bulb illuminated the unmarked entrance into the club. Another basement that was converted to a club, this time under a police station. I marveled at the brashness of whoever had pulled off the recent assassination here, literally under the noses of the police above. Or perhaps with the blessing of the police above. I would never know.

Kolya gave the guard at the door the password for the evening. We were eyed with scrutiny to ensure that we passed the "face test" that was *de rigeur* of all clubs. Despite the fact we had the password was not a guarantee of entry — we also had to look presentable in the eyes of the bouncer. I held Kolya by the arm and did my best bored *devushka* pout while the bouncer took a good look at Natasha's and my black spandex mini-skirts.

We were waved inside where the next bouncer asked (almost courteously) if he could check our weapons. He offered a check tag, like what you would usually receive for a coat, and gestured to a safe where the weapons would be locked. We brusquely responded that, no, we weren't carrying weapons. The bouncer looked a bit surprised, but in any case let us continue on in. No search or inspection to see if we were actually carrying weapons, of course. We just had decided not to check in anything and that was all he needed to know.

Now downstairs, we were inside the club that, until recently, had been the small rat-infested basement of a Police Station. The décor was simple brown and beige. I looked around and was surprised to see not a dance floor but a pool table. Possibly the only pool table I had seen to date in the former Soviet Union. And no music. Yes, it was still early (maybe 1am), but still, to come into a club and be met with total silence was a bit odd. Only a few others were hanging out in the back room. Every word of every conversation could be overheard. Foreigners were not welcome here. My American accent would be overheard in a moment, inviting the bouncer to throw me and my companions back out onto the street – or worse.

Kolya parked me at the bar with a glass of champagne in hand while he and Evgeni tried to demonstrate their prowess at billiards. It was rapidly apparent that they had played maybe twice before in their lives. The guys laughed quietly and bantered and attempted to look stylish and sophisticated. I again was excluded from their conversation and attempted to turn to Natasha, who was sitting next to me with her own glass of champagne. She returned my advances with a stare that was not entirely cold but simply said silently that it was not appropriate for me to be chatting with her, no matter how quiet I was trying to be.

I therefore had no choice but to continue to play the role of the subdued pouting *devushka*. So I sat back on my barstool and recrossed my legs and attempted to look the part.

This is what I had wanted out of a Russian dating experience, wasn't it? Kolya was taking me places that would otherwise be inaccessible to me as an American. He was introducing me to corners of Moscow society and experiences that I knew existed but had not yet seen for myself. I even found myself a bit pleased at my new secret identity as a Russian *devushka*. Kolya had whispered to me that my legs looked "exquisite" with the black mini skirt and heels.

I took the compliment, but I knew that this was just a charade. This is not who I really am. Strong willed American women expats are not mentally equipped to play the role of Russian *devushka*. Yes, I was sitting quietly on the sidelines and being told what to do next, but this was an effort for me, not my nature. I was engaged in a social science research project of what life would be like dating a Russian man and I was getting it. Kolya was a good guy. I will say nothing negative about him. But each moment that I sat obediently doing what was expected of me rather than what I wanted, I felt rebellion growing inside.

The situation with Sergei Glebovich in Ekaterinburg had come to its conclusion that week. Nadya had done what was expected of her and handed over documentation that would serve as evidence of "corruption." Raymond had then dutifully made a statement to the Russian Privatization Center that Arthur Andersen had no choice but to request the removal of Sergei Glebovich from his position as Director of the Local Privatization Center. Again, not what he wanted to do, but exactly what was expected of him. The RPC had thanked Raymond and Arthur Andersen for our diligence and then very quickly and publicly ousted Sergei Glebovich. The nominated replacement was described by Nathan simply as "utterly boring" and someone who just sat at his desk waiting for the next set of instructions from the RPC. Everyone had played their role in the event exactly as had been scripted by some unseen hand. The balance of power had been retained.

I had been furious of course, but powerless. The treatment of Sergei Glebovich was not fair, but what was the alternative? He had been found to be engaged in corrupt practices by our own accounting team. Of course Raymond had to act. I had stormed around the office frustrated with my inability to do anything at all that would be promoting the side of truth and justice.

Returning back mentally to the White Cockroach, I finished my glass of champagne and then laughed to myself with irony. Who was I to criticize others for playing their part in the grand spectacle that was Russian power politics? Here I was pretending to be something I clearly was not. I was neither madly in love with Kolya, nor a Russian *devushka*, nor an aspiring social climber in the Russian social elite. So why the act? How could I critique Nadya and Raymond while carrying on this charade of my own on a much smaller scale – and clearly much more voluntarily. I was offering criticism by day, but playing games of my own at night.

The contradiction had to end. If I was going to eventually leave Russia with anything resembling my mental stability, at least I would need to attempt to live a consistent life. My actions needed to be because of my own decisions. I was not a pouting *devushka* quietly pleased to be Kolya's decorative object. My actions with him were not my natural behavior, but that of an alternate character I had assumed. The silly game of make-believe was over. My social science experiment in Russian dating was coming to an abrupt conclusion.

As soon as I had come to this realization I was on my feet and giving Kolya a quick kiss goodbye and walking out alone into the Moscow night. I certainly left Kolya totally baffled. What had happened just then to cause me to abruptly end not only the date but our relationship? (If you could call it that.) I tried to explain later but I was never sure that he fully understood. I needed to live my life with consistency before I would allow myself to critique anyone else.

My Russian dating experiment was over.

20   THE GIFT

August 1995

As it turned out, the whole Moscow chapter of my Russian expat life was over as well. With the departure of Sergei Glebovich and the mounting evidence that our Local Privatization Centers would be able to do nothing that was not centrally mandated from the RPC, I became rapidly demoralized with my role. The whole stated purpose of the project was to establish local consulting centers that would be able to provide on-the-ground services to recently privatized enterprises. Yes, the centers were fully USAID funded to start with, but were supposed to start to build a fee-based clientele and eventually be self-supporting. In the end the LPCs were government entities, not private consultancies. Although millions of dollars of taxpayer money had been sunk into the exercise, I realized that the LPCs would never become independent consulting centers – their focus was on pleasing the officials in Moscow, not understanding true client needs and delivering services in their Regions. Without the ability for the LPCs to do any projects of their own, all we had really achieved was establishment of a framework to keep certain people on payroll within the approved power structure.

In addition, the whole direction of my data collection project had been resolved unsatisfactorily with USAID making the statement that it was "empowering" the Russian Privatization Center to define future projects that were in the best interests of promoting economic development and foreign investment – including how this data would actually be used and maintained. With the hollow phrase of "empowerment," the last remaining scraps of my hopes for the project had been shredded. The completed data base was spirited away to the Russian Privatization Center for those in positions of authority to determine exactly who and under what conditions would have access to information about the privatized companies.

The final blow to my morale was when USAID actually awarded our company with a "phase 2" round of funding for the LPCs. Yes, despite everything USAID and the Russian Privatization Center actually declared our project to be a success and therefore worthy of another year of funding. From the perspective of a pure read of our work order, yes, we had accomplished everything that was specified – establishing offices, hiring staff, providing computer equipment, collecting data on privatized companies. This was all that was formally expected of us. And yes, we had delivered. The higher, loftier premise of promoting private enterprise did not have any measurable goals or activities. Therefore no one in higher levels of authority held us accountable for such things. And I was coming to realize that Raymond, Joseph, Nathan, Sergei Glebovich, Alyosha, and I were the only ones who were actually bothered by this.

Under the premise of promoting private enterprise, our US government aid project had in fact only served to strengthen the role of the Russian central government and its control over what would and would not happen in regional Russia. Of course, with a bit of reflection and observation I should have come to that realization much earlier. But my optimism had blinded me to what was really happening on the project. I wanted to support the growth of Russian independent private businesses throughout the country. Therefore, in the face of everything I had seen, I had still wanted to believe that our project to be worthwhile.

But no more. The energy was completely drained from me. I wasn't quite ready to give up on Russia entirely, but I needed a new project where I could *really* make a difference this time. I turned to Raymond for advice and guidance.

I've said it before, but I'll say it again. Raymond was simply one of the best mentors/managers that a young eager consultant could ever hope to have. As he was a retired partner who had come to Russia entirely for his own amusement, he was above the petty politics that are omnipresent among those battling their way up the corporate ladder. His recent decision to "expose" Sergei Glebovich for corruption came from his deep loyalty to the firm as a whole, rather than any personal aspirations. He epitomized the "Think Straight, Talk Straight" motto that had been much parroted in my consultant training camp in St. Charles.

So therefore I came to Raymond pleading with him to help me sort out a better situation for my career and for my mental stability. I was not disappointed.

My request coincided very neatly with the problem Raymond was facing about what to do in the aftermath of the negative audit results and the heightened crackdown from Moscow on any rogue activities of the LPCs. In South Russia Joseph continued to be miserable and both he and his ally Noah (the Peace Corps volunteer who I had met earlier that summer) were effectively prevented from initiating any independent consulting activities in the Region. Meanwhile on another Arthur Andersen project in St Petersburg, the in country project manager had recently abruptly returned to the United States – a new project manager was needed. A rotation of roles would solve many problems at once. Joseph would move from South Russia to Moscow and take over my role here. I would then be dispatched to St Petersburg to take on the real estate registration project based there. There would be a friendly face on the team in St Petersburg waiting for me - my friend/colleague Paul had joined the team several months earlier as a junior analyst.

The prospect of the project excited me. Real estate registration! This was at the heart of what was needed to build the foundation for a true private Russian economy. Although the apartments across Russia had been "privatized" and handed over to their occupants, the legal framework for property title validation and transfer was still shaky. My knowledge of property title registration processes was non-existent, but this did not stop my enthusiasm. Property title validation was fundamental to the creation of new small businesses. Without a functioning property title registration and validation process, banks would not be able to issue loans or mortgages – crippling the growth of private wealth and independence. Yes, I could see real purpose here! I was thrilled at the role I was asked to play with the growth of the vibrant Russian future.

The Russian girls on my team were not happy about the planned changes and did their best to try to talk me out of it. "*Eto myilo za shchilo*" they all warned. The translation literally means that you are trading piece of soap for a comb, but the purpose of the expression is more ominous – you are trading one worthless object for another. I was bright eyed and eager about the idea that this *next* project would be different. Somehow in St Petersburg I would be able to *really* make a difference for the future of Russia. Nadya was much more skeptical. Certainly the fact that the project had been through about four different project managers in the last year should be some warning that I should heed?

I kept the farewells short and unceremonious. Really I wasn't saying goodbye to Moscow and my team here just yet. I would just be seeing them a lot less often. I promised that I would be back regularly. Although my new project office was in St Petersburg, Moscow was still Arthur Andersen's main headquarters for all the USAID projects. The new partner I would report to, Patrick, agreed to let me keep my Moscow-based apartment after we quickly calculated that even if I had to be in Moscow for just four days each month, the cost of hotel rooms in Moscow was now so extraordinary that the apartment could be justified.

Change seemed to be sweeping through many people's lives at once in those weeks. But then again, change was one of the few constants in Russia at that time. Gloria finished her role as the HR manager for the team and returned to the Arthur Andersen offices in Washington DC for her next challenge. Oksana was promoted to be the new HR assistant under Robert's watchful guidance as the Office General Manager (I laughed to myself the ridiculousness of the situation.) The American Advisor to the St Petersburg LPC abruptly left the country in the wake of some mysterious event there.

(This LPC was managed by a different consultancy, so I did not know much of the details, but could only draw my own conclusions.) Noah, the Peace Corps volunteer in Stavropol, had accepted the role as his replacement. He was close friends with Joseph, so why he agreed to this assignment after seeing what was going on with Joseph was a complete mystery to me.

And my friend Spencer had been accepted to Harvard Business School.

Spencer and I needed to catch up for a farewell beer before his departure. The concept of a bar where you catch up for a drink after work really didn't exist much beyond Rosie O'Grady's, the Irish pub that somehow bizarrely seemed to fit in with the rapidly evolving landscape of Moscow. We decided, instead to meet at the collection of aluminum kiosks near my office at Park Kulturi that was more consistent with a scene from *Blade Runner* than a biergarten. The haphazard sheds sold the staple items of dried fish, Coca-Cola, cigarettes, and Snickers bars, but then other items appeared and disappeared at random intervals – shoelaces, pens, dried noodles. Black Death Vodka, with its striking skull and crossbones logo, was becoming increasingly popular we noted. Not the sort of brand that would sell in the United States, but here in Moscow it seemed to be totally appropriate.

Change was everywhere. Maybe it was the summer air. Maybe there was a revitalized growth spurt in the Russian economy. Orange juice in boxes imported from somewhere in Western Europe was a pleasant surprise in one kiosk. Then we had to laugh at the name of the brand – Taraxa. This is "cockroach" in Russian. What numbskull of a marketing genius decided to try to sell their brand in Russia without even doing the basic research to find out what their brand meant in the local language? Okay folks, line up here and buy your "cockroach" orange juice! Well, at least we were not the only ones suffering from idiocy back in the home office..

We commiserated with the shared understanding of the terrible truth that after a quick visit to a five star hotel in Moscow, those from the home office could retreat back to Washington DC and declare themselves to be "experts" on how things "really worked" in Russia. We had signed on to years of hard work in Russia with a sense of adventure, a belief that we would help to make a positive impact on the country, and conviction that somehow the experience would be good for our careers. Was any of it true?

My rant moved from the unknown marketing team of "Taraxa", to Denise and the auditors, to the latest source of such frustrations – I had encountered a British backpacker in Moscow just a few days earlier. His presence had baffled me. The Russian bureaucratic hell to obtain a tourist visa and the complete lack of budget accommodation had thus far served as an effective barrier to entry to such travelers. Even more baffling was that I had encountered him with a heavy tome of *The Brothers Karamazov* (in the original Russian) in one of the most western of Moscow restaurants – Patio Pizza.

At first I had been impressed. Dostoyevsky was challenging enough to read in English. I certainly did not have nearly the Russian language capability to be able to read such heavy literature in Russian – even after six years of studying Russian and now over 18 months of living in the former Soviet Union. How long had he been studying Russian and living here to be able to achieve such a level of literacy?

No, the backpacker responded, he had not actually read a word in Russian before he arrived in the country last week. He had simply decided that the way to learn a country's soul was through its literature. So he had the enormous tome of *The Brothers Karamazov* on the table and on his lap he was pecking through a dictionary – looking up one word at a time.

"What an arrogant poser!" Spencer laughed the obvious point. "Gaining a deeper understanding of the Russian soul – at Patio Pizza."

"And the most frustrating thing to me is that he actually believes it," I replied. "He will return back to London and tell everyone about his accomplishments and struggles. Denise returned back to Washington DC with her little *matryoshkas* and ticket stubs from the Bolshoi. And both will exert a moral superiority that they understand Russia better than we do."

Spencer could only respond by buying me a warm beer and crackers (close to expiration date) from a nearby kiosk. The next kiosk over was simply a charred blackened skeleton – the remains of some dispute that went badly for the operator apparently. A few plastic chairs were poised by a grizzled man cooking skewers of *shashlik* over a burning oil drum. After purchasing a bit of charred meat each, we settled in for a lovely warm August evening. The backpacker could have his pretentious moment at Patio Pizza. We would appreciate the bleak beauty and raw energy of our *Blade Runner*-style biergarten.

Change was visible everywhere. From our position I could see my office building. Although the exterior of the building still looked like it had barely survived an air-raid, progress had started with rebuilding the exterior wall on the 10th floor. No scaffolding or safety barricades, of course. But still progress appeared to be going in a forward direction. Soon Kolya's and my illicit rendezvous spot would be forever enclosed and turned into some Russian version of a modern office space.

Looking in front of us, renovations were also underway at the Park Kulturi Metro station. A pile of concrete rubble and jumbled escalator parts looked like they had just been vomited from the depths of the Metro and deposited unceremoniously on the street. We sipped our warm beer, ate our charred flesh, contemplated the scene, and were content. Life was good. Change was coming to Russia. Maybe some of it even would prove to be positive.

A stream of humanity passed in front of us. The working day was over and everyone gravitated to the metro station. A *devushka* passing by sported a fashionable short hair-cut, carefully styled. Wow, that was new. To date I had mainly seen blunt cuts where the objective was practicality rather than style.

Then we saw three men running through the crowd. Or more accurately two men carrying what looked like Kalashnikovs, chasing a third. The one in the lead was clearly desperate to escape and attempted to elude his pursuers by scrambling over the pile of concrete and metal rubble. The men behind him were too quick, however. They caught their target and wrestled him to the ground, then dragged him by the arms into the cavern of the Metro Station. None of the three were in police or other official uniform. I couldn't say if that made me feel any better or worse for the guy who had just been abducted. I was just glad that the ones openly carrying weapons had decided not to open fire.

Others had certainly witnessed the scene, but no one had paused or batted an eye. This was everyday life in Moscow. It was someone else's crisis not your own. Better to not be involved – whatever that was. Would any bystanders report the abduction to the police? Almost certainly not. Nothing good could possibly come of raising a hand to be noticed by either the police or whatever shady characters were involved in that scene.

"So how will life at Harvard compare to this?" I asked Spencer as a punctuation to the event we had just witnessed.

"How can you even compare the two?" Spencer simply responded. "Moscow and Harvard exist in two alternate planes of reality. Harvard represents the essence of continuity and a predictable future. And Moscow – only the present matters here."

"You say that although you know that the city is 750 or so years old," I responded.

"You know the Russian expression – 'the only thing more uncertain than our future is our past'," Spencer smiled. "Even history is not constant here, as each new leader seeks to rewrite it. I'm done with Russia. Yes, this all is wildly amusing. But I want a future – and here, that is an unreasonable expectation."

Spencer was saying the same things that Sarah had said to me a few months earlier with her departure. He had reached some point of no return and had mentally cut himself off from Russia. Exactly what had happened so that he knew it was his time to go?

"You just know when it is your time," he said cryptically. "When it is your time to leave Russia, there will be no doubt at all. You will just leave."

Like with Sarah I started to suggest that maybe I should go as well. My last project had not finished well. In fact, in my opinion, none of the projects I had worked on in Russia or Kazakhstan were stunning examples of success. Certainly not worth the blood, sweat, and tears – and taxpayer money – that had gone into them.

Spencer shook his head, no. I still had optimism about the future of Russia. Just listen to how I described Sergei Glebovich's activities and so desperately wanted him to be successful. Listen to how I described the importance of private property and how much I wanted to be a part of promoting this in Russia. And although Spencer's own emotional reserves were exhausted, it was still important for people with optimism to remain here and do what we could. Look at the girls on my team. I was inspiring them. Despite everything, Nadya was still determined to go to business school the following autumn. Even if I was changing just a few people's lives, wasn't it worthwhile to continue on while I could?

And with that Spencer pulled a small bundle wrapped in newspaper from his coat pocket. A parting gift for me.

I unwrapped the newspaper to find a small home-made gadget. A square four pronged telephone adapter was the base. The plastic casing for the adapter had clearly been removed to add the upgrade of an additional standard phone modem connector spliced together with a plastic coated wire that ended with two small metal clips. I squealed with delight, immediately realizing the prize that I held in my hands.

"Did you build this? You are an absolute genius! No wonder Harvard Business School wants you!" I gushed praise at Spencer while inspecting my new device.

Spencer was the only American I knew who rivaled me in the number of Aeroflot "frequent survivor points" he had accumulated. He was one of only a handful of people I knew who had been to Uralsk. But more impressive in my eyes was the fact that he had managed to establish a dial up connection from Uralsk and send an email. A true pioneer! And here was evidence of how he had connected to his email service from a Soviet-era hotel room. The phones in the hotels were, almost without exception, hard wired to the wall. How to establish an internet connection through such a phone line was an essential skill that regular travelers like Spencer and myself, took pride in. To date I had just used my Swiss Army knife to peel back the plastic casing on the phone line to expose the bare wires. I had mutilated a modem cable to create partner wires to establish a connection. The result was shaky – but generally worked (as long as no one sent me emails containing ridiculous graphics to download).

Spencer's solution was brilliant. I would still have to peel back the plastic casing of the telephone line, but rather than work with the frayed wires directly I now had two little metal clips to connect the phone line on one end to a proper modem connector on the other. In the unlikely event that I ran across a four pronged telephone wall jack, I could use it also to connect to the phone line rather than the metal clips.

This was honestly one of the best gifts I have ever received in my life. The practicality and engineering was spot on. But more than that, Spencer had given me a deep symbolic gesture that I was not alone. With this simple gift I would now have a constant reminder that at least one person understood what I went through just to accomplish the most basic of everyday tasks here. And where there is support there is courage and the will to carry on.

Yes, I still had enough optimism for one more project in Russia.

21 BEWARE OF YOUR TELEVISION

September 1995 — St Petersburg

Another crumbling Soviet-era office building smelling of wet dogs and unwashed clothing. No matter how much things change they always stay the same. Isn't that the saying? I had plenty of time to contemplate the subject. I was sitting with two colleagues — one American and one Russian — while waiting for a government bureaucrat to grace us with an audience. Perhaps he would see us today. Perhaps he wouldn't. The posturing for seeking dominance over a relationship continued. New city, new project, but still the same old story.

All I could do for the moment was to stare at the cold stark concrete walls. My colleagues Alan, Ruslan, and I were packed together snugly on a small wooden bench in a stairwell at the government agency. Not a waiting area by any stretch of the imagination, simply a dark, dank stairwell, lit only by a bare light bulb dangling precariously from its socket above. Ruslan and Alan were engrossed in conversation, so I stared off into the dark cavern of the stairwell and contemplated life.

Life was good, I quickly concluded. No, life was amazing. Every day in Russia was a reaffirmation of what I privileged life I had. Yes, I was now sitting on a cold wooden bench in a dank hallway (with rats probably living in the walls), but this reinforced my sense of amazement for my life. I was living a fantasy that belonged to some wealthy heroine from classic Russian novels, not a 28-year old American who just recently escaped graduate school. I was now a regular at the Bolshoi Theater or Moscow Circus (depending on my mood that weekend) — with caviar and champagne at the intermission, of course. I could be wandering in the mysterious ancient cemetery in

Novodevichy one day, then browsing the art in the Hermitage the next. The *Krasnaya Strela* first class overnight train would whisk me between Moscow and St Petersburg. A driver would drop me off at one train station and another would be awaiting my arrival and ready to carry my luggage at the next. I had an apartment in Moscow and soon would have another in St Petersburg. Any time I wished, I could indulge in fresh bread and Danish cheeses.

I smiled and contemplated my new fashionable boots – purchased during a weekend trip to Vienna. Yes, Russian reality guaranteed that they would be battered beyond all recognition soon enough, but for the moment they were a concrete piece of evidence of the amazing life I led. Who at age 28 has an apartment with a housekeeper and a driver in Moscow and (soon) another in St Petersburg and takes weekend trips to Vienna? I could be carefree while helping others – Nadya now was my house-sitter of choice in Moscow and she was totally happy to stay in my Moscow apartment and look after my cat while I was in St Petersburg or beyond. My travelling was not only an incredible professional and personal experience for me, but also provided a benefit to her.

But I then had to revise my initial thought. No, I was not a heroine from some Tolstoy novel. As decadent as their lives were, I was actually better off than them! Anna Karenina was entirely dependent upon the favors of the men in her life. Here I was, a single woman, able to afford all of this on my own – independently and accountable to no one but my own whims.

Looking at my beautiful leather boots in the contrast to the dank Russian government stairwell, I fully appreciated what the girls in my office had said to me at our International Women's Day festivities. I was living a total dream life – but they saw me as a real woman, not some fictional character. If I was able to achieve such things, then they could too. They were inspired and invigorated. Russia was changing and they were not condemned to becoming toothless *babushkas* mopping the floors in rat-infested buildings.

I was obviously on an emotional high and in the honeymoon stage of my new project in St Petersburg. The grand vision of the project seemed so noble and important – and still unblemished by reality.

Property title registration in Russia. What could possibly hold more significance to the future of Russia? Throughout Russian history, property was at the heart of all major uprisings and revolutions. And now, here on the front lines of building Russia's future, property held the key to true individual self-determination, entrepreneurship, and lasting economic growth. The first wave of property privatization was complete, but in its wake the process to validate who now owned title to what was complex, uncertain, and still heavily dependent upon currying favor with the right people in the right places. If Igor wanted to sell his apartment to Ivan, Ivan would want to confirm that Igor actually truly owned the apartment to begin with. This simple title validation process could take upwards of two years. Yes, two *years*. To improve this process would mean unlocking individual wealth, self-determination, and (as the financial system stabilized eventually) to be able to draw a loan against a property to be able to start a business or other venture.

I was truly doing something *important* with my life. The extravagant life I led was *earned*. Yes, I knew that the journey ahead of me would be challenging. I would be working with the St Petersburg government. Where my other projects had questionable accomplishments, here I would succeed. I was certain of this. More than any prior project, I truly believed in the core principles for what we were striving to achieve. And now I had years of experience on my side.

The long-term expatriates on the project team had looked at me with a sideways glance when I bounced into the office with enthusiasm on that first day. Why was I possibly excited about joining the project? Did I have the slightest idea what I had agreed to? The project had been underway for just over a year and I had been brought in to replace the prior project manager who had just returned to the United States.

"You heard that the previous project manager 'returned' to the United States?" Paul had asked me with a tone of disbelief mixed with sarcasm. "Well, that would be more or less accurate. It was the logical thing for him to do – to return to the US – after he was deported."

Deported? Oh yes. In fact I was about the fourth or fifth in-country manager for this project. The door to the project office was revolving with ever-increasing speed. During my time based in Moscow I had heard persistent whispers that St Petersburg was a difficult city to work in. The city government politics were completely chaotic, broken into warring factions that struck up then shredded alliances without batting an eye. Permits were offered then retracted for foreign investors, or revoked with the statement that they were not issued by the proper authority in the first place. Taxes were levied, forgiven, then demanded. The more savvy international companies kept their distance. Rumor had it that McDonald's had assessed the situation and then refused to open a restaurant in the city under such conditions. McDonald's had backed out of the city. Good grief. If the most persistent international missionary of American business practices was reluctant to do business in St Petersburg, then what were we, mere novices, attempting to accomplish here?

We were working with not one, but five different government agencies in St Petersburg. Each of these agencies controlled some aspect of the property title registration process. And each of these agencies was deeply suspicious of the actions and aspirations of the others. To the government agencies, reform and streamlining the title registration process would mean loss of power, control, and prestige. The battle lines in the political war games were underway. None were going to concede any territory to the others. Progress and information sharing and process improvement were all fighting words and had to be stopped at all costs. Eventually conflicts with the city government escalated to deportation of the project managers.

Deportation. A harsh word. Never mind. I would be able to emerge victorious where others had failed, I convinced myself. I was the first in-country project manager to speak Russian. The first who had prior experience working with government agencies. The youngest (and therefore, I assumed, most resilient to hard blows). I had taken Russian secretaries from answering the phone "*da*" to "Good Morning! Arthur Andersen, how may I help you?" When compared to all my predecessors in the role, I was clearly the best positioned to take on the challenge of transforming St Petersburg. I was also incredibly naïve.

My first few days in St Petersburg had only reinforced my view that I would succeed where others had failed. As evidence for this I only had to look at Alan, my American colleague, who had arrived in St Petersburg a few days before me.

Alan was a consultant sent from Washington DC to define an appropriate training program to enable the adoption and ongoing maintenance of the new title registration software. He spoke no Russian, had never worked on a project in the former Soviet Union and (to my knowledge) had never travelled outside the United States. When Alan learned that the current manual property title registration process could take upwards of two years, he nodded thoughtfully and said "Our clients will welcome the software we are building to automate the process and save time and effort."

Of course, I knew by now that the directors of the government agencies would not have "process improvement" at the top of their agendas. We would have to understand their underlying agenda to achieve anything at all. Today's appointment would give an indication of how fast Alan could absorb this lesson as well. The meeting had been organized by my predecessor, with the objective to outline the necessary training requirements for implementation and ongoing operations of the title registration software. Although training program definition was Alan's area, I was tagging along as the new overall program manager on an attempt to learn something firsthand about the political context in which we would be working.

Alan sat primly on the bench, wearing his fresh blue suit and clean sharp tie. (I eyed up our wooden bench and wondered if he would shred his suit on his first expedition to a government office. My business clothing was now demolished beyond recognition from such furniture.) Alan talked innocently and naively about how excited the Russian agencies would be to receive this new labor-saving software. Just imagine how much more client-oriented they can be once they can process and validate property transactions in a matter of hours rather than months!

Alan looked around the dimly lit stairwell and nodded his confirmation to our mission. Of course. We were here on a sacred quest to improve the processes and systems of the St Petersburg city government. Look at how decrepit this stairwell was. The outside of the building was visibly deteriorating. There was no signage or even street numbers on the exterior of the building. How did the public ever find this place and lodge their documents to conveyance properties? Here we were in the stairwell waiting interminably for our appointment. The air was heavy with wet dogs and unwashed bodies – although the concrete space was empty save the three of us. This place was ripe for process improvement. USAID had made a wise choice in the selection of St Petersburg for the site of this project. Efficiency and customer service! That is the ideal! We, the American project team, have it as our sacred duty to spread the good word.

My eyes drifted across the ceiling. One solitary exposed light bulb dangled precariously from a wire, vainly attempting to illuminate the stairwell. The light fixture had deteriorated years ago to the point where just a dangling light socket remained. Not that the lighting was ever very high quality to begin with. The wire from the light socket was tacked to the ceiling in various places and then ran down the wall to the light switch. The switch looked like it had been constructed by simply firing some sort of weapon at the wall and embedding a light switch in the resulting cavity. Bare wires dangled out of the crevice in the wall and I wondered how many people had electrocuted themselves by turning on and off that light.

At this moment I noticed an aging poster, tacked carelessly on the wall above the alarming light switch. It was just a simple poster, black and white, rather aged, dusty, and frayed at the edges. It had obviously been nailed to the bleak wall many years ago and forgotten. In capital letters the poster warned the readers – "Beware of Your Television!" The poster featured a rather blurry photograph of a burning television set and a charred apartment. The smaller text below explained that exploding televisions were the leading cause of house fires in Russia. Owners of televisions should beware and always be sure to unplug their televisions when not in use. Children should not be allowed to watch televisions in a room unsupervised, since the television may explode at any time.

I was thoroughly amused by the scene. I asked Ruslan what he thought of the poster. He shrugged his shoulders and replied with complete lack of interest. "There really is no purpose for the warning. Everyone knows that televisions explode." I then translated the poster for Alan, my American colleague. He nodded his approval and said, "That is a very good public service announcement." Such typical Russian and American comments. Both of which, in my mind, completely missed the point.

Someone somewhere in the Russian government saw exploding televisions as enough of a hazard that this merited a public service message. However, this poster provided merely words not actions. What could actually be *done* to reduce the risks of exploding televisions? For starters, I am fairly confident that when given a choice between exploding televisions and non-exploding, that most people would choose non-exploding. Japanese televisions were safer and more reliable than Russian, simply because consumers in the west actually have a choice. If a product is dangerous or unreliable, the news will spread and customers will shop elsewhere. In 1995 however, personal electronics were subject to a 65% import tax — raising the cost of such items to be prohibitive for ordinary Russian families.

Certainly some people will then say "oh the safety standards for those Russian televisions needs to be improved." I actually have little doubt that safety standards did exist for the Russian televisions, but like with everything else in the realm of Russian government operations, the enforcement was entirely ad hoc and discretionary and probably in the hands of bureaucrats who had not been paid for months and therefore their interests were not necessarily aligned with public safety. One layer of government regulations to prevent the import of safer, more reliable televisions is not best addressed by another layer of regulations to attempt to counterbalance the effects of the first.

The amazing thing to me was that the Russian government acknowledged the situation — Russian televisions are dangerous. They actually put together a public service announcement on the subject. This was the one and only time I had ever seen a public safety announcement on any subject. There were so many potential hazards. Why were exploding televisions singled out among them? Why not missing manhole covers? Why not radioactive concrete? How about heavy metals in the drinking water? Fish reeled in from the Moscow river were rumored to be flammable — you shouldn't eat them! Or what about the fact that the air quality was equivalent to smoking two packs of cigarettes a day? No. None of those hazards were considered to be worthy of a public safety announcement. Exploding televisions, however, were. I was baffled for why this particular hazard was targeted for a public safety announcement. I was certain that somewhere in this poster was a clue to unlocking deeper mysteries of the Russian psyche.

My contemplation would have to wait a bit longer. Finally we were granted an audience with the government official. Ruslan, Alan, and I collected our coats and notebooks and scampered into the office at the invitation. The project team had struggled for so long for this moment. We leapt at the opportunity to meet with the bureaucrats. Our quest to improve and automate the processes of the St Petersburg City government had taken the next dramatic leap forward.

Or maybe not. A few minutes later I was sitting bewildered in the background of the meeting between Ruslan, Alan, and the designated government bureaucrat, Yuri Mikhailovich. In the required introductions I explained that I was the new project manager and had invited myself along to the visit as a way to meet him — as the head of one of the key agencies we would be working with.

Yuri Mikhailovich paused briefly then beamed with genuine enthusiasm. He was *so pleased* to meet me. Finally he had the opportunity to meet one of the project managers. We would have so much to discuss regarding opportunities to improve the property title registration process. He had so many ideas. He was so looking forward to sharing them.

I was thrilled by his enthusiasm – this was the complete opposite to the reception I had expected. His smile was genuine. His words were sincere. He truly wanted to improve the title registration processes.

So why hadn't any of the previous project managers made contact with him and engaged his support? Yuri was professing his enthusiasm for the project (we were on informal names basis already). But I didn't want to hijack the agenda for the day. I kept my questions to myself and just let a cartoon question mark drift over my head in silence. I would be back soon, I promised.

Ruslan, Alan, and Yuri rapidly become engrossed in a discussion about the theory of training principles (Ruslan translated at intervals for Alan). Computer training is good. Computers are the way of the future. Everyone needs to be trained on how to use computers. The three of them were in complete agreement, nodding and smiling together.

There was only one problem. The government office was notably lacking computers. Not one. Alan, Ruslan, and Yuri were smiling and happy and welcoming the future of the information age into their offices with their feet firmly planted in the clouds of theory. What exactly did they think was going to happen here? What would we be training on? To whom? For what purpose? How would it actually benefit anyone if there actually were no computers at the end of the day to execute this wonderful plan into the future?

I restrained myself during the meeting, as the three of them were having such a wonderful time planning the computer training and I (after all) was a newcomer to the project. In the car on the way back to the office I asked the obvious question. Obvious to me at least.

"So can I ask a) how exactly are we going to provide computer training to an office of 50 people without computers, b) what are they going to do with this training? And oh yes, aren't these the people who are supposed to be using our wonderful new custom application for property registration? Our task order from USAID is to provide the custom software and related servers and infrastructure. Where are the desktop computers for the end users coming from?"

Alan and Ruslan looked at me like I was from another planet. Their conversation paused for a few seconds while they gave me a blank stare. They then resumed their conversation, analyzing the various elements of the organizational hierarchy of the government agency we had visited, determining the various facets of training required to their personnel to make them entirely computer literate. Multiple dimensions of training required really. First there was basic computer literacy. What to do with a computer. This is a mouse. This is a keyboard. And then they would have to learn basic

266 ☆ PHAEDRA FISHER

software applications. No wait. Microsoft training was outside the scope of our project. Therefore they would leap directly to the training on the custom Oracle application we were developing.

"Does this make any sense at all?" I was in the front seat of the car leaning back over my shoulder attempting to interrupt their discussion. "We are going to be delivering computer training for people without computers!" Ruslan and Alan continued their planning session with high animation, oblivious to my interjections.

Our driver, Sergei, suddenly exclaimed – "Bananas. Look – bananas are being sold over there." With a violent lunge, the heavy Volga swung an abrupt U-turn in the middle of the street. I had not even seen what had caught Sergei's eye. But I had learned that Russian drivers have extra sensory perception far beyond the normal spectrum of Americans.

Sergei had been breathless with excitement when he was behind the wheel. His demeanor changed abruptly as he began a round of haggling and debate with the driver of the Lada. Crush or be crushed. Take the upper hand or be taken advantage of. As with any transaction in Russia, one would come away the victor and one the loser – the idea that the negotiations would result in a mutually beneficial outcome was an impossible foreign concept.

So now Sergei was engrossed in negotiations with the driver of the muddy Lada over some bananas that may or may not exist. Alan and Ruslan were oblivious to our delay and continued to sketch out their training plan for the Russians who required basic computer skills training at the privatization office – despite the fact they had no computers. I could not participate in either discussion without questioning my own sanity, so I turned my gaze to the pedestrians on the street just outside the car.

An old grizzled man in a WWII Red Army uniform caught my eye. Actually, WWII is incorrect – in Russia the correct term is "Great Patriotic War." War veterans wearing their full honor regalia were still a fairly common sight and I had to admire them. These men had endured not only the horrors of the Great Patriotic War, but then had returned to face the onslaught of the Stalin regime and then survived every crisis since. The veterans were always weathered and dusty and pierced you with an icy glare that confirmed their status as survivors of brutality that neither you nor I could even begin to imagine.

I watched the veteran for a moment and then realized with horror that he had no arms. The sleeves of his uniform were hollow and fluttered empty at his sides. Even worse, the elderly man was now begging for coins from the passersby. Begging without hands, so instead he opened his mouth at the pedestrians and tried to coax them to drop a coin in. Drop a coin into his mouth! If this were not enough, a filthy gypsy child scampered up the street and started jumping and clawing at the old man, attempting to grab the coins from his mouth. The veteran clamped his teeth shut and kicked vigorously at the street urchin. A violent battle ensued. The gypsy child screeched and jumped and grabbed at the man's face, attempting to grasp even one coin. The man could not call for help – he clenched his jaw in determination to hold onto his coins, kicking violently at the child.

Sergei, meanwhile, had coaxed the owner of the Lada to open the trunk of his car so he could assess the quality of the contraband bananas that were available at a price. In their own alternate universe, Alan and Ruslan continued to discuss the theory of computer training for the government bureaucrats who had no computers. I was simply stunned into silence by the whole scene. I was just waiting for the red velvet curtain to appear and a dwarf to start dancing and singing along to the hypnotic theme from *Twin Peaks*.

This was the world I had entered for my next project in Russia. Somehow I would be expected to bring the project to its conclusion. Successful completion of the project would raise my professional profile within the firm and hasten my re-entry to the United States and promotion within the Washington DC consulting practice. Or at least that is what Patrick, the partner on the project, had told me. I watched the war veteran issue a decisive blow to the knee of the gypsy child. The street urchin howled in pain and ran off down the street. This was the context of my project. Patrick was based in Washington DC. How would he possibly understand the world we were operating in? No wonder that the previous five project managers had been deported and the DC office had been unable or unwilling to do anything about it.

One way or another, the project was certain to end over the next year. It had to – we were going to run out of money. The entire question was a) exactly when we would run out of money and b) to ensure that our project plan resulted in us finishing *before* that critical date, not after. My predecessor had left numerous spreadsheets and documents on floppy disks for this purpose. I was still untangling and analyzing them trying to understand what had happened over the past year, mixing this archeological evidence together with stories from Paul and the others who could help fill in the details.

The total budget for the project was $11 million dollars. In the early days of the project (well before my time) money had flowed like water. The belief was that eleven million US dollars would last forever. The Grand Hotel Europa – one of the "Leading Hotels of the World" – served as the base of operations. By day the team worked in conference rooms that opened to an airy atrium with a water feature that cascaded in careless ripples over polished marble. By night the expatriates lived in luxury rooms with damask linens, fresh flowers, and immaculate service.

The project had blasted through $9 million out of $11 million in the first year. Patrick advised me that I was now responsible for holding the spending to $2 million for the second year. The days of frivolous spending were over and austerity must begin – immediately. Shortly before I joined the project, the operations relocated over to the similarly named, but decided downscale "Evropa". Where the Grand Hotel Europa's restaurant featured fresh seafood over homemade linguini with a light herb sauce and accompanied by crisp champagne, the Evropa cafeteria featured warm beer, boiled eggs, and pickled mystery vegetables. Once austerity had been decreed, the long term expatriates had all quickly found apartments to rent. I was a newcomer, therefore I would be staying at the Evropa until my own arrangements could be sorted.

The Evropa was everything I had become accustomed to during my months of travelling to regional Russia, but still a bit frustrating knowing that my predecessors had ended their working day with white fluffy bathrobes, indulgent deep bathtubs, and little mints left on their pillows at night. Here at the Evropa, the water smelled of sulfur and was stone cold. The television emitted a piercing howl no matter how I manipulated the battered rabbit ears. The door and lock were so flimsy that one night the lock actually fell apart when I was *inside* my room – putting me at the mercy of the hotel maintenance staff to release me from my orange, brown, and green prison cell.

And this would be my home in St Petersburg – unless I could find some apartment to rent for less. I wanted to be optimistic about my project, but without a sanctuary to rejuvenate me at the end of the day, the honeymoon would soon be over.

On a positive note, although the cafeteria at the Evropa was dire, at least there were real restaurants in St Petersburg in 1995 – you just needed to know where to find them. Unfortunately my first week on the project I really had no idea where they were. I would be at the office after the others had left for the day – only then would it occur to me that I should have asked for a bit of local advice. Yes there actually was a published guide book for St Petersburg at this time – but like in Moscow, the pace of change was too rapid for traditional publishing to keep up. Restaurants would appear and disappear. Great gems would be hidden behind unmarked doorways down unlit alleys. Yes, the restaurants of the five star hotels were obvious – but they also were far out of my budget for a regular nightly meal.

This is the background of what lead me to the St Petersburg location of a restaurant chain that I will call The American Café. As far as chain restaurants go, The American Café is one of the better ones – you can actually pretend to have healthy options. In St Petersburg, the American Cafe was a bright beacon of neon on Nevsky Prospekt. Perhaps the only western owned restaurant at the time in the city and the easiest to find for a newcomer. I honed in on it like a moth to a flame. I needed food and the American Cafe offered sandwiches of reasonable quality. I ordered a massive sandwich and sat at a table by the window and devoured it in full view of the passersby.

Okay, it didn't taste like a real American Cafe sandwich. The bread was less than spectacular. The meat was definitely leathery and the cheese was a bit chalky. That didn't faze me for more than five seconds. No matter what its limitations, this sandwich certainly far exceed the offering of hard boiled eggs, and pickled vegetables back at the Evropa. And I knew that somewhere out in the St Petersburg night, awaiting discovery, were other restaurants as well.

My mental ramblings were abruptly interrupted as I noticed a man pounding on the glass of the window in front of my face to gain my attention. How obnoxious. But then I took another look. Noah! Good grief. I had met him earlier that summer as the Peace Corps representative in Rostov. I had heard that he was now the American advisor for the Privatization Center in St Petersburg, but I had not yet had time to hunt him down. Noah urgently beckoned for me to come out on the street. He most definitely did not want to come into the restaurant.

I was pretty much done devouring my meal in any case, so I pulled together my coat and belongings and joined Noah out on the street. After brief and requisite hellos and pleasantries I had to ask him why he had to drag me away from the American Cafe. Was it such a terrible place to come in off the street for a moment to chat?

"Well actually, yes," he answered. Noah paused for a moment to organize his thoughts. "The American Cafe is boycotted by the whole of the expatriate community here. If you are at all attempting to promote a decent society here in St Petersburg you will join our boycott." The American Café – a subject of protest? Really? Isn't this just about as mundane an organization as you can imagine? I certainly was not following his logic and asked for details.

I took his arm and let him lead me through the streets of St Petersburg. Noah told a story of enterprise, intrigue, and deception. The American Cafe had opened in St Petersburg as a joint venture – as all companies in Russia were required to have at least 50% local ownership. The local partner had been endorsed by the city government and the American Café executives were assured that the Russians would be a silent partner. An American woman named Michelle managed the joint venture in St Petersburg. All went well for the first year. Very well. Too well, you might say. The restaurant was profitable and Michelle explored the idea of opening a second location. The local partner assessed the situation and decided that they wanted a larger percentage of the profit. But no, said the American Café executives, the agreement was that the Russians were 51% owners, therefore they were entitled to 51% of the profit and that was it. At this point the City stepped in on the Russian partner's side and stated the case that the Russian partner had to be given a larger percentage. The American management back in the United States continued to say no. Michelle was stuck in the middle between the American Cafe HQ and the St Petersburg city government.

The Russian partner appealed to their buddies at the St Petersburg city government for a bit of intervention. Someone in the city government came up with some reason why the restaurant had to be closed and issued a statement as such. Michelle was advised that she was not to re-enter the restaurant or their warehouse until certain conditions had been met. The management back in the United States viewed the letter as a personal request from a single city official rather than a true legal requirement. The American management cried foul and instructed Michelle to continue business as usual, while a legal consultation and resolution were underway. What to do next? She was a sweet young American woman, attempting to run a business deep in unchartered territory. She returned to the restaurant and attempted to carry on.

At this point Michelle received a phone tip from a friend within the city government. A warrant had been issued for her arrest for re-opening the restaurant despite city orders. The police were on their way – *now*! Michelle did not even pause to hear the next sentence. She dropped the phone in mid conversation and ran for the train station. Like all experienced expatriates in Russia, she carried her passport and several thousand dollars cash on her at all times. Within an hour Michelle was on the next train to Helsinki – not even passing by her apartment to pick up a toothbrush or a change of undies.

Michelle never returned to Russia. She was caught in limbo in Helsinki for far too long. The corporate headquarters in the US demanded that she return to St Petersburg. She protested, arguing that she faced arrest if she returned to the city. The corporate head office argued that her job was in St Petersburg – if she was in Helsinki, then that was holiday, not work. Michelle was caught between the mythical rock and the hard place. Eventually she had to resign and return to the US. She was certainly not going to return to Russia with an arrest warrant waiting to greet her.

The Russian business partners managed to gain access to the warehouse and to the restaurant and seized effective full control over the operations. The expatriates took perverse pleasure in the rumors that the quality of food and service was deteriorating on a daily basis. We had to boycott the American Cafe, Noah concluded. If we were to patronize the restaurant, that would be support for the evil business partners who had chased dear Michelle out of town. We were all in this together. Yesterday it was Michelle and the American Cafe caught in the trap of the St Petersburg city government. Tomorrow it could be any one of us. We had to do what little we could to stand up to the octopus of the city government.

What a story. I was completely engrossed. Power, corruption, intrigue. And just a little too close to home. But in a perverse way this was why we loved life in Russia. We faced challenges that people back in the United States could not imagine. We survived, persevered, excelled despite all odds. We heard people say "no" and retorted "oh, but that's your opinion." No does not really mean no. It just means that things will be more difficult than you initially believed. In Michelle's case, however, "no" did eventually win out.

"So where are you taking me anyway?" I finally started to take in my surroundings. We were walking down one of the many small canals that wound its way through the heart of the city. Fierce elaborate facades of imperial architecture loomed over us and disappeared into the night sky. The endless city dirt scuffed under our feet, intermixed with a refreshing crisp crunch of fallen small tree branches. The canal was silent and black. Away from the main thoroughfare of Nevsky Prospekt the city fell into darkness. Every building façade was the same – grand, bleak and watchful. No streetlights. No signage. Like anywhere in Russia in the mid-1990s, you had to have a local guide to find anywhere interesting.

And then Noah paused and opened a door to another world. Light, warmth, and laughter poured out onto the street. I looked at him and smiled and walked through the entrance. "Welcome to the Magpie," he smiled. "Australian hospitality here in St Petersburg."

Carlton Draught poured in pints and schooners. Ian and Peter, the Aussie master-minds of the pub, chatted up the girls with a smile and a wink. It was a fictional place really. An artificial haven away from the reality of St Petersburg city life. I looked at Noah with disbelief. Thank you for bringing me here. This was exactly what I needed tonight. A respite from the reality of St Petersburg where I could recharge and be pre-pared for whatever tomorrow may hold in store for me.

The Magpie was the height of the expatriate social scene in St Petersburg that sea-son. Okay, it was really the only pub available on the expatriate social scene. Therefore by default it became the height of fashion as the place to go when you wanted a break from the Russian reality. Not too much of a break – I noticed with a wry smile. Lack of health and safety standards still were the norm, even in such places. With perverse pleasure I watched a group of drunks playing darts. The small sharp weapons flew in the general direction of the opposite wall. Fine. That was standard practice in Australian and British pubs I knew. (American bars, of course, no longer have sharp objects and drunks intermixing out of fear of lawsuits.) I was horribly amused, however, to notice that the flight path of the darts crossed the main thoroughfare to the restrooms. How appropriately symbolic of our existence – Aussie pub life meets Russian reality.

I bought schooners of Carlton for Noah and I, while he scanned the room for his friends. No he had not planned on meeting anyone that night. He just knew that there would always be someone he knew there. And we were not disappointed. We quickly located a table of Americans who were watching the dart game as a sort of spectator blood sport – placing wagers on when the next injury might occur.

Introductions were brief and I was asked the obligatory question of when I had arrived in St Petersburg. Just this week really, I said. But I quickly added that I had been working in Russia and Kazakhstan for well over a year and a half already. I was not a newcomer. I had an apartment in Moscow and was now looking for some place to stay in St Petersburg that would be an improvement over the Evropa.

My new friends (like all expats) were eager to share their insider knowledge on all the rumors for who was coming and going from St Petersburg, and within minutes I had leads on a number of apartments that would be soon vacated as the expats returned to the United States or Western Europe. Few apartments in St Petersburg were modernized to the level of Moscow expat apartments they warned, keenly observing my reaction. But no, I had no intention to repeat a *remont* exercise. If some prior expat had found the apartment to be habitable, I should be fine. They laughed and exchanged meaningful glances and I could tell I was silently being accepted into their circle.

Well good, they said. I should join them on their periodic weekend adventures.

"Of course," I smiled. "What do you get up to for entertainment here in St Petersburg?" I knew that the answer would not be soccer matches or picnics or anything else that smacked of American normalcy. The young expat community in Moscow had organized ski weekends to civil-war torn Georgia and a Halloween party in a castle in Romania. We were young, well-paid and had lost all touch with what constituted a "normal" existence some time back. If we were playing high stakes political games during the week, the adrenaline had to be released somehow on the weekend. Sedate dinner parties would just not do.

Apparently I had just missed "Tank Day".

The guys had been here at the pub one night and had been thinking about how fun it would be to drive a tank. Then they realized the obvious – why not? All they would have to do would be to find the local army base. Certainly they would then be able to find someone there to slip a hundred dollars to give them a tank to drive for the day. This is Russia, after all. Anything is possible. You just need to have the nerve to try.

I laughed. These were my sort of people. Never listen to "no." Keep going. Work hard and play hard. We saw the rules being bent every day at work. Why not bend them a little bit in our favor when playing? Use what we have learned about how to operate in Russia for a bit of weekend entertainment.

"Are you up for a round of darts?" Noah asked, holding out a handful of small weapons for my perusal.

"Sure, why not," I fingered the sharp metal daggers and then let them fly at the opposite wall – narrowly missing a young woman who just emerged from the Ladies room.

St Petersburg was a dangerous place and it was in motion. I was now part of it. In my first week I had struck up a positive relationship with a key official at one of our stakeholder agencies while political confrontations had led to the deportation of my predecessor. I was certain that I would succeed where others had failed. I had allies within the St Petersburg expat community and was ready to accept a Soviet-era apartment that I had never even set foot in. And I couldn't wait to see what would happen next.

22   GULAG ARCHIPELAGO

September 1995

The next day I bounced into the office with a huge smile. I was recharged from an evening of expatriate camaraderie and filled with optimism. After all, hadn't we managed to meet with a director at an agency yesterday? Yuri Mikhailovich himself had said that no one had done that previously. Clearly the project was going in the right direction. We would bring real estate title registration to the city of St Petersburg – and the agencies would embrace us. The future of St Petersburg was bright and we would be the project leading the way.

Clear procedures and access to title records would mean that properties could be bought and sold with confidence. With ownership able to be readily validated, then there would be the possibility to obtain home financing. Banks could provide loans against properties as equity – unlocking funds to enable millions of people to start their own businesses or invest in other ways. Title registration would be the first step towards helping the people of St Petersburg build their local economy, establish their own life savings, invest for the future. Older women would no longer be battle-weary veterans but instead have the fresh carefree smile of Rita. All of this would be possible because of property. And we would be at the vanguard of helping the Russian people achieve it.

My dreamy reveries were rudely interrupted by a door slamming and a hostile middle-aged Russian woman with a body resembling a fire hydrant barking at me.

"Larissa wants you to call her," she snapped without introduction or pleasantries. "She is not happy at all."

I stared blankly for a moment at the fire-breathing figure while slowly compiling the scene. This was Ludmilla, our translator. Paul had told me that a separate office had been arranged for her – on a different floor of the building. Why put the translator in her own room, I had asked. Paul had laughed, shook his head and refused to answer the question directly. I would figure it out for myself, he had said. Now as her black aura eclipsed the sun and smothered my bright shiny moment of optimism, I understood. She radiated a dark hostile energy that clearly had to be sequestered and contained.

"Why isn't Larissa happy? What did she say?" I finally responded.

"It is not my place to ask such things. I am just the translator," Ludmilla turned her nose to the ceiling, spun on her heel and violently exited the room.

I stared with disbelief at the door that was still shuddering from being slammed a second time within a matter of minutes. The real question, I quickly realized, was why was Larissa calling Ludmilla in the first place? And why did we tolerate having such a person as a translator? I wanted to pick up the woman and toss her out on her ear. Paul just laughed and muttered something incoherent about a ship and a drowning witch.

Frank Zappa lyrics, I quickly learned, was Paul's way of advising that there was no rational answer. Structured English language sentences could not possibly convey the complete message – therefore he was reduced to babbling.

After further coaxing and a few interjections of Zappa lyrics I did get the full story out of him. Larissa, our key contact with the St Petersburg city government, had instructed the prior project manager to hire Ludmilla. No one on the project team liked her and the prior project manager, David, was ready to refuse – but Patrick, our US-based senior program manager – had instructed David that he had to do it. A small favor to Larissa that would help to improve the relationship with the St Petersburg government.

"And so now Larissa calls *Ludmilla* when she wants anything to happen on the project, but doesn't want to talk to anyone here directly," Paul concluded.

Granted I was a young, inexperienced project manager. That being said, I knew enough to understand that this was a symptom of deeper problems with the project than I had ever begun to imagine. The client had no interest in talking with the project team directly and instead went through her personally-selected contact – who had no formal role in the project management structure.

And, of course, this meant that the woman with the black aura was completely immune from anything resembling real management. Any bit of pressure, or a request she disagreed with and word would get back to Larissa that she was being mistreated by the American imperialists. Only then would Larissa contact the office directly – advising that we needed to treat our staff with respect.

"So Ludmilla calls Larissa regularly as well?" The situation was getting even worse as the conversation continued.

Paul muttered and spun a pen expertly across his fingers, then looked at the door through which Ludmilla had departed. "Why do you think we have sequestered her on another floor of the building? It isn't just the black aura. We don't need her reporting every word here back to Larissa."

A spy in our midst. Something that is supposed to help us, instead poised to lash out at some unsuspecting moment. A Soviet-era television sitting quietly that could explode at any moment and burn the house down. At least the televisions could be unplugged. With Ludmilla we had to settle for attempting to quarantine her.

Paul turned in his seat and hunched over his keyboard, the Soviet-era chair creaking precariously as he moved. I contemplated the situation and then finally said to no one in particular "well, I guess that if Larissa is unhappy I have to call her and find out what is going on."

Paul continued to type at his keyboard with an exaggerated display of mock focus. While keeping his back to me, he pointed purposefully to a fax that had been printed out and posted over his desk.

"You're an expatriate... You drink yourself to death. You become obsessed by sex. You spend all your time talking, not working. You are an expatriate, see?"

Classic Hemingway. Although the quote was over 70 years old, a more fitting mantra for the American expats in Russia could not be found.

I had not yet been formally introduced to Larissa as the project manager. Patrick had promised to do so, but hadn't. In this country of protocol, demonstrations of power, and prescribed formalities to start any relationship I felt completely out of place having my first conversation with her as a response to a complaint from my translator. Aren't relationships supposed to start with a horrific scene of vodka and night club strippers? Then again, I already knew the answer. As much as I dreaded the ritual of keeping up with the Russian hosts shot for shot, I knew that a far worse proposition was not being invited to vodka at all at the start of a relationship. Larissa had decided that her first contact with me would be via the translator to tell me she was not happy. Clearly this was not a good sign of where the relationship was going.

You can probably already anticipate the conversation that followed. Larissa's sharp tongue reached through the scratchy telephone line and cut me with layers of abuse. What pretensions for me to go to the property agency without her approving the visit first!

"But you did approve the visit of the team to the property agency," I was staring at the authorization fax which clearly had her signature on it.

Larissa was stunned that I would debate the point with her. After catching her breath, a fresh string of insults was hurled my way. I was not paying proper respect to the protocols on the project. The authorization clearly stated that the subject of conversation was to be the computer training for the agency. Why was I, the project manager, even visiting the agency? I was not the trainer. I was not going to be involved directly in the computer training. Therefore what was the purpose of my visit?

I explained that as I was new to the project I wanted to meet the directors of the agencies that we would be working with.

"Exactly," said Larissa sharply. "That is a purpose for a visit other than what you were approved for. You have violated the protocols of this project. Ensure that you do not do that again."

And then she slammed down the phone and that was the end of our first conversation.

"It is an honor to work on this program with you," I said to the dead void on the other end of the line.

As should already be evident, the expatriates were prone to endless discussion about the events that swirled around us. This natural state was exaggerated further in our open plan office in St Petersburg. Large industrial desks were pushed up against each other at awkward angles to make the most of the space in the Evropa which served as a project office for the team. Every conversation was overhead and then repeated and analyzed. Immediately after I hung up the receiver with Larissa, everyone except for me broke out in laughter. I had completed my first round of hazing – I had been abused by Ludmilla and endured a conversation with Larissa. I was now officially indoctrinated into the project.

"So is this the best challenge you can offer?" I forced a smile. "Are you trying to say that these petty nuisances are all that stand between us and a successful project here?"

"Oh no," responded Brad, the technical team leader. "You haven't met Vincent yet."

Vincent. A new name for the mental database.

"Who is he?" How could the challenge be worse than what we were already facing with Larissa and Ludmilla?

"The Prince of Darkness," answered Paul in a matter-of-fact tone.

The room fell silent. Obviously Paul's answer was sufficient introduction in the others' opinion.

"Could you be more specific? Exactly how has he been awarded the title 'Prince of Darkness'?"

Brad and Paul gave each other a meaningful look.

"Vincent is the general manager of Flis, our Russian subcontractor for Oracle development work."

Of course, it is a bad sign if a key business partner is referred to as "the Prince of Darkness". I had to learn more. The general situation was quickly outlined to me. Per the terms of our work order from USAID, a portion of the software development had to be by local contractors. Totally sensible from the pure perspective of aid and building local expertise. The problem was that the city of St Petersburg had advised that its preferred Oracle development company was Flis. No, Flis probably would not have won the work if subjected to a pure competitive bidding process. And yes, this meant that

Flis was just as difficult to manage as Ludmilla – their true loyalties rested with Larissa, who had helped them obtain the contract – rather than to their nominal "client".

"This is just so not-good," I stated the obvious. And then added with my last remaining shreds of innocence – "Why didn't anyone stop this? If it is against USAID requirements to contract without a competitive bid, then how did the city get away with it?"

Paul laughed. I had so much to learn about the real workings of this project. The documentation would show clearly that there *was* a competitive bid. And in regards for someone trying to stop it – had anyone explained to me the reasons the previous project manager had been deported?

So we had an arrogant subcontractor, managed by the Prince of Darkness. David, my predecessor, had initially attempted to quarantine the potential damage by allocating trivial pieces of development work to Flis. Hence the buildup of the American team of developers and the massive budget over-run for the first year – to cover the fact that the expectations of the local partners were about zero. But the team had been blocked from meeting with the government agencies to validate business requirements for the software and as a result the American contractors were burning a hole in the budget rather than making real progress with the system. To stretch the budget into the second year, the number of American developers was being cut back – which meant that (like it or not) the project was now dependent upon Flis for key developments.

The capabilities of the subcontractor were questionable, but the documentation would show that our consultancy had selected them through a competitive bid. And what were they developing anyway? We had to demonstrate some forward progress with a title registration system – but we were not allowed to talk with the agencies to define future processes and systems. Larissa relished pulling out the initial proposal from Arthur Andersen quoting the firm's commitment to bring in "best practices" and "proven methodology". If Arthur Andersen was employing foreign experts and bringing in an experienced team and a proven approach, then why was there any need to disturb the agency officials with the details of the project? Larissa used the firm's proposal to support her own argument – the local officials did not understand best practices, therefore the Americans should be given free rein to design and develop a system as they saw most appropriate. Oh yes, and ensure that we engage and pay the local subcontractors.

My head was ready to explode and this was only my first week on the project.

Over the weekend I made my escape back to Moscow. The urban mecca. The promised land. My wonderful nest of an apartment away from the combat zone of privatization.

I was rapidly joining the ranks of the expats (and Russians) who saw Moscow as the center of the civilized universe. Moscow was civilization – decent food. Marvelous bannyas. Great nightclubs and far far away from the horrors of my St Petersburg project. Each return trip to Moscow warmed me with a satisfying smile. For just a few moments of bliss I would be in control of my own life again.

Craig, my dear comrade from my Kazakhstan days and Sochi, was visiting Moscow briefly. He was considering taking a job offer in Moscow and I was determined to show him why Moscow offered a superior life to Almaty. Spices beyond salt and pepper and paprika could be found in shops. The opera and ballet is indisputably the finest in the world. Our mafia tough guys drive better cars than the Kazakh hit men. There is more construction underway, more neon signs going up. Everything is a work in progress and improving. Moscow was at the epicenter of the economic and political changes sweeping the former Soviet Union. Back in Uralsk, Kazakhstan, did your efforts even matter if there was no one there who noticed and shared what was happening with the international audience?

Craig recoiled a bit. Perhaps he had been living in Kazakhstan too long. The bright lights and carpeted floors of the Roditi shopping center disturbed him. Everything was too clean. Too polished. Too organized. Quite depressing really. Where is the challenge of survival when everything you need is laid out in front of you? How do you know you are really alive if you are not continuously challenged? Without a struggle there is simply existence. The same existence day after day until suddenly five years have slipped by.

For Craig, through the lens of years in Central Asia, Moscow was indistinguishable from any other western city. He did not want to live in the west. He had chosen chaos. He needed chaos to reinforce that he was alive and participating in the dramas of history. Craig was not about to relegate himself to the role of the middle manager, driving a sensible car and parking in the garage with his monthly permit. That would be a long-suffering death.

Really – the expatriates in Moscow lived on the edge! We took risks and needed adrenaline just as much as the expats in Kazakhstan! Credit card roulette had become standard routine when a number of expats went out for dinner together. Four, five, even ten people going out to dinner together. Everyone would throw their credit card onto the table. Heads or tails would show on the cards. We would keep tossing them until there was one card odd out and the owner of the card would pick up the tab for the table. High stakes for twenty-something year olds. Craig just laughed and replied that I was being ridiculous. Kazakhstan was an all cash society. Credit card roulette would be impossible in Almaty. Besides, had our lives become so predictable that we had to *invent* games for an adrenaline rush? What ever happened to the unexpected wilds of daily life?

I paused for a brief moment of reflection. How predictable and formulaic had my lifestyle become? Was it just an illusion that we were living on the cutting edge of new world? I was now trying to justify my life to myself as well. So what else could I show Craig and help to demonstrate that we were not entirely domesticated in Moscow? Jim's video store! A visit to Jim would show Craig that we were not living in western suburbia. Here the front line of capitalism was smudged a bit grey into the abyss of the black market. An American expatriate with a blurry identity and a Russian girlfriend, renting out pirated videos to the expat community. That was the leading edge of capitalism — and it wouldn't be too sterile for Craig, would it?

The zap of the door buzzer echoed through the concrete hall. Jim opened his steel door, tumbler of scotch in his hand. And judging by the glazed look in his eyes, it was not his first for the afternoon. He gestured for us to come in and mumbled something appropriate.

We stepped across the threshold. In traditional Russian style, Craig shook Jim's hand in greeting only once safely across the threshold. I don't believe either of them were conscious of the gesture, or of the implication — if we are subconsciously assuming these Russian customs, then what else have we absorbed into our daily routine and simply accepted to be standard?

My musings were interrupted as I felt my shoe sink into the slop of wet mushy carpet. I jumped with a few slurping steps to the relative dry land of kitchen linoleum and then turned to Jim with expectation. The Russian girlfriend, Lydia, shrieked a despairing howl and appeared momentarily in the living room. She sobbed bitterly for a few moments, wailed some unintelligible curses in Russian to no one in particular, and retreated to a back room with a dramatic waving of the arms.

"We've had a bad day," Jim said slowly with an astonishing degree of understatement. He had already finished his glass of scotch and was now pouring another.

Jim told his story quickly, punctuated by a few shrieks and howls from the girlfriend in the back room. They had just returned that morning from a week-long trip to Greece. (Absolute paradise, Jim noted as a sidebar.) They were all nicely relaxed, tanned, ready to face work again when they opened the front door and found this... Jim gestured with his refreshed tumbler of scotch towards the water-soaked floor. They had turned on the dishwasher right before they walked out the front door on holiday. ("You have a dishwasher?" I interrupted, completely inappropriately.) Apparently one of the hoses had become disconnected and for the entire week water had poured onto the floor of their kitchen — soaking their apartment. And the apartment below on the fourth floor. And the apartment below that on the third floor as well. Plus the second and the first floors. Craig's and my eyes widened with horror. We had both lived in the former Soviet Union for long enough to anticipate what Jim would say next. This was a country without homeowner's insurance or viable civil courts of justice. The neighbors would be taking direct and swift and convincing action to recover their losses.

"Within ten minutes of arriving home we had our first demand for money. Ten thousand US dollars cash – from the neighbor below us. That was followed within hours by demands from the other neighbors – each for $10,000." Jim sculled the rest of his drink and slammed the empty glass on the kitchen countertop. "They will be returning tomorrow to collect. We are leaving tonight."

What more was there to say? That, unfortunately, was the only answer. Their life in Moscow was over. If they did not produce $40,000 cash by morning the street justice would be swift and violent. I shuddered at the memory of Igor with his sledgehammer in my apartment. He had said calmly that he would collect money from the neighbors to pay for the damages they caused. He did collect the money, quickly, and without further comment – as if he had done it 100 times before. That was the way Moscow worked. Actions have consequences. Justice may not be recognizable to western eyes, but it will be swift and to the point.

"Now if you'll excuse us, we have to pack what we can carry out without drawing attention." Jim escorted us to the door and locked the steel fortress behind us.

I returned a week later to Jim's apartment – hopeful that I had overdramatized the scene in my mind. On Jim's door was a simple hand-printed sign: "*zakrit*" (closed). Fresh dents from a crowbar punctuated the door frame – but the steel door had remained intact. Jim and Lydia were clearly gone. I have no idea whether they found sanctuary elsewhere in Russia (they certainly would not have remained in Moscow) or if they fled the country entirely. I hope they are still alive. Who knows. I never saw either of them again.

As strange as it sounds, the visit to Jim's invigorated Craig. His eyes were wide with the possibility of Moscow. Perhaps a change from Almaty would be good – a new challenge. He would definitely follow up with the job offer that he had in Moscow. I was pleased. I was looking forward to another friend nearby. Too many expats had left in recent months. The stresses of daily life pushed them finally to crave a bit more stability. Not Craig, however. He was ready for a new adventure. But first he would go for a relaxing trek through the Tien Shan range of the Himalayas in Kazakhstan. A good way to challenge yourself and let you know you are still alive.

A quick kiss under the gorgeous chandeliers at the Arbatskaya metro station. Till we meet again.

Back at my Moscow apartment, I picked up the mail from my dilapidated ancient letterbox. Not that there was ever anything for me. All my "real mail" arrived via the office in a courier pouch from the United States with the rest of the American expat mail. Much more reliable. The community notices filled the box and at random intervals a telephone bill arrived, so I did check the mail. But this day was different.

Intermixed with a few requests to contribute money to the apartment building maintenance fund was a small brown postcard that was barely holding itself together – addressed to me.

The card was hurriedly handwritten in Russian, so it required a bit of work to decipher, but finally I decoded the message – my presence was requested as a witness in the trial of Mr. Kr - , Mr. Yu-, and Mr. Zh-. I blinked for a moment and then grasped what I was reading. It was really happening – the three men who had attacked me many months before were really going to trial.

To say I was astonished would be an understatement. Since the day I had given my statement to the police commissioner I had heard nothing. Absolutely nothing. No communication of any sort from the police, the courts, or the prosecuting or defending attorneys (assuming those people even existed). I had just assumed that the case had been dropped and the men had gone free to torment other young women on the streets of Moscow.

I was wrong.

I called the court to try and understand what would happen in advance. Of course that was a futile exercise. The shrill voice at the other end of the "information line" instructed me to arrive at the courthouse at the appointed hour. I would receive further instructions after that.

The wheels of the Russian legal system were in motion. I had absolutely no idea what would happen next. I only knew that I was petrified of being held in contempt of court. My Russian colleagues were unable to provide much further insight – everyone, however, was fascinated and jockeyed for the opportunity to provide moral and translating support as required.

On the nominated day, I found the court house identified on the postcard, accompanied by Marina, the interpreter on the team. Although in general I worked without an interpreter, I had decided that I needed Marina today both for moral support plus assistance with whatever might happen in the court room that was beyond my daily vocabulary. The building would have been magnificent once but now was more akin to an inner city crack house that an official government building. But no, the address was correct. The front door was wobbly on its hinges. A single light bulb hung precariously on a strand of wire in the entranceway. The concrete shell of an interior was devoid of color or décor of any sort. A front door watchman (I can't bring myself to say receptionist) gruffly examined my postcard and directed Marina and I to a room upstairs. The halls were silent. Perhaps we were the only people in the building today. Out of sight a door slammed closed, echoing through the cavern.

A grand staircase curved up to the second floor. With a dramatic window soaring above the scene would have been majestic once. But now the window was opaque with filth. The stairs were dim and the railing in the center of the spiral was missing, so we kept close to the wall. A few of the concrete stairs were crumbling. Bits of stone were torn loose by our footsteps and fell with a sinister crash into the abyss below.

We finally found the courtroom. It was furnished with benches and tables that would have been rejected by the Salvation Army. My clothing snagged on a shard of a bench. A stark metal cage lined the right side of the room. For the defendants perhaps? We were alone. And waited.

And waited. An hour passed. There was no one to consult – had proceedings been postponed? Why were we the only ones here? Queries at the front desk were futile. We were simply instructed to do as we were told – go and wait in the courtroom. So we waited. I did not dare leave without permission. What would the Russian court system do to uncooperative witnesses who were not where they were told? I did not want to find out.

Eventually a man and a woman entered the room and talked together for a few moments and then left. Not a word to me or to Marina. What exactly had happened? I returned (yet again) to the front desk and learned that the defense and prosecution had agreed on a postponement.

"Until when?" I asked.

"Such pretensions!" The front door clerk had had quite enough of our questions. "You will receive a notice in the mail."

So that was it. That was my introduction to the Russian legal system. There was a process of some sort in place but it certainly was on a "need to know" basis. Clearly witnesses/victims did not need to know.

I returned to the office to the eager questions of my colleagues – what had happened? How did the trial go? And then a phone call – Craig was dead.

Yes, it was that sudden and yes, I was that stunned. What happened? How was this possible? He was quite alive when I had last seen him just a week earlier. Quite alive and looking forward to the new challenge of Moscow.

It was a terrible hiking tragedy. Just as he said when I last saw him, he had decided to go for a trek in the Tien Shan range. Not a true trek, just a good day hike. It was late summer so Craig and his friend took a lunch and a sweater and looked forward to a wonderful day in the mountain air. They crossed one small ridge and went down into the next valley when disaster struck – a freak snowstorm howled through the mountains and descended upon the unwary hikers. They had a lunch and sweaters but they were completely unprepared for the full fury of a Himalayan storm. What to do next? An argument ensued – seek shelter in nearby trees until the storm passes, or attempt to hike back to safety? Craig was headstrong and insisted to hike back to safety. His friend sought refuge in the trees. They quickly lost each other in the storm. The friend survived the night – barely – with severe frostbite. But Craig was nowhere to be found. A helicopter search and rescue team found his body a few days later.

The expat community was stunned. This was not supposed to happen. The dangers of the former Soviet Union are manmade — mafia, violent street justice, home brew alcohol, radioactive vegetables, rogue criminals, but not natural disasters. We were immortal against anything nature had to offer — look at everything we survived on a daily basis. How could Craig possibly have survived a brutal attack with a screwdriver to the chest nearly two years earlier only to have been killed in a hiking accident? The ways of the world are too mysterious. Perhaps he had become too Russian in his ways. Perhaps he had seen the dangers and shrugged them off — real men do not concern themselves with hazards. We wanted answers for what had gone wrong and what we had to learn from the tragedy.

"Fate," the Russians shook their heads and looked at each other knowingly. "You cannot fight the will of Fate."

No, you can't. But wouldn't it be nice if Fate offered a bit of an explanation sometimes?

Fate, however, did not offer an explanation for its actions. Neither did the Russian legal system. The initial scene at the courthouse repeated itself three or four more times over the following months. Eventually I became convinced that I would return to the United States before the case would come to trial. Perhaps that was the hope of the prosecuting attorney and the reason for all the delays. That is conjecture only. Actually I have absolutely no idea. Not one person ever spoke to Marina or I during those long hours in the courtroom. Each appointed day blended to the next. I did not dare miss one session however, perhaps my absence would be noted and I would be captured and held in solitary confinement for not following the court's orders. I had no idea. No one would explain the rules to us.

And then one day everything changed. As always, Marina was at my side, and instantly we knew that something more interesting would happen. The back rows of the courtroom were filled with sobbing middle-aged women dressed in mixed prints and florals and layers of coats and shawls. Low income women. Desperate women. The families of the criminals.

All eyes turned to me as I walked in the room and in a moment I was surrounded by wailing sobbing women pleading with me on the son's behalf. "They are good boys," they cried. "We have nothing without them. No income at all. You cannot let us go hungry." A teary woman took my hand with her massive paw — worn from a lifetime of a harsh existence. "You know how boys are when they are drunk," she sobbed. "They are good boys. Please have mercy."

It was a horrific scene. My testimony held their livelihoods in the balance. I knew nothing about these people. Perhaps these families were honest and hardworking. Perhaps they weren't. And with a word I could change the scene for everyone.

Complete strangers were turning to me for desperate mercy. And these tormented women saw me as a foreign girl with their fate in her hands.

I did the only thing I could with a clear conscience. I turned to the families and said as simply as I could: "This is your country. All I can do is say the truth. Your country will decide what will happen next."

This quieted the sobbing and the protests. The women paused for a moment, conferred and then decided that this was a satisfactory answer. They resumed their seats in the back row. Still sniffling in their handkerchiefs and lamenting the plight of their sons – but hopefully assured that I was not an evil woman wishing misery upon them all.

And then, I noticed the men. Dark jackets. Dark turtlenecks. Dark glasses. And smoking at the back entrance to the room. (Yes, in the court room.) Chechens. Of course. I had nearly forgotten that the three criminals had been Chechen. I felt their eyes studying me. The women may have stopped their protests but the men might have more powerful means of persuasion. Marina held my hand tightly as we sat down. "My god, Phaedra," she whispered in English. "What have you got yourself involved in?"

There was no way out. The trial would proceed. If I testified, I faced the stern Chechen men piercing the back of my head with their stares. If I decided not to testify, I would incite some mysterious clause of the Russian legal system that I knew nothing about. At least if the going got tough I would be able to flee the country – assuming I had a whisper of advance warning.

With some unspoken signal, the remaining participants in the proceedings filed into the room. Marina's knowledge of the Russian criminal system was entirely based upon what she had picked up from local television dramas – which was still more than my understanding. This account, therefore, should be viewed from the perspective that I have absolutely no real knowledge of the Russian legal system and is really just impressions of my experience plus advice from a Russian girlfriend who watched a lot of television – rather than a practical legal exposition.

First a swarm of uniformed police officers escorted in two defendants. Two? Why two? There were three who jumped me. Where was the third? No idea. The men were thinner, paler, disheveled, and their heads had been shaved. They were pushed unceremoniously into the cage on the side of the room. The men surveyed the room, recognizing friends and family and then me. We locked eyes. Their icy stares paralyzed me. Finally I had to turn away. Marina was breathless as the reality of the scene hit her. "They dragged you behind the building…" she said under her breath. She held my hand, terrified – looking, probably for the first time in her sheltered life, at real criminals.

"It's okay," I reassured her. "They can't hurt us now."

Next a man and a woman entered the room. The same man and woman I had seen on the previous occasions. I had quickly concluded that they were the defense and the prosecuting attorney – although who was who I could not say as neither had yet said a word to me.

Next the judge and jury filed in. Yes, there was a jury. At least that is what they were called. An elderly man and woman, each proudly wearing a handful of mysterious Soviet era medals, took seats at desks at either side of the judge.

"Two jurors?" I asked Marina. "Where are the others?"

No, she replied. There are just two jurors. Permanent jurors, in fact. People were awarded a permanent position of juror as a high honor from the state. Typically it was granted to military heroes, or "Heroes of the Labor Collective" or similarly recognized distinctive achievement. In any case it was viewed as a free ride and a position of honor – nothing was expected of them. They had a title of distinction and were paid for it. In all, it was a pretty good retirement plan for military heroes.

So everyone was in position now – families, witness/victim, defendants with police escort, prosecutor, defense, jurors and judge. Then a young Russian *devushka* slipped into the room. Actually she was the sort of girl who could not really "slip in" anywhere quietly – except for into a scene of utter chaos, like a Russian courtroom. She had peroxide blond hair, heavy blue eyelids, and pink leather shorts over fish net stockings. The outfit was complete with a fluffy angora sweater and stiletto metal shoes. She carried a notebook and loudly snapped her bubblegum as she took her seat. The court stenographer had arrived.

Let the show begin.

And I do mean "show." What followed could only be described as a bizarre cross between a David Lynch movie and the Jerry Springer show. Although there were nominally other legal participants, it was the judge's show and he was not about to concede the spotlight to anyone.

What happened next would be viewed to be complete pandemonium to the untrained eye. The judge shouting instructions, the prosecutor and defense retorting swiftly and sharply. The defendants protesting loudly – the *militsia* vigorously beating nightsticks against the bars of the cage to intimidate the criminals into silence. The families wailing and protesting. But this was chaos only to the untrained eye. To those of us wizened to the alternate universe of Russia, there was a process under the madness.

The judge introduced the case very quickly in a blinding flash of drama and pounding of paper. In a matter of moments many questions that had built up over the previous several months were answered in one fell swoop. The three men had been charged with the crime of "group attack". If found guilty, the maximum penalty would be four years of hard labor. They already had served nine months in prison already... (I ceased to hear what was said next as this information slowly registered. They had been imprisoned since that fateful night the previous winter. It hardly seemed possible.) One of the men charged had been found to be criminally insane (Thug A – Kh-). Therefore he had been committed to a mental institution. I looked at Marina in horror. I had wanted these men to be punished for attacking me. But a mental institution in Russia for the criminally insane? I had seen the top tier hospital facilities Adrian had stayed in – what did the mental institutions look like?

After this brief introduction, the judge conducted a survey in the room. Did anyone see any reason why the case should be postponed further or could it continue today? The judge started his survey with defendant #1 (Thug B), then defendant #2 (Thug C), moving on then to me, then the prosecution and finally the defense. Defendant #1 gripped the bars of his cage and argued that the case should be dismissed because his rights had been violated. He had not been allowed to talk to an attorney until six days after his arrest and he had been held without bail ever since. The *militsia* saw the fingers protruding from the cage and seized the opportunity for target practice with their billy clubs, slamming at the defendants' fingers and rattling the iron bars of the cage until the defendant retreated to the relative safety of the back wall.

The judge barked a question "do you have a lawyer now?" The defendant answered yes. "Well, then," said the judge quickly, shuffling his papers, "there is no problem then, is there? The case may continue." And on the proceedings charged.

My entire view of the American legal system comes from many hours of watching night-time drama television and sitting through jury selection several times (although I have never actually been selected). As far as I could tell, the proceedings in this Russian courtroom were galloping forward at a pace about 20-30 times the speed of the standard American court room. The judge had complete control of the room. What he said happened. No debates, no challenges. He was the sole source of legal opinion that mattered. All other arguments were dismissed swiftly.

The defense attorney argued that the case should be dismissed because of discrepancies in the arrest records between the defendants. If the three men were arrested together for the crime of group attack, then certainly their arrest records should be identical? But no – the defense attorney read different dates and different places of arrest from the records of all three criminals.

Of course this would invalidate the whole case. I secretly hoped that the judge would agree and the defendants would go free. They had already served nearly a year in the horrors of a Russian prison for a crime that would hardly earn a wrist slap in the United States.

The judge was clearly irritated that the defense would waste time with such trivialities. He bickered a bit with the defense attorney – why was he wasting the court's time with such silly matters? But the defense attorney held his ground and finally the judge agreed to consider the matter further. He declared a recess. He retreated from the room (perhaps to give the impression he would actually consider the matter further, although personally I was of the view that the judge had no such intentions.) The *militsia* opened the cage and herded the defendants from the room. The stenographer pushed her chair back from her table and began filing her nails.

The remaining participants and observers just milled about listlessly. The mothers of the boys started a fresh round of sobbing. The men at the back of the room conferred in low voices and smoked putrid Russian brand cigarettes. Low level Chechen mafia muscle men – I concluded. The higher tiers of shady underworld characters would smoke nothing but western brands. No one spoke to Marina or me. My clothing snagged on the splintering benches. I craved a glass of water or anything to drink, but of course there would be nothing available in the building, save for the rust-colored water that would shudder out of the clattering pipes in the ladies' room.

After about an hour the prisoners were escorted back to their cage and the judge and jurors returned. The stenographer blew on her fingertips, willing her nail polish to dry a bit faster. Finally she could postpone the inevitable no longer. She gingerly picked up her pen, turned to a fresh page in her notebook and began to scribble furiously.

After everyone resumed their positions, the judge read a brief statement. Basically he said that it was irrelevant that there were errors in the arrest records. There were no doubts that the three had been arrested together. The trial would go forward at once.

First the judge read all the arrest records, my statements, and the criminals' comments to my statements. He sped through this bit of the proceedings at lightning speed – obviously as a formality only. The judge then assumed the role of talk show host and directed the first "guest" to take the floor – defendant #1, come on down! Actually he stayed right where he was, in the cage. There was none of the process I expected as part of an American trial – no one was sworn in and directed to "tell the truth, the whole truth and nothing but the truth. So help me God." There was not even a witness stand or agreed area for people to make their statements from. But although bizarre to me, there were underlying rules that kept the scene moving and gave a sense of controlled chaos to the event.

Defendant #1 was directed to give his statement to the court. He addressed the judge, the jurors, the attorneys, even me. The room was his audience. When he had finished with his statement, everyone was given the opportunity to cross-examine him. And I do mean everyone – each of the key players was invited to ask questions in a round robin around the room. First defendant #2 was given the opportunity to cross-examine defendant #1, then me, then the prosecution, and finally the defense attorney. The judge also interjected questions of his own as the mood struck him. The two elderly jurors sat perfectly motionless and stared off into space. The stenographer hunched intensely over her notebook and scribbled frantically to keep up with the pace of the proceedings.

I sat watching with astonishment as defendant #1 was cross-examined by defendant #2 – both in their cage, gripping the metal bars and calling out loudly to each other.

The militsia saw a hand extend just a bit too far out from the cage and quickly swung at it with their nightsticks. A smack as the club connected with flesh. Some shrill yelps and protests from multiple corners of the room. Then nightsticks hammering loudly on the cage — whether it was intended to subdue or stir up the criminals, I cannot say. The circus continued.

The criminals had a new story. They both testified that they were forced into participating in the group attack against their will. It was the third guy, Kh-, the one who had been found to be criminally insane, who had masterminded everything. He had threatened the other two into participation. Defendant #2 stuck with his story that he had given in his original police statement that he was trying to rescue me.

The story then turned from simply denial of guilt to the level of ludicrous. The defendants argued that they a) never asked me for money, b) they did not really understand what Kh- was doing. They thought he was just trying to "*poznakomitsa*" — you know, "pick me up". Then they concluded with c) I was never really restrained and I handed over money (and my business cards) to them voluntarily. This last statement was so over the top that even the defense attorney was laughing.

The discrepancies between the police records and the defendants' new story were obvious to everyone immediately. The judge interjected and started to re-read sections from the criminals' initial statements at the time of their arrest. He asked why they did not raise the issue then that they had been coerced into participation? They said that they were afraid of Kh — he's criminally insane, you know. So why were they with him in the first place if they were afraid of him? Oh, they just met him about half an hour earlier because they had just arrived by train and were trying to find their aunt's house. Kh- offered to show them how to find the street, so they followed.

After the defendants gave their statements and were cross-examined through the surreal round robin, it was my turn. The judge simply told me to recount my story and then my turn at the center of the trial began. Mind you, there was no swearing in of any sort, nor a designated spot from which witnesses gave testimony. I was only instructed to stand and speak. A bit odd – should I at least swear to tell the truth? But the court was waiting and so I began. My university Russian language teacher would have shot me for the massacre of grammar which followed. I justify this because I was painfully nervous. The environment was not exactly conducive to thinking clearly. The two men who had attacked me gripped the bars of their cage and opened their mouths to protest and insult. A menacing step forward from the *militsia*, brandishing their Billy clubs, quickly subdued any spoken protest. Voices were stilled, so their eyes communicated the message.

I made the mistake of meeting the ice blue eyes of Defendant #1 and stopped mid-sentence. The back of my skull suffered burn marks from the laser stares of the families. What would the repercussions be if I appeared to be too eager to lock their sons away? But then again, what if someone accused me of deviating from my original police report? I did not know Russian law. If I changed my story at this time, terrorized into silence by the presence of the families, then what future would I face at the hands of the Russian police. My mind was thinking about every aspect of my current situation – except for Russian grammar. Finally I surrendered to the inevitable – I could listen in Russian, but the stress of the situation would only allow me to talk in English. Marina snuggled close at my side, as much for her own sense of security in the situation as moral support for me. She translated patiently and accurately. I dutifully followed American-style testimony (at least the Hollywood version of it), trying to stick to the facts only without opinions. But this apparently was not the standard in Russia. The judge asked me if I believed that they acted together. Did I believe that #1 was trying to rescue me? I tried not to offer opinions, but actually it was strange that he was pinning my arms behind my back if he was trying to rescue me. Then the judge asked if they were drunk – another opinion requested. Yes, of course, they were all sloppy drunk. But to the court I said only that I did not really know. At this point I was trying to hit the middle road – anything to survive this ordeal without being accused of betrayal by either terrifying side.

After my statement I was about to sit down, but the judge sharply stopped me. I was done with my statement but now the cross-examination would begin and everyone would have an opportunity to join in. First the defendants cross-examined me! Yu- asked me if I had been drinking earlier in the night. At this, the judge swiftly interjected with a slam of his gavel on his desk. The court stenographer squeaked with an involuntary yelp, paused for a moment, and then continued scribbling in her notebook. Her feet were wound tightly around her chair legs and her eyebrows were furrowed in deep concentration.

The judge sharply ordered me not to answer and then yelled at the defendants to ask only relevant questions. Yu- started to protest that the judge had asked me if the defendants had been drunk therefore it was only logical that...

"Enough," the judge barked. The *militsia* took this as a cue to smack the defendant with their clubs yet again. Yu- took the not-so-subtle hint and announced that he had no further questions.

Then it was Zh-'s turn to cross examine me. He asked me how many times I saw the *militsia* hit him while he was at the police station. Christ. How to answer this one, with both the *militsia* (fully armed) and the devoted Chechen family looking on? I answered, honestly, that I really was not counting, but he was already in the middle of being beaten against the wall when I arrived. He was then thrown to the floor and kicked and beaten by several men, then taken to a back room out of sight – but I still heard shouting, yelps, and thumping of fists and walls and clubs against flesh.

This statement ignited a vocal outrage from all participants in the court. The defense attorney leaped to his feet and started shouting at the *militsia* and the judge. The family joined the fray. Everyone was standing and gesturing violently in protest. The Chechen men in the back of the room hurled insults generally towards everyone representing the Russian legal system. If they reached inside their coats... I was certain that we were a fraction of a second away from a shootout in a Russian courtroom. The air was explosive. Anything could happen. The judge, like any strong talk-show host, eventually regained control of the room.

The defense attorney demanded a postponement for the case while there would be an investigation into whether the defendants' rights had been violated. The judge denied the motion and retorted swiftly that perhaps excessive force was used in the arrest, but that was irrelevant to today's proceedings.

The judge had tolerated the impudence of the defendants for long enough. Right. Their opportunity to cross-examine me was now officially over. It was (once again) the judge's turn to ask questions. He started a new line of questioning with me – basically trying to coax me into either definitively confirming or refuting the story that the two defendants had "involuntarily" participated in the attack. The judge asked me whether Kh- was threatening the other two (as they had just testified). I responded that the three of them had all been yelling at me rather than each other, so that might suggest that they were cooperating.

I knew my testimony that day differed from the police report on some details. Such as, in my police report I stated that Kh- was gagging me while Zh- was strangling me with my scarf and pinning my arms. That would have required three arms (at least) on the part of Zh-. In my courtroom testimony (and the way I now believe things must have occurred) Kh- was gagging me and strangling me. (He was also planting scary sloppy kisses all over my face which the *militsia* had refused to enter into the official record, so I did not recount that here.) Zh- was restraining me and Yu- was searching and frisking me. I braced myself for the torture the defense attorney would certainly put me through for such inconsistency. But then – I breathed – there was none. No significant questions from the defense at all. My testimony, miraculously, had come to an end.

The next person invited to make a statement was the prosecutor. She gave a nice summary speech of the events and concluded that this was clearly a case of group attack. The round robin continued and once again everyone in the room had the opportunity to question her. Finally it was the defense attorney's turn. He produced a large stack of letters from family and friends of the defendants, all testifying that the boys were upstanding members of society. A few were read for the record before the judge interrupted – his patience was wearing then. He conducted a poll of the room – would anyone object if they were all entered into the record – without any further recitation? No objections – so with a wave of the judge's hand, that was done. Next subject. The defense attorney simply repeated the defendants' story that they had been coerced into participation by Kh- and therefore all charges should be dropped.

The two jurors then were offered their turns in the round robin. I had nearly forgotten that they were there at all. The ancient man and woman were motionless, dusty, and practically furniture during the proceedings. Quiet grunts confirmed that they had nothing to say.

So the judge moved straight into proposed sentences. First the defendants were asked if there were any extraneous considerations that should be made. Zh- said that they had to work to support their families and claimed health problems. I was asked if I had any opinions of the sentence. (Would this happen in a western legal system? I don't think so.) I said I had no opinion. The prosecutor asked for the maximum penalty – four years in a labor camp. The defense attorney said that since the defendants had been in jail since January 1995, they had served enough time and should go free.

Then the proceedings were over except for the final event. As far as I can tell, criminals in Russia have two rights – the right to an attorney (which may or may not be acknowledged in a timely manner) and the right for the last word at the trial. Ever since I had heard of this, I had been looking forward to their "last word." They had been rotting in jail for many months and therefore had sufficient time to think of something interesting. Yu- said nothing. Zh- , however, turned to me and gave a long, prepared apology which rambled along aimlessly in monotone Russian. No particular point to be made. No dramatic statements or accusations or revelations or political statements about the plight of the Chechen nation. Nothing intellectually challenging or provocative. Then suddenly everything was over. How disappointing. But realistically, I was subconsciously projecting my Hollywood version of courtroom dramas onto this bizarre but very real scene. And in real scenes sometimes things just end without memorable quotes.

So that was it. The testimony and arguments were over. Beginning to end the whole trial had lasted about three hours. The judge declared the court adjourned and said the verdict would be announced in a few days. We were no longer required. With these words Marina and I fled the building – we did not want to spend one more minute under the paralyzing eyes of the defendants' families.

Over the next several days Marina called the court house continuously until she finally learned the verdict – guilty of group attack and sentenced to four years in a labor camp in Murmansk. I was in shock. Labor camp. Four years. Murmansk. The sentence read like a passage from a Solzhenitsyn novel. In the United States the case could have been dismissed for a dozen or more reasons. I had no doubt whatsoever that the men were guilty. And definitely they should be punished for their crimes. But really – four years in an Artic labor camp? That was a death sentence. They had attacked me and robbed me, but I had no substantive injuries. I stared out my office window and contemplated what I had told the criminals' families – I would tell the truth and their laws would decide. I hoped the families believed it was their son's actions and their country's laws that resulted in the sentence. Hopefully they would not blame me. Revenge from an angry Chechen family.... I cut off my wandering thoughts. If I actually thought about the situation I would certainly become hysterical. Better to just continue leading my life as always. There was nothing else I could do.

A few days later I was at home deeply engrossed in my latest attempt to purge the cockroaches from my apartment (a futile effort, of course) when a sharp zap of my door buzzer snapped me into reality. Someone was at the door. My door. Uninvited. People just do not drop by uninvited in Moscow. Who would possibly come by uninvited? I could only think of the Chechen family. And Jim's irate neighbors demanding $10,000 cash. And Igor and his sledgehammer demanding compensation for the damage to my apartment. Of course my residential address was on the police records. And of course the Chechen family had obtained them. And now I would be required to be sacrificed in retribution for their sons' sentence.

Gingerly I peered through the eyehole in my steel door to assess what was awaiting me. Two middle-aged women with the requisite *shapkas*, cardigans, plaid woolen skirts, etc. They may or may not have been in the family of the criminals. I could not see their faces clearly through the distorted lens of the eyehole. But in the corridor they had seen a shadow cross the eye hole. They knew someone was home.

"*Devushka!*" they cried out and buzzed the door again. The disturbing harsh electric zap split my skull. "We know you are home. We have wanted to talk to you for several days but you are never home." They zapped the door again. They were going to torment me with my own horrible door buzzer until I submitted to their demands and opened the door. To what?

"We are from the building management collective," the women barked with increasing agitation. "You have not paid into the maintenance fund. We need to collect from you."

Of course. I nearly collapsed with relief. Intermixed with the court summons had been notice to pay the dues to the maintenance fund. I had assumed any money I paid would actually go towards some clever Russian's vodka fund, so I had simply ignored the notices. Now they were here to collect. Fine. It was just the building collective. All things considered, I would be delighted to pay them.

I opened the door with a warm smile of relief. The two women were indeed from the building collective. They immediately realized that I would be receptive to anything they had to say about the maintenance fund. They had a little prepared presentation that they talked through – explaining the benefits of the maintenance fund and the accomplishments to date. The lights in the corridors and ground floor were replaced quickly without fuss when necessary. The lift had been repaired six months ago and was actually now quite reliable. It was a real success. For the next year they wanted to increase the annual contribution for each apartment to cover the cost of installing a real security system at the front door — where all tenants would have their own codes to punch in to enter the building. They had a business case and cost estimates to support the proposal!

I looked at the women in complete disbelief. Were they truly from the same culture that produced the legal circus I had just participated in? How could these *babushki* wearing floral house dresses create a true business case while St Petersburg city government would not even return my phone calls? My emotional state took a violent swing from panic to joy. I was now lightheaded and barely able to string two sentences together. I wanted to embrace them and tell them that they had renewed my hope in the future of Russia. But I restrained myself and instead produced a 50,000 ruble note for them. (About 20 USD, but a lot of money to everyone in the building collective!)

Perhaps it would just go into their vodka fund. But I was delighted to hear such a good story and was willing to pay for that privilege.

23   ESCAPE FROM VALAAM

November 1995 — St Petersburg

It started off as a "bad Russia day." The term sounds silly, I know, but it was understood universally by all expatriates, so I have to use it here. A "bad Russia day" is
when a string of petty frustrations just build one on top of the other until you are left
screaming for mercy and researching options for the next flight out to anywhere in
Western Europe.

First you do not notice what is happening. In the morning you turn on the lights
in the kitchen and count to 10 — but open your eyes before the cockroaches have scattered to their dark corners. You find squirming maggots in a spoonful of sugar you are
about to stir into the morning tea. This is what happens in Russian kitchens. You had
already seen it 100 times before, so you shrug it off and toss out the sugar and move
on. Perhaps then you break a zipper in the morning or lose a glove. So what, you might
think, zippers break all the time and everyone loses a glove every so often. But in Russia
the agony you had to go through to replace such trivial everyday items was excruciating.

Outside the front door the first early hint of winter assaulted my senses. Soon we
would once again be in survival mode to get from home to the office without turning
into an ice cube. Not everyone made it. Some mornings you would see a corpse frozen
solid, huddled against the side of a building or a tree. And I do mean a corpse. Drunks
who stumbled on their way home the night before. In the summer they would simply
be unconscious until morning. As the temperature plummeted, however... The first
time I saw a frozen corpse, near a Metro station in Moscow, I stopped and looked, wondering what to do next. No one else stopped or even gave the body a sideways glance.
The expatriates called them "popsicles". Everyone had found one. You had to give a
bitter laugh and move on. The locals certainly did. If you truly stopped to think about
the suffering that surrounded us, you could be driven to madness.

So I retreated back from the real world into my own personal hell. Ignore the pain of the world and focus inwards. Cold sleet churned dirt from the street into a deep brown sludge. Vehicles would wallow through the muck, splattering everything within range. No proper storm drains anywhere. The sludge had nowhere to go – except into your boots. Your feet would be frozen solid, wet and slimy by the time you trudged to the office.

And today I had forgotten to bring fresh cozy socks and shoes to wear at the office. So I peeled my feet out of my miserable mucky boots and tucked them into cold impractical heels that were stashed in my desk.

This particular morning, like every morning, the first order of the day was to wipe a layer of greenish brown grit off my desk. A single wipe from an old rag would cut a shiny path across the surface. Papers that had been standing untouched for more than two days needed to be shaken off. Clouds of the mysterious grey-green dust would catch the sunlight in the office – or at least the feeble rays of light that managed to penetrate the slime-covered windows. What exactly was in the air that we were breathing here anyway? I coughed as the dust grated my lungs.

Natasha, our admin assistant, was out for the day. I appealed to Ludmilla, our hostile translator, to request her to help out on the phones for just one day. She turned up her nose with a huff and stated that she was a highly qualified professional. Answering the phones was not in her job description. Why wasn't I prepared to answer the phones myself? The Russian men looked at me with astonishment when I asked them to assist with answering the phones. Receptionists are women! They couldn't possibly answer the phones.

Why does everything have to be so difficult? Crush or be crushed in the Russian world. So my new colleague, Brian, and I (the two most senior people in the office) found ourselves answering the phones for the day.

Ah yes, Brian. Brian had been engaged by Patrick to support the relationships with all the St Petersburg government agencies – despite the fact that we still were not actually permitted to talk to the government agencies. I had protested Brian's assignment to the project simply on the basis that our project burn rate could not possibly support one more expatriate salary. Patrick had responded that Brian was necessary for the project and it was up to me to manage the budget and ensure that the software and related hardware were delivered per the statement of work with USAID.

Olga, our accountant, brought me the office phone bill, which had finally arrived from a few months ago. The total amount was $2000 more than she had expected. A large amount of money for most people – astonishing to Olga, who was paid $600/month. She offered a quick explanation for my benefit: Patrick had visited the office shortly before my arrival. He had connected to the internet not through a local dial up connection to St Petersburg, but back to the Washington DC office. He had left the dial up internet connection open for hours at a time. Patrick was criticizing us for not managing the budget more efficiently, and now here he had burdened us with a $2000 phone bill. Olga pleaded with me to talk to Patrick. She was diligent in her efforts to attempt to control our expenses – and now this!

I sighed and promised to talk to Patrick – another point of agitation. I could already hear Patrick's response. He would simply shift the responsibility back to me to manage the budget more effectively. I had to plan on telephone expenses at an appropriate level and obviously I had underestimated. In the early days when I had just joined the project I was dissecting the excel spreadsheets for budget forecasting that were handed over by my predecessor and had discovered an error in some formulas. After my correction, the remaining available funds for the project suddenly dropped from $2 million to $1.25 million. $750K had simply evaporated. I called Patrick to protest (with the hope that my predecessor would be held accountable for the mistake). But no, he had simply replied to me that I needed to manage within the available funds and deliver the project to completion. The ground had shifted but expectations remained the same.

(One small improvement to our burn rate was that Alan's allocated time on the project had mercifully come to an end. The document he left behind included such pearls of wisdom as "Training must include both general computer literacy as well as training on the final software application. Training must include both classroom training as well as ongoing hands-on exercises." Alan had spun out the revolving door of consultants on the project, leaving Brian and I the task of trying to figure out how to actually implement such generic drivel.)

As the day continued, annoyances mounted. First a phone call from the landlady of my St Petersburg apartment. She had found a German couple who wanted to rent my flat for much more money on a two year lease. I began to issue a variety of protests that would be appropriate in the United States – I had a six month lease. She couldn't just kick me out because she found someone who would pay more. Also this implied that she had been parading people through the flat without my knowledge. I opened my mouth to protest and then shut it again. Why bother. I had no avenue to recourse unless I found a hit man bigger than her hit man. Any complaints would just make the process more painful than it already was. I took a breath before just confirming the date she wanted me out of the flat. Two weeks. I needed to be out of the flat in two weeks.

One painful call down and inevitably there would be more to come. I could see this would be a bad Russia day and just waited to see what would reveal itself next.

The phone rings again. I am playing receptionist this day as well as project manager and surprise myself by answering the phone with a semi-hostile traditional Russian "Da, slushayu vas" – Yes, I'm listening to you. (How much coaching had I given to my Russian receptionists to use the American "Good morning, Arthur Andersen. How may I help you?")

A pause on the other end of the line, followed by a Russian woman asking "Phaedra is that you? Why are you the receptionist today?"

Immediately my mood brightened. It was Svetlana – one of my favorite new business acquaintances. As our relationship with Flis, our St Petersburg Oracle subcontractor, deteriorated even further I had been searching for a potential alternative local Russian firm to partner with and had been introduced to Svetlana through the expatriate grapevine. She was a Vice President at a firm of Oracle consultants based in Moscow called RossDev and she had pleasantly shocked me with her level of professionalism, organization, and courtesy.

Svetlana was calling to talk through some questions she had while preparing a proposal for the scope of work that would bring the local components of the development work to conclusion. Ah yes, such rational questions about how the business requirements would be documented and provided to her team. Expectations for the level of technical documentation to be provided. How the test cycles would work with the clients. Expected involvement of her team with the handover of the end product and training with the client. It was almost like she wanted the project to be successful!

I reveled in the fact I was having such a professional goal-oriented conversation with a potential business partner. I fantasized about how pleasant and orderly the project would be with RossDev as a partner and Svetlana as my main contact.

There was only one severe problem – the development was still contracted to Flis, who was making no visible progress. We had nothing to show for the upcoming next milestone on the contract and something had to change. I was determined to fire Flis for non-performance and then bring in RossDev to finish the work. Of course non-performance is always a tricky business with subcontractors – even more so in Russia. I had recently engaged Oracle directly to perform a third-party quality assurance review of Flis's work. Their incompetence, I was certain, would be reconfirmed by the independent assessment of the Oracle review. We would then be free to end the Flis relationship and engage a new contractor.

So it was with enthusiasm that I discussed the scope of the subcontract with Svetlana and answered her questions to help her prepare an appropriate proposal. The report from Oracle would be delivered any day now. I wanted to have an alternative ready to go as soon as we were able to pull the plug on Flis. And then in mid-sentence we both paused and heard a distinctive metallic click on the line. I heard a sudden sharp gasp from Svetlana, which she then promptly attempted to cover with a cough. We continued the conversation – slowly and methodically. But we both knew what was happening – our phones were now being tapped.

Svetlana ended the call as courteously and as rapidly as possible. She promised to visit me in my offices soon. The message was clear but unspoken – no more phone conversations discussing her company's business.

"So our phones are now tapped, big deal," I attempted to shrug off the latest news with Brian. My moment of optimism while talking with Svetlana was rapidly spiraling into a black abyss.

"We are now part of the 'in crowd' I guess," Brian answered, with an effort to be light-hearted. Where this would lead us, neither of us could venture to guess.

Tapping the phones was a clear statement on the relationship we now had with the city of St Petersburg. One more notch of restraint around the throat of the project team.

Ever since my first week on the project, when Ruslan, Alan, and I had our computer training planning session – with the agency that had no computers – we had been denied audience to meet with any other city agencies. Our designated primary point of contact with the St Petersburg city government, Larissa, strictly forbade us from work-ing with the agencies directly. All communication would have to be approved by her. And so far, she had denied all requests for communication. No need to bombard the agencies with senseless requests for information. We were supposed to be the experts. If we did not know the answers then we should just pack up and leave town. Oh actu-ally, we shouldn't really pack up. We should just go – it would be fine for us to leave behind our computer equipment.

Larissa asked continuously for an exact inventory of the servers, computers, rout-ers, hubs that we were planning to deploy with the delivery of the registration system. Her voice choked up with excitement as her eyes skimmed to the bottom line on the inventory - $2 million USD of hardware, software and networking infrastructure. Sun Sparc stations. Cisco routers. Laptops, desktops and lightpro projectors for training and presentation purposes.

"When this equipment is transferred to the city at the close of the project it will help modernize their title registration process," Alan had said with a firm authoritative nod.

"If the hardware actually ever arrives and if there actually is a working system to go along with it," I commented bitterly and entirely sincerely.

As difficult as the hardware procurement exercise had been for my prior project, the level of angst was taken to a whole new level with the property title registration project. At the core of our project was the delivery of custom software to be deployed to five different government agencies throughout the city. In the days before there were such things as hosted services or web-based applications, this meant that we had to purchase every piece of necessary infrastructure ourselves – from the Sun Sparc sta-tions that would host the Oracle databases to the dedicated lines that would connect the five locations. The ordeal to comply with the resulting procurement and administrative nightmare was the entire reason for existence for Paul. And he was becoming slightly loopy as a result.

The good news of the day was that the SunSparc stations had finally been purchased and were in process of delivery. The bad news was that the country of origin for the servers was Ireland (if I remember correctly – in any case, not the United States). For

USAID to reimburse the project we had to have all equipment sourced from the United States. The fact that SunSparc stations were not actually built in the United States was not a legitimate response. We had to provide backup information regarding what alternatives were explored, why they were not viable etc. Paul now was in purgatory writing essays for mysterious USAID procurement rules explaining why SunSparc stations were necessary to run Oracle databases, and (the logical next step) why we had decided to go the route of developing on an Oracle platform vs other options available.

I knew that every other USAID, EBRD, World Bank and British Council project had similar administrative requirements. My head would explode if I thought about what percentage of our so-called "aid" budgets were being spent just complying with documentation requirements. Somewhere along the way the stated objective of supporting the privatization and development of Russia had been replaced with the new mission of preparing nice paperwork.

The next phone call of the day was from Yuri Mikhailovich – the director of the city property agency who I had met my first week in St Petersburg. My last words with him had been the earnest promise to meet with him soon to work through the business requirements and process improvements for the title registration project. That promise had been shattered. No fault of my own (I attempted to justify the situation to myself), rather due to Larissa's severe restrictions on contact between the project team and the agencies.

Yuri Mikhailovich was in a state of heightened excitement. He was waiting for our return visit. When would the American experts be ready to work with him on the plan for how the property registration activities would be restructured? The future of his agency was at stake – and, therefore, his own political future. He was anxious to assist the project however possible.

I explained that I had been reprimanded for participating in the on-site visit some months earlier and since then had attempted (without success) to gain permission to visit the agencies again. Each proposed agenda had been reviewed and denied with the underlying theme that all the proposed questions reflected a lack of preparation by the Americans. Only once we had clear future processes that were a rational proposal would she grant an audience. (Of course we required input from the agencies to create such a rational proposal of future processes – how wonderful are circular arguments.)

So no, dear Yuri Mikhailovich, we would not be seeing you any time soon. But no, don't give up – he argued. Rationalization of the title registration process was essential to limit the growing power of the St Petersburg central government. He understood that a structured process would support the individual citizen gain a bit more control over their lives. Abstract randomness benefits only those in power – and the people who curry favor with them.

I agreed with Yuri Mikhailovich. The project goals on paper were quite noble. Although I had issued many requests to Larissa for a working session with the agencies, I promised that I would not give up and would try yet again.

Shortly after hanging up the phone with Yuri Mikhailovich — a call from Larissa with a sharp reprimand. Why did we persist in contacting the agencies directly? We were unreliable contractors — going behind her and having conversations with the city agencies directly. Conversation with the agencies was out of line. We had been warned before.

I was impressed by how effective Larissa's monitoring efforts had become and then promptly dismissed her call to the back of my mind. We knew she was watching us. We knew she did not want us communicating with the agencies directly. Nothing new had been learned in that phone call. Just another bit of harassment as we attempted to get our job done.

And then an agitated phone call from our program director of USAID, Greg. "Why were we being so difficult?" The program director demanded. "There are certain rules of conduct for working in this city. Your team is showing complete lack of respect for the process and unwillingness to partner with the city."

Of course I opened my mouth to start to ask whether tapping our phones was a good partnering gesture by the city, but restrained myself at the last moment. I took a deep breath then said what was expected of me. I agreed that I would submit a request in writing (yet again) for permission for a discussion with Yuri Mikhailovich.

So this meant turning to Ludmilla, the translator, for assistance. Would she please write a letter for us to the city council requesting an opportunity to meet with Yuri Mikhailovich to review proposed changes in the registration process.

"I cannot do that," Ludmilla replied with a smirk. "I am just a lowly translator, not a project manager. I cannot make assumptions of what you want to include in such a letter. You must write the letter in English and give it to me to translate."

She turned her back and marched away without waiting for my reply. I stared in disbelief at her retreating figure. Such attitudes are completely foreign to Americans and I was utterly ill-equipped to deal with her. I turned to Brian for advice and he suggested that we shoot her. A pleasant thought for a moment, but not really practical. And also I concluded that although Brian's appearance had thrown a wrench into the budget management, it really couldn't be held against him personally. It would be good to have an ally in battle.

Paul had been watching me with Ludmilla. He was always quick with some sarcastic comment, so I asked him if he had any advice other than shooting Ludmilla. Perhaps something a bit more actionable. Paul solemnly and silently pointed to the quote from Ernest Hemingway taped prominently over his desk.

Never mind that those words were written seventy-five years ago — they served as our simple outline of modern expatriate existence. Yes, when would we ever get anything done. Someone please get me a drink. And the sex…. Well, everyone knows what a great stress reliever that is. And in the temporary state of mind of the Russian chaos and expatriates, you just could live for the moment. No worries about tomorrow. Do what you want to do. With who you want to. It doesn't matter. This isn't your real life anyway, is it? Expatriate life is just a fantasy existence to experiment. Do what you want. Reality is back in the United States.

And then a phone call for Paul. Witty, sharp-tongued Paul who had completely entered an alternate reality as a defense against the strains of every day Russian existence. He would spontaneously break into song with a refrain from "Skip to my Lou", or would mutter obscure Frank Zappa lyrics to himself. A bit of release to allow equilibrium with the world. But this phone call shocked Paul's expression into total seriousness. Quite unusual, so we knew it was bad news.

It turns out that not all apartment blocks had building collectives as friendly as my own. Back in Moscow, Alex and Everett continued to share an apartment together and lived a life of stereotypical American bachelor debauchery. The morning after a particularly rowdy party there was a knock at the front door. Building collective! They took a deep breath and braced themselves for the verbal abuse that would surely be forthcoming from the noise the night before. Through the peephole they saw a *babushka* bundled in a wooly scarf. As they opened the door, three burly aggressive Russian men suddenly appeared and pushed their way into the apartment and viciously attacked the two friends. The *babushka* had been planted as bait to coax the Americans to open the door. Within moments they were bound hand and foot and being tortured to reveal the whereabouts of their stash of cash.

Of course, Americans keep their money in banks, not stashed under mattresses, but the Russian men did not believe that. This was especially true as Alex was a native Russian speaker, so in the invaders' minds, he must obviously save money the Russian way – secured somewhere in the apartment. No one in Russia trusted banks. These Americans were wealthy. They had money – lots of it. And therefore it had to be hidden away somewhere in this apartment. The invaders beat and tortured the Americans (with obvious lack of success to determine the whereabouts of the hidden treasure), then proceeded to demolish everything in the apartment in their quest. In the end the brutes had to make do with stealing all the electronics in the house, including the watches off the guys' wrists.

Yes, Alex and Everett would be fine. No, they were not leaving the country. Violence was a fact of life in this place. Eventually it would touch everyone. Touch us, but not hurt us. We were survivors and would continue on. We would insulate ourselves from the reality of the Russian existence by creating an alternate universe for ourselves where this was just a game.

"They'll be fine," said Paul. He shrugged off the phone call and moved on. Sounds callous I know, but we had to. If you actually dwelled on the implications of such a call and took it seriously, you would be paralyzed to ever open the door to your apartment again.

The day progressed and Brian wrote the letter to Larissa formally requesting permission to meet with Yuri Mikhailovich. Ludmilla read the letter – written by Brian in English - and then handed it to me with a smirk. The letter was completely unsatisfactory, she declared with a distinct overtone of malice in her voice. There are certain protocols for how formal letters to the city government are to be written. This letter will be rejected by the city as unacceptable. It would be a waste of her time to translate it. Ludmilla thrust the letter at me triumphantly.

"Ludmilla," I barked back at her. "Can I remind you that earlier you were informing me that you were 'just a translator.' If I wanted political consul, I would ask for it. Just translate the letter." I had simply had enough of her for one day.

Ludmilla turned to her desk and gave me a sideways glance to let me know that she intended to come out victorious over me. Every encounter in Russia is a battle for supremacy. There are no partnerships, just winners and losers. Ludmilla would not be defeated. She had something planned. I could only watch her and attempt to stop any sabotage.

But I was too slow. Ludmilla had snapped up the phone and dialed Larissa's office at the city government. With perverse pleasure she was now explaining to Larissa that she had no confidence in our ability to write letters that adhered to proper protocol. Our team would require special attention to ensure that no inappropriate letters were circulated. A malicious smile slowly spread across Ludmilla' s face as she listened to Larissa's response and then put down the receiver.

"I have just confirmed that the city will not accept a letter that does not conform to the proper protocols," she said with obvious delight.

I was too furious for rational words at this point. "Well then ensure it does conform to the correct protocols," I snapped back at her.

"I cannot do that," she shook her head. "I am just a lowly translator. I do not have the necessary training to write sensitive political documents."

And so my day at the office continued. Just another typical day of confrontation, agitation and a tiny hint of possible progress forward. Then hope would turn to illusion. And then Paul would break out into song with "Somewhere Over the Rainbow." It would lighten the mood, but it wouldn't solve anything.

And my friends back in the United States wonder why all expatriates are alcoholics.

A few weeks earlier, as the grind of Larissa's continuous abuse was beginning to get to me, I had turned to Noah for commiseration over a few beers at the Magpie. I had expected sympathy and a friendly ear and similar stories of frustration, but instead

Noah simply waved his hand in dismissal. I was taking everything too seriously. I just needed to sit back and enjoy the ride. He had been Joseph's friend in South Russia and I had expected that he would approach the role as American Advisor to the St Petersburg Local Privatization Center in much the same way as Joseph had – hitting the challenge head on and suffering from continuous frustration and setbacks in his attempts to provide real consultation to real companies. Instead I found that he had settled into the same sort of philosophy as Carl in Krasnoyarsk. Noah made an early decision early on to simply become a "Pet American." He would go to meetings when requested, shake hands with people on demand, and drink toasts to the future of Russia. If something was not explicitly requested by his Russian partners, he wouldn't do it. Absolutely zero initiative.

Noah's predecessor had been expelled from St Petersburg in much the same way that Joseph had been ejected from South Russia. "Why rock the boat?" was Noah's simple mantra. If the Russian partners wanted him to do nothing but sit at a desk until he was summoned to the next official pony show, then why not? He wouldn't accomplish anything by beating his head against the brick wall of the St Petersburg government anyway, so why even try. The nominal objective of the project was achieved simply by placing an advisor in St Petersburg – therefore his consultancy and USAID could check the "complete" box. Everyone was happy and Noah could just sit back and collect his paycheck.

I could hear Noah's arguments but could not internalize them. Maybe he had completely given up on the project to establish self-sustaining local consulting centers, but I still deeply believed in the objective of my project to streamline and automate the property title registration process. Success on this project would dramatically improve the lives of so many. It was worth fighting for!

I needed allies and a bit of girly camaraderie and therefore called Jennifer, an American I had befriended through the St Petersburg expat circles. She lived in a massive Soviet era apartment nearby with another expat, Valerie, as a flatmate. After the opening line of "I have had such a bad Russia day," Jennifer quickly invited me over to their apartment for drinks and dinner that night. And, she added, if my Russian landlady was serious about throwing me out of my apartment in two weeks, of course, I was welcome to crash on the sofa in their living room while I sorted out a more permanent solution.

My mood lunged from lonely despair to shared delight.

Hours later, the stresses of the day were obliterated by several bottles of red wine and a much-needed evening of girlie camaraderie. My girlfriends and I were snuggled up together on the sofa. A thick woolen blanket covered our bodies and bound us together in warmth and companionship. I had splurged and spent $45 on three pints of Haagen Daz at Stockmann's. Yes the price was extortionary – but the indulgence was a fabulous counterbalance to the pain of the day. The Haagen Daz was creamy, rich, perfect, dreamlike. We swirled spoons in our individual tubs of ice cream and moaned with obscene pleasure as the clouds of chocolate melted in our mouths. Our mood improved further from content to deliriously happy when Valerie revealed her surprise for the evening: Courtesy of her sister back in Boston, we now had a video tape of episodes of the new popular American television show that none of us had yet seen – "Friends."

After a moment of a contented lull in the conversation, Jennifer sighed deeply. "I'm so happy right now, I could just cry."

She spoke for all of us. The emotional rollercoaster of Russia had flung us into new heights. It is only when you are at the pits of despair when you truly appreciate the basic pleasures of life. The worse your agony and frustrations, the deeper the primal pleasure from such very simple luxuries. Good friends. Red wine. Companionship. Chocolate ice cream. Warm blankets. Cozy sofa. Escapism American television. Wow we had a great life. Look at the lives of ordinary Russians. We were living a life of complete decadence and indulgence.

It was in the context of the contented warmth of friendship and Haagen Daz ice cream and escapism American television comedy that Jennifer suggested that we all take a cruise boat up the Neva River to Valaam. A cruise ship. The Neva River. Valaam. No, none of us knew anything about Valaam, but it sounded wonderful. It was outside the city and we imagined that we would have fresh air and a last adventure outdoors before winter settled in. Life was good. We could rally all the St Petersburg expats for a weekend away together. On a river. We hummed with contentment and agreement and fantasized about this mythical place called Valaam.

A Russian cruise boat. What were we thinking? The term "cruise boat" evokes glamorous and relaxing images. Leisurely champagne-drenched meals, warm breezes, the smell of the sea, laughter, music, and dancing. The destination does not really matter. A cruise is about enjoying every moment of the journey. Of course, we all knew that the Russian cruise boat would be a completely different experience. If my tour of regional Russian hotels was any guide, I knew that we would be treated as suspects rather than guests. "Shut up and relax" was the unofficial motto of the Russian *bannya*. I knew that Russian restaurants served boiled grey meat and potatoes three times a day. And yet – somehow, despite all this, we were all seduced into the tantalizing idea of a weekend on a Russian cruise boat – an expedition to Valaam.

Once the warm glow of the dinner party had faded, we realized what we had agreed to. But still we looked forward to it. Why? Well, why do Russians dash from the sauna to the ice cold pool? Why punish your body with a long brutal run? Why go white-water rafting? Or come to think of it, why do anything at all? It is for the contrast, an experience to get the blood going and let you know you're alive. A challenge, something new. Only death is constant. Life requires continuous action and stimulation. The everyday chaos of St Petersburg had become background static in our lives. We needed a new experience.

The expats were always up for an adventure and it was relatively easy for us to round up a group of about twelve of us. Our motley crew included Noah, Paul, Valerie, Jennifer plus a number of other expats—among them Sonya, who would be returning to the US soon and declared the weekend to be her going away party.

Our first sign of what we were about to experience came as we organized our gear in our cabins after check-in. I laughed out loud as I read a statement left prominently on each of the bunks: "In case of necessity to abandon ship, the residents of this cabin are assigned to life boat number 14." Oh, of course. As the boat is sinking all the residents must proceed to their assigned life boats. No further advice on where we could find life boat number 14. No map of the cruise boat with an "X marks the spot" or anything else. I laughed this off and tossed aside the formal notice. We were in a river. Who cared if we had to board an assigned life boat. We could wade to shore if we chose.

As would be expected, our friends all collected at the dining room for dinner. We gathered like a group of giddy American college kids escaping for a spring break holiday. Rowdy, excitable, and intending to have a fun-filled weekend – no matter what. The vodka was flowing already. Russian tradition meets American expatriates. Here in Russia it was socially acceptable to be completely drunk by dinner time – and some in our group had a head start on the festivities of the evening. We are in Russia – therefore do as the locals do. Or at least we would choose from the local traditions that seemed to be of interest to us.

We all gathered at a table. And then a few more joined us and we moved around some tables and chairs to accommodate the rest of our friends. One chair creaked ominously and shredded at someone's clothing. We swapped it for another. All of this is standard American practice, but it was just a bit too much for the Russians. The restaurant staff sharply reprimanded us for moving around the tables and for not sitting at our assigned places.

What assigned tables? Surely they were kidding. But no it was quite serious. A stern Russian man barked at us that we were occupying his assigned table. We were instructed to vacate two seats at table #64 immediately because this Russian couple were the approved diners at that table. A room of hostile faces turned in our direction as we argued the point. Weren't there about a dozen tables that were completely empty? Why was it so important for Boris and Natasha to sit at this particular table? We were a group of friends who wanted to sit together for dinner.

"Such pretensions!" huffed the waitress with obvious disdain for the foreigners.

But we had learned our lessons of life in Russia well. Arrogance must be met with arrogance. There are rules for everything. But the rules can be ignored if you hold your position with enough determination. We ordered another bottle of vodka and held our table without flinching, ignoring the icy stares surrounding us.

We laughed and poured rounds of vodka for the table. We were victorious. Toasts and congratulations. A toast to the host and the guest of honor and to all the women at the table. We followed the process in classic Russian tradition. The predicted meal of boiled meat and potatoes was brought to our table. (No menus at this restaurant. You will eat what you are told and you will be grateful.) We continued with our laughing and carousing and being generally obnoxious. But our general lack of social graces soon did not matter as the rest of the Russian patrons quickly caught up to our level of intoxication with life and liquor.

The restaurant closed and we were tossed out to return to our cabins. Of course we had ample supplies of alcohol to keep us socially lubricated for the rest of the evening. Sonya's farewell added another layer to the frivolity. We packed into a tiny berth and began bestowing parting gifts on Sonya with much fanfare. A bottle filled with St Petersburg tap water – murky and in its raw unfiltered state. A bottle of "Black Death" vodka, St Petersburg subway tokens, a "*perchatki*" bag – a little mesh bag everyone seemed to have in their pockets at all times "just in case" you ran across something interesting to buy, Russian hair dye, a dried fish, plastic cups from Aeroflot.

Then gasps and applause as Scott produced a GAI baton – the stick wielded by the traffic police as they waved cars over for their collections of fines. Everything else presented so far was easily accessible as part of our daily life – but a GAI stick... This meant that Scott somehow had managed to bribe one of the GAI to part with their baton! Scott gestured to his girlfriend, Katya. She was the one who should be credited with such an accomplishment. A round of toasts followed for Katya. She smiled and waved to her new friends.

Twelve people cannot easily pack into one berth on a Russian cruise ship, so we spilled out into the main corridor. We began to intertwine with Russians who were carousing and joined in drunken renditions of various Russian folk songs. Empty bottles of vodka rolled on the floor. Bad luck, of course, to leave empty bottles on a table. For some reason Noah had brought newspapers and after just a bit of provocation, an intense competition of folding paper sailor hats was under way.

We were now all properly fitted out with our Russian sailor paper hats and bottles of vodka and were toasting and harassing and congratulating everyone we encountered. Our new Russian friends toasted us in return and offered pickled herring, dried fish, chalky chocolates from dilapidated Soviet-era paper boxes, and yet more vodka. At some point even the Black Death vodka was (unwisely) shared around. A bleary-eyed

Russian staggered down the corridor away from us, wearing one of our paper hats — sliding down over his eyebrows.

In all, a classic Russian evening – complete with a few pouting *devushki* silently posing at the side of their designated men for the evening.

The next morning we awoke (or "came to", as a more appropriate term) to find our ship docked snugly at a tiny island that featured one small dilapidated ancient fortress. Perhaps this was a tourist stop before we reached our final destination of Valaam. No advice or announcements from the ship's crew.

The gangplank was down to the island, allowing passengers to disembark and have a look around. A fierce gale of a northern wind battered any exposed flesh. Still, this looked like an interesting spot and worth an inspection. Ancient fortresses and ruins always attract the Americans — as we have nothing like it in the United States. With the exception of Katya, the Russian *devushki* yawned with boredom. They did not want to venture out into the bitter wind and opted to stay back in their cabins.

Unusual for a Russian historical site, these ruins actually had a fact board providing a few tidbits of local history. We were inspecting the Oreshek Fortress which was first constructed in 1299. As Oreshek Fortress is on an island at the south end of Lake Ladoga and only 35 kilometers away from St Petersburg it has been a strategic part of defending the city for nearly 700 years.

Wait a minute. Thirty five kilometers away from St Petersburg? South end of Lake Ladoga? Valaam was at the north end of Lake Ladoga. We looked at each other with cartoon question marks looming over our heads. Didn't we depart St Petersburg at 6pm the previous evening? Hadn't we been motoring along all night? Apparently not. We had travelled only 35 kilometers. And in our raucous state we simply had not noticed. Now it was 10am on Saturday and we were still about 150 kilometers away from Valaam. On the wrong side of the lake. A few quick calculations and we concluded that we would never reach our destination and back to the dock in St Petersburg within the prescribed schedule. A moment of silence as we all stared at each other and then, as if on cue, the wind picked up a notch and a cold violent sleet started to pelt our inadequately protected bodies. We scampered back to the boat for shelter and information.

Well, at least we got shelter. Information, however, was far more difficult. All attempts to obtain a scrap of information from the staff was met with rough "such pretensions!" or "there will be an announcement." Nothing more useful. We were the pesky Americans asking questions.

Katya flirted with some of the male crew to get a bit of the inside information. We quickly learned that the storm of wind and sleet we were seeing here was far more severe out on the lake that we were yet to cross. Four meter waves at least and this little boat was not built to be able to handle such conditions.

We were all amazed: The captain had actually elected to dock the boat safely. In our collective opinion, the standard Russian male response would have been to declare "ah, but I am a superior seaman. I can helm my ship through these conditions where others would fail." And then surely we would have ended up on the bottom of the lake — especially since none of us had taken the time the night before to note where our designated life boats were.

I was about to make a statement about how I was going to have to seriously re-evaluate my opinion of the Russian psyche. Before I could do so, however, Paul joined us and filed his report: "In case you're wondering, the captain and his crew are now in the restaurant working on their next bottle of vodka."

I closed my mouth without saying another word.

After much effort of stalking around the boat attempting to find someone sober and with a bit of authority, we finally found a stern woman in an official-looking uniform who grunted when we asked her if she had any information about what was to happen next.

"If we aren't going to be going up to Valaam, then when will we push off from this island and return to St Petersburg?" Scott asked.

"Tomorrow evening," she said curtly and turned to leave.

A dozen eyes opened wider with panic. A trip to Valaam was interesting and amusing. We had already spent a few hours inspecting the ancient Oreshek Fortress. Another day or so sitting docked in a storm of sleet was hardly a good use of a weekend. We quickly stepped in her path and asked another question with disbelief.

"But why don't we just return to St Petersburg now if we have to abort the trip to Valaam?"

"This is a two day trip. We will return to St Petersburg as scheduled," she barked at us severely.

A moment's pause as we all registered the fact that we were essentially prisoners on the boat for the next day and a half. But no. We refused to accept this. The basic rule in Russia is that there is no such thing as "No." You hear "No" every day. But in the end "no" is just an opinion. The official said that we would not return to St Petersburg until the next night, but that was just her opinion. We knew that, if we were resourceful enough, we could get back sooner.

Perhaps we can figure out where our designated life boat is. Perhaps we can bribe the crew into returning early. Perhaps we can take over the boat ourselves. Based upon prior experience, all of these were potentially viable solutions.

And then we noticed a man puttering along in a small motorboat on the Neva, not too far from our docked island prison. Aha! We could escape with the assistance of another boat. If only we could convince him to give us a lift. We called out to the man in the boat, but our words were caught in the force of the wind. Then with some quick thinking, we changed our approach to a more universal call for assistance: We pulled American dollars out of our wallets and flashed the greenbacks at the passing motorboat. Almost instantly, he made a U-turn and circled back to see what we wanted.

Farewell Russian cruise ship and all your silly rules. We will make our own rules. And now we have decided to go.

The driver of the motorboat was happy to take our cash, but not willing to take us any further than the closest shore of the river. There we were unceremoniously dropped at the muddy banks, left to hike in the sleet through a field then a small farm – and onwards in our quest to return to St Petersburg. Our spirits were still high. At least it was more interesting than being confined on the boat for another day.

Mercifully the cold sleet eventually stopped. And, even more important, we found a village. At least by some definitions it could be called a village. In reality it was simply a small muddy collection of collapsing buildings with hand painted signs declaring "Bar" on virtually every other shack. The village appeared to be completely deserted with the exception of a half dozen men leaning against each other, sitting in the mud outside one of the huts marked "Bar". They had not shaved for some time. Certainly had not changed their clothes or bathed for much longer. And probably had been sitting in the very same spot in the mud for the greater part of the previous month. Blind drunk. Swaying, even while attempting to lean against each other while seated. Empty jars of odd shapes and sizes laid scattered around the men. Home-stilled vodka apparently.

We all stopped, as if on cue. Our frivolous discussions about our adventures of the morning or mud seeping into our boots were silenced in mid-sentence. Rarely in our protected American lives had we witnessed such a scene of total despair. What can you do? What can anyone do? Their shattered remains were left as a warning to others. It was a lesson to us, in some way, I was certain. We were living frivolous expatriate lives in Russia, but they were living the real thing. Our daily stresses included arguments with Russian government officials, attempting to gain access to talk with more Russian government officials. This was trivial in the face of what these men were living through. But what were we to do about it? We could appreciate the extreme relative luxury that we lived in, but realistically what could we do that would help these people? Better just to keep moving towards our goal and return to St Petersburg.

Eventually we found a small battered bus full of villagers about to depart for the city, wallowing in the bog that served as the village's main street. The driver protested that the vehicle was already over capacity and we would have to wait until the next bus – the following day. Yet another rule. Yet another protest. No. We had heard too many "Nos" and would not tolerate another one. None of us even paused to listen to the hollow predictable threats and insults of the bus driver. We wanted to be on this bus. We would take seats on this bus, or stand, or sit on each other's laps. "No" was just his opinion. We wanted to return to St Petersburg. Our will was stronger than his in the end. Calmed down with a handful of rubles, he relented. We emerged victorious from another confrontation. Win or lose in every encounter. Crush or be crushed.

Our moods soared as the bus labored through the trenches of regional St Petersburg muddy tracks en route back to the city. Obstacle after obstacle had been cast in front of us and we had emerged the clear winners with each one. We had achieved our goal of a total Russian experience, a team-bonding weekend with the friends, and a small expedition out of the city. It was still Saturday, now late afternoon. The sight of the despair in the rural village had invigorated us rather than depressed us. Look at so much that our lives had to offer! We led such privileged lives! What did we really have to complain about anyway? The weekend was still young. How to celebrate our small victories and work off some of the adrenaline boiling in our veins?

A full session at the newest hot spot in St Petersburg was in order - Tribunal. We reconvened that night around 11pm or so. Early actually for the clubs. Tribunal was yet another rat-infested basement that had been converted into a club. This one, at least, was the rat-infested basement of a gorgeous 19th century building, featuring low ceilings and dramatic arches separating a rabbit warren of dark secretive rooms. The rats were certainly still living there, in rodent form as well as human.

Techno music vibrated through the brick walls. The air was heavy with sweat and cigarettes – European cigarettes. No one coming to Tribunal would allow themselves to be seen smoking Russian cigarettes. No real ventilation. The air was stirred only by the churn of the dancing bodies. Life was a daily struggle. We survived and thrived. We claimed our place at the top of the victors' platform for the day. We were young and strong and nothing could defeat us. No one could say "No". We were tired of rules and would make our own.

I surveyed the swirling crowd looking for friends as they arrived. The next table over was occupied by New Russians, alternately posing with their mobile phones to ensure we were all aware of their wealth and status, then studiously ignoring the unwashed masses that were beneath their rank to associate with. I watched with amusement as a Russian man at the table took a *devushka* by the arm in a display of ownership. He leaned towards her and said something to the *devushka*. She attempted to free herself from his grasp and replied with words that were lost in the general din of the club. The man immediately responded with a sharp blow to her face that nearly knocked her off her chair. The *devushka* then quickly composed herself and continued to sit at her place as if nothing extraordinary had happened.

My instinct was to do something, anything, in support of this woman. Katya, Scott's Russian girlfriend, had also seen the blow but quickly pressed my shoulder down in restraint and camaraderie. "Don't let it bother you," she advised. "There is nothing you can do. That is all part of the job of being the girlfriend of a *biznisman*."

My heart sank, but Katya was right. There was nothing we could do. In the eye of the Russian law and Russian social norm, nothing unusual had happened. What did I really expect to do? Tell the man he shouldn't hit his girlfriend? Tell the *devushka* she shouldn't put up with this sort of treatment? And then what would happen? Did I expect her to leave this man who was obviously wealthy and able to provide an amazing lifestyle for her? Did I expect her family to be supportive? No. Her situation was appalling in my mind because I was financially independent and able to make my own life decisions without consideration of any benefactor.

No, I did not know this *devushka's* actual situation, but I knew enough of her world to make certain assumptions and to be frustrated by her lack of options. Unfortunately Katya was right. We all had aspects of our jobs that were disagreeable. A blow to the cheek every so often was what this *devushka* tolerated in return for other benefits of her role.

I was powerless and had to turn away.

Then a familiar face caught my eye in the crowd. Ian, one of the Australians who co-owned the Aussie pub, the Magpie. He was not dancing, but sitting at a table in the shadows with a drink. Strange actually. It was Saturday night, shouldn't he be down at his own pub? I was curious and wanted to talk with him, but hesitated for a moment. It seemed like a betrayal – we patronized other clubs in the city beyond the Magpie, and now we were exposed.

Nevertheless, I smiled and invited myself over to his table. Then I noticed crutches parked against the wall. My eyes flitted down to an extensive brace up his leg.

"Open manhole cover? Fall on the ice?" I asked. Both were very common causes of injury in the city.

"The Russian partners decided they wanted a larger share of the pub's profit," Ian answered simply, taking a long gulp from his pint of beer. "At least only one kneecap was shattered. The other leg was just badly bruised."

My gaze unconsciously slid from the brace on Ian's leg, to the *devushka* who now had a black eye that was blossoming quite visibly, despite the dim interior of the club. We knew that the world of Russia was crush or be crushed. We knew that "No" was just an opinion that could be argued or fought. We knew that battles were won and lost on a daily – or even hourly – basis. We were victorious now, but our triumph could be just fleeting. We had to celebrate this moment, because tomorrow, the next battle would be waged. Another battle – my friends and I had won today, but what about tomorrow?

Carpe diem for tomorrow may never come.

24   IMMORTALITY AND IMMORALITY

February 1996

When you are dreaming, do you ever achieve that glorious sensation of awareness? Not enough to wake yourself up, but enough consciousness to be able to make true decisions about your actions? Nothing compares to the empowerment of such a sensation. Once you have achieved a state of awareness in your dream, you can fulfill your most outrageous fantasies – without any consequences at all. No one will ever know.

Once you achieve self-awareness in a dream, what is the first thing you do? Usually it is a continuum of how you would behave in the real world. You might give a politically correct answer in an argument, or flee an attacker, or make other decisions that focus on self-preservation both physically and psychologically. Your personal reputation is at stake with every decision you make. By the time we are adults, most people have decided on the sort of image we want to project on the outside world and make every decision accordingly. We are civilized to people who we despise. We drive our vehicles in an orderly fashion. We see an attractive person on the subway, but stay quiet and just enjoy gazing at them over the top of our magazine. We stand at the edge of a cliff and enjoy the view, but do not seriously consider jumping.

But what if there were no consequences for your actions? What if the next day everyone's memories of the incident were magically erased and your body could be repaired if needed? What would you do then? Would you give a piece of your mind to that horrific boss? Would you turn and battle an attacker to the death? Would you see exactly how fast you could drive your car around the turns on that treacherous mountain pass? Would you lunge at that gorgeous person on the subway? And, would you dare to jump off the cliff into the unknown?

Have you done this? I have. Some nights I have reached a state of awareness in my dreams and behaved with total and complete recklessness. All codes of civilized conduct can be dropped. For just a few vivid moments you can achieve your most insane fantasies. Your actions have no consequences. You face no true physical threats. The confrontations with those who you despise will not have repercussions tomorrow. You can do anything you please. Absolutely anything. There is no moral code of conduct in dreams, is there? Or are you really such a repressed person that you do not allow yourself to dream a bit on the wild side? No one will ever have to know your darkest dreams – what you could do, what you have done, in the corners of your mind where no one else can see you.

So why are we so eager to push our limits in our dreams? My theory is adrenaline – one of the most intoxicating and addictive drugs around. Oh the delicious surge of life through your body when you push yourself beyond your natural limits. Leaping off a cliff and gliding through the wind, charging into a packed session of Congress to steal the microphone and give the politicians a piece of your mind. Of course these actions aren't real, but the surge of adrenaline certainly is.

In the morning you are flushed, invigorated, and ready for the challenges of the real world. Perhaps facing the day with a bit more restraint than you showed in your dreams, but still empowered by the knowledge that you were able to beat your attacker into a quivering pulp, you were able to seduce the beautiful stranger on the subway, and you actually were able to soar like an eagle as you leaped off that precarious cliff. The surge of adrenaline boosts your confidence and lets you coast through the day, drifting slowly lower and lower until you are able to get your next hit. Possibly that next night. A better hit this time one that will enable you to relive that victorious sensation all the following day. There is nothing wrong with this, is there? After all, we are only talking about our actions in our dreams – in our own private world without consequences.

Can such a high be achieved in the real world – without the use of drugs? Of course it can. Any time we achieve the impossible, or push the boundaries of our known world we release a shot of adrenaline. Just a small shot. Enough to give a bit of a high and leave you craving a bit more. Oh please, what can I do to gain that feeling again? Bring every nerve in my body to life, make my scalp tingle, bring the world into technicolor. Adrenaline brings the world into sensory overload – smell the sweat of the bodies near you, hear the whisper of a breeze through the grass. Is this what it is truly like to be alive? Then bring it on and give me more.

In the United States how do you achieve an adrenaline rush? Truly mad behavior is ruled out for the basic reason that our actions have consequences. If you charge a microphone at a public event to give the world a piece of your mind, you would likely be arrested. If you pick a fight with your manager, you put your job on the line. And only a madman would leap off a cliff. Our behavior is guided each minute by layer upon layer of social norms and expectations. Deviate from them and you are called a madman. Follow them and are you truly living your own life as an individual? What if I feel like running naked down the street or seducing a married man? No, I can get a rush doing these things in my dreams if I choose. But clearly the basic codes of social and moral behavior restrain our actions in the real world to a predictable pattern.

Of course there are ways to achieve a reasonably satisfying adrenaline rush within the confines of acceptable society. Sport is the obvious area to turn to for a fix. You could take that run on the ski slope just a bit faster than you know is sensible. You could go rock climbing on a death-defying cliff, just a bit more precarious than last time. Or you could join 60,000 screaming fans in Candlestick Park cheering the 49ers to a victory snatched from the jaws of defeat. The adrenaline surges through each body, invigorating each person into a unified mass of ecstasy.

The adrenaline rush is gained by casting off your inhibitions and living a fantasy – if only for a moment. You conquered the mountain – you are invincible. You are alive on the dance floor at the disco – your business world image is long forgotten. You approach the stranger at the taxi rank and ask him out with confidence.

If living this life gives you such a rush, then why don't you do it every day? Well, then you would actually have suffer the consequences. Bones may get broken at high speeds on the ski slopes. The stranger at the taxi rank may reject you in front of your friends. Isn't one of the basic fundamental laws of physics the principle that every action has an equal and opposite reaction?

Ah yes. What a wonderful law of nature. This law of nature keeps society in equilibrium for the most point. People know their own boundaries. If I do this, then the effect will be that. People are rational and think through their actions. Life hums along in a predictable state of balance. So stable and gentle and comfortable. And oh my god, how boring.

Now, what if we could change the laws of nature? I mean what if your actions did not necessarily bring on an equal and opposite reaction? What if tomorrow no one remembered your actions? What if in the real world you were able to act with as much abandon as you did in your dreams? Such a world is possible only if there is no future.

That statement sounds like a premise to a science fiction story: imagine a world where there is no future, no past, only the present. How would such an existence alter our behavior? Certainly the question has been asked by Hollywood. Bill Murray dropped all inhibitions when he realized that he was trapped in time in *Groundhog Day*. He spoke his mind, did as he pleased, and discarded any concerns for the standards of society. Tomorrow was never going to happen. He did not have to suffer the consequences of his actions. Moral principles and social norms that guided the rest of society were irrelevant to him.

But that is Hollywood and not reality, right? Such a situation certainly could not exist in the real world, could it? I mean, there is always a future and a past. This is a fundamental law of nature. This basic principle serves to keep society moving in an orderly fashion. Actions have consequences. There is always the future to consider.

No. Not necessarily. Even the first doubt of a future begins to alter our behavior. What about the neighbor who is moving to a far corner of the earth and who you would never see again? Would you take this moment to reveal how you had been infatuated with him all these years? Why not? You have nothing to lose. If events continued on their present course you never would see him again anyway. Your personal risk has dropped, so you are tempted.

What about when you have a great job offer in your pocket and are savoring the moment you will push away from your current employer? Isn't that a great feeling? You are no longer confined by the same code of conduct. You are free to do as you please. You are no longer stifled by trivial demands. You have no future here those petty people can go to hell. They no longer matter. You can live without consequences. Bliss and freedom.

So that is if one person is able to behave free from the tyranny of the future and the consequences it holds. But what if a whole society questions whether tomorrow will ever come? What will happen then? The binding premise of society is then smashed – good deeds will go unnoticed, treasons will go unpunished. My behavior does not really affect anyone else because there is no future. There are no consequences and therefore why is there a moral code? If my actions do not harm anyone, then why can't I do as I please?

What happens to a society when the people see no future? This is not just an idle academic question, but a scene that has repeated itself throughout history. I wish I could remember where I read this, but somewhere I know I have read an account of the Black Death Plague in Medieval Europe that detailed the moral depravity of the survivors. All inhibitions were abandoned in the face of near certain death. Shops were looted, old grudges ended with murder, and ecstatic orgies conducted on the graves of loved ones. The depravity of such a scene cannot possibly make sense within the context of orderly society. How could people do such a thing? How could a woman fulfill her wildest sexual fantasies in a cemetery, rolling in the turned soil of her husband's fresh grave? People reading such accounts while sitting on their back deck under a crisp shade umbrella will certainly slam the book closed and turn away in disgust. Impossible. Such people were clearly heathens to begin with. And besides, what does life during the Plague in the Middle Ages have to do with modern society anyway?

Sipping a latte at a café in San Francisco, this question is academic. In the tumult of the post-Soviet era it was quite real – anything could happen tomorrow. Make the most of today.

One day Ian was happily serving pints of beer to expatriates at the Magpie, the next day his knee caps were shattered. Hitchhiking home after a night at the clubs could result in a friendly random Russian singing along to Boney M on the raspy stereo in his

Lada and offering you parts of a dried fish – or you could be kidnapped at gunpoint and tied to a chair and subject to Russian roulette. When there was knocking at the door of your apartment it could be the building collective rounding up payments for a new security system or a group of thugs ready to invade your apartment and take everything you own. This enticing red tomato at the open air market could be the most flavorful and juicy home grown tomato ever or it could have been sourced from somewhere near Chernobyl and emitting radioactivity. Your family could finally celebrate the completion of the years-long *remont* project on your apartment, then receive advice the following day that the building was condemned and would be razed in a month's time.

Driving through southern Russia on the way to Stavropol we had expected a standard long evening of vodka toasts and meat and potatoes. Suddenly the Chechen civil war escalated to a major hostage crisis nearby and instead we found ourselves skinny dipping under the stars with Russian government officials. How far were we really from rolling on the graves of loved ones in a state of total debauchery?

When we take a small step across a line one day, how big of a step are we willing to take the next? What if the social norms that constrain us are slipping away? The future is uncertain, the rules are vague, and we were surrounded by examples of questionable activities on a daily basis. In the memorable words of the American businessman, before he deliberately charged the Russian border control at Sheremyetovo: "In Russia we have no rules – only suggestions." A compass does not work if it is placed on a magnet. Here in Russia, we were surrounded by magnets. What chance did we really have of using our moral compass?

Once social constraints are blurred and removed, how close are any of us from sliding into a state of depravity? Look deep within yourself. Look at how you behave in your dreams. My god. *Hello, I am your little voice of conscience. Have you listened to me recently? Look at the things that you are willing to do if you know there would be no consequences whatsoever.* Outrageous! What are you accusing me of?

Okay then, let's pull back and just look at the small transgressions in daily life. Minor really that would generally go unnoticed. Perhaps you signed a credit card receipt and then walked out of the restaurant carrying the clerk's pen. Did you mean to do it? Maybe not. But did you actually return the pen? It isn't your pen, so didn't you just (gasp) steal? It is just pen – this isn't really stealing. Are you seriously citing walking out of the store with a pen as a breach of moral code? *Really? So exactly where are your lines of what constitutes ethical behavior? Or is this definition flexible – stretched just a bit further with each action?*

For example, if you know that payments in dollars in cash are illegal, why isn't your housekeeper on some sort of payroll? Valya is a single mother who left a job in a nuclear weapons factory. Of course, I should do what I can to help her income! Russian employment laws are deeply mysterious. It would be impossible for me as an individual to employ

Valya if I were attempting to follow the Russian employment laws. If I had held to strict legal lines, then Valya would have less income for her and her daughter! I am also helping Valya by paying her in dollars – rubles are so difficult to convert back to dollars and she needs some financial security for her and her daughter! Yes, she will be stuffing all the dollars literally under her mattress, but this is because the Russian banking system is in such a mess and hyperinflation would demolish any savings in rubles. My transgressions are minor in the face of a higher purpose of keeping food on the table for a single mother. *Is this another step down the slippery slope of an amoral life?*

So with the cash payments you justified this by helping out a single mother. What then is the justification for passing off the counterfeit money? It wasn't like I wanted to do it. I just found the dodgy $100 note in my wallet. I could tell it was counterfeit because the ink smudged slightly between my fingers. Perhaps it appeared in my wallet when some other expat or a colleague had asked me to break a $100 and had passed it on to me. I don't know where it came from. What was I supposed to do next? If I held the $100 counterfeit note, then I would have effectively lost $100 – not a small amount of money. I had to find another expat – a stranger – in a dark restaurant and ask him to break the note into smaller bills for me. Then I made a hasty exit. *But this was in your own self-interest. The story that you were helping someone else out doesn't work here.* This isn't something I do every day! I had the choice of being a victim or a perpetrator. I will not be a victim!

Dealing with counterfeit goods isn't something you do on a daily basis? Really? What about all the Russian language software on the computers of the project team? We paid for the licenses, but the software did not arrive. What exactly were my options here? If I had stripped all the unlicensed software from the project computers, then the computers would have been virtually unusable by the Russians. They were just getting familiar with the idea of a mouse and keyboard. English language software would have been too much of an obstacle for them to overcome. To keep the project moving we had to install the pirated software. *So this was endorsed by higher levels of the project management?* Not exactly. I was just being evaluated by how we were progressing against the project timelines. If I had raised the absence of software licenses as an excuse, then I would have been criticized for not figuring out some way to keep the team moving forward. Damned if you do and damned if you don't! *Hmm. Interesting argument.* Besides, the pirated software was going to a good cause – we are building the future of Russia! I am helping a generation of Russians learn invaluable computer skills and we are building a real estate title registration system. We will help the average Russian build their financial future as they will be able to obtain mortgages to buy an apartment, rather than pay all cash. They can obtain loans against property and have capital to start a business. Entrepreneurship and personal financial security all comes back to the ability to enforce your rights against your property and being able to maximize these assets to their full potential. We are on the front lines here - building the future of Russia! The software licenses are just minor in the greater scheme of things! *Exactly what message are you sending to the people you are trying to help here? Is anything sacred in the name of a higher cause? Haven't all the major transgressions in history started with the justification of the means for a higher end?* Oh shut up. I am talking about software licenses, not the Spanish Inquisition.

And that is how we would finally silence the little voice in the back of our mind. We were good people – here in Russia to help. The minor ethical violations on a daily basis could easily be justified in the face of a higher purpose. What were pirated software licenses in the face of the grand goal of rebuilding a country after total political and financial collapse? The moral code of the country as a whole was unstable. In this context, our transgressions were barely worth mentioning. After all, a beautiful new road had been built in Ekaterinburg rumored to be at the personal request of the President. Assassinations happened at the White Cockroach – literally under the watchful eye of the police station.

The whole country was in motion while the ground shifted rapidly underfoot. Exactly where should we be standing anyway? Where was it even possible to stand still for a moment and assess whether an action was right or wrong? There were no legal taxis therefore we *had* to hitchhike. *Dezhurnayas* commandeered my hotel room in Uralsk to watch their favorite night time soap opera. They weren't stealing anything from my room, but still the room was mine for the night. What right did they have to it? Back in Kamchatka, Dmitri of the Volcanology Institute had redirected the helicopter hired by US Government money without authorization. Was this stealing – or helping out his colleagues in distress? When really could you say that something was legal or illegal in this uncertain time? And what exactly would you expect the Russian justice system to do about it?

In the trial of my assailants I had secretly cheered on the judge as he dismissed all the accounts of inconsistent police records, violence against the abused, and lack of access to an attorney. But then I was horrified with myself. Yes, I knew that these thugs were guilty and wanted to see them held accountable, but what were the larger implications of the judge's discretion? The legal system did not rely on rule of law or impartial standards – rather the discretion of those in power swayed decisions. Those in positions of influence could use the so-called legal system. Those on the outside had to find their own means to set things straight.

Michelle, of the American Café in St Petersburg, understood this. When the Russian business partners used the power of the St Petersburg government against her, she knew that she had no legal recourse. Michelle did, however, have an American passport. She could flee to Helsinki. Russians, however, generally had nowhere else to go. Those who were aggrieved or threatened and without connections into the power structure had to find alternate methods of resolution.

Shells of gorgeous ancient buildings were crumbling out of neglect, then painstakingly restored, only to be bombed in a blast of retribution from one angry *biznisman* against the next. What other options did the aggrieved *biznisman* have to settle a dispute if he wasn't a political insider? When the ceiling in my bathroom collapsed, destroying thousands of dollars of fixtures and fittings, what were my options? No renter or home owner insurance. No functioning civil courts. Therefore my options were to send Igor and his sledgehammer to collect the money directly or for me to suffer the financial loss in silence. Perpetrator or victim. Crush or be crushed. And as Jim knew all too well, the roles could easily be reversed tomorrow.

So what sort of person would volunteer for such a life? People who truly lived by the motto *Carpe diem!* Seize the day. No need to worry about the future.

The expatriates who thrived in Russia almost universally fell into three categories – 1) recent graduates – who did not yet have a future defined; 2) new divorcees – who had their future ripped away from them; or 3) retirees – who were free to enjoy the moment, because they were completely satisfied by their past and had no definite demands of the future.

The most tormented souls in Russia were the family men who had been relocated against their will to Moscow with their families. They had a plan. They had a future. They had a career that was important and going in a particular defined direction. The senior executives in the home office in Chicago or Washington DC had declared that this move was important to the family man's career – with the ominous undertone that it would be a serious mistake to say no. What option did he have? He arrived in Moscow determined to prove himself and earn the most elusive of rewards – a promotion to a new role back in the home office.

But with the madness and chaos of Russia there was no future, only today. How could a career-oriented person survive in such a state? He cannot. He cannot plan and then see the plan through. That simply does not happen in a state of chaos. The term *carpe diem* does not resonate with him. He cannot live for the moment, because he cares about his family and the future. Yet there is no future in Russia, only the present. The responsible family man will be in denial that this is the case. He will block himself and his family behind the safe walls of his compound and try to create a predictable world. He will have to pretend that Russia really does not exist, or he will snap.

We knew that the family men existed in Russia. Estimates varied widely regarding exactly how many expatriate families lived in Moscow and St Petersburg at the time. The most elusive of creatures were American children, which were rarely spotted outside the walls of expatriate compounds. Then, at a Christmas party sponsored by an

Embassy, suddenly all the children would appear. The young expats would be astonished by the unexpected numbers of this mysterious species that had been rumored to be on the verge of extinction.

The family men worked physically in Russia. Their children were sequestered somewhere safely within the Russian borders. But we, the young expats, *lived* in Russia. We were liberated from thinking about the future. We thrived by embracing the present.

What was not to enjoy? Our income was astonishing by local standards. Astonishing by standards of our classmates who had accepted desk jobs back in the United States.

Look at me. I had one apartment in Moscow and another in St Petersburg. In Moscow I had a Russian friend, Nadya, house-sitting and looking after my cat while I was away, plus a driver and a housekeeper. In St Petersburg I had moved into the living room of Valerie and Jennifer's gorgeous and massive classic flat. We learned that the prior tenants of the St Petersburg flat were not one but *three* families — one family in each of two bedrooms and one family in the living room — all sharing a single small bathroom and kitchen.

Of course Valerie, Jennifer, and I had a housekeeper in St Petersburg. This was *de rigeur* and just the starting point for the expatriates. In addition to a housekeeper, Valerie also found us a hair stylist who would do house calls to our flat. In the luxury of our own kitchen, we sipped champagne and snacked on caviar while taking turns having our hair cut and styled. Back in Moscow, my friend Heather took things one step further. After the revelation of how wonderful it is to have a housekeeper (and how inexpensive in Russia as well), Heather then took the next step of indulgence and hired a personal cook who stocked her fridge with tasty homemade *pelmeni*, soups, roast chickens, and other treats twice a week.

Honestly, where else but Moscow in the mid-1990s could a twenty-something single woman have a personal cook, a housekeeper, and a driver plus a brilliant career? How decadent is that! But we would just smile and laugh and say that it was not extravagant at all — we were putting real green dollars in the pockets of hard-working Russians who would otherwise have no income at all in these desperate times. Yes, we lived an outrageous life, but Russia too would benefit in the long term.

Outside the walls of our apartments, the life of luxury continued. Trips to the *banya*, massages, weekend excursions on a cruise boat to Valaam. Okay, that cruise boat was not exactly luxurious, but we loved the *idea* of it more than the reality. We went to hockey matches, to American football matches, to the opera, the ballet, the circus, the nightclubs. We took lessons in painting, lessons in horseback riding and show jumping, lessons for ballroom dancing. We would hire string quartets, nightclubs, and riverboats for private parties, and tanks and helicopters for private adventures. We haggled for original oil paintings, Azeri kilims, antique samovars, and ancient Russian icons. Everything was accessible to us at a fraction of the cost of what it would have been in the United States. And nothing was found in the Yellow Pages.

Half of the adventure was the pursuit and the negotiation. During the day we were in a state of continuous argument and negotiation with everyone around us. What would today's argument be? A battle to attempt to get an early glimpse at the code that Flis may or may not be working on? Another round of debate with Larissa regarding the lack of a data sharing agreement between the city property agencies? (Without a data sharing agreement, none of the agencies would allow our system to access their data. Larissa of course would twist the situation back at us – no system is yet ready, therefore the lack of a data sharing agreement is irrelevant and an obvious distraction from our own shortcomings to deliver a working piece of software.) And someday soon we would receive advice that our hardware shipment was stuck in customs with a demand for 43% import tax – a tax that I knew would never be reimbursed by USAID, therefore we had to figure out some way to make it go away. Crush or be crushed. Perpetrator or victim. This was our work life. We needed release in our play life. Therefore in our off hours, of course we took a bit of liberty with our ever increasing skills in navigating through the labyrinth of Russia.

It was a badge of honor to achieve some quest where others before had failed. Tickets to the Bolshoi or Marinskii theater were never available through their box offices – other sources were required. The objective of obtaining tickets for the Bolshoi was never just simply about the performance itself, but also to demonstrate the quality of your scalper connections and to win the respect and awe of your fellow expats. Anyone could go to a five star hotel and pay well over a hundred dollars per ticket somewhere on the main floor, but I could secure box seats for Swan Lake at the Bolshoi at $30 per pair and therefore claim one more point in my expat credibility status.

I could pay full (western) price for the Hermitage, but why? Somehow a visit to the gallery was more satisfying when I wore my *dublunka* and hot red lipstick and passed as a Russian for a fraction of the entry price. Yes, I could afford the western price, but where was the adventure in that? In addition, why wait in the big line for entrance? Far better to spot a tour group being escorted into the building through a side entrance. Okay, today I am a German tourist. I can play that part too.

What could Russia offer us today? What were we capable of? How could we push our limits a bit further? Push push push – it was the way of Russia. Every situation has a winner and a loser. There is no concept of a mutually beneficial outcome. No one wants to be the loser, therefore we must be winners. Everything was a point of contention. Every price negotiated, every action debated. On the cruise boat going to Valaam, none of the expats had budged when we were told that we were sitting in reserved seats in the restaurant. We wanted the seats, we would take them. Same thing when we found the bus going back to St Petersburg. The fact that the driver said that he was at capacity was completely ignored by the expat Americans on a mission to get back to the city. "No" was just an opinion. Resolution is a question of nerves and willpower. The actual rules were irrelevant. We did as we pleased.

We embraced Russian literature. What had been perplexing and academic in university now resonated as a logical key to help understand our lives. *Master and Margarita* was the favorite among Moscow expats, while those in St Petersburg relished *Crime and Punishment*. The expats had naturally gravitated to novels that were set in their respective cities of residence, but the underlying themes were strikingly similar – when social norms are in motion, really where does depravity begin? What constitutes immoral behavior? And look at how we can justify our own actions! We read these books with fresh eyes. The authors reached across generations to us. Who hasn't wondered what it would feel like to kill someone? Dostoyevsky asked the question. We passionately debated Raskolnikov's actions and torment. And then we plotted our next adventure.

The guys in St Petersburg were impressed with themselves that they had managed to drive a tank for the day – until word spread that other expats in Moscow had scored rides in MiG fighter jets. Now the ante was upped just a bit more. What would we do next? We were limited only by our own creativity.

Observing the actions of the New Russians, we became students standing in awe of the masters. Where we were impressed when we could circumvent the queue at the Hermitage, we watched in amazement as the New Russians deftly sidestepped airport security at Domodedovo airport. The Americans could talk our way onto buses that were over capacity, but the New Russians boarding a plane in Ekaterinburg could pay off the flight crew to redirect the flight from Moscow to St Petersburg.

The message was clear – whatever you wanted was possible, if you had the money and the connections and the nerves to pull it off.

We could not redirect planes – yet – but we could use our money and influence in other ways. For the expatriate men wielding dollars and a western passport this generally meant a fantasy of access to beautiful compliant Russian *devushki* that would have been unimaginable in the United States.

On American college campuses, guys compete to see who can actually secure a girl for the night. In Russia, however, that was a rather irrelevant challenge. If you want a girl, you will be able to obtain one. The challenges then became more outrageous – how fast they could get a girl to come home with him? How little effort would it take to get a girl to go to bed with him? Was dinner at a nice restaurant really necessary? How about just a burger and fries at McDonald's? (The Russians, conveniently, still viewed McDonald's to be a high end date place.) What about after just one drink? Just a cigarette? Just a piece of gum? Could we convince these *devushki* to cooperate in a *ménage a trois*? Where else could your fantasies lead? What else would she agree to?

No, the American guys would never have behaved this way back on their home turf. But they had *dreamed* of this a thousand times. And now here in Russia their fantasies were becoming reality. Or at least a temporary reality. When they eventually returned back to the United States they would be thrust back into the American dating scene

— where they would have to make a bit more effort than flashing a US passport and a pack of gum to get a girl for the night. Wait, why am I even mentioning the American dating scene? That is the future for these guys — and therefore irrelevant. All that matters is the present moment.

One person who would soon be faced with the harsh reality of the American dating scene was Paul. In the efforts to manage our project against our budget, it was painfully obvious that the number of expatriates in St Petersburg had to be cut. This wave of reductions included Paul and one of the American developers, Keith. Brian and I had managed to secure a transfer for Paul from St Petersburg back to the home office in Washington DC. His role of managing the procurement of all our hardware, routers, servers, etc would be picked up by Mikhail on our technical team and, of course, Brian and myself. Keith, however, was a free-lance contractor, not an employee to Arthur Andersen. He was totally at ease with the prospect of his contract ending. This was early 1996. Demand for Oracle developers was booming. He would be fine.

We decided that the farewell party for Paul and Keith would be a decadent Sunday brunch at the Nevski Palace Hotel. On a bleak winter day, there was no greater pleasure than spending hours at the five star elegant dining room of the Nevski Palace with bottomless glasses of champagne and endless trays of blinni with caviar. Outside the city would be shrouded in shadow as the sun crept along the horizon during the few brief hours of anemic twilight. Absence of sunlight and warmth drove us in pursuit of bright sparkling chandeliers and alcoholic anti-freeze — and we found it at the Nevski Palace brunch. Of course this was far beyond the price range of our Russian staff, so for Paul and Keith's farewell we decided to split the total cost for the full team among just the expats and treat the entire Russian staff to the day of debauchery.

The first glass of champagne was poured around 10am and did not stop flowing until about 4pm. Yes, a long decadent brunch — just like we promised. The buffet groaned under burdens of smoked salmon, caviar, blinni, sautéed mushrooms, fresh berries, tiny perfect almond pastries, and dozens of other delicacies. Rose petals were scattered on the white tablecloths and crystals dripped from the chandeliers. Waiters stood attentively in the shadows with ice buckets holding bottles of champagne glistening with sweat, waiting for us to lift a finger to summon them.

I casually dipped a gorgeous ripe strawberry in my champagne. I bit into the perfect fruit and laughed, then discarded the green top (with many others) on a small side plate. Natasha watched me attentively, then haltingly mimicked my gestures. If this is what the wealthy Americans do, then it must be sophisticated and correct. She gave a forced laugh as she placed the top of her strawberry carefully on her plate. Of course she does this every Sunday — not.

Brian designated himself as the master of ceremonies for the day. First the toast to the guests of honor — Paul and Keith. Then Paul responded in classic style with the second toast from the guests to the host, Brian. We had actually drunk many bottles of champagne before the toasting had started. All was well in the world. We were amongst friends, among the people we loved. Or at least the people we wanted for particular reasons. Even Ludmilla was smiling after a few drinks. The Russian *devushki* (and this term excludes Ludmilla) slid their hands down the legs of Brian, Paul, and the other American men. Brian lifted his glass of champagne with his right hand. His left hand was hidden around the waist of Natasha, now visibly in motion somewhere under her shirt. The third toast was to the women at the table. Of course. Natasha turned to Brian for a passionate kiss. But then he turned to his right and met the lips of Masha. Of course. The American men are such the prize for the Russian girls. Who wouldn't be attracted by that shiny blue passport with the eagle on the cover? Elsewhere at the table, Paul's hands were nowhere to be seen as he moved his chair a bit closer to Olga.

Now Paul was smiling as the center of attention. The farewell party was for him and he would make the most of it. "Okay girls, would you line up and give me a goodbye kiss?" He said with a wink and a clap of his hands. And sure enough, they did. Each *devushka* from the office dutifully took their turn giving Paul an affectionate kiss. I was now just pushed back from the table and contemplated the scene while drinking probably my eighth glass of champagne and working through serving four or so of the salmon roe and blinni. Some months earlier I would have tried to stop the excesses of Paul and Brian, but now it just seemed pointless to intervene.

Would Paul behave this way back at an office party in the United States? Never! So why the alternate behavior here in St Petersburg? Why not? He was surrounded by beautiful Russian *devushki* who had a different view of what was standard practice than American women. Here the women were more compliant and the men more direct with their requests and demands. We were in an alternate reality where these very average guys attracted absolutely astonishingly beautiful women – just by the mere fact that he held an American passport and was therefore likely to treat the *devushki* better than their Russian counterparts. Next week he would return back to Washington DC. No one back in America would ever know what he had done in St Petersburg. There he would have a fresh slate. His actions here had no consequences.

My eyes wandered around the room and settled on a table of Russians. Men with crisp Italian suits and flashy watches and perfect polished shoes. Ridiculous displays of wealth. The women fluttered their eyelashes and posed for the men and flirted and pressed their bodies just a bit closer. Russian *biznismen*. I watched the lead man at the table, holding a glass of champagne. Toasting the women at the table, now leaning to kiss the attractive blonde closest to him.

And my gaze returned to our table, where Brian now had his hand wrapped around Natasha in a display of ownership – at least for today. One table spoke English and the other table spoke Russian, but besides that, what was the difference? It was easy to criticize the New Russians for their ease of bending the rules to their own advantage. But meanwhile Brian and I were actively pursuing options for how to bury or remove the import tax that would be levied when our hardware shipment arrived at customs. How different were we really in the end? Tomorrow the rules will change again. We have to make the most of today.

I looked at the Russians again. They were mirroring our actions from a few moments before. Or were we becoming them? Brian snapped his fingers and summoned the waiter to the table for another round of champagne. Another toast – to the future of Russia!

His words were in English but the actions were Russian. I could have been at the table of Ivan Ivanovich in South Russia. Brian was the master of ceremonies today and he would determine what we would do next. Power. Control. Isn't it great to clap your hands and have champagne arrive at the table on cue?

In the final scene of *Animal Farm*, the pigs and the farmers are laughing together. I saw the faces of the Russian Mafioso and Brian side by side. Laughing and toasting each other. Were we here to help these people? Or having discovered the ways of the ruling class was it more enticing to join them?

Were we changing Russia or was Russia changing us?

25 LOOK ON MY WORKS AND DESPAIR

March 1996

"Al Capone, one of the most notorious figures of the history of the underworld, was brought down on the charge of tax evasion. We could expose the underbelly of the St Petersburg mafia through a public review of subcontractor invoicing."

Clearly the ravings of a lunatic. Where did that comment come from? What has possessed her? People averted their eyes and compared notes. She's not quite all with us anymore. Perhaps we should just smile, give her another Bear Beer, and move on.

I saw the faces before me. Three heads. Or maybe six heads. A cold beer was put in my hands. A distraction. I fumbled with the key tab. Someone opened it for me.

Perhaps she will quiet down now that she has a beer to keep her occupied.

Another beer. Had I had one earlier? I couldn't remember what I had been drinking earlier. What had led to this point.

Smiles and mumbled words. It's safe for us to move on now.

A swirl of hair and fabric and colors mixed into the crowd.

"I am not dangerous. It's them. They are the dangerous ones," I sputtered off to the retreating figures.

Who were these people anyway? I was in my own apartment, but did not recognize anyone. My apartment – but also Valerie and Jennifer's. Actually their apartment and I was a permanent house guest – ever since my unceremonious eviction from my prior flat. Life was uncertain but often had happy endings. At least happy moments. A happy moment to celebrate so we decided to host a party. It must have been the only event on that weekend, because the entire expat community and most of the Russians we knew seemed to have shown up. And even more who I did not know.

Ouch. I bumped off a floor lamp. Who put that there? To clear room on the dance floor. The living room (also known as my bedroom) was apparently being converted into a dance floor. I collapsed into an armchair parked in the hallway. Better vantage point to watch everyone coming and going.

And with a good eye on the front door – to monitor for any unwanted visitors.

A reasonable precaution. Violence was circling closer every day. Just hours after our brunch of drunken debauchery at the Nevsky Palace Hotel, there had been an assassination in the very same dining room. It was just dumb luck that somehow we had paid and bill and left before the violence had been erupted. Who was the target? Perhaps the very New Russians who I had observed as eerily similar to ourselves. Details were difficult to obtain and for some reason I had felt compelled to return back to the Nevsky Palace as if the place itself might offer some explanation for what had happened and what it meant for me.

I couldn't tell you what I had expected to find at the scene of the crime. Perhaps a sign on the door of the restaurant explaining that it was closed until further notice with a word of condolence to the family. Perhaps some temporary plastic wrap covering the damage to the beautiful interior. What I found instead, actually disturbed me even further – just days later the interior had already been completely restored to its prior luxurious décor. Patrons and waiters ambled about the dining room as if nothing unusual had happened there.

Was assassination in public places becoming so commonplace that it no longer left a visible mark? The chandelier sparkled and the tables were shrouded with crisp linen. Patrons casually sipped wine and studied menus. The past was already forgotten. Tomorrow was uncertain. Live for today.

Yes, I knew that the only way to maintain mental stability in Russia was to brush aside the future with a laugh. This, however, was becoming increasingly difficult. As violence closed ever-closer the obvious question was whether I would be next.

I lunged between being convinced that I would be the next one on the casualty list to then laughing and dismissing my thoughts as a sign of frayed nerves. But still the actual events were difficult to ignore – a few nights ago someone had been pounding on the door at 3am, insisting that I come out and talk to him. He called by name. I looked out the peephole in the door and saw a burly Russian – polyester track suit, gold chains, oily hair. The standard uniform of the Russian mafia – or more accurately, the standard uniform of their muscle-men. I stood behind our steel door and watched him - said nothing, did nothing. And eventually he went away. This time he went away.

Why did he call me by name? Because he wanted to make a point that he knew where to find me. Tonight would not be the hit. But another night…. If I did not cooperate…

A call from Svetlana a few weeks ago had unnerved me as well. She had travelled from Moscow up to St Petersburg to present the development proposal of RossDev. A fabulous proposal, everyone in the office agreed. I was still working on trying to end the contract with Flis. Once that was done we would sort out the next steps to conclude the agreement with RossDev. Only the dark aura of Larissa lurking in the back of the room blackened the moment.

Our driver Sergei had escorted Svetlana to the station for the overnight train back to Moscow. First class in the Krasnaya Strela was the only way we all traveled between Moscow and St Petersburg – booking the whole cabin for safety. But when she reached the station, she was told there was some problem with her tickets and was placed in a second class cabin. She found herself confined for the next seven hours with three very large men who had an uncanny knowledge of her interest in subcontracting on our project.

This could be interpreted as an unpleasant coincidence or an organized plot to harass potential competitors to Flis. I wanted to simply believe the former, but the tone in Svetlana's voice when she called me to advise that she was withdrawing her proposal told me that she believed the latter.

In St Petersburg, disputes were resolved with harassment, threats and violence. I reflected on the rumor that McDonald's had halted plans for operations in the city. If McDonald's saw the business climate as too challenging – what chance did we have? The harassment was becoming more intense. At what point would it escalate to violence? The *biznismen* at the Nevsky Palace Hotel certainly had not anticipated a hit. When I last saw them they were laughing and toasting each other with rounds of vodka. This round of violence was too close – both physically and emotionally. Wasn't I just commenting how similar we looked and behaved side by side? How far would the similarities with the Russian *biznismen* go? At what point should we be seriously worried about a hit as well? Obviously the table of festive *biznismen* did not see it coming. Would we be similarly oblivious when our time came?

Back in my apartment, a tall dark Russian man bumped against my armchair in the crowded corridor. Reasonably attractive. Actually what am I saying. Russian men are so rarely attractive. Must have been the Bear Beer talking to me.

"Come with me," he said as a statement and took my hand.

"No, I will never come with you," I spat back venomously in Russian, ripping my hand from his grasp.

The Russian quickly stepped back and retreated into the crowd. Jennifer's face appeared from the swirling shadows.

"Phaedra, he was trying to take you onto the dance floor. Why refuse? Live for the moment. What is with you tonight?"

"I will not cooperate with them," I answered.

"You aren't making any sense," Jennifer said, with a bit of concern.

"No, actually for the first time I think that everything is very clear," I answered. "It's everyone else who does not make sense. I see the truth now."

An arm wrapped itself around Jennifer's waist and pulled her away from me. Lips met in a sudden kiss. A surprise encounter. Or perhaps not. This way to my bedroom. Never mind the raving lunatic. She'll be fine when she sobers up.

Yes, everything was so clear to me now. Why didn't I see it earlier? How could I have missed the warning signs?

I mean seriously, if the average salary of Russians in state-sponsored jobs was $100 USD per month, then how possibly was Larissa able to afford her holidays abroad? In the time since I met her, she had taken weekend or week-long trips to Sweden, Spain, Denmark, and Switzerland. Rather difficult to afford on a government salary.

Why didn't anyone ask that basic question – "Larissa, how do you afford such extravagance?"

And then, look at the next obvious point – the political explosion that had resulted after Oracle had delivered its QA review of the project. The very professional analysis had given the development effort by Flis an "unsatisfactory" rating. What further evidence was required to validate my assertion on the current trajectory we would never be able to deliver the required software to support the city's property title registration processes? I had counted on the findings to support my recommendation to remove Flis and install RossDev as the local development partner.

Larissa's response was to sweep the report to the side with a shriek that we were using the report as a stall tactic for paying Flis against the development milestone.

Outcries from Larissa rapidly reached Patrick back in Washington DC. He called to reprimand me for failing to meet the client's expectations. I replied that I was attempting to introduce quality control over the subcontractor's work and we couldn't pay the subcontractor because they didn't deliver. On the current trajectory we would not be able to deliver against the stated goals of the project. I passionately believed that a streamlined property title registration process would improve the economic situation for all of St Petersburg. One of the key obstacles we faced, however, was that we had a development subcontractor that did not deliver and did not care.

"You must continue to work with Flis," Patrick said sternly. "They are the identified subcontractor. You are responsible for managing them. If their quality is unsatisfactory, you will be held accountable. You must ensure that they achieve the necessary quality to pass the milestone."

With that, the conversation with Patrick was over. And I was forced into the obvious situation of handing the work of Flis back to the American developers to fix before it could pass the milestone. Now the American developers, who already disliked Flis, were unhappy with me as well. If I had just let the quality of Flis slide there would be no scrutiny of an independent review by Oracle. But now that we had this "unsatisfactory" rating, we had to clean up the mess ourselves.

Eventually we did achieve the "satisfactory" rating from Oracle, then we paid Flis.

A day later Larissa had both approved the related milestone on the project and had booked a trip to Ireland. Despite the completed milestone, there was no victory party. Everyone was angry with me – Larissa for me delaying the payment to Flis, Vincent (aka The Prince of Darkness) for attempting to do anything resembling managing the subcontract, the American developers for being the source of additional work on them, and Patrick for my antics irritating the city of St Petersburg yet again.

Only Brian and I gave each other words of encouragement – over shots of vodka and some oily stew at the restaurant of the Evropa.

A face materialized out of the crowd into focus. Valerie. And some man circling around her in a protective orbit. Her face was flushed – with alcohol, dancing, excitement, romance. Or all of the above.

"Oh Phaedra, that's where you are," she gushed with a sudden convulsion of affection. "I can't believe that you are sitting out here all on your own. There are so many gorgeous single men here tonight. At least some of them are single." Then she turned to the man hovering at her shoulder. "You are single, aren't you?"

"I am whatever you want me to be," he answered.

"Oh good," she smiled with relief.

"Tell me," I asked the couple in front of me. "What is the difference between prostitution and consulting?"

"Is this a joke?" Valerie asked. She curled up coquettishly in the man's arms. "Do you know this joke, sweetie?"

"Not a joke," I said. "I'm just curious what you think."

"The paperwork," the man replied. "Prostitutes aren't exactly bothered by paperwork."

"The wardrobe," Valerie added. "You can tell a prostitute from a consultant by the wardrobe."

"The wardrobe. Is that a fact?" the man smiled coyly. "So what sort of wardrobe are you wearing tonight? Consultant or prostitute?"

"You'll just have to tell me," Valerie flirted back.

"Perhaps a very special type of consultant."

And with that, the couple vanished. Engulfed by the spinning chaos, pulsing to the rhythm of the dance music.

Nope. No real difference between prostitutes and consultants. Except for the wardrobes. And, yes, perhaps the paperwork. The consultants had to actually make it look like they were doing something. The prostitutes had a much simpler way of establishing project completion.

And billing. Hourly rates. Isn't that what prostitution is all about. And consulting, come to think of it. The only difference there is that consultants are expected to have nice clean documentation for how they arrived at their final figure. Quotes, estimated level of effort, resources, and deliverables.

That's what was expected with the project documentation. I had to ensure that every dollar spent was properly documented. Billing and milestones. That was all that Patrick ever worried about. That was all that really mattered in the world of government-funded projects. Clean documentation.

Well, I had documentation. Whether it was "clean" or not was an entirely different matter.

Larissa returned radiant from her holiday to Ireland and immediately advised me that Flis's participation in the next set of project deliverables was essential. Shortly thereafter the project leadership was presented with a quote for $50,000. Actually to call it a "quote" would be to make the document sound reasonable. It was essentially a letter from Flis stating that they required $50,000 for the next project milestone. No further explanation of how they arrived at the amount or what would be delivered to earn the payment.

Brian and I nearly doubled over in laughter at first. Vincent and Larissa really were going a bit too far this time. $50,000 for a milestone that was about 6 weeks away. That meant just over $8,000 per week. Given prevailing wages for Russian developers and a reasonable overhead charge, that would have meant a team of about 30 developers would be working on the project for the next six weeks. Realistically we believed the work that was scoped would require no more than three competent technical people and a team leader. And furthermore, we didn't believe that Flis even intended to staff the project with those minimal four resources.

After we recovered from our laughing fit we called Patrick back in Washington DC. He would have to recognize how silly the situation was and just call a halt to us working with Flis. The important thing was that he would have to do so from Washington DC. If the St Petersburg government or others in the food chain believed that Brian or I could actually sign off on subcontracts or payments, then we would be facing local direct pressure to change our minds – pressure Russian style. I had seen enough results of such pressure to know that any communication regarding our subcontracting relationship would have to come from someone with authority far far away from St Petersburg. Anyone local would have to be viewed to be powerless and completely without any influence.

And what did Patrick say? It should have been predictable. I was increasingly coming to understand that Patrick had not supported any of the previous four project managers in St Petersburg. My predecessor had been unceremoniously deported. Why should I expect any differently for myself? Why hadn't I followed the logical path of his directives to date to anticipate his response? And, more importantly, why did we make the phone call from the office, where we knew our phones were being tapped?

In hindsight his statement was so in character – Patrick and I were simply instructed: "The selected subcontractor is Flis. You have to work with them and manage them effectively. If the quote is for $50,000, then you better have the documentation to back up the quote and billing. You are the project manager, so you have to take care of this."

"But Patrick," I protested. "That's the entire point. They don't have the documentation. They couldn't possibly have the documentation. The quote is so far beyond anything that is reasonable that any documentation would be pure fiction. And anyone with an ounce of common sense would see that."

Of course, our office did not have any technology as sophisticated as a speakerphone or three-way calling, therefore Brian and I did our best to attempt to share the receiver, listening to Patrick's response over the scratchy international line.

"Well you are the manager for this project," Patrick retorted. "If you can't manage your subcontractors and meet milestones effectively for a little Russian project, then how could I ever place you in a project management role back in the US?"

I gasped. Brian clenched his teeth and gave me a look that showed that he felt the blow as well. We were being cut off and being held out to dry. Patrick was not stupid. He knew exactly what was happening here. And he also knew that he did not want any speck of it to taint his fingers. In the (unlikely) event that we would find some way to manage this project to successful completion, he would certainly stand up and declare us to be "his team". But now that we were heading towards a fiery disaster we were effectively cut off. We would be labeled as "incompetent managers", dismissed and Patrick's reputation would remain unblemished.

The next morning we received an agitated but direct phone call from Larissa. If we needed documentation in order to sign off the statement of work, then we would get documentation. We would receive it in a day or two – project plan, staffing requirements, overhead calculations. That's what we required, right? Would we then sign the statement of work and stop being so difficult?

Yes, it is exactly what we required. Not exactly a lucky guess on her part. The phone taps were definitely paying off. With the one phone call to us she was able to reinforce, yet again, that she was the one in the position of power here. We were just pawns in her little game. And it was so convenient that Patrick was playing along. She would get her cut of the fee, the aid agency would get their paperwork, the US taxpayers would be told that another milestone had been achieved in the great push forwards to democracy and capitalism in Russia. Then once all that was settled, Patrick would be able to take the credit for the success of the project. So simple really.

But if it was really so simple then why was I drinking myself stupid each night and still unable to sleep? Why had I taped a note on my bathroom mirror with the agitated reminder "Leave Weapons at Home!"

A few days later, a burly man walked into our office uninvited. Natasha, the sweet demure receptionist, attempted to ask his name and hold him at the front desk. He held a crumbling cigarette, still smoldering, in his calloused hands the size of bear paws. Not exactly the hands of an office-worker. He grunted at Natasha then brushed by her to stalk over to where Brian and I were sitting. He nodded recognition to Brian and me. I gave a sideways glance to Brian. I didn't recall ever having seen this man before.

Why was he casually acknowledging us as if he knew us so well? Perhaps he had been watching us, following us? Or was the tactic just another game of Larissa's? My mind raced and I tried to smile and look relaxed.

"I have a message for you from Vincent," mumbled the man in Russian.

He took a drag from his cigarette, his fingers nearly black from nicotine and other abuse. Hard labor of some sort had taken its toll. Except for Ludmilla (who was quarantined in her own office) the project operated out of a single large room, and now every eye was turned to this Russian. Fingers poised over keyboards, motionless.

He looked at Brian and me and thrust his hand purposefully inside his coat. A ripple of a silent gasp around the room and the team tried not to watch what was happening, but yet could not avert their eyes. We were under pressure from unsavory characters, and everyone knew what the next steps for that pressure could lead to. A hand inside the coat was never good.

And a moment later he thrust a fistful of crumpled documentation into Brian's chest.

"Vincent says that this is what you need," he stated simply. "You should be ready to sign the contract once you have read this."

A pause while the man took another long drag from his smoldering cigarette, while giving a meaningful look at Brian and me. He had our attention. He commanded the audience. He relished the moment of being the center of our miserable existence. Our visitor then dropped his burning cigarette to the floor and crushed the smoldering butt under his battered boot heel into our parquet floor and strolled casually from the office.

A breathless silence while we listened to the footsteps of the departing figure echo then fade. A moment later the project room exploded with a release of tension. Every Russian team member had an opinion on what to do next. "Go along with Larissa and Vincent – it is the Russian way, you have no choice." "No you need to hold your ground. Someone needs to stand up for basic principles against the corrupt powers in the government." "What is the point anyway? This situation has been played out again and again for the last 500 years or so. Just play your part in the grand game." "No, Brian and Phaedra should just leave St Petersburg and to go Helsinki tonight. It is no longer safe for you to stay here."

Isn't it wonderful how easy it is to have opinions about how others should conduct their lives? But once you are embroiled in a situation yourself, it suddenly becomes real. Real events, real consequences. All those wonderful grandiose statements about morality and history and cultural sensitivity become a bit irrelevant. From this point forward the question was survival. How would we exit Russia intact? Our careers, our mental state, our physical bodies even were at risk.

Brian and I just looked at each other while the Russians engaged in enthusiastic but somehow abstract debate about our future.

"Is it too early to have a shot of vodka?" Brian asked me.

"It must be noon somewhere in Russia. Therefore let's go," I answered quickly.

We retreated to the dive of a restaurant in our building for some watery stew, hard bread and a few shots of vodka and a quick read of the papers. As we suspected, the documentation was laughable. We knew it was fiction and we would be essentially acknowledging that the whole contract was a cash handover to some unsavory characters if we agreed to it.

The vodka bolstered our nerves. We had to confront Vincent about the "documentation" and quickly. We would expose the fact that he really did not have 30 team members, all paid extraordinarily well. Plus the price of office overhead that could only be justified if the company had hired a German engineering firm to completely modernize their accommodation, complete with ergonomically correct chairs and task lighting for everyone. Perhaps if we caught him off guard we could get him to work with Larissa to reduce the figure to something that was at least plausible.

Our driver Sergei delivered us to the address cited as the Flis offices. We had actually never even been to their offices before. We had never been invited and Larissa had argued that we should never ever arrive anywhere uninvited. We were not even confident that we would find anyone at the address – perhaps it would turn out to be the address of a sports stadium, a la *The Blues Brothers*.

The grey building cast grey shadows into the grey twilight of the never-ending grey St Petersburg winter. With total seriousness, Sergei asked how long he should wait outside before he should flee the scene and call for backup from Yuri Mikhailovich. Brian and I laughed and said we would be fine – we were just discussing contractor invoicing. Sergei muttered that we were in far over our heads and should have a more intelligent plan other than simply "discuss the quote."

He said he would keep the engine running and would watch the windows of the building in case we waved anything like a distress signal. Sergei pulled a crumbling Russian cigarette out of his pocket and lit a match in a cupped hand against the cold wind.

"I'll wait for you," he finally said with resolve. As if this were a substantial decision. And, to Sergei, it probably was. He wanted nothing to do with what was about to occur at the offices.

"You and your roommates sure know how to throw a good party, Phaedra," a drunk unsteady voice brought me back to the present tense. Back in my apartment – with nearly a hundred strangers, or so it seemed.

My eyes slowly focused on the American man in front of me. It was a senior manager from Valerie's company. Over from New York for a fly-in-fly-out senior management session. The kind of manager who knew nothing about Russia except for the five star hotels in St Petersburg and the headlines from CNN. And now one of his arms was wrapped around a Russian *devushka*. She was quite sober, wearing the standard predatory uniform of black spandex miniskirt, body-skimming faux fur-trimmed top, and stiletto heels. She clearly had focused on this American as her target for the evening. All other women were cleared away from her man with a hiss and a show of red claws.

"You girls have such a good life here," he said – either to me or to the *devushka* in his orbit. "Valerie is always carrying on about the hardships in Russia. I think she is exaggerating a bit. This is a fuckin' party every night here. How did I ever get suckered into paying her a hardship allowance?"

Too much talking for the *devushka*. She knew she had limited opportunity to work on her target before he and his American passport would potentially disappear off into the wilderness again. She glared at me for interfering with her plans, and silently slipped a finger through one of his belt loops. A tug. You are mine tonight. No looking at other women.

"Hardship allowance," muttered the American to himself, taking a swig from his beer. "Hardship, my ass." He was pivoted around by the *devushka* and propelled back into the darkness of the living room.

"Lord, protect the expatriates from their managers." I whispered a fruitless prayer into the hollow microphone of my empty beer bottle.

Yes, we knew how to throw a good party. We played hard. We played like there was no tomorrow. Because at times we all realized that tomorrow may never come. Live for today.

Brian and I were astonished to discover that Vincent actually did work at the address provided on his quote. Tick that off as being one piece of accurate information. The next question was whether we could reasonably believe there would be 30 people dedicated to this project working with top quality office space and infrastructure to justify a three-fold overhead rate.

The lighting in the hallway was out of order. The corridor had the standard Russian government building aroma of wet dogs and fermenting mud. The door to the Flis office was thin plywood that could have been kicked down if we were drunk or angry enough. We were actually admitted through the door by a surly receptionist with blue eyelids and bleach blond hair. We were to go no further and not to talk to anyone, she said sternly after we introduced ourselves.

Not that there really was anyone to talk to anyway. We were in a small reception area, but it was the same scene I had seen countless times before in Russian offices – Salvation Army reject furniture. No sign of electrical equipment at all, save for a bare light bulb dimly overhead. No fax, no computers. The blue-eyed woman gave us a sharp glance and then pulled out a nail file and began working slowly on her manicure.

The air held a stale dead taste of inactivity. Bodies at rest, collecting dust and cobwebs. My wooden chair creaked ominously as I leaned over to compare notes with Brian.

"Oh yes, definitely I can support their overhead rates," I said bitterly in English. "This fine architectural detail and careful attention to efficient special design undoubtedly commands top dollar in the market."

"This office space is extremely prestigious and difficult to obtain," Vincent appeared suddenly in a doorway – and he was speaking with a hiss – in English.

A pause in conversation. Vincent understands English. Why was he revealing this only now to us?

A twisted smile. He smirked with pleasure to have unnerved us, but still was clearly irritated that we were there at all. He talked to us standing by the receptionist desk. No we were not going to visit the interiors of his office. There was no point. What would we accomplish from the visit anyway? We were here without an invitation and that violated the agreed protocol. Why were we asking so many questions that were irrelevant? He had provided a breakdown of his cost structure. We should stop interfering where we did not belong. Was this any way to treat a business partner?

As we were escorted from the building Vincent said firmly, "I will have to tell Larissa that you are being disruptive."

Silence from Brian and I. That was a threat and we knew it.

That evening Brian was having dinner on his own, enjoying yet another glass of wine and savoring a moment away from the office. A man slipped into the restaurant and invited himself to an empty seat at Brian's table. It was Yuri Mikhailovich – the one government official who we believed honestly wanted to make the project succeed.

"Brian," he skipped formalities and launched straight into his main point without wasting a breath. "You cannot let Larissa have her way. Your project is the first real chance we have to diffuse the power of the *apparatchiks* in this city."

"How did you find me here?" Brian was understandably unnerved by the sudden appearance, even if he was a friend. Far too many people were keeping tabs on our movements.

"It is not important," Yuri gave a dismissive wave. "The *apparatchiks* thrive on the current real estate registration manual processes – they have control. They can decide which applications to process, which to delay. Their favors are required to do anything with a piece of real estate in this city. An integrated real estate registration system would change everything. A process that does not require favors means no more power for the *apparatchiks*. No more opportunity to cash in on favors. Everyone knows this. Especially Larissa.

"But if you sign another subcontract with Flis, you will continue to ensure that the project goals are not achieved and she gets money in her pocket as a bonus. You cannot continue to strengthen her position."

It wasn't a threat, but the pleading of someone who saw a door shutting closed before him. With a bit more agitation, however, the pleading could become a threat. Another side weighing in their views on the situation. Yuri Mikhailovich passionately believed in the potential benefits to the people of St Petersburg. His passion helped to rebuild our resolve. We would have to persevere onwards. All our agitations would be worthwhile in the name of a higher purpose.

Strangers showing up uninvited are never a good thing. And strangers wearing military uniforms are definitely bad. Back at the party my eyes attempted to focus on the forms of about a dozen men who had just walked through my front door. Long military wool coats. Short cropped hair. Leather gloves. Heavy boots. They stood in the entrance way taking in the scene, deciding what to do next. Blocking the exit, should I attempt to escape.

Had Larissa dispatched troops to intercept me? Why else would a dozen military personnel now be in the entrance hall to my apartment. Crowds of drunken guests obscured a clear view from the front door. I slipped from the armchair and maneuvered towards the back of the apartment. The front door was the only "real" way out. We were up only one story. If I were cornered I could rip a sheet and climb down a makeshift ladder out a window, couldn't I?

In my retreat to the back of the apartment I came to the door to Jennifer's bedroom. Door closed. Room occupied. Locked. I raised a hand to knock and looked anxiously over my shoulder. What would I say? "Hello in there, the Russian military appears to be pursuing me. Can I jump out the window from your bedroom?" Somehow that did not sound rational.

Before I could summon the nerves to say that ridiculous sentence, the men were walking down the corridor towards me. One of the expats led the way. "You're looking for Phaedra? I think I saw her go this way." She smiled and bounced along in front, happy to be useful.

Behind her, one of the men looked at me, focused clearly and reached his hand inside his coat. I felt everything moving in slow motion. No, this really couldn't be happening. How did I get so far in over my head? Expatriate life was supposed to be interesting but this was more than I had counted on.

"Phaedra," the American girl called out to me cheerfully. "These guys are looking for you."

I just looked blankly at the man at the front of the group. How could my friend be so daft and lead the military right to me? She knew the sort of peril we all lived in each day. She knew about Michelle fleeing arrest from the St Petersburg police on the train to Helsinki. Yet she smiled and was oblivious as the military man pulled his hand out from inside his coat and.... Handed me a bottle of vodka.

"I wanted to give this to the hostess of the party," he said in clear English. "Thank you for inviting us."

"And you are?" I could not breathe.

"Lars Gunderson. Swedish Navy. We heard about your party tonight from Amelia."

Who was Amelia? And how did... But stop. It really didn't matter. The main point was that I had a dozen Swedish sailors now in my apartment. Not Russian military about to kidnap or shoot me. But gorgeous blond, fit Swedish sailors out for a night of shore leave in St Petersburg.

Lars smiled at me. "Can I pour you a vodka?"

"Yes, please," I was about to black out from the emotional rollercoaster of the evening. The vodka wasn't helping either. Or was I drinking Bear Beer earlier?

I held the drink unsteadily in my hand and surveyed the living room. Our apartment was massive – but still I couldn't imagine that just a few years earlier four or six or more people across multiple generations had lived in this one room. This evening half of the space had been cleared for an impromptu dance floor. Sofas and chairs had been moved into the hallway or packed into the other half of the room – giving the area a feel more like a furniture show-room than an apartment.

But in the half-darkness, I could tell that no one really minded the clutter of sofas crammed against each other. In fact, as my eyes adjusted to the light I could see couples squirming around on the couches making the most of the chaos and dim lights and extra sofa space. The American single girls now set their sights firmly on the handsome new Swedish arrivals. For the first time ever, the ratios were firmly in the favor of the expat women – and they were all poised to make the most of it.

Lars was still attentively at my side. He smiled at me. I pressed my forehead against his chest and closed my eyes. It was so incredibly reassuring. Feeling a strong warm body, the rise and fall of his chest as he breathed. A protective arm around my body. Just make the rest of the world go away. I want to stay right here where I am safe.

Was I safe? What did that really mean?

After Brian relayed his encounter with Yuri Mikhailovich, we decided to call Patrick in Washington DC again. He would have to take control of the situation from Washington. We could not be perceived to be in any position to make decisions. The decision-makers were the ones with broken kneecaps or shot in their own bathtub – unless they were safely back in Washington DC.

But where to make the phone call from? Our office phones were tapped. As were our homes. What about the Grand Hotel Europa? The meeting rooms were just off the main atrium. If we could slip into one of the rooms there and organize a relay AT&T call from a local number to the USA then the call would not be over-heard. If we could use one of the meeting rooms at the five-star hotel unnoticed.

Brian and I laughed nervously with each other as we planned the exercise. We were American management consultants, not highly trained counter-intelligence officers. We had no idea what we were doing and were improvising based upon what we had read in spy novels. My mood during the planning process wavered between hilarity at how ridiculous the situation was to despair that if things went terribly wrong... I just did not want to finish the thought.

We decided to have Sergei drop us off at the Grand Hotel Europa and then simply drive away. This would leave the impression with all the hotel staff that we were simply American business travelers coming back to the hotel after a day of meetings – which would generate less interest than if we were arriving and had a car waiting for us.

We had both been to the Grand Hotel Europa many times and knew the floor plan very well. The conference rooms were conveniently located along the side of the central atrium – which meant easy access for us – but the rooms had glass walls, which meant that everyone passing through the atrium would see us in the conference room.

Brian, who was a world-class bull shitter when required, assumed the task of diversion, chatting up all the nearby hotel staff in ridiculous conversations about borscht recipes and the renovations of the Marinskii theatre. I slipped unnoticed into one of the meeting rooms and placed the call to Patrick.

Miraculously I reached him on the first attempt. I knew that I possibly only had a matter of a few minutes before a hotel employee would evict me, so got straight to the point.

Once again, I attempted to emphasize to him the fact that he needed to make it perfectly clear to everyone in St Petersburg that all the project decisions – especially those regarding finance, contractors, and milestone sign-off – were made from Washington DC. If people thought that Brian and I could make decisions, then we would be in real danger. He had to act quickly as they were getting impatient and the threats were becoming more ominous.

"So you're saying that you can't hack it being a project manager?" Patrick responded.

No, that wasn't the point at all. Just he had to understand that a certain type of positioning was required with the St Petersburg government was required.

"Look if you can't handle managing this project, then I can't possibly nominate you to run any projects back in the US," Patrick said simply. "American clients are far more demanding."

Again, a threat. How many people were going to threaten Brian and me from every angle? He raised though the threat about my future. Expatriates can float above the chaos of everyday existence in Russia only because we see it as a transient state. The future is in America. But what if that future is cut off? Then the present becomes real. We have to deal with the current situation in order to move on. But how?

"Patrick, please," I tried not to sound desperate. "Our phones are tapped. We're calling from the Grand Hotel Europa. You have to understand what is going on here."

And then Patrick did the most damaging thing to my fragile remnants of sanity – he laughed. "Oh, cut it out with the cloak and dagger stuff, Phaedra. You and Brian really need to get a grip. You have been reading too many Tom Clancy novels. All you need to do is manage a subcontractor properly. It really is not that difficult. Stop coming up with excuses!"

And that was the end of the discussion.

"Too many Tom Clancy novels?" Brian repeated with astonishment as I recounted the conversation to him later.

"Well yes," I muttered. "That was Patrick's spin on the situation. Maybe he's right. Maybe we are completely losing our grip on reality."

"Tom Clancy gets his material from somewhere," Brian answered.

So who was right? My face scratched against the heavy fabric of the sailor's uniform as I closed my eyes and pressed closer to feel the warmth of his body. Were Brian and I incompetent project managers? Or were we being set up as pawns in a struggle for power and money within the St Petersburg government? There clearly were arguments for either position.

I certainly was living on an alternate plane. How else could one explain the sudden appearance of a dozen gorgeous Swedish navy boys in my apartment? This sort of thing did not happen in real life. Was I just suffering from dementia and too much vodka when I thought they might be Russian militia coming after me? Maybe I was living in a fantasy world after all. Well, that's okay. I like my fantasies. Especially those which are living and breathing.

A hand slipped under my shirt and found flesh and I was abruptly snapped back to the present moment.

I pushed back from the Swedish sailor. Lars Gunderson. A few hours ago I never even knew he existed. What was I doing here with him? I staggered out of the living room into the bright lights of the corridor and kitchen. Valerie, who obviously had been watching me, quickly darted over to my side.

"Phaedra, what's wrong? The sailor boy is such a catch. Make the most of it."

"Maybe I've been reading too many Tom Clancy novels and I'm living in a fantasy world," I muttered. "What is real here anyway? The Swedish sailor boys can't possibly be real."

"*Carpe diem*,"Valerie answered. "That is our motto. Don't question it, just seize the day."

"Yeah, live for the moment. Because do we have a future anyway?"

"Phaedra, what has gotten into you?" Valerie asked with a fragment of concern, which was quickly forgotten as an arm wrapped itself around her waist.

"I thought I had lost you," said her man of the evening.

"Of course I was coming right back. Why would you say something like that," she flirted back.

"Never mind," I muttered as I shuffled off towards the bathroom where I could have a moment of respite from the chaos.

I closed the door behind me and closed my eyes as I sighed a deep breath of relief. For a few moments I could seal everything off and forget.

I opened my eyes and in one corner I glimpsed a stranger in the room. Who was that! In here with me in the bathroom. But I took a closer look. My own reflection in the mirror. And I did not even recognize it. I looked terrible.

My hair stuck out at strange angles. As I attempted to calm it down, it came out in clumps in my hands. My face was a pastry white and sagged with massive purple bags under my eyes. My eyes were bloodshot and did not focus. My shoulders slumped under the strain of... of everything.

In short, I had the same face I had seen every day on the trams, on the subways, in the markets. I was becoming an old *babushka*. Or, more accurately, an old alcoholic *babushka*. The ravages of a vodka and potato diet were all too plain. My hair was falling out. How long before I started to lose teeth as well? In a fit of confused terror I checked my clothing to ensure I hadn't matched florals with plaids. That would be the last straw. Fortunately I seemed to be respectably dressed.

Weren't we supposed to be young, successful, and beautiful? Isn't that the standard description of jet-setting expatriates in exotic locations? We took our holidays in Turkey or Austria and did our shopping on weekend trips to London. We worked hard and played hard. We were models of health and glamour. And timeless. We lived in the present moment – fictional people without a past and certainly no sign of aging or moving towards the future. Only the present where we could do as we pleased with no consequences.

I stole a side glance in the mirror back at the battered *babushka* who had replaced my youthful face. Harsh undeniable evidence that actions have consequences. If we sign the subcontract with Flis then we have sold our souls to the St Petersburg mafia and become pawns in their grand game. If we don't sign, then we are discarded on the trash heap of expat consultants who have passed their "use-by dates" – the firm certainly would not bring us back to the US in the near future and the St Petersburg government... a few people there might literally try to throw us on a trash heap – wrapped in a bit of plastic. If I continued to stress and drink myself into oblivion each night then my deterioration into a shell of a tortured *babushka* would certainly become irreversible. Actions have consequences. How much damage had I already done to myself already? How much more could happen because of my actions?

How could I make it stop?

I stumbled out of the bathroom into the dim smoke-filled air of the apartment. Empty bottles lined the walls along the floor. A perilous moment as I tripped over a few vodka bottles and, in an unexpectedly agile move, I grasped a bottle neck as it was about to spill its remaining contents on the floor.

I stood at the entrance into the living room and surveyed the scene. Writhing bodies moving in the near darkness. Mostly upright on the dance floor – in various other poses on the collection of sofas. Lars, still standing along one of the walls, spotted me as I paused, contemplating this life. He reached out to me and smiled. A few weeks earlier I would not have hesitated for a moment – here is a handsome shadow with only a name. No past, no future. But no, this no longer made any sense. I was now a spectator at a bizarre performance where people played out their fantasies. I was a spectator and I needed to find a way out of this theatre. Where was the real world anyway?

I backed away from the crowded mosh pit of a living room. I had to get out. I swung open the steel door into the corridor of the building and stumbled down the grand staircase towards the street. Grand at least in memory only – now a sweeping statement of crumbling concrete softened only by layers of filth and broken light fixtures.

On the street I took in a deep breath. What was I expecting? Some healing breath of fresh air? Our apartment was along one of the minor canals of St Petersburg. In the western world canals evoke visions of romance, peaceful walks, a glass of wine, flower petals floating gently on the water. But that was in an alternate version of reality from St Petersburg in the mid-1990s. My little canal was effectively an open sewer. The stench of rotting rubbish pierced my lungs as I attempted to cleanse myself with the night air. Everything is just too difficult and so futile! I can't even have a breath of fresh air when I need one! A final blow that would drive me the one final bit closer to madness.

I was still clutching the half-full bottle of vodka. I looked at it and seriously contemplated taking a swig. Straight from the bottle. What sort of person had I become? Isn't this what we came to Russia to help stop? Did anything we worked for really matter anyway?

In a fit of hostile vengeance I hurled the bottle of vodka against the wall of the building. It shattered in a satisfying explosion of glass and liquid. Satisfying for a moment at least. Vengeance against what? Some abstract frustrating concept that I could not quite summon the words to articulate.

And then deep within the corners of my dusty memory a poem came to me that I had memorized in literature class in high school. As a teenager I had dutifully committed the words to memory. But only now, in a drunken state of agitation did I truly understand them. Words to synthesize my incoherent laments of futility and despair. I called out the words into the still night.

> *I met a traveler from an antique land*
> *Who said:"Two vast and trunkless legs of stone*
> *Stand in the desert... Near them, on the sand,*
> *Half sunk a shattered visage lies, whose frown,*
> *And wrinkled lip, and sneer of cold command,*
> *Tell that its sculptor well those passions read*
> *Which yet survive, stamped on these lifeless things,*
> *The hand that mocked them and the heart that fed;*
> *And on the pedestal these words appear:*
> *My name is Ozymandius, King of Kings,*
> *Look on my works, ye Mighty, and despair!*
> *Nothing beside remains. Round the decay*
> *Of that colossal wreck, boundless and bare*
> *The lone and level sands stretch far away.*

As I finished my rant, a drunk Russian man wandered past me, muttering to himself – hopefully on his way home. He did not even acknowledge me. Apparently a drunk American woman reciting Shelley to no one in particular while standing in shards of glass along a canal in St Petersburg was not a sight that deserved a second look for him. Come to think of it, the scene seemed perfectly natural to me as well.

I only wished I had brought a second bottle down onto the street so that I could hurl it against the wall as well. One more fleeting moment of satisfaction to stall the inevitable march towards tomorrow – and whatever the future would bring.

26   THE FISH ROTS FROM THE HEAD

April 1996

On Monday morning Brian and I each found a glowing email waiting in our "in boxes" for us. Patrick was singing our praises, recounting the accomplishments of the project (all milestones to date had been signed off by the St Petersburg city council). We obviously were very talented project managers, therefore he was "empowering" us with the full control and ownership of the project. He was reducing his involvement to only a cursory oversight role. He had full confidence that we, as the in-country project team, would be able to conclude necessary arrangements with subcontractors and bring the relationship with the city government to successful completion.

He had contacted Larissa and Vincent to confirm that Brian and I had full authority to agree work orders with subcontractors. We should be pleased with this level of autonomy granted – it demonstrated the firm's utmost confidence in our abilities.

In short, Patrick was completely washing his hands of us. Anything that happened on the project from this point forward he would unequivocally be able to be pin as being the fault of the in-country management team. He was going to claim no direct knowledge of any project activities other than the sterile project status reports that we submitted. My attempts at writing a more colorful account of the events of the project had been met with Patrick rejecting the status report as being inappropriate and subjective.

We laughed bitterly as we read the emails. The words were all politically correct, precisely chosen, but carried a clear message that was written in invisible ink – you have been cut off. You are on your own out there. If you fail, we will disown all knowledge of your actions. In the (unlikely) event you will succeed, however, we will claim the credit for the great steps forward in Russian-US relations. The author's mastery of double speak would have made George Orwell proud.

With the words of "empowerment" and "delegated authority" and "trust", Patrick had managed to crush our last vestiges of hope. There would be no one from Washington ready to stand up for us and give us support in the trials to come. So much for all the wonderful slogans that were repeated endlessly in official HR materials, happy-clappy training sessions, and annual reports – trust, mutual respect, integrity. The words of corporate principles look so nice in print. But what does it really mean in practice?

"Of course we are practicing our core principles," I could almost hear Patrick's voice echoing in response to my resentment. "Read the email again. Every word in the message reflects empowerment of you as a manager and our trust in our team in Russia. This is what our firm is all about."

And of course the haunting voices pounding my skull were correct. This was what the firm was all about. I had to agree with the voices there.

And at the fragile age of 28, I realized that I would never be a partner in the consultancy. I did not have what it would take to get to the next level – the dark genius of double-speak. My fatal flaw was that I would always speak my mind.

"We are so totally screwed," Brian announced to the general public in our office.

I revised the last comment to myself – Neither Brian nor I would ever be partners. We were both compulsively open about our opinions. We were physically incapable of toeing the party line when our instincts led us in a different direction. And often knowing full well that the consequences would be dire.

Brian and I looked at each other silent for a moment. Then he summarized the situation succinctly.

"Yesterday we stood on the edge of the abyss. Today we took a step closer."

We needed an ally. A strong ally. Someone who would help us stand up to Larissa and Vincent. Someone who could help us hold a meaningful position that we would not sign the ridiculous work order.

"What about the USAID representative?" Brian suggested.

It was really our last chance at finding an ally. USAID was providing financial backing for the project. They should be interested to know that we were being cornered into a position where we were being asked to sign away tens of thousands of dollars more than were reasonable. And this, we knew, would only be the beginning. The total project budget was $11 million. And the city knew it. Once Larissa and Vincent confirmed that they were able to pressure us into signing this scope of work, we would be opening the door for further demands. We would have proven our vulnerability and be ripe for the taking.

"But we have never initiated contact with USAID before," I protested without conviction. "Patrick has the primary relationship."

"Patrick did say that we were fully empowered on all aspects of the project," Brian quoted from the email.

"I guess that if we now are fully empowered with all major project decisions, then at a minimum it is our responsibility to let him know what is going on here," I agreed slowly.

Bur really, who was I kidding? Why did I entertain the idea for a moment that USAID would be a bit more sympathetic to our plight than the partners back in Washington DC? In retrospect the conversation was entirely predictable. I was nominated to have the phone call with Greg, our USAID representative, as I had a few more interactions with him in the past and Brian thought that I had something of a "rapport" with him. Whatever that really means with government officials. So I made the phone call.

Greg listened correctly and attentively. I rambled on. I carried through the history of the project. The subcontract concluded against our will. The threats that the City would not sign milestones until certain demands were met. The demands were small now. We acknowledged that $50,000 was hardly a serious amount of money given the total volume of aid flowing into Russia at that point. But with each subsequent milestone we knew that we would be exposed for future demands. And Larissa's choices in holiday destinations were certain to become more exotic and expensive. We would have to keep up or the sign-off of the project would be jeopardized. And where would that put USAID? We would be unable to guarantee actual delivery of the project per the agreed scope if things went on their current course.

I needed USAID to step in and tell the St Petersburg city government that we were not going to use Flis as the subcontractor.

At the end of my rant there was a moment of silence.

"So, if I understand your situation correctly," Greg slowly and deliberately summarized the conversation. "Essentially you have a subcontractor that is charging too much and under-delivering."

"Well, that's only the superficial point of what is going on," I stammered.

"Those are the facts of what is happening. Your team is unable to properly manage the subcontractor. Is that correct?"

"This is not a subcontractor that we wanted to work with," I objected.

"Like and dislike are subjective statements. Part of the terms of the USAID agreement is that you are to work with Russian subcontractors."

"True," I agreed. "But we were compelled to use this particular subcontractor. We did not choose them."

"Do you have any evidence of threats that led to the signing of the agreement?" Greg asked.

"Not exactly. I know that the previous project manager left the project suddenly."

"So nothing in writing?"

"No," I could see where this discussion was going and resigned myself to the inevitable conclusion. "The only thing we have in writing is the signed subcontract."

"So the bottom line is that you do not like your subcontractor and are looking for a way out. Despite the fact that you have a signed subcontract?"

Of course he was right. Of course that was all that the paper trail of evidence would ever prove. We had a subcontract with Flis and we were unhappy about it. Any lack of performance of the subcontractor could be attributed to poor management on our part. Any extortionary pricing would be simply the result of our inability to negotiate properly to define an appropriate scope of work.

In summary, USAID had the same formal conclusion as the Washington DC partners.

"So are you trying to tell me that you are not capable of managing this project?" Greg asked.

"No, of course not," I had to reply.

"Well, then," Greg said in the tone of a discussion that had reached its logical conclusion. "My recommendation to you is to learn a bit of cultural sensitivity for how to work more effectively with your Russian subcontractors. If you have any more situations like this then I will have to consider recommending removing you and your company from the short list for future contracts."

I hung up the phone wondering how I too could master the dark art of double-speak.

Brian could see from the look on my face that the conversation did not go well. I answered his expectant eyes with a summary of the ordeal.

"He told me that we need to improve our cultural sensitivity for how we work with the Russian subcontractors. And he never wants to hear of our problems with subcontractors again."

"In short, if we have no evidence that we are being threatened, then we are simply incompetent," Brian summarized. "But if we actually do produce evidence that we are paying underhanded sums of money to the city government...."

"Then we will be hung out to dry," I finished his sentence. "Everyone will say that they had no idea that this was happening.

It was only a matter of hours before we received the inevitable phone call from Vincent.

"So, shall we finalize our work statement?" he said simply. Even over the phone I could hear him smirking. He had Brian and me in a corner and he knew it. No one, absolutely no one was going to support any position other than for us to sign the work statement. And that being said, no one would be actively endorsing the signing of the work statement either. The decision was "empowered" to us as the in country management team and we were expected to reach the appropriate decision.

We would meet him over dinner to discuss the details. An instruction, not a request.

Where shall we meet you and when? I asked, pen poised.

A laugh from Vincent. A pause. No. He was not ready to disclose where we would meet. He would call later, at 6:30 pm. Only then would he tell us where we would meet him.

"As if we would have a backup muscle-man organized somewhere in the wings," I muttered to Brian.

"Perhaps we should organize a sniper," Brian answered – only half joking. "I'm sure there must be a few available in St Petersburg. With just a few phone calls and a small handful of cash…"

I sat silently for a moment, looking at him in disbelief. "You do realize that we are being completely set up here. No matter what we do from this point forward, we are totally screwed."

"That's why I am going to call in the sniper," Brian said, lifting the hand set on the telephone. "I'm sure we could find one in the next few hours. Yuri Mikhailovich probably could help. Or who was it that organized "tank day" – they know some people in the Army willing to take some cash payments. Maybe your new Swedish navy boyfriends…"

"Seriously, Brian," I reached over and gently pressed his hand to return the handset to the cradle. "We're consultants. We are silly white-collared project managers. We don't have a chance against the likes of Larissa and Vincent. Do we?"

"Phaedra, we have to fight this," Brian dropped the phone and became serious for a moment. "You know the system here well enough to understand why. It's not just a matter of this one work statement. But then the next one, and the one after that. Once they think that we can sign work statements for them, they have us."

"But…" I just did not want to believe what was happening around me. "What if Patrick is right. What if we have been reading too many Tom Clancy novels?"

"Tom Clancy gets his material from somewhere," Brian retorted. "It is compelling reading because deep down everyone knows that what they are reading really could be happening somewhere. We now happen to be stuck right in the middle of that somewhere."

"Are we?" My instincts told me that Brian was absolutely right. "But really, who will believe us when we say we are worried about being entangled with unsavory underworld elements in St Petersburg?"

The project team erupted in a vigorous debate for what we should do next. All pretenses of meaningful project work came to a complete halt for the rest of the day as the entire team of Americans and Russians analyzed the situation, re-analyzed it and offered bits of advice to Brian and me.

I was convinced that Vincent was deliberately trying to unnerve us. Only in elaborate suspense scenes of *Godfather*-esque movies did people say "I'll call you later with the rendezvous spot."

"Or, he could be calling around for restaurant reservations," said Ludmilla smugly.

I glared at Ludmilla. She was now inciting violence deliberately. Trying to destabilize our understanding of the situation. But then, I had to pause for a moment. Yes, she was right. Vincent could simply be calling around for restaurant reservations.

Natasha, our admin assistant, together with our accountant, Olga, were unified with their recommendation that we run to the train station immediately and never return. They said they could just close down the office for us. Of course, this wasn't a real option for Brian and I – if we left the country now, we would be thoroughly abused by senior management, USAID and the city of St Petersburg and probably be fired on the spot. If we cared at all about our futures with the firm, we would have to attempt to see this through.

But then again, didn't we both already conclude that we had no future with the firm? If we were behaving rationally, then we should be simply moving into survival mode – which would mean a train ticket to Helsinki. The firm had already discarded us, hadn't they? I re-read the email from the morning. All the words were correct – the firm was supportive and empowering, and enabling Brian and I to "take the next steps" as project managers. Maybe if we pulled through here then we really would be on track for re-instatement to the United States and promotion. If we pulled through here.

Besides we were just totally average American consultants managing a project. What sort of delusions would lead us to believe that anyone would consider us to be influential enough to threaten seriously? Jumping on a train to Helsinki is a radical step. It would be a decisive move that would sever all chance of further opportunities with the firm or with other privatization projects. It also would essentially throw away all the work we had done to date on this project. All my blood, sweat, and tears in Russia would be worth nothing – as the project would be abandoned incomplete and the firm would just remember me as the consultant who fled the scene when the going got too tough. I would be without a job, without a home, without a recommendation in my pocket to make a fresh start.

I would have to try to make this work.

"You don't want to get mixed up any deeper with Vincent," advised Sergei, our driver. "He is the worst type of *biznisman*."

The room fell silent to hear Sergei's advice. One of the implicit understandings in St Petersburg was that all drivers had an ear into a network of news and information deep below the surface in the city. Sergei did not offer his insights often, but they reflected relationships that reached far beyond our office.

"Vincent is a minor figure with the *biznismen*. He is extremely dangerous because he is small. He has obviously made promises to bigger people. Or he owes them money. In any case, he will need to deliver what he has promised. And his insistence on this work statement – And Larissa's insistence on the work statement, for exactly $50,000 – shows that someone has been promised this money. Vincent himself will be under pressure for this money. He will do whatever it takes to get it out of you. You know the expression 'the fish rots from the head?' This is what you are dealing with here. The source of the problem is much higher up."

And so the debate continued. We worked ourselves into a frenzy. Why not just sign the damn work order? But we knew that there was not a shred of truth behind the proposal from Flis. Their proposal over-staffed the engagement by about six times the number of people actually required. Their response gave no insight into their proposed approach to the project or even a grasp of what was requested. The failed Oracle audit provided further external confirmation that the few developers they did have working were by no means actually focused on delivering a quality product that met the documented requirements.

The odds that Flis would actually deliver the scope of work on time and have it meet our requirements were pretty close to zero. Our ability to manage them was laughable – as every attempt to provide meaningful oversight had been slapped back.

We would inevitably be in a position where we would have nothing to show for the next program milestone. If (or more accurately "when") everything fell apart we would certainly have the long nose of US government auditors sniffing around our handling of the project – potentially to ruin our professional careers forever. Yes, we signed the work order. Yes, we realized that it scoped out a team of 30 when we had never actually met a single developer from Flis. Yes, we knew that they had previously failed Oracle QA audits, yet we continued to grant work to them anyway.

No one wanted to have that discussion with USAID auditors.

So how to get the Prince of Darkness off our backs without selling him our souls? Hours of debate later, at the witching hour of 6:30pm, we still had not figured out the answer to that critical question.

At 6:30pm Brian, Sergei, and I were the only people left in the office. Vincent was exerting control over us by forcing us to wait in the office until 6:30pm for further instructions. This was well before mobile phones were omnipresent. Even if they were, I am convinced that Vincent would have said that we needed to wait by the main phone at the office. Just on principle to make us uncomfortable and tired – and to therefore give him the advantage.

So 6:30 passed then 6:35. A few more minutes. Every agonizing minute of wait was a harsh reminder that Vincent held control over the situation now. Finally the phone rang and a brief request for us to come to the Hotel Oktyabrskaya restaurant – VIP section.

"Just Brian and Phaedra. No one else," said a voice gruffly. Not Vincent but some deeper growly voice. Oh great. Now he had his lackeys making phone calls for him! Not exactly a threat, but it still sounded a lot like what I had seen in Robert de Niro films. Just enough innuendo to send a very clear pointy message – you will do what we say or else...

Sergei chuckled quietly when he heard he would be taking us to the Hotel Oktyabrskaya. As American newcomers to St Petersburg we needed some explanation.

"This is the place where deals are done. The place where the real backroom deals have always been done – for decades. The place to be seen to make a particular political statement – or to disappear. It is so far out of the mainstream St Petersburg social circuit. It is guaranteed that no one you know will see you there. And those who do see you there will have an implicit understanding of what is happening and will stay quiet."

Not the sort of comforting words we were looking for.

Sergei was willing to drop Brian and me off at the Hotel Oktyabrskaya but flatly refused to wait for us after the dinner session with Vincent. All bribery of overtime pay etc fell on deaf ears.

"If we disappear tonight, you'll tell everyone that we were last seen with Vincent at the Hotel Oktyabrskaya," Brian said as a parting comment as he was getting out of the car.

"No I won't," Sergei said simply. "I have a wife and two kids. If you disappear tonight I'll say that you sent me home early and you decided to hitch a ride. Oh yes, have a great dinner!"

Thanks for the support Sergei. Go team.

Like many relics of the Soviet era, the architecture of Hotel Oktyabrskaya would be more appropriate in the eternal semi-darkness of Gotham City than the exuberance of the St Petersburg classical style. The hotel was in a totally unknown section of the city, perched on a small hill – one of the only hills I recall ever seeing in St Petersburg. A menacing driveway curled up to the snarling entrance.

The moment Brian closed the car door behind him, Sergei slammed his foot on the accelerator and his heavy Volga squealed out of the driveway, leaving a scent of scorched tires.

"Sergei never spins his wheels," Brian commented to no one in particular. "It is too hard to find replacement tires in Russia."

We stood for a moment looking at the retreating vehicle. A lifeline to the outer world was vanishing. We would have to face Vincent on our own.

We turned and faced the entrance to the Oktyabrskaya, which was poised waiting to devour us whole. The concrete stairs crunched and crumbled under my metallic heels. (Yes, I too was now having my shoes repaired with old coins as reinforcement on the heels.) I reached for the door handle, half expecting a demonic figure to be etched on the handle as a sinister portent of what would await us inside.

As we stepped inside, the temperature dropped several degrees and dampness enveloped us. In the semidarkness I instinctively watched my step, knowing already that the ratty red carpeting would certainly contain holes and wrinkles ready to trap unsuspecting visitors. Oily heavy dark paneling closed in on us – only us. No other signs of life in the inner passage.

"No matter what happens tonight – no side comments in English," Brian whispered to me in Russian. His voice vibrated against the wood panels in the empty chamber.

Right. No English. We had agreed that earlier as one of our basic rules for the evening. Like all expatriates, side comments in English were compulsive and almost involuntary. Now knowing that Vincent understood much more English than he had previously disclosed, this could be a major liability. We would have to rely on more rudimentary signals – such as sharp kicks under the table and meaningful stares. Whatever it is that we would have to warn each other about.

"No matter what happens tonight, we cannot sign anything," I switched over to Russian and said with more conviction than I felt. This was the second rule we had made for ourselves. In the hours of leading up to the rendezvous, we still had not determined the best way to get out of this situation. We had agreed, however, that signing anything would weaken our position even further. We would have to figure out some other way to leave the building alive.

Leave the building alive. I laughed to myself at the thought. Were we over-drama-tizing the situation? This was just a dinner with a Russian business colleague. I had been out on dozens of dinners with Russians at similar Soviet-era hotel restaurants. Vodka, meaningless toasts, boiled meat, potato, pea and mayonnaise salads, probably a bad sound system and dancers and strippers. I had done the drill before and managed to get home with everything intact except my liver. Objectively why would tonight be any different?

But we knew it would be.

We walked through the dim entrance hall towards a barricade of doors. Involuntarily we paused and looked at each other and took a deep breath before pushing through to the unknown. Yesterday we stood on the edge of the abyss. Today we took a step closer.

Finally, the main dining hall. A sweep of a few steps down to a sunken main floor. The scene would have been grand at one point in the hotel's history, but was now precarious with rumpled carpets on the stairs and wobbly hand rails. An enormous interior space lit erratically by some upward sconces and some downward dusty chandeliers, some working others broken or off to conserve money. Shadows flickered, distorted further by images from floor to ceiling mirrors unevenly planted along one wall. Tables were placed unusually far apart – perhaps in a futile attempt to give the impression there were more patrons in the restaurant than a simple headcount would reveal. Or to accommodate the unstated traditional purpose of the hall – allowing private conversations at tables unable to be overheard by others. The hall was only a quarter filled, if that. If the tables were laid out in a standard configuration, the living would fill only about ten percent of the tables.

The Soviet-era ghosts filled the rest of the hall. Good lord. Sergei had warned us that this was the place where people were summoned to dinner and were never seen again. Even without the warning, we would have drawn the same conclusion ourselves upon breathing the stagnant air of this place. One did not need to be a clairvoyant to feel the presence of souls in agony that they were being taken to their last meal. I tried to breathe deeply to calm down, but felt my lungs constricted by the damp air.

We scanned the room for Vincent. No sign of him. No hostesses either, so Brian took the initiative to guide me to a table near the center of the room. I argued that it would be better to have some place where I could have my back against the wall. Brian's logic was that there were multiple exits and entrances. In the center of the room we would have equal opportunity to run rather than be cornered.

Again, we were management consultants, not trained undercover operatives. Were we really having this conversation? My head started to spin as I gratefully took a seat (in the center of the room). We waited in silence for Vincent to show.

Abruptly my thoughts returned to my first week in Moscow. Laughing in the sunshine at the Dinamo stadium reading the article in the *Moscow Times* about the American consultant found shot in his bathtub. The shooting was linked to the mafia. A vague statement that everyone simply nodded and agreed with and dismissed. The only things we had in common with the dead consultant were that we were all American and managers at Big Six consultancies. We never would be involved in the underworld in Russia. What had we thought at the time? The dead consultant must have lost his way. He must have turned greedy, unethical. Anyone who got themselves involved in the mafia should understand the consequences. He had it coming. We had closed the newspaper and turned to watch the second half of the football match. The nameless consultant had moved to the dark side. We would stay in the light. We were here to support privatization and the glorious future of Russia.

But then what about Michelle, the American Café girl, who fled to Helsinki without even stopping by her flat to pick up a toothbrush? What had she done wrong? What about Ian the Australian with his cracked kneecaps – who just wanted to run a pub and enjoy life. Jim and his girlfriend had made the fatal error of leaving their dishwasher running as they left for holiday. I had no idea if they were alive or dead. And Andrew had remained silent about how he had extracted payment from upstairs neighbors for the damage to my bathroom. Igor, I'm sure, could be very persuasive. And I was on the grey side of the law with whatever happened there.

"The fish rots from the head." Who or what was the head? Not Vincent. Probably not even Larissa. No, if Larissa were removed from the project, another like her would sprout up in her place. The root cause of our problems was the whole nature of our project, the whole nature of the aid work to Russia. Larissa and the City of St Petersburg were nominally the "clients" – but this was in name only. In a normal client relationship, the client has actually identified a problem and is willing to pay for the service to resolve the problem. This is true whether you are just taking shoes to be repaired or a company seeking to implement a new accounting system. But here in Russia, our nominal client, Larissa and the City of St Petersburg, had not recognized any issue on their own. And they certainly were not willing to spend their own money to resolve it. Why would they support the automation and improvement of the property title registration process? This would only reduce their own areas of influence. No, Larissa and Vincent would be engaged in our project only to the extent that furthered their own interests. And at the moment their interests were firmly focused on the $50,000 associated with the next scope of work.

"There he is," Brian said sharply and quietly. "And it looks like he brought Big Boris with him as well."

My heart stopped as my eyes met Big Boris's from across the room. Boris had no real job description with Flis that I was aware of. The last time I saw him was when he had personally delivered the written quote to our offices.

"I like my kneecaps," I attempted a feeble joke with Brian.

He was transfixed as well by the sight of Boris and my words were met by silence.

"This is where you are supposed to tell me that I am over-reacting," I kicked Brian under the table and hissed.

"You aren't over-reacting," the color was draining from Brian's face. "I am now trying to decide which will be the safer course of action – get them totally blind drunk, or restrain from alcohol altogether this evening."

Yes, Brian was right. Didn't Russian relationships always come back to alcohol? But we were paralyzed by the sight of Vincent and Boris walking across the room to us. Conversation was impossible. We did not have agreement on our alcohol strategy – which was (now I realized) a critical aspect of the pre-planning which we had neglected. I looked at Brian and attempted to read his mind – sober or blind drunk? Which approach would serve us best this evening? There could be arguments either way.

Vincent and Boris approached in slow motion. The rest of the evening was being set into play and we were filling our roles. Vincent wore the greasy bottle green polyester suit that was so much in vogue with the lower rungs of the mafia. Actually the term "mafia" is so inaccurate. "Biznismen" is how they were referred to in Russia. Was there really any meaningful distinction between "biznisman" and "mafia"? None that I could piece together.

Vincent's face stretched into a forced smile when he reached the table. He grasped my hand and lifted it to his face for a poisonous kiss. I was relatively pleased with myself for resisting the urge to slap him. Vincent then turned to Brian. Brian, however, was poised and ready and was reaching *across* the table to shake Vincent's hand. I barely suppressed a laugh at the gesture. A total insult to shake hands across a barrier. Brian smiled and said the correct pleasantries, but he was stabbing an invisible knife through Vincent's ribs.

Who would control the evening? Control or be controlled – it was the Russian way.

Boris was introduced with a grunt and a powerful handshake. He took his seat to my left and across from Brian – keeping his hands conspicuously on the table. Hands that did not belong to an office worker, or even a driver, but to someone accustomed to hard manual labor. He flicked some dust off the plastic flowers in a cracked vase set as the centerpiece for the table. I instinctively recoiled and pulled my chair a bit closer to Brian. Vincent looked at me with a satisfied half-smile. Bringing Boris along to dinner was having the desired effect. I took a deep breath and resolved to not be so obvious with my reactions. This was going to be a long evening.

Vincent barked and summoned over the requisite pouting waitress with blue eye shadow. He ordered a round of vodka shots. Not a full bottle, mind you, but just one round of shots. What that meant, I could only guess. As much as round after round of shots was painful, it was still a generic symbol of whatever passed for mutual cooperation in the Russian business world. Anything less than one round of shots per person at the table would be an insult and a sign that the relationship was not on solid footing. Here Vincent was deliberately ordering only one round of shots. He had seized control of the situation now by commanding control of the waitress and by dictating the pace of the evening.

The waitress delivered the round of vodka shots to our table with a puzzled expression. If there were four people at the table, then certainly there would be four rounds of vodka shots at a minimum throughout the evening – sixteen shots of vodka total. Traditionally this would require a bottle on ice, not individual glasses. She put the glasses on the table – and then placed the menu in front of Vincent. One menu for the table. Only the host would have the menu here, of course. We would all have to comply with whatever it was that he decided to order. Yet one more demonstration of control.

The traditional first toast, of course, was from the host to the guests. Vincent lifted his glass to Brian and me. "To your new promotion, Brian and Phaedra. I understand that you are now the full managers of the program here in St Petersburg. Congratulations on your success and we can now toast your new-found authority."

The message was clear. He had us cornered and he knew it. I looked at my shot glass and momentarily wondered what it would feel like to simply toss the contents at Vincent. I decided that I needed the relaxant more than the momentary emotional release. Gratefully I swallowed the liquid fire.

Vincent smiled with self-satisfaction. The balance of power of the evening was definitely going his way.

The warm glow of the vodka pulsed through my veins and gave me strength to look around the room. Did anyone else notice the scene that was going on at our table? The waitresses were nowhere in sight. A few Japanese businessmen were being escorted to a long table with a number of Russians in bottle green jackets. Perhaps a parallel scene was being created over there. But then again, judging by the wide smiles and gracious body language of the Japanese businessmen, clearly they were at a much earlier stage in their relationship with the Russians. Ah, just wait, grasshopper. You have much to learn. I smiled with an evil twist of *Schadenfreude*.

My attention was then diverted to a couple at a table against the floor to ceiling mirror. A *devushka* with intensely black hair was clearly pleased with her reflection in the mirror. Her date was pushed back from the table and could not have cared less. The *devushka* wore long black opera-length gloves – over the elbow and completely inappropriate for this sleazy Soviet-era crumbling relic of a restaurant. But then again – I paused and watched her pose dramatically in front of the mirror, reveling in her own image – the *devushka* was exactly in the correct context. She was caught up in her own version of reality, as was the table of Japanese businessmen, as were Brian and I at the table with Boris and Vincent. Our versions of reality only loosely intersected here in the dining hall of the Hotel Oktyabrskaya.

As if to emphasize the point, a blast of static erupted from the far corner of the room. A non-descript man dressed in brown polyester battled an unruly tangle of audio system components. A peroxide blonde woman in a black spandex miniskirt and blood red lipstick stood silently nearby, holding a microphone, waiting for some signal to begin her performance. The hall was still only at about ten percent capacity and the cavern of space sucked all conversation into a black void. The static of the sound system shredded the dull silence.

Behind the spider web of speaker wires loomed a heavy red velvet curtain. The uneven lighting cast bizarre shadows across the face of the blonde singer who waited for her cue to begin. Or perhaps she was waiting for the midget to emerge from behind the curtain and start singing along to the hypnotic notes of the *Twin Peaks* theme music.

I turned back toward Brian, half-expecting to see a zebra standing under a ceiling fan. The real and the surreal were melding into one.

Brian ordered beers for him and me. Deliberately excluding Vincent and Boris. Deliberately ordering beer rather than the next round of vodka shots.

Bear beer in a can. Warm and rather revolting really. Brian poured his can into a glass and drank it without offering a toast of any sort. I smiled and followed suit, amazed at how hostile the simple act of drinking without offering a toast could be.

Vincent stared blankly at Brian, not offering any reaction to the blatant show of hostility. He then turned to me and opened what could be superficially called a "conversation."

"You have been in St Petersburg for nearly nine months now. Have you had the opportunity to experience much of the Russian culture after the work day is over? Hopefully you have seen more of our grand city than the office and your apartment?"

I was taken aback. What was his point here? He could not possibly be interested in anything resembling pleasantries. I stole a side glance at Brian, attempting to gauge how to answer this seemingly innocuous question. I started with an innocuous answer.

"Of course, as a visitor to St Petersburg I have spent far too much time at the Hermitage. It took me probably about ten visits before I felt like I had actually been through the whole palace. The depth and scale of the collections there are absolutely staggering. Virtually every piece is priceless in its own right. Then to see the whole collection together under one roof is rather overwhelming."

"Actually, the acquisition price was probably lower than you might expect," Brian joined in with his opinions. "Having the army help with the acquisitions definitely helps with expanding a collection at a low cost. It can also result in quite the range of art and objects."

Vincent studiously ignored Brian and asked his next question of me.

"The Hermitage has recently introduced dual pricing – a low price for Russians and one about ten times higher for foreigners. Which price do you pay?"

How to answer this one? Whatever my answer here, Vincent would certainly have an insult ready for me. I decided to answer with the truth.

"I wear my *dublunka* and red lipstick. I dress Russian and I am given a ticket at the Russian price," I smiled sideways at Vincent.

"So you do not represent yourself honestly and truthfully to the ticket vendors at the Hermitage? You are cheating the national museum from much needed funds to keep it in operation. I expected you to be more solid with your principles for doing the right thing to support the future of Russian culture."

Ah yes, Vincent had now found his angle to make the first jab at me.

"But what would you have said if I told you that I always paid the foreigner price at the Hermitage?" I responded quickly. "You would have told me that I was naïve and that I did not understand how the Russian system really worked. You would have reminded me that only the tourists and outsiders pay the full foreigner price at the museums and theatres."

Vincent paused and then pursed his lips with a curly creepy half-smile. "I see we are beginning to understand each other. You really are becoming *nashi*."

Being called *nashi* was usually a compliment. You are one of us now – accepted in the inner circle. Coming from Vincent, however, I did not like the term.

"Exactly what am I supposed to understand?" I heard the words falling out of my mouth before I could stop them.

Vincent visibly withdrew a bit. I had crossed some unspoken line of agreement. Apparently we were not supposed to be discussing things explicitly.

With a sharp snap of his fingers, Vincent summoned the waitress. He handed her the menus back without glancing at them. Spoke to her sternly but quietly. The commands were given for our meals – commands from Vincent to the waitress that would be obeyed. Brian and my opinions were irrelevant.

That task complete, Vincent turned back to me with a smile of growing black confidence.

"Yes, I actually could see you passing as a *devushka* if you wanted to deceive someone. You studied Russian in university at Berkeley. Right?"

Yes, he was right – but no we had never had a cozy discussion reminiscing about our college days. This was a deliberate demonstration of power – if he knew this tidbit about me, what else did he know? And how? I did not recall ever discussing my university history on my work or home phones. His sources of information were clearly expanding.

Brian's glare turned from chilled to icy. He had picked up on the purpose of the comment as well.

"Berkeley is in California," Vincent continued talking, casually noting our reactions with cold pleasure. Feeding his confidence further. "California – home of sunshine and palm trees and beautiful people playing on the beach and swimming in the ocean. Why would you ever leave such a paradise and come here?" His arms swept the post-apocalypse interior design of the Oktyabrskaya.

"Berkeley is in Northern California. You are thinking of Southern California," I corrected Vincent. "San Francisco is the city of fog and cold ocean and wind. People do not play on the beach in bikinis in San Francisco."

"No. You are wrong," Vincent retorted evenly. "California is the home of beach volleyball, and blonde women driving convertible cars." He waved his hand to dismiss the frivolity of such activities. "Why would you choose to leave? What are you running from?"

I kept silent. Vincent was clearly just trying to provoke hostility. And now I was in the miserable situation of either reacting to his provocation to defend my version of the truth or to let him have his way. In either case, he was holding control of the conversation. I was silent. He had battered me into submission (for the moment at least), Vincent's attention next turned to Brian.

"Brian, you have a California girl available so close to you," he gestured towards me with a vicious smile. "It is the dream of so many men – a California girl. So why do you prefer the Russian *devushki*? And you do not seem to be able to find one to satisfy you. Are our *devushki* not good enough for you?"

The knives were stabbing deeper with more toxic venom. And how did Vincent know Brian dated an assortment of Russian girls? Actually, as with all expatriate men, it was probably a safe guess even without any inside information. Most American men were like kids in a candy store – amazed by how easily and cheaply the sweets were available and wanting to try everything.

Brian smiled and found his opening for a return volley.

"Yes. There are so many Russian girls available to the American men. It seems that they do not find the Russian men to be adequate. I do my part to improve the lives of the Russian women."

I clutched my napkin to my mouth to keep from squealing too obviously in delight. One goal for the Americans.

"I am also working on a social research project," Brian continued. "You see, many of the expatriate men have a theory that within every Russian *devushka* is a lesbian waiting for the right moment to come out. I will bring two or three girls at a time back to my apartment to test this theory."

Okay, that is enough now. Brian was crossing a line from balance to deliberate provocation. And he was clearly enjoying it.

Big Boris entered the conversation.

"Americans are all the same. Bringing your depravity to Russian and corrupting our culture."

The continuation of his thought was implied and unspoken: "In the good old days the government would send your type to the gulag. Now happily the responsibility falls to good Russian citizens to uphold the standards of decency for the good of Mother Russia."

On cue the waitress appeared with the meals which had been ordered by Vincent. As I suspected – non-descript meat and potatoes both of which looked like they had been boiled to within an inch of disintegration. An open bowl of grimy salt placed on the table was the only spice included in the meal. I reached for a pinch of the gray-ish salt and as I dusted my food with dirt that most Americans would have shunned I reflected that yes, I was *nashi* at this point. I did understand the way Russia worked. As bizarre as this evening was from an objective view – none of it was actually surprising.

Over at the table of the Japanese businessmen, one of the Russians was standing and narrating a long rambling toast. An interpreter leaned in to the Japanese men and offered the translation of the words. I observed the scene and wondered how much they were braced for the cultural side of the toasts as well. The speech ended and the rest of the table sprang to life with a rousing refrain of "to Russia's future". The Japanese men struggled to their feet just a bit slower and with less focus. The Russians smiled and slapped each other on the back and looked at their new business partners with pleasure. The Japanese were showing a bit of weakness with the vodka. This was a good sign for the Russians. The relationship was being launched exactly according to plan – the Russians would have the upper hand here.

The sound system erupted with a pulse of static, then crooning from a bland brown man who was now tangled in the microphone cabling.

The Russian woman with sleek black hair and opera gloves continued to revel in her own alternate version of reality. Perhaps the version of reality where this restaurant was the scene of glamorous socialites and moneyed new Russians. She examined her gloves with a self-satisfied smile and adjusted her skirt and arched her back in a display of indulgence. "I belong in a glamorous world. Look at me." If the glamorous world did not exist in reality, she would create it in her imagination and find that a perfectly adequate substitute. At least for the moment.

Big Boris had finished his meal and was now examining the cutlery on the table. As was standard in most Soviet-era hotel restaurants, the cutlery looked like it had been accidentally tossed in a cement mixer and then retrieved and unsuccessfully cleaned. Boris traced his fingers along the mangled tines of his fork and then calmly bent each tine back into place. He scrutinized the spoon and adjusted the curvature of the handle with an easy touch. Next he picked up his knife and tested the blade against the plastic tablecloth.

I was transfixed by Boris's massive paw casually holding the knife. What was his role with Flis anyway? What chance did Brian and I really have if Vincent had Boris on his team to "persuade" us to sign the statement of work? At what point would intimidation escalate to real violence? The *biznismen* at the Nevsky Palace Hotel certainly did not see the hit coming for them. Michelle only had a few minutes of warning. But worse, she was running not from hired thugs, but from the actual city police who had a warrant for her arrest. Did Larissa have the level of influence necessary to put that sort of pressure on us? She knew that we now had our computer shipment stuck in customs while we figured out how to obtain a waiver for the import tax. (The tax that legally we were supposed to pay, but USAID would not accept as a valid expense. Damned if you do. Damned if you don't.) Could she use this as a pretext for instructions for us to be arrested? And if we were arrested – we would be at the mercy of whatever the police and judges decided to do. I had witnessed police brutality and judges dismissing evidence that they thought to be irrelevant. Vincent had Boris on his side. Brian and I had…. only each other.

We were in a country governed not by rule of law but by the whims of those in positions of power and influence. And Brian and I were certainly in a position of far less influence than Larissa and Vincent.

Vincent was also watching Boris playing with his knife and decided it was a good opportunity to begin the business part of the discussion.

"Now that Patrick has granted you the authority to sign contracts, I see no further reason to delay the next phase of our project." Vincent was speaking with incredible directness and pulled out a set of papers from his briefcase. "I have the statement of work here with me and I believe you are now authorized to sign it."

"Vincent," Brian replied as evenly as he could "You know we have not been happy with the quality of Flis's work. You know we do not want to sign an additional work statement."

"This is not about what it is that you want to do. It is about what is best for Russia's future. Personal opinions are of no consequence. This project is for the improvement of real estate title registration in St Petersburg. Your delays are hurting this cause."

"We have told you that we cannot support your proposal," Brian repeated what he had said to Vincent in numerous prior conversations. "The price cannot be justified and we are not confident in the quality of your company's work. I do not know how much more clear I can be."

"But Brian, the United States is providing aid to Russia. You must work with Russian companies. We are your partner. It is the responsibility of the American companies to transfer knowledge and skills to the Russian partners. If Flis has failed then your firm has failed to transfer knowledge to us."

"If Flis has failed this could also mean that your company does not have the skills or ability or interest to complete the work," Brian lit a cigarette and pushed back from the table.

"Of course we have the interest in completing the work. Flis is a strategic partner of the St Petersburg City Government. Larissa herself wants us to be the partners for this development effort."

Partnership. Mutual cooperation. Knowledge transfer. Such wonderful words with such vacant meaning. If Flis did not demonstrate sufficient ability, then it was our fault for not transferring knowledge. If the pricing was not clear, then it was our fault for not supporting Flis with documentation of an appropriate proposal. Larissa wanted the project to be a success, Vincent emphasized. Success meant knowledge transfer to the local partner companies. Without a local partner – without Flis – the city government would not be able to endorse the project.

If we did not agree to the statement of work, then the project would fail, as Larissa would refuse to endorse any future milestones of the project. A local Russian partner was essential. And if we did agree to the statement of work, then our team was fully responsible for the knowledge transfer to Flis to make the project successful. Failure was not an option. Failure was the only option. Sign this document and Vincent would leave us alone. Sign this document and we would be bound to Vincent for the next six weeks. The next six months. The next six years.

It is just a statement of work. The project has the money. The money was of an inconsequential amount to the US Government. The contractor has been approved. What is the problem? The fact that we do not believe the contractor will deliver. Well, is that actually a fact? No. That is an opinion. An opinion that cannot be substantiated. The City did sign off the last set of deliverables, didn't it? Yes the Oracle QA review had come back negative. But wasn't that due to the fact that we had not outlined the requirements clearly to Flis in the first place?

All our instincts told us not to sign the work statement. The logic we provided did not satisfy anyone. The price was too high. We knew the contractor would not deliver. Wasn't that enough? But no. Per USAID this was a sign of our failing, not the contractor's. We were empowered to sign the work statement. We would be held accountable for the delivery of the project. But it was not acceptable for us to say no.

The lights dimmed in the dining hall and a disco ball began to twirl. The slow crooning singer gave way to the pulsing beat of European techno music. Two girls wearing gold sequined bikinis and stilettos appeared from behind the red curtain with a pout and predatory stare. Immediately they focused on the table with the Japanese businessmen as the prime target for tips and began to strut and dance and thrust their way towards them.

"Finally, some good classic Russian culture," Brian could not resist another opportunity to nip at Vincent.

The restaurant had faded. A nightclub was just waking up. This cannot possibly be happening. This is a fantasy. All of Russia is a fantasy, isn't it? This is just a temporary place. What we do here doesn't really matter – because some day I will be back in the USA and no one will remember what I have done here. What I have seen here? If we just signed a document, everything would go away.

Brian finally, definitively pushed the statement of work back to Vincent. No. We cannot sign this. How many different ways did we need to make this statement? The price is ridiculous and we do not believe the work will be performed in any case.

Vincent slowly withdrew the papers and tucked them in his briefcase. The bill was delivered to the table. Vincent very deliberately counted out notes to cover exactly half of the bill.

I took a side glance at Brian and nearly broke down laughing in nervous exhaustion. A final insult from Vincent. Invite us to dinner and refuse to pick up the bill.

I gathered my handbag and coat, ready to flee the restaurant. Brian was putting on his coat. Vincent sharply hissed at us. "I am certain you will come around to our perspective soon enough. Wait here. I need to make a phone call."

Boris, who had been silent for the greater part of the evening, suddenly spoke. "Vincent said you must wait here," he gestured sharply at our chairs.

I let out a quiet yelp (which was lost in the pulsing techno beat) and sat as I was told. Brian was clearly taken aback, but not ready to argue with Big Boris. Once Vincent was out of earshot, Brian leaned over to me and broke into English. "This is where Vincent will call in the hit."

"Should we run?" I asked Brian, only half-joking. "We could beat Boris to the rear exit."

"No, we can't. What would get back to Patrick, Larissa, and USAID? We had dinner with our subcontractor, refused to sign the work statement, and then ran. We will lose even more credibility than the shreds that we have now."

Big Boris was now cracking his knuckles, as if to emphasize the ridiculous situation. Brian was right. We had to see through the evening as calmly as possible. Besides, running would only reinforce to Vincent that he had the upper hand at this moment.

We were performing our assigned role instinctively. I did not know, however, how the act would end. I am not accustomed to being told to sit down and wait by a large intimidating Russian. From an objective perspective it was just a simple polite request – he had to make a phone call. Couldn't we just wait until he was done so that we could leave together? If that was all there was to it, then why was I holding on to the table to keep the room from spinning? I did not drink much over the evening.

No one else in the room took notice of us. The Japanese businessmen were now captivated by the Russian girls in the sequined dance outfits. Flashes of greenbacks from wallets tucked not-so-discretely into the dancers' clothing. The rest of the room had vanished for them. They were absorbed in the moment. Live for the moment. Feel the techno beat.

I had been at that table in Kazakhstan and in South Russia, and who knows how many other times. The table is caught up in the moment of the frivolity of the senseless toasts, the endless rounds of vodka shots, the meat and potato and mayonnaise salads. What other scenes had been playing out at other tables when I was caught up in the moment of the vodka-induced frivolity? Brian and I could disappear at this moment and no one would notice. No one would remember that we had been here, at the Oktyabrskaya for dinner this night. Live for the moment for tomorrow may never come.

Vincent arrived back at the table and was quickly putting on his coat and escorting us to the door.

"I did not see your driver outside here," he noted as a factual point. "Let us drive you home. Phaedra, you live on the Griboyedev canal, don't you?"

Yes, he was right. And no, I had never told Vincent where I lived. Vincent glanced at me to see if his comment had the desired effect. I breathed deeply and attempted to reply with an even tone.

"Brian and I have made other arrangements."

Of course we had no one waiting for us. Once Sergei had abandoned us our only real option was to just walk out on to the main road and hitchhike – per standard procedure at the time. But we weren't going to tell Vincent that.

Vincent paused and then took my hand with an exaggerated gesture of civility and kissed it. "Always a pleasure, Phaedra. I am looking forward to concluding our business arrangements in the very near future. I am certain you will appreciate our position soon."

Brian took a step backwards and nodded in Vincent's general direction. He did not want his flesh contaminated by Vincent's.

Vincent then gestured for me to take the first step from the hotel out to the street. "So where is your car waiting? I will see you off."

He was looking at us just a bit too attentively. He knew we did not have a car available. Instinctively I did not want to stand on the street hitchhiking with Vincent watching. I stood, just waiting for Vincent to disappear. He didn't.

"So, where is your car?" Brian finally said.

"Right this way,"Vincent's mouth slid into a satisfied smile. He turned and began to walk towards a waiting black Volga, expecting us to follow.

With his back turned, Brian and I could resist the urge no longer. We turned in the opposite direction and nearly sprinted across the front courtyard of the hotel towards the nearest street. Throwing all caution aside, Brian and I made the same reflexive gesture of pulling US dollars from our wallets and using them to flag down a passing car. Generally not the smartest way to get attention, but always effective.

A rusting Lada pulled up to the curb a moment later. Following standard procedure with hitchhiking, I opened the passenger door and leaned in to talk to the driver, assess his relative sanity, and agree a price for the trip. We may be fleeing two creepy characters but I did not want to jump into a car with another one.

At this moment a squeal of tires a hundred meters away and flash of headlights caught our attention. An engine gunned and raced towards us at an alarming speed through the night.

Brian flung open the back door of the car. "No time for pleasantries. Let's go."

I slammed the front passenger door of the car closed and was pulled into the back seat by Brian. The roar of an angry engine drew closer. The headlights shone through the back window of the Lada at full high beam glare.

"Shit, it's the hit." Brian said what had already crossed my mind, but seemed too ludicrous to say out loud. We wedged ourselves low in the back seat.

The car wasn't moving. "So where do you want to go?" The driver asked casually, taking a drag of his toxic cigarette with nicotine-stained fingers.

"Anywhere. Just go." Brian answered quickly.

The driver looked at us in the back seat and then at the headlights behind us and slammed his foot on the accelerator.

"Brian, we aren't really being followed, are we?" I asked slowly from my contortioned position. If the car behind us would start a round of gunfire, we should be low enough to be relatively safe – at least until the driver was hit.

Brian, for once, was silent. Yes. We had passed the boundary of ridiculous some time back. We are just average American consultants trying to manage a rather minor and mediocre project in Russia. This was clearly just our over-excited imagination getting the better of us. We had been reading too many Tom Clancy novels.

"Why is this Volga following us?" The Russian driver shattered my thoughts and I gulped for air. I heard Brian take a sharp intake of breath as well. There goes our last possible thread to clutch on to which could tell us that this was all in our minds. External validation that we now had a hostile Volga following us at altogether too close a range.

"Angry Oracle developers. They want money. Please just lose them," Brian replied.

The driver did not need to be told this twice. He clenched the cigarette between his teeth and took the next right turn at full speed. The headlights swung around the corner and followed us. He did not ask again about the Volga following us – probably figuring that he would be better off not knowing what was going on and simply getting rid of us as quickly as possible. Or possibly the driver had prior experience with angry Oracle developers.

Conversation at this point was impossible. We twisted our bodies to keep a low profile, half expecting the back window to be shattered by gunfire at any moment. The little Lada surged and lunged and braked, then turned and surged again. The driver was silent and focused on the task at hand. After what seemed like an eternity (but realistically was probably only a few minutes), the bright lights faded and the driver slowed down to a standard speed. We had lost our pursuers – for the moment at least.

We gave new instructions to our driver and minutes later the car pulled up in front of my building. I paused a moment before opening my door. The street was quiet. Too quiet. Only a few steps from the car to the front entrance of the building. But the front door never latched properly. Anyone could be inside that main entrance. Or in the unlit stairwell – lit only by incidental light slipping through the dusty windows. I found my keys in my handbag, and prepared myself. A pale light from a window in my flat. A shadow moved past a curtain. Someone was in my flat. I had to hope it was Valerie or Jennifer.

I opened the car door quietly and closed it gently behind me. Who was I kidding. Anyone lurking for me would have heard the car pull up to the front entrance. I glanced back at Brian looking on attentively, then sprinted through the front entrance, up the blackened labyrinth of a stair case and burst through my front door. I slammed the steel trap behind me, closing the events of the evening behind the barrier. I flashed the lights on and off – a signal to Brian below that I was in the flat safely. I heard the Lada pull away from the curb and drive away. I then took a deep breath and felt all remaining pretenses of emotional stability drain from me, collapsing into a nearby chair.

Valerie appeared before me and looked me over. "Rough day at the office?"

I stared blankly at my friend – utterly incapable of speaking in complete sentences. Valerie looked at me with alarm for a moment, then quickly and reflexively pulled our bottle of vodka from the freezer. At first she was going to mix it with tonic (as the Americans tend to do). But then she decided I needed it straight up and poured it into the tumbler and handed it to me without a word. I gratefully welcomed the tranquilizer.

I was huddled in the chair, still with my coat on, holding the empty glass when the phone rang. I was immobile, staring blankly. Valerie answered and stretched the cord out to hand the receiver to me. It was Brian.

"You know our phones are tapped. Why are you calling?" I was only able to pull together brief sentences of paranoia.

"I won't be in the office tomorrow. But don't worry about me."

"Where are you going…" but wait. A click on the line.

"I'll be fine. I'll be in touch." He hung up and was gone.

My head was pounding with the events of the evening, the previous day, the previous week, month, years. The brute powerful force of Russia – which years ago I had climbed on to with reckless abandon – now was destroying me. Not a personal attack, but rather the nature of such an animal would always result in destruction. The creature was moving, galloping, towards a destination I could not quite understand. Until recently I was riding the beast, relishing the wind in my hair, closing my eyes and smiling, not caring where the ride might end. I felt the sweaty body and pulsing heart and churning muscles of the animal as life, pure adrenaline, surged through my veins. But then I opened my eyes and decided I didn't like where the beast was taking me. I tried to change direction, but it was too late. The animal was in control. I was powerless. Now I was being tossed, thrown – in danger of being dragged with my ankles caught in the stirrups, while the beast galloped onwards, oblivious to those it was crushing along the way.

I gasped for breath. The air in the apartment was stagnant. My sofa in the living room still reeked of cigarette smoke and stale vodka and sweat from the party a few days earlier. I stumbled out onto the street into the pale glow of the St Petersburg white nights of late spring, gulping the crisp air.

The canal was still and silent, lying as a deadly no-man's land between two opposing armies of massive apartment blocks. The imposing buildings eyed each other up across the water, poising and posturing. Which side would pounce first? One of the buildings across the banks twitched, I was certain. Gathering itself to lunge at the defending fortress on my side of the canal.

Stomping of feet and sounds of a crowd in the distance. At this hour of the night? What was going on? I turned a corner and found myself engulfed by a crowd, masses of people, marching and carrying torches. Their voices were those of liberation. People who finally had found freedom after living a life of despair. I joined them and felt uplifted. Momentary relief. I dared to laugh with exaltation.

And then I noticed blood. The men walking on either side of me were flogging themselves with barbed wire. Blood was splashing against my face. I looked at the men's eyes and they were turned up with pure ecstasy. Then one closed his eyes and collapsed. The crowds continued to march, stepping on him as they proceeded.

"What is going on?" I asked the man next to me with alarm. He whipped his flail of barbed wire across his back and took a few peaceful breaths before answering.

"We are gaining control of our lives in the most profound way possible. We are seizing complete control of our lives – and our deaths. It is true freedom. Are you not on this march for the same reason?" The man picked up a flail from a body on the ground and handed it to me.

I extended my hand as a natural reaction to having something offered. But as the cold metal touched my flesh, I recoiled and the weapon dropped to the cobbled street, splashing in a puddle of blood.

"No." I said simply. "I do not want that." I stopped still and the marchers continued around me, moving onwards to some unknown destination, singing with glorious salvation. So tempting, but no.

The marchers continued their procession past me – howling in pain, howling in ecstasy. Involved and absorbed in their own suffering. And in a moment of clarity I reflected back on my drunken recitation of Shelley alongside the canal. The staggering Russian man had ignored me not because the scene was too common, but because he was so caught up in his own pain to register the pain of the others around him. Suffering is everywhere. But in the end everyone suffers alone.

A drop of water hit my face. A tear? But then another and the skies opened and beat down with cold lashing onto the earth. The marchers did not notice. Their mission continued unabated, the flails flying dangerously close to my face, nicking my arms. My feet splashed in rivers of blood. I had to get away, to some place safe – away from the flails and out of the rain.

I negotiated my way to the side of the crowd and saw a warm inviting light through the torrential downpour. I ran towards the light and found a familiar man with arms outstretched, inviting me out of the rain. The rain drummed against a tin roof. I was safe now. Protected. The pain would soon end. The rain pounded down all around, but I was secure in the arms of a trusted friend. I felt warmth, comfort, security, and buried my face into his chest – willing the rest of the world to go away. I could stay here forever. Finally I looked up into his face and saw Craig – calm, smiling, and welcoming me.

I woke myself up with my own screams.

Being rescued by a dead friend is never a good sign. I had to take control of my life. The suicide march had been rejected. I needed another way out.

27 MARGARITAS ON THE ROCKS

May 1996

"The future of Russia can be seen in the eyes of the youth," Adrian took a drag from his cigarette and surveyed the scene with a satisfied smile.

"If that is true, then Russia has a bleaker future than even I assumed," I took a swig of beer and nestled deeper into the welcoming deep booth seat of the bar. I was curled up next to Adrian and attempted to absorb his positive energy. Every thought that came to the surface, however, was progressively blacker and blacker.

I was back in Moscow. In hiding in Moscow. In denial that St Petersburg even existed.

The day after the dinner with Vincent, I had been scarcely capable of a coherent sentence. I went to the office and sat at my desk and stared at the laptop screen. Incapable of conversation. Incapable of action. Brian had called me from Helsinki. He had told Patrick he was going on holiday for a few weeks – leaving the door a bit open that he would return to the project and attempt to close this whole thing off intact. But how? I was paralyzed in St Petersburg – utterly incapable of thinking, talking, walking out the front door without visions of Ian and his broken kneecaps overwhelming all other conscious thoughts.

I came up with the most flimsy of excuses for why I needed to be back in Moscow for a few weeks and told the project team that I would return soon. They undoubtedly saw the terror in my eyes, but did not ask any questions.

A few days ago I had been with Brian, Vincent, and Big Boris in the cavernous dining hall of the Oktyabrskaya. A relic of the Soviet era but totally appropriate in the context of modern violent Russia. Now I found myself in the very latest uber-hip venue in Moscow. A bar that had emerged from the rubble of some faded Soviet artifact and stood as a monument to Moscow's present and future – the Hungry Duck – a bar that took every image and stereotype of American college antics and debauchery and turned up the intensity to a whole new level.

On the surface the Hungry Duck was an American bar — blonde waitresses, enthusiastic service, modern music, gleaming new décor, Western European beers on tap, booths to cozy up with friends in a crowd, and cardboard beer coasters.

Superficially the Hungry Duck could have been a bar from any American college town — loud shrieking women, even louder music, beer flowing freely. Every week now it seemed like a new venue was opening — bringing the West ever closer to Moscow. Stylish interiors, printed menus, professionally trained staff. I had seen this before, breaking through the tired ruins of the Soviet era. Change was everywhere and continuous. A march forward, to where. The crowds swirled and squealed and smiled.

That was it. People were smiling. And not just the Americans. The Russians were smiling. There were Russian *women* smiling — hair cut just a bit more European, clothes a bit more stylish. Not the pouting sulking *devushki* who cling to the arm of their bottle green clad *biznismen* boyfriends, but these were real Russian women.

Real Russian women — most with American or European dates. Laughing, smiling, dazzled by this new world that was opening up to them. Their dates handed them a beer. A beer! Draft with the head pouring over the side, German style. *Devushki* don't drink beer. They pout and sit perched quietly on a chair and sip champagne. But no — something was definitely changing here at the Hungry Duck. The *devushka* accepted the beer from her date and — *smiled*.

"Moscow has changed in the past few months while I've been gone," I stated the obvious to Adrian.

"Russia is not such a horrible place, Phaedra," Adrian gestured to the scene in front of us. "young happy people. Optimism for the future. Things are turning around here. You'll see."

"Spring is here," I replied. "Sunshine affects the brain. Add alcohol and of course everyone is in a good mood. Alcohol is also a wonderful way of washing the rest of the world away."

"Alcohol is also a traditional way of celebrating in just about every culture. Celebrating the wonderful things in our lives in the present moment. Looking forward to the future."

"Adrian," I turned to him with astonishment. "No one seriously talks about the future in Russia. *Carpe diem*. That is our motto. Live for today. Tomorrow may never come."

So are they excited about the future or trying to bury their pain? Or did the expats here even have any appreciation for what was happening just outside the door? Adrian worked on academic analyses safely inside an English speaking office in Moscow. Valerie's American manager, who stumbled through our house party, was just flying through St Petersburg for a few days. Both were nominally working in Russia, but neither were actually on the front lines of the battlefield.

Valerie's manager had laughed at the idea of "hazard pay" believing that life in St Petersburg is one long party. And Adrian was simply baffled to see me muttering to myself and guarding my beer protectively. If others nominally working in Russia did not understand what I was going through, how would the last few weeks and years possibly be appreciated by those back in their air-conditioned offices in Washington DC?

I stared at my beer, lost in thought. Back in graduate school, expatriate life had sounded so adventurous and glamorous. How exciting to be on the cutting edge of history promoting the cause of economic development! But now I realized that they say the "cutting edge" for a reason: people do get hurt.

The frothy head of the beer had receded a bit, leaving the glass a bit emptier. Wasn't the glass full just a moment ago? I had only taken a sip. Now the beer was exposed for what it was – a bit less than expected. (Adrian, of course, would say the glass was more than half full.) This was the correct way to pour a beer for the Germans. The Australians would have been outraged. Who was right? I watched as the cheery froth rolled down my glass and then disintegrated into a pathetic puddle. I had seen the little cardboard coasters, but somehow did not have one myself.

An American was bumped by the swirling crowd into my table, beer in one hand, arm possessively around a *devushka* with the other. He glanced at our table first as an obstacle, then he noticed my glass sitting in a miserable puddle of beer.

"Coaster! She needs a coaster," he called out at full volume.

Somehow he was heard over the din of music, laughter, and full volume scraps and shouts of conversation. The call from the American was met by a volley of beer coasters being thrown at me from every corner of the bar. The American smiled, unwrapped his right arm from the *devushka* so he could pick up a few coasters and hurl them back into the crowd. In a moment the air was filled with flying whirling projectiles.

Back in the United States this would be the moment when the bartender would call out with a loud whistle and threaten to throw people out into the street. Someone could lose an eye. Throwing beer coasters in a crowded bar. It was against the rules. There could be injuries. And (more importantly) someone could sue the bar management.

And here is where the Hungry Duck proved to be truly a Russian bar with only a superficial American disguise. The bartender surveyed the scene, smiled and then actually himself began tossing beer coasters into the fray. The air was alive with random missiles. I shielded my eyes. The shrieking from the girls raised a pitch higher. Ah yes, it is all fun and games until someone gets hurt. In the United States this would end with a lawsuit. But here in Russia, what if the favorite *devushka* of some biznisman were injured? Then what? They have Big Boris on their side. Do you have Igor with his sledgehammer ready to support you when needed?

I curled up next to Adrian to protect myself from the onslaught of beer coasters — and everything else that was being thrown at me, both real and imaginary.

An American woman scrambled up onto the bar with a smile and a shriek and a boost from her friends. She stood triumphantly atop the bar in fashionable high heel suede boots — which clearly had not yet been subjected to the Moscow acid rain — and then took a handful of beer coasters and threw them in various directions. All attention was on her now and she loved it — tossing back her gorgeous long hair and dancing. Enjoying the moment. To be young and beautiful and the center of attention.

But not for long. A Russian *devushka* lifted a graceful hand to her date and stepped from the floor to a barstool to the bar countertop. The American girl was no longer alone in the spotlight. The *devushka* glanced sideways at the American with a satisfied smile and proceeded to dance with the air of assurance that all men in the room were now interested in only her.

Loud whoops and whistles erupted from the onlookers. Other women quickly elbowed their way into a corner of the limelight. The American women exuded just a bit more desperation than the Russians. Even the American women who were clearly newcomers seemed to understand that they had hardly a chance in the harsh dating world of Moscow when pitted against the beauty and availability of the Russian women.

As if to emphasize the point, the Russian girl deftly slipped off her shirt — dropping it into the hands of her date below. All eyes were on her now — or more accurately all eyes were on her perfectly formed body and European lingerie. She milked the moment expertly, turning to a second Russian girl who had just joined the growing crowd of women on the bar. The topless *devushka* placed one manicured hand on the waist of the newcomer as she danced to the pulsing Euro-house music. Ran her other hand through her own hair — a deliberate display of casual sensuality. Aware of her audience while studiously ignoring them.

Adrian, like all the other western men in the bar, was now completely transfixed. The Russian *devushki* were staking their claims over the western men. The American women did not have a chance against these predators.

I felt myself disappearing into the shadows as the Russian *devushki* consumed all available light and attention. They were the present moment. They were the beautiful intense all absorbing passion of the expatriate men. They represented fantasies and better yet, they were actually here in the flesh delivering on those fantasies. Here and now.

Devushki represent the present moment. The youth represent the future of the country — isn't that the phrase that is used by every politician? The youth are eternally young — how can they possibly be the future of middle aged shapeless, toothless muttering women wearing floral shirts with plaid woolen skirts?

"Not me" — the *devushka* shouts silently with every thrust of her hips and flutter of her eyes. "I will never ever age. I am eternally young — just look at this gorgeous skin. See how the men are unable to look anywhere but at me."

Is it hope or denial? When Rita floated through the office, the office *devushki* were transfixed. They had never seen a beautiful older woman. It was unnatural to be beautiful, healthy, and happy over the age of sixty. Their gaze had followed her movements with longing and the first seeds of hope. There were other options in life to becoming an embittered hostile old woman. Show me the secrets of grace and beauty.

The secret, of course, was that Rita had lived most of her life in the west. She had good food, clean air, a loving husband, healthy exercise, and the greatest stress in her life was determining which charity event to favor. Virtually none of this was available in Russia. Or, more accurately, none of this was readily available to the Russian masses. In Moscow in the mid-1990s everything was available – for a price. Healthy vegetables (not from radioactive parts of Ukraine) could be found in the well-stocked shelves of the extortionately-priced Swedish supermarkets. Clean air could be found far from the city – or on overseas holidays by the Mediterranean. Loving husband? That was where the western boyfriend came in. But loving may be a bit of a conceptual stretch. The first requirement was a western passport – which would obviously provide access to wealth, fabulous holidays, great restaurants, beautiful clothes. The western boyfriend also was probably not an alcoholic or abusive – therefore several levels of improvement beyond the Russian norm. Exercise and charities? What are those anyway? Foreign concepts.

Eternal youth is found in the west. Here in Moscow our youth will be ripped away from us tomorrow. Seize the day. Enjoy the moment. Plan for the future by plotting your escape from Russia. Now.

Sarah had said that something happened when women turned 30 in Russia. They lost their sense of style, lost their confidence, their looks, their teeth, their hair. A few weeks after turning 30 women would suddenly be wearing brown ambiguous shoes and their legs would be shapeless to a sagging cankle. Hair would stick out at strange angles and they would begin to talk to themselves wandering down the street. Was it genetic or something in the water? Sarah did not want to find out. A few weeks before she turned 30 she had left the country abruptly, never to be heard from again.

My attention returned to the *devushki* dancing on the bar. Now several girls were topless – including the American. Were they dancing with exaltation in the moment, hope or desperation? The moment was all that mattered. Grasp it. Seize it. For tomorrow may never come.

I was already becoming a *babushka*. My hair was coming out in handfuls. I was muttering to myself. Rocking myself to sleep. A bottle of vodka in the freezer at all times, helping me to blur over the sharp edges of the day. Muttering and hostile about all the dramas that cluttered my vision. My skin was pasty and soon my teeth would start falling out. The American men were only interested in the illusion of the gorgeous Russian *devushki*. The Russian men had been sampled and put to the side. And the Swedish sailor boys? That was some bizarre temporary fantasy that could not have any basis in reality on this planet. I was clearly destined to be living alone with my cat and a house full of cockroaches.

There was a point not too long ago when I would have been on the tables dancing as well. When did it all change? *Carpe diem* – that is the mantra of the expatriates. Seize the day. Enjoy the day. We are young and the world is ours. All our efforts and pain and suffering by day was worthwhile because we were making positive *impact* – and then we celebrated our victories and camaraderie at night. We were in Russia to help change the country for the better. Our work was so *important*.

The revelers were celebrating the possibilities – the endless possibilities – of what one could do in Moscow. They had money, energy, a thirst for adventure – and no rules holding them back. Anything was possible. They were celebrating the adrenaline rush of living in a lawless society. But did they understand the consequences? In a land without rules, every day, every encounter is a new challenge for who will win and who will lose. Yes, today they were riding the emotional high of victory. And like with any drug, the higher you fly, the lower you crash. Did they understand that the very lawlessness they celebrated also would someday bring Igor and his sledgehammer to pound on their door?

The music, the laughter, the bodies and energy. It was all closing in on me. This was not my world any more. I was suffocating. I had to get out.

I grabbed Adrian by the hand and dragged him from the bar out into the street and took a deep breath of the night air. While Moscow air never could be called "clean," it certainly was refreshing compared to the demons' nest I had just fled.

Adrian assessed my glazed eyes, fragments of sentences and shaking body and took me by the arm – leading me onwards somewhere into the evening. Forms shifted and emerged and sank into the shadows. Voices muffled. Now clear. But what language were they speaking? And now background – rippling. I am walking a straight line. Aren't I? Then abruptly Adrian steers me to the right – around an open manhole cover. Lurking. Waiting in the shadows for its next victim before pouncing.

Now garish bright lights. Enclosed space. Dank and stale. Are we safe? The lobby of the Hotel Intourist.

"Excuse me, do you speak English?" An American voice. Woman. A blurred image moved in front of me. Two women. Tourists. Adrian must have said something. The American woman continued.

"Do you know where the Bolshoi Theater is? Our tour guide left us. We have tickets for tonight's performance but we don't know where the theater is."

I stared blankly ahead. Were these women for real? The Bolshoi Theater was less than two blocks away. One of the most easily recognizable building facades in the city

— just after the Kremlin itself. Had these tourists even looked at a map and taken two steps outside their hotel?

Again some words from Adrian. He was doing the decent thing and giving them instructions. I just stared silently.

"Oh. Two blocks away," her voice shook with nervous tension. "Would you walk us over there?"

It is just two blocks! Certainly the Americans were capable of walking two blocks without a guide.

"We are afraid of the mafia," the second woman clarified.

This really was too much. Two middle aged American women separated from their tour guide and afraid of – the mafia. I could not restrain the bitter laughter and tightened my grip on Adrian's arm.

"You are perfectly safe from the mafia. You are meaningless to them. What would they possibly want with you? It is me who they want."

Adrian made some apology for my behavior and pushed me past the women towards the lift.

"Mafia. They are afraid of the mafia," I was spitting with fury at their ignorance. "Do they even have the slightest idea what the mafia is?"

"Phaedra, ever consider the possibility that you are over-dramatizing? Just a little bit?"

Adrian escorted me into the lift – a relic of the 1960s which shuddered as it began its ascent to the top floor. He was guiding me towards Azteca – one of the original Moscow expat hangouts. Always popular due to the views of the Kremlin, 24 hour service, and real margaritas. My friend commandeered a table, hunted down a waitress and ordered margaritas for the both of us. Either he read my mind (fairly easy – I was clearly in need of yet another drink) or he was becoming Russian himself. He had not asked where I wanted to go or what I wanted to do next. But a margarita would do fine. Thank you.

Although Adrian had made his comment sincerely and with good intentions, the effect was completely the opposite. My own friend was trivializing and dismissing the angst I was suffering. Patrick had laughed at me and said I was reading too many Tom Clancy novels. Greg, the USAID manager, had told me that I needed to show more cultural sensitivity. And now Adrian was saying that I was perhaps over-dramatizing. I was the victim of domestic abuse that turns to the police only to overhear the officers commenting that the husband seems like a nice guy. If the people who are supposed to be at the core of my professional and personal support network did not appreciate what I was going through, then I was well and truly on my own.

"Don't you start with the 'it's all in my mind' stuff as well," I retorted sharply to Adrian, just short of a bark. "Seriously you are an academic economist here. Do you think that the mafia come around with business cards to identify themselves? Do they even call themselves the mafia? What do you mean by mafia anyway?"

"Mafia are criminals who operate businesses and consider themselves to be above the law. They bribe and infiltrate the government to get favorable treatment and decisions."

"Do you really think it is that simple? Crap, you really have been in academia too long. Do you think there is a little club in Moscow called "the mafia" where people pay dues and elect a president? No. You really never know who is in and who is out. You don't know if you yourself are in. Everything is just all shades of grey."

"I think I would know if I were in the mafia. The mafia seeks to control the rules for how the game is played. They manipulate the government to define the rules." Adrian kicked back from the table and lit up a cigarette. He was clearly enjoying this conversation from a perspective of professional interest. I was about to leap out of my skin and throttle his neck. For me this was not a matter of academic analysis and contemplation. This was real.

"The rules in this place are impossible to follow. We all play our part in the machinery that keeps this country moving. To obtain a simple driver's license is nearly impossible and will take years (if ever) if you follow the rules. How did your driver get his license? He would have paid someone something to 'expedite the paperwork.' Then how about petrol? There aren't any real gas stations anywhere. Have you been with your driver when he fills up the gas tank – down some dark alley with some unmarked petrol truck? And how did your office renovations get completed so quickly? The standard wait is two years to get a phone connection – yet your new office was up and running in a few months. How do you think this all happens? Everyone is a cog in the machine here – the entire question is how close you are to being crushed or the one doing the crushing. For me – I have something the city of St Petersburg wants – a nice cheque for $50K. The problem is that they don't actually care what happens in reality, as long as they get their $50K."

"I am not sure I would call it mafia," Adrian said slowly, knowing I was emotionally unstable, yet unwilling to agree for the sake of calming me down.

"I don't like the label either. But really, didn't you just say that the mafia bribe and infiltrate the government to get favorable treatment? What do you think is happening with my subcontractors? This is definitely not a normal client – contractor – subcontractor relationship. The so called client is not actually interested in the services being delivered – just whether the subcontractor is paid."

"Adrian!" our conversation was interrupted by a familiar face – a British colleague of Adrian's with a standard issue gorgeous brunette Russian *devushka* on his arm. She was silent and glared at me for occupying the same space as her target, this Brit. "You aren't actually talking work are you? Always analyzing everything. Lighten up, mate."

The Brit gave Adrian a hearty slap on the back. Just a bit too hearty. Obviously it was important to give the impression that they were best of mates.

"Have you met Natasha?" But he did not pause for an answer or even acknowledgement. He was too clearly enthralled in the moment, a beautiful woman on his arm, witnessed by a colleague who would be able to verify the fact on Monday morning. "We were eating upstairs and were just leaving. It is a beautiful evening for a stroll through Red Square."

Natasha was silent. Too much talking for Natasha. Her eyes glared that she wanted to get to work on her project of the evening – the British passport. She tugged his arm and the pair departed.

"He really doesn't give a damn about her. It is all about the image," Adrian stated the obvious with amusement.

"And she has no interest in him except his passport – that was fairly apparent as well," I added.

"Yet he so wanted to put on this impression that this is some wonderful deep and meaningful relationship. Dinner and an evening stroll," Adrian sighed at his departing colleague. "Guys are so predictable – needing external validation to bolster his own self-image."

"You know something, Adrian. Acknowledgement is the first step towards recovery," I smiled and laughed. "Have you learned something from this encounter?"

"Perception is more important than reality, of course. I thought you had learned that lesson already. It is the theme of the day my dear. Just look at my colleague and his love interest, the American tourists and their fears of the mafia. Look at the amazing candidates for president in the upcoming elections here. Zhirinovsky is promising to stop capital flight abroad by canceling all flights from Russia to the western world. Of course air flights have precious little to do with the reality of capital flight – but he has actually managed to gain a following of people who believe this perception."

What is more important – perception or reality? In the end, it is perception that makes people act, not reality.

But actually wasn't that really the theme of my life these days? Would Vincent ever direct Boris to crack my kneecaps? I believed it – therefore I was terrified and hiding in Moscow. Brian believed it and was somewhere in Helsinki. The reality of Vincent's intentions was unknown. All that was important was the perception that with a simple phone call by the Prince of Darkness my life could be totally demolished.

And I needed a drink. Where were our margaritas anyway?

I scanned the room. The waitress was serving beers to people who had arrived long after us. I sighed at the injustices of the world.

I stalked my waitress and pleaded with her to hurry up with our margaritas. She advised me (with an air of recent customer-service training and over-confidence that she was saying the right thing) that my margaritas would be coming soon. But why the delay? Many people are receiving drinks now who arrived long after us.

Ah yes. You see, we ran out of ice and are now freezing more.

This was the final straw for my fragile mental state. This Russian waitress was perfectly self-satisfied that she was providing top-notch customer service. We ordered margaritas. We would get margaritas. She was even going to the lengths to freeze additional ice for us.

I gripped the edge of the bar to balance myself and prevent any sudden lunges for the waitress's throat. I opened my mouth to begin a lecture about customer service and how completely ridiculous it was to make us wait for more ice to be frozen.

Why was everything so difficult? Why was I the designated one to be the crusader for the improvement of life in Russia? But then no. I just cannot do this anymore. Let the Russians have their crappy customer service. If it doesn't bother anyone else, then why am I shouldering the effort to try to improve the situation for everyone else. I ordered two beers and sat back at the table with Adrian.

I paused. Could it really be that simple? If the crappy customer service doesn't bother anyone else, then why should I let it bother me? Here at Azteca the answer for how to achieve a peaceful evening was simply to stop insisting on margaritas and opt for a beer instead. I needed to stop hitting the problem head on and look for an alternate solution that just worked with the existing situation.

I took a deep breath and pounded my fist into my forehead. How had I been so blind to the obvious? Image vs reality. Image is so much simpler. It is visible. Why ask difficult questions when the image alone can give you the answer you want?

The lesson Sarah was trying to teach me with the gypsy girl on the Old Arbat finally fully registered. Why were people giving money to the gypsy girl? They wanted to believe they were helping her in some way. Yes, the reality was that the men who controlled her would keep the money. How many people paused to think through what it would take to genuinely help her? No one. The question was too difficult, too complex, and beyond anything they as an individual could realistically accomplish. Therefore it is much easier to just go with the image that they were helping her and move on. If anyone asked about what they did today to make the world a better place they could smile and say that they gave money to a gypsy girl. The reality that in fact they were paying her captors and reinforcing the system would not be raised or discussed. Why would it be? Look at the evidence – I gave money to a poor child. Tick this off as an act of charity and move on.

The lessons of the years in Russia suddenly were visible in bright Technicolor. Everything came back to vodka diplomacy. Every dinner with Russian partners was filled with proclamations of mutual cooperation and toasting the future of Russia. The symbolic gestures of success and cooperation were important to everyone – with flowery toasts and hearty slaps on the back . But any perceptive observer for such a dinner will note that although the words are correct, all the participants have different objectives for what they want out of the relationship.

It was the symbol of success that everyone needed. With the gypsy girl this was simply handing her rubles as a symbolic gesture of assistance that could not be refuted or openly criticized. The person who tried to really help her would be taking on a monumental project with limited probability of success. By directly tackling the problem they would also opening themself to a higher probability of failure.

For my project in St Petersburg, Brian and I were the only people who were consumed by anxiety over the horror that Flis would not deliver anything against the Scope of Work. The reality was that no one else was looking anything beyond the symbol of success – documentation. All that the St Petersburg city government officials wanted was for their favorites to be paid and to receive the computer equipment and to be left alone. All the DC management cared about was signed documentation saying that the project was completed on time and within budget so they could be paid. USAID just wanted to be able to tick off another success story in the name of building mutual cooperation and building democracy.

The success of the project would be measured by the paperwork, not by whether there actually was a viable title registration system. As long as there was a completion certificate in the files everyone would be happy.

New mission objectives – get the paperwork signed and then get out. As quickly as possible.

I could feel the stresses of the past year lifting. Like with many complex problems, when the best answer presents itself you are left with astonishment at how simple the solution can be. The black clouds of my mind started to part and a tiny ray of hope was permitted to penetrate the darkness. There was a way out.

I smiled as I drank my beer and felt an inner calm as all my anxieties melted away. Like a master in Judo who had learned to use his opponents' moves to his own advantage, I was done fighting. I was prepared to cooperate with the system now. Or at least I was prepared to cooperate to the extent that it served my purpose to declare victory – and exit.

Sarah and Spencer were right when they each said "when it is your time to leave Russia, you will know." My time had come. Yes, I would be able to declare victory – on paper – but I did not have the strength to fight another battle. Everything I had endured in Russia and Kazakhstan had been accepted as the price to be paid in the name of the higher objectives of the Goals of the Project and the Future of the Nation. But now the masquerade was over and I was certain that no one actually truly believed in the Goals of the Project. Pain for a cause is martyrdom. Pain without purpose is simply masochism.

Once the fire of purpose had burned out, all I was left with was cold ash.

28 INDEPENDENCE DAY

May 1996

Somehow I did find the reserve energy to go through the motions required to close off the project paperwork. With the new mission objectives defined, everything else fell into place incredibly quickly. Everyone's goals were now aligned. There was no longer any need to battle. Flis had agreed to a scope of work that would encompass the whole of the remaining required project milestones. Larissa was delighted that the Americans were planning on exiting sooner than expected and leaving all the computer equipment in the hands of the City. USAID could proclaim that another aid project was successfully complete and a Russian subcontractor had been empowered. Patrick was pleased that the final accounting of the project would show us coming in exactly on budget with all milestones signed off. And even all our paperwork for the computer equipment was now nice and neat as somehow all import duties had been waived shortly after we advised Larissa that we were preparing for a handover immediately after delivery.

Brian and I regrouped back in St Petersburg and got down to business creating the final sets of documentation to close the project. A revised scope of work for Flis to perform all the remaining project activities. Certificates to be signed by the City of St Petersburg acknowledging completion of all major deliverables and acceptance of responsibility to oversee the integration and deployment – effectively exonerating Arthur Andersen from any further obligations. Certificates for transfer of all servers, computers, networking equipment, printers, and even office telephones from the project inventory to the City of St Petersburg. And, unfortunately, letters of redundancy to all of the Russian staff in our St Petersburg project office.

As we were closing down the project, this was the end of the line for them with our consultancy. The team mostly received the news with a shrug of acceptance. They knew the project would not last forever. They were not surprised that this American firm would not be keeping its promises of ongoing employment after the end of the project. They had enjoyed a good ride – at several times the average wages in Russia at that time – and now were being cast aside.

What ever happened to all the grandiose statements that we were in Russia to make a difference? Weren't we here to change the system? To help to get the government out of people's daily lives and to lay the foundation for the future development of private wealth by ordinary people?

"The project will be completed. The title registration system will be established. The only thing that has changed is that the City will oversee the completion of the remaining pieces of the program. This is all part of deepening the ongoing partnership between USAID and the Russian Government. The Russian government has been asking for more control over the programs and less involvement of western consultants. This will further that objective," I explained the plans to the team with the correct words. But my sentences ran hollow. I know I am a lousy actress. I did not believe these statements myself. Why would I expect my team to believe them?

Never mind. The documents all said the right things. Everyone could smile and declare victory. Of course the concept of a mutually beneficial outcome is a foreign concept in Russia. In Russia every situation must have a winner and a loser, therefore Brian and I had to put on a show that Larissa and Vincent were actually gaining the upper hand with all the arrangements. If they had suspected how happy we were to close this chapter in our lives, they would have then paused and believed that somehow we were taking advantage of *them*. For them it was conceptually impossible that both sides would come away with what they wanted.

Larissa, of the City of St Petersburg, was delighted to take possession of $2 million USD of hardware and software. When she opened the back doors of the truck delivering the goods to her office, her eyes lit up and she clapped her hands with excitement like a child on Christmas morning. All her wishes were coming true – she received her computer equipment, her favorite subcontractor was being paid, and these pesky American consultants were packing up and leaving town. Vincent (aka the Prince of Darkness) did not actually express pleasure of any sort – but he did sign and return the revised Scope of Work within hours of receiving it. And I never saw Big Boris again.

The only person who was visibly distressed by the change in plans was Yuri Mikhailovich. Throwing all caution aside, he drove over to our offices to meet with Brian and me as soon as he heard the news. He pleaded with us to change our mind and tear up the final round of project certificates that we had created and Larissa had signed. Rather than pushing the cause for freedom and economic advancement, our project now would entrench the city government power structure even further. We were leaving the city worse off than when we arrived, he argued. Now Larissa had even greater political strength, with a war chest of modern western hardware and software for her to use as leverage with whatever she wanted to do next. We had paid off her favorite subcontractor – ensuring that the system of power, favoritism and extortion would remain. The individual agencies were left with nothing and were powerless.

What did we have to say for ourselves? Yuri had delivered his message in person because he wanted to see our real reactions to his arguments – not just some correctly chosen words over the phone or in a letter.

Yuri's words hurt because they were true. I had bounced into his office months ago on my first day on the project with wide eyed optimism and cheerful promises of working towards establishing a true secondary market in real estate in the City of St Petersburg. Many Russians now owned their own apartments – due to the first round of privatization – but without the ability to easily establish title, all the real benefits of ownership would be lost. Banks would not extend loans against property when title could not be validated. Purchase of property through cash alone was out of reach for most people. And those with property – what then? The key to economic development is leveraging assets with credit – the ability to draw a loan against your property to start a business. I had enthusiastically endorsed the objectives of the project to Yuri in our first meeting. Yuri had understood the importance of the program well before I had discussed it with him. He wanted the project to be successful.

Yuri had genuinely endorsed the documented objectives of the program where no one else would. And now that I held the documentation stating that the program was complete, he waved aside the completion certificates with revulsion and dismay. This program had started with the potential to make a real difference – but instead it went the way of all the others – just to reinforce the existing power structure. A positive step forward for Russian and US government relations – government to government relations. But not such a great result for the real Russian citizens who wanted to improve their daily lives.

"Yuri," Brian and I pleaded desperately. "We didn't have a choice. You know that the City had our phones tapped. You know that we were all being threatened unless we did what was asked of us. This was the only way we could close the project safely and be sure that we would all get out of this place in one piece."

Yuri was clearly disgusted by us at this point and stood up to leave. "You always have a choice for what to do next. You have chosen the easy path – like so many before you – and as a result the system here continues to be strong. You have the advantage of being able to leave this place with your tidy completion certificates. You do not have to ever look back. I must live here the rest of my life. The future of this country means something to me. To you it is just a job. I had thought that you were different."

Yuri turned and walked out of our office, not looking back. His departing footsteps echoed in the corridor and the room fell silent.

Silence. Deafening silence for a few moments as if to punctuate that this was one of those moments that would forever define our lives. Yuri was taking one path and Brian and I had taken another. The chapter of my life with the City of St Petersburg was now closed. But where I would be able to return to the United States and start afresh, he would remain behind. The expatriates could be frivolous because we were just passing through Russia. For Yuri, this was his country – his past, present, and future.

And then mercifully, a phone call to rescue us from any damaging moments of self-reflection.

Paul. He was now back in Washington DC. He was nominally calling us to work on the close out documentation. But from the tone in his voice I could tell there was more to what was going on.

"Don't come back to the United States, you will hate life here," he said with overly dramatic desperation in his voice. "Everything is too safe and boring. There are barriers around the open man-hole covers. The carpeting on stairs is neatly nailed down. The biggest decision in my life is where to go on a Saturday night. And then when I do go there, the women here are so harsh and uninterested. And I haven't had a date in weeks."

"A place where you are not the center of attention with all the beautiful girls? Obviously America is hell," I smiled.

"It is worse than that," Paul said conspiratorially. "Everything is so sterile and controlled and predictable and politically correct. I can't even try to pick girls up without getting into trouble."

"So the days of just flashing the US passport to get a girl's attention are over I guess. I feel for you, I really do," I said with a voice that reflected exactly the opposite, relishing his pain in the American dating scene.

Paul grumbled that I would understand soon enough. America was not the promised land. It was a place of rules and procedures and any vestige of personality or interesting variable would be sued out of existence. On a whim and with a handful of money you just could not hire a tank or get a lift on a passing boat.

Yes, true, I replied. But I responded that he probably did not have irate subcontractors hiring people to scare him into believing that his knee caps might be shattered. What was boring to Paul sounded like bliss to me. I was done with the suspense of what might happen next. I wanted to be able to take a taxi home rather than take my chances hitchhiking. I wanted to be able to leave my house with the television plugged in and not worry that it might explode. I needed predictability and calm and lower levels of stress in my life.

I moved the discussion with Paul on to the real business of the day – project closure documentation. So far we had sorted out the project completion certificates, scope of work for Flis, final payments to Flis, transfer of equipment, canceling our office lease, and redundancy notices for the staff. Only a few items remained unresolved – like what we were supposed to do with all the office furniture that our project had acquired. No one could remember exactly how the dozen or so giant industrial metal desks and oversized bookshelves had been acquired and I was asking Paul to investigate whether it was documented in any project records back in Washington, DC.

Paul confirmed exactly what I wanted to hear – there was no record of any office furniture acquisition for the project. No one exactly knew where the furniture had come from.

"And now no one needed to know where it was going," Paul whispered with barely restrained excitement. He clung to the activities in St Petersburg as a lifeline to a previous existence where daily life provided a much-needed dose of adrenaline.

The desks and furniture of our project office were far superior to the standard issue semi-demolished Salvation Army rejects that inhabited most Russian offices. Brian and I quickly agreed that they would make nice parting gifts for our Russian team. They would undoubtedly be able to resell the furniture for extra pocket cash. Each of our Russian staff was given rights to the desk and chair that they sat at – then we held a lottery for the furniture used by the Americans and the common-use bookshelves.

Within hours of the furniture lottery, the Russians had fully mobilized with their plans to remove the furniture and sell it on the open market. Sergei, ever the resourceful driver, obtained use of a truck for the day. The team sprung into a communal activity of removing the furniture from the office at lightning speed – perhaps to ensure that the furniture was well and truly off the premises before the Americans had a chance to change our minds.

Sergei laughed as he picked up one end of a desk and worked his way through the narrow doorframe.

"See Brian and Phaedra. This project is successful after all. We are privatizing. Isn't that what you wanted to do? Privatize the property here in St Petersburg,"

I opened my mouth to correct him about the true definition of privatization. But then I closed it. This was privatizing in the mind of Sergei. And he was happy. I was done arguing and was just going to go along with what made people happy.

"Privatizing" the office furniture definitely lightened the mood during days when we were helping the team cope with their imminent redundancy. Per Russian labor law we were supposed to pay out a substantial sum of money to every employee that we let go. But of course this would have been disallowed by USAID as unrelated to the project. Once again we had put ourselves in a position of breaking one set of rules in order to comply with other rules. The USAID project required us to have a certain percentage of the team as Russians. The role by definition was temporary, yet there was no way legally to contract Russians for two years. Therefore we were forced to violate the rules somewhere. For the most part, the Russians in our office just shrugged it off. They had expected this would happen at the close of the project. We wrote glowing letters of recommendation for all the team and were thrilled when Natasha and Olga were picked up by the local growing office of Nokia. They had a promising future and were an inspiration to others.

Ludmilla, as always, was the black cloud darkening the mood. She protested loudly that she had been hired by the firm as a permanent employee and was due an ongoing full time role. Of course Patrick was outraged when I raised the issue to his attention. With frustration he declared that this was the sort of thing that I needed to handle myself in St Petersburg and he did not want to be bothered with the details.

Ludmilla raised her cause to her close friend Larissa in the city government. Larissa called me directly to let her know that she was not pleased. The project was now officially closed. Officially, of course, she had no stake in this. But of course things are always more complex than that. Larissa let us know that there would be consequences if we did not honor Ludmilla' s contract.

A wave of panic hit me. A threat again. I did not need more threats. I needed a way out. The pleasant waves of peacefulness that had been washing over me ever since the signing of the completion papers were rudely replaced by fears once again of my kneecaps being crushed under the hands of Big Boris.

Brian and I once again retreated to the café of the Hotel Evropa to attempt to devise an exit strategy – while reviewing the employment contract in question. We wanted to attempt to do the right thing legally – one more set of rules being ignored by the Americans would drive a further wedge between our ideals and what we were actually doing. We wanted to follow the Russian legal framework – even though we easily could have just walked out of the office and jumped on a train, never to return again. That being said, we did not owe any favors to either Ludmilla or to Patrick at this point.

How to follow Russian labor law, but not go out of our way to help either of them? Brian was the one who discovered the exit strategy. It was so simple really. The company name on the employment contract was Arthur Andersen's legally registered office in St Petersburg. The *real* office of the consultancy, where real accountants and tax advisors and management consultants worked with American and Russian companies – not just on temporary aid projects. Better yet, the signatory on the contract was Patrick himself – who probably did not have signature authority on behalf of the St Petersburg office. But none of that was our concern. All we would have to do would be to redirect Ludmilla over to the consultancy's St Petersburg office, holding her employment contract and give her the details of the local HR director. It would then become the problem of the local office what to do with her – and Patrick would be the one to take the fallout from any consequences. Our names were nowhere associated with any piece of Ludmilla' s employment contract and all we were doing was following local law.

Who could fault us for that?

I smiled. I too could play the game of vodka diplomacy.

With the resolution of Ludmilla' s employment contract, Brian and I had the final pieces in place to close our project in St Petersburg and close the door behind us – but then what? The notable outstanding question was what would become of Brian and me?

By USAID's and Arthur Andersen's objective standards we had closed the project successfully. On time, on budget, with satisfied clients and documents validating that the goals of the project were achieved. Brian had been promised a role with the Moscow office and I had been promised a transfer back to Washington DC. Nothing in writing, however. And in the end we knew that nothing would matter except the written word.

Then the written word did come – by email.

Brian received his first. Patrick was very sorry but the strategy of the Moscow office had changed. They had explored all options but unfortunately there would be no opportunity to place Brian in a permanent role with the Moscow office. His employment contract would therefore be terminated in two weeks' time.

A few phone calls to close contacts in the Moscow office quickly confirmed what we suspected. Patrick had not even reached out to the senior partners to explore the possibility of placing Brian in their office. Of course, our inquiries were off the record and no one was willing to stand up to support out allegation back to Patrick that he had not even lifted one finger to place a phone call to Moscow. Brian attempted to call bullshit and called Patrick to protest. Predictably he received an earful of hollow compliments for how he helped bring the project to successful completion and vacuous apologies that the strategic direction of the firm was not able to support bringing on board another manager at this time. Brian started to protest, became incensed and was on the verge of hostility when abruptly he stopped – breathed deeply, hanging up the phone on Patrick mid-sentence. He picked up his coat and walked out the door into the late afternoon. Undoubtedly in search of a vodka somewhere far from the Hotel Evropa.

I was up next. I had been promised repatriation to Washington DC once the project was over. A reasonable request – and one with plenty of precedent. (Starting with the fact that my employment contract and W-2 forms stated my home office as Washington DC.) I had lost track of the number of consultants who had rotated in and out of the projects in Russia, but to date all had been repatriated back to Washington DC once their tour of duty was over.

The catch in my case, I soon discovered, was that my tour of duty was not yet over.

The email from Patrick held all the right phrases – congratulating me on the successful completion of the project. On time, on budget with satisfied clients. The clients (USAID and the Russian Privatization Center) were so pleased in fact that our consultancy had been awarded a follow on project to do the same real estate title registration project – this time in the southern Urals region – based in Chelyabinsk.

I read onwards. The project would be six months long. Given the fact that we had already established a basic methodology and system in St Petersburg (a two year project) the logic was that I should be able to deploy to three cities in one quarter the time of the original project. Three times the scope, one quarter the time and budget. Given the limited time and budget, there would be no allowance for me to keep my Moscow apartment and no reason for me to return to Moscow for the duration of the project. I would be based in Chelyabinsk until the project was completed. My reward for a job well done – a one way ticket to Siberia. Quite literally.

I called Patrick to protest. His response, predictably, contained all the correct phrases. The job had been completed successfully. It was a compliment that the client wanted a follow up project. Of course, we had established a repeatable methodology, process and system – that was all in the project goals for the St Petersburg project. Didn't I just get that signed off successfully? Was I suggesting (gasp) that perhaps we *didn't* have a reusable methodology? The client had requested that I lead this project. It was just for six months. After *that* I would then be repatriated back to the United States.

Couldn't someone else do the project in Chelyabinsk? I protested.

Alas no. My skills were too valuable. I spoke Russian fluently, was recommended by USAID and the RPC and already had established relationships in Chelyabinsk through the project I had implemented the previous year.

"In consulting, you have to go where the clients send you," said Patrick with just a bit too much condescension. "If you aren't client-oriented enough to undertake a six month project that has been requested by your client, then perhaps you shouldn't be in consulting."

Patrick had me in checkmate and he knew it. As difficult as the project was in St Petersburg, the one in Chelyabinsk would be virtually impossible. With a fraction of the budget, time and far away from the supportive company of the expatriate community. Plus now we had written documentation stating that the original pilot was completed successfully, so obviously we must have established processes and systems that could readily be deployed in Chelyabinsk.

A little over two years earlier I had jumped onto a plane to Uralsk, Kazakhstan with the enthusiasm of the young and naïve. Two years can age a person and make one bitter, hostile, and intolerant. I had done my time in Siberia. I was done arguing. I just wanted out.

I knew immediately that I would never board that one way flight to Chelyabinsk. Where once I had a sense of adventure and belief I was doing something *meaningful,* now was only dread and emptiness. I was done with expatriate life in Russia. And if

Arthur Andersen was not going to return me to the United States, then the answer was obvious — I would have to take matters into my own hands and resign.

I made a decision. I set a date. I set the engine in motion for my exit. And suddenly the world was a much brighter, happier, optimistic place.

The days snapped by in an impressionistic collage. The dull grey of Moscow buildings, clothing, sky — all were swept away by a vibrant kaleidoscope of color and sound and motion. The sky was blue. Women laughed and wore bold colors. Fresh fruit appeared in baskets for sale at the metro stations. In the wasteland of the empty lot near my apartment block, a brave single flower attempted to bloom. The white nights lifted the city's spirits.

Farewells with the team in the Moscow office were teary but joyful. Champagne flowed freely as Nadya announced that she had been accepted to an American MBA program. Nastya received an offer for a more senior role from a top tier financial institution. Oksana confided with excitement that Robert wanted to take her with him back to the United States. And Tatiana, who had never used a computer before she had joined our team, was brimming with confidence and enthusiasm as her responsibilities expanded in the wake of the others moving on. My dear housekeeper, Valya, marveled at the ingenuity of the Tupperware that I left with her as a parting gift.

The joy and optimism of the women near to me was infectious. The hollow void occupied by the paper accomplishments of my project was now overflowing with satisfaction that, despite everything, yes we had made a positive difference in at least a few people's lives.

Change was in the air. Bright bold colorful change. Energetic change. Democratic change. Colorful illustrations on McDonald's placements educated Moscow about process to expect at the amazing new concept of a "drive through restaurant". The bright green and yellow shield of BP drew attention to the first *modern* gas station in the city, complete with shiny new pumps and a canopy to protect patrons from the weather.

The Xram Xrista Spasitelya, which had still been an unfulfilled promise at the time Sarah left Moscow, now opened its magnificent doors. The gleaming white and gold cathedral boldly proclaimed that a new era of Russian Renaissance had begun. Color erupted along the Old Arbat as brick walls gave way to shop windows filled with handbags and jewelry and enticing pastries. A giant hole opened up in the ground within sight of the Kremlin with the rumor that it would soon be filled by a high end luxury shopping center. As if to punctuate all this energy and renewal, at the epicenter of Red Square, the mature woman who had gazed calmly at Lenin's Tomb from Estee Lauder's window at GUM in 1994 had quietly left and in her place was Elizabeth Hurley bursting with youth and vitality.

The energy of optimism built towards a crescendo with the Independence Day celebrations – marking the anniversary of Russia declaring its independence from the Soviet Union. The first post-Soviet elections were only days away. *Babushkas* were walking arm in arm, singing, and smiling and chanting simply *"Yeltsin – Da!"* My friend, Sally, and I had started the day with plans for a general stroll through the center of the city, but now found ourselves swept along with the celebration. We were embraced spontaneously by a passing *babushka*, handed Russian flags, and flowed with the bubbling current down Tverskaya towards the beating heart of the city – Red Square. Sally was a good friend from my graduate school days in Washington DC and had recently arrived in Moscow to start her own tour of duty, just as mine was ending. The symbolism of the moment was not lost on either of us. Out with the old. In with the new. Fresh young energy to take this country to the next point in its history.

The toothless *babushkas* marched and laughed and waved their banners. Then a shout and shriek – a cavalcade of young rollerbladers swept by. European haircuts. Stylish clothing. Rollerblades! I had never seen anyone rollerblading in Moscow before (for starters, how was it possible on the horror of the Moscow asphalt?) – and now we were surrounded by a hundred or so healthy Russian college-age kids – gliding by and flying a Russian flag in their wake. The crowds surged forwards towards Red Square. Towards the epicenter of Russia's past, present, and future.

Two years earlier I had been at Red Square to witness the return of the last of the Russian troops from Eastern Europe. The event had been a throwback to the days of goose-stepping troops and thundering tanks. Giant banners had proclaimed that the troops were heroes leading the country into the future. But the mood was reserved and withdrawn and clearly the door was simply closing on a final chapter of the past.

Today the mood was nothing short of exaltation of the promise of the future. Strangers greeted each other with smiles (rare in Russia, needless to say Red Square). Friends walked arm in arm. People spontaneously sang Russian folk songs and led cheers into the crowd. *"Yeltsin – Da!"* The crowd surged forward through Red Square towards the embankment – where Yeltsin would be speaking later. (No one yet knew he also would be dancing!) The energy was more like a build up to a rock concert than a series of election speeches by a presidential candidate. Sally and I smiled and walked arm in arm and made our best effort to sing along to the Russian folk songs and spontaneous cheers in the crowd.

This was what I had been fighting for. Positive energy from the crowd radiated optimism. The darkest days are behind us and now we are moving forward. Together we are working towards making Russia a better place. Maybe Adrian was right. Maybe I was too harsh on Russia. Perhaps six months in Siberia would be a wonderful experience and I could help lift Chelyabinsk and the South Urals into a new world of capital ownership – where homeowners could mortgage their apartments to have cash to start their own businesses. The future was bright. Anything was possible. I laughed as a stranger spontaneously kissed me on the cheek and congratulated me – in the abstract way that Russians congratulate each other on holidays.

And then suddenly we were stopped.

The OMON. A human wall of black battle ready anti-terrorist special forces. Heavily armed. Dressed for combat – helmets with visors down, steel tipped boots, bullet proof vests, heavy gloves, clubs and guns at their sides. They stood shoulder to shoulder, arms locked – forming an impenetrable human wall and blocking our progress from Red Square to the embankment. Their motto is "We know no mercy and ask for none" and everyone knows it. Even if you didn't know their actual motto – one look at the immovable human wall would give you a pretty good idea of their mission. The Russians near us instinctively pulled back at the sight of the OMON, thrusting Sally and I into the front of the fray. We were pressed against the men's chests. They were heavily armed, hostile, and we had no idea what their objectives were.

Just on the other side of the OMON was a parallel surge of the crowd. I glimpsed over the shoulders of the OMON to see faces of *babushkas* trying to get from the Embankment to Red Square. None shall pass. The reason, however, was not clear. A black gash through the center of the celebration.

The joyous cheers of the crowds were muffled and a glaze of panic crossed the faces of the civilians near me. The Russian civilians tried to scramble back away from the OMON. These were the violent ruthless special forces of the government. Who exactly controlled them was never clear. Maybe they would be friendly to the Yeltsin supporters. Maybe they were here at the bidding of Zhirinovsky and his allies – to put an end to the Yeltsin era. Anything was possible.

Sally was still new enough to Moscow not to have the instinct to pull back from the OMON. She looked through the human wall and saw the surge of pro-Yeltsin supporters on the far side – trying to cross the barrier to our side. No obvious reason why we were prevented from going south and they were prevented from going north.

"Why can't we cross through to the other side?" Sally innocently asked the OMON nearest her. Her words were in Russian but her understanding of the situation was not. The civilians near me recoiled in anticipation of a conflict.

"You cannot pass," was the response. Not an answer really, but just a statement of the obvious.

"But why?" Sally protested. Her questions fell on deaf ears. No one ever asked "why" to the OMON. They just cooperated.

A hostile glare in our direction. The OMON were locked arm in arm to defend their line. Despite this a few hands reached for their billy clubs. Would they break ranks to keep the inquisitive American in her place? I took Sally by the hand – we had to keep moving.

Sally looked back over her shoulder.

"I don't understand..." her voice trailed off.

"This is Russia," I answered simply. "I can't explain what they are doing. I just know that there will be another way through. There is always another way."

The surging crowd pinned us against the human wall of the OMON. I pulled Sally to the left, down the Embankment towards the Moscow River. We struggled to stay together as the crowd became agitated, nervous, trapped against the OMON.

And then suddenly the human wall ended. We had to stop and take in the scene. The final man in the chain gritted his teeth and locked his arms with the man on his left. His stance was braced against the crowds surging around him – going *around* the human wall. A more pointless display of aggression could not be imagined.

I saw the end of the human wall and saw the opportunity to get around to the other side – towards the stage where politicians were droning on and Yeltsin would soon appear. Sally paused and looked at the final link in the chain.

"But..." she was attempting to find reason in the moment, and took a step forward to talk to the OMON.

"No, Sally, don't talk to him," I nearly shrieked in English. "We can get through to the other side. That is all that matters right now."

"But I don't understand," the rational American was having a difficult time processing this very typical Russian scene. She was very much in the first stage of the expatriate experience – attempting to process what she saw around her and classify it in a standard American framework. I had definitely moved on.

I gestured back towards the OMON behind us. "That is an executive summary of why I have to get out of this place. Rules for the sake of rules. What they are doing makes no rational sense whatsoever – but everyone involved cooperates and pretends that it has a purpose. In the end people just do what they want anyway. Just going around the blockade and do your own thing. You may be beaten into submission for asking questions. The OMON management will probably be congratulated for a successful day out here. Doing what? Absolutely nothing useful whatsoever. But on paper their mission will be accomplished." I paused from my rant and then concluded the obvious: "I have to get out of Russia!"

I struggled back to my apartment block at the end of the day. Emotionally drained from the highs of chanting and singing with the pro-democracy *babushkas* and then plunged to the low heart stopping moment with the OMON. Once again I was focused on the vision of the bottle of vodka that was safely tucked in the freezer of my apartment. A bit of liquid fire to take the edge off the turmoil of the day, steady the nerves a bit, and let me slip quietly into the evening.

And then – what. The front door to my apartment block was locked. Locked!

But how. Earlier that day there wasn't even a lock on the front door to the building. I looked again and laughed. Yes, there really was a lock on the front door – complete with a keypad and an intercom. All nice and modern and fully operational.

I had totally forgotten about the *babushki* who had collected money from me months ago and their plan to install a building security system. They had actually done it! They had delivered a modern security system, complete with all the wonderful features of locks, an intercom and a personal security code to get in the front door. And I was on the outside of the building looking in.

I sat on the front step of my building and broke down in hysterical laughter mixed with tears. The *babushki* had a rational plan. A business case. A budget. They delivered as promised and it would benefit everyone in the building. The OMON had their project as well – which made no sense to the rational observer. But undoubtedly they would also be congratulated at the end of the day for completing their project. Whether the goals of the project made sense or not was not actually part of the question. The *babushki* were part of the grey market in Moscow in the mid-1990s. They had no legal body. They exerted influence and got results. The documentation would show that the OMON's project was completed successfully. A crackdown on black market activities would strive to eradicate the efforts of the *babushki*. Russia was moving forward – towards what.

After a few minutes another resident of the building returned home. Someone I had never met before. I was leaning against the wall of the building shaking with something between laughter and crying at the scene. He shrugged and decided I was harmless and let me in the building.

For every rule there is always a way around the rule. We have no laws, therefore no laws have been broken.

29 ANYTHING TO DECLARE?

17 June 1996

The date is significant because the country's first real election for president had taken place the day before. And significant for me because I was leaving Russia this day – officially ending my tour of duty. Russia was starting a new chapter of its history and, in a symbolic parallel, so was I.

"Russia will not let go of you lightly," my expatriate friends had warned – both those still in the country and the few who had remained in touch after their departure. The warning was directed at both Russia's psychological hold as well as physical.

I knew that leaving the country would not be just a matter of buying a plane ticket, summoning a taxi, and waving farewell. Everything always was more complex than would be expected in a rational world. But to the Russians everything made sense. I was the one questioning my own sanity.

Why were my knuckles white, clutched possessively around the handle of my cat carrier. Why was I sitting on the cold concrete floor in a shadowy corner of Sheremyetovo airport shaking and avoiding eye contact with everyone. The Russians in my office would have scolded me that sitting on a concrete floor causes infertility. I smiled at the thought and then was pained that I would not ever actually hear that scolding from them.

The remnants of a vodka tonic sat on the floor beside me. I wasn't quite native enough to order a straight shot to calm the nerves. The tonic, however, was just window dressing to say that I had not yet lost my sanity. It was 10 am and I had just cashed in my last handful of rubles at the bar. The bar at Sheremyetovo inside passport control and customs. This represented the final test of whether you really understood the system here before you would be released. Passport control had a very sternly worded sign "no rubles beyond this point". And then just a few steps beyond the airport bar, which served cold vodka in chipped semi-washed glasses, only accepted rubles. A cruel joke and consistent with Russia's approach to the end. The rules are deliberately set up to conflict. At any time anyone could be found to be in violation of the rules – therefore an enemy of the state, at the whim of the state. Actually "the state" made it sound all too organized and following some sort of formal rules. More accurate would be "at the whim of someone who had a bit of authority to inflict a personal vendetta".

I had been through Sheremyetovo enough times to know the drill – save a handful of rubles for use at the bar before the flight. Calm some frayed nerves. Plus gain the bitter satisfaction of seeing others who were not so savvy be baffled that their dollars or Deutsch Marks are not accepted.

Then again, at 10am only the locals and the war-weary expatriates are queued up at the bar. The casual visitors are appropriately shocked to see me staring vacantly, muttering to myself, muttering to my cat, and examining my glass to see if there are any friendly drops left at the bottom.

Then, unexpectedly, a familiar faces in the waiting area. Laughing, clean cut, with fresh clothing and perfect hair. Yes this was out of place, but I knew them so I would have to get up and say hello. I struggled to my feet but then realized – wait – they are Tom Brokaw and Dan Rather. Of course I recognized them – as did every other American in the holding pen. But they were not my kind. They were invaders from a different universe. Here in Moscow. Oh yes. They must have been here to cover the presidential election. So did they fly in three days ago? Two days ago? Did they have a few deep and meaningful interviews and then somehow be bestowed with the authority to pass judgment and share their thoughts on Russia with the universe? And now they were on their way back to New York for their next engagement – covering…. I could not even think of what they would possibly be discussing the next day, smiling into the camera with their perfect teeth and perfect skin. The Russian election would be over and no longer of interest. Less than 24 hours after the last ballot and they were already here at Sheremyetovo.

What had Tom Brokaw and Dan Rather shared with the rest of the world? Were they focused on stories of corruption – urging the new leadership to "do something about it"? Or did they offer stories of hope and optimism – USAID projects that transferred skills to Russian companies and modernized the systems and processes of the Russian government. Did they understand that just underneath the veneer of the press releases, the two stories were really one and the same? Sergei Glebovich had engaged fully in the stated objectives of the project in Ekaterinburg. He had offered an opportunity for businesses and individuals to advance themselves – without currying favor from those in positions of influence. As his efforts gained momentum, allegations of corruption were raised and he was removed. Officially, of course, there was no relationship between the two parts to Sergei Glebovich's story, but those paying attention could draw their own conclusions.

What, I wondered, would become of Yuri Mikhailovich in St Petersburg?

Tom Brokaw placed one perfectly polished cowboy boot casually on the plastic broken thing that was called seating in the waiting area. He rested an elbow on his knee and leaned forward engaged in friendly conversation with his network rival. Crisp white shirt – freshly pressed at some five star hotel no doubt. Freshly laundered blue jeans and polished boots. Nope. He was definitely not from around here. And he did not talk to anyone except his peer. Laughing again, sharing some casual joke, no doubt.

Did they see the bar here at Sheremyetovo and really understand its significance? The last point before release into the western world. The last obstacle to be overcome – bring your rubles, but no, you aren't allowed to have rubles. The rules are contradictory. There are no rules. There are rules everywhere and it is at the discretion of those in influence what will be enforced when. There were other expats like me in the waiting area, staring vacantly, holding half-empty drinks. Hair sticking out at strange angles. Our clothes ragged from years of acid rain and hostile office furniture. Another woman with a cat carrier in hand looked at me – gave me a battered half-smile of recognizing a kindred spirit before shuffling onwards.

Would Tom have possibly understood my last few days and put it in the context of his great hope for the future of Russia?

I held the cat carrier close, attempting to shield it from view of anyone with any degree of authority. Just because I had managed to get my dear kitty this far was no guarantee that I would be able to board the plane with her. Everything was a battle – including (surprisingly) the right to take my cat *out* of the country.

My friends had been right. Russia would not relinquish its grip lightly. The entire suspense was where the difficulty would be. I knew that the United States would require a health certificate for my cat upon arrival to JFK. I was given the name of a veterinarian and told to obtain the health certificate within 48 hours of traveling. By now I was experienced enough to know that it would not be a simple matter of walk in with cat and walk out with cat and health certificate, but I was in suspense regarding exactly what the catch would be.

Forty eight hours exactly before my flight I discovered the catch. The veterinarian advised me that before he could issue a health certificate he would have to be sure that my cat was free of rabies. To do so, he would have to inject something into my cat today, then we would come back in *three months* and he would perform a test to determine if my dear kitty was still healthy. Also I needed to have a certificate proving that she was not an exotic species prohibited from being exported from Russia.

I protested that this was all ridiculous. For starters, I had brought Nikko into the country with me. She was American. I had the paperwork to prove it. She was not some endangered exotic Russian species. I was just returning her home. Second, she was current with her rabies vaccines – therefore can't we just assume that she does not have rabies?

Logic, of course, was not part of the procedure. I did not have the necessary Russian documents, therefore I would not receive the health certificate. And of course my major lesson of all this time in Russia and Kazakhstan was that "no" is just an opinion. For every "no" there is always an alternative. I just had to figure out the solution.

I offered an "administrative surcharge" to cover the fact that I did not have the necessary supporting paperwork. The veterinarian was shocked and shrieked that he was an upstanding member of the medical profession and under no condition would be accepting bribes.

So one option down. What else? Then I realized the obvious answer: documentation. Everything is about documentation. The Americans wanted a health certificate. This veterinarian was distressed that I did not have rabies clearance and an exotic species exemption. So I just asked the veterinarian to add an asterisk to the health certificate and write a notation on the reverse identifying his complaint and his reservations. The whole thing was in Russian, of course. With the right stamp, certainly it would pass at JFK. In any case JFK would not care about the exotic species exemption or the rabies test. Document document document. And the documentation will set you free.

Two days later, after waiting for two and a half hours in the line at Sheremyetovo for airline check in and customs questions I was questioning my approach. What would Russian customs say if they looked at the kitty health certificate? A pair of New Russians arrogantly inserted themselves into the line in front of me without a backwards glance. Waiting in the long line was for the little people. They were the new elite and belonged at the front of the line. An American behind me protested (in English) that they were not following the rules. Rules? What rules? In Russia we have no rules, only suggestions. Didn't I learn that on my first day in Moscow a lifetime ago? The American behind me looked with despair at the backs of the New Russians. He sputtered that it was not right that they cut in line. I did not say anything but just found myself looking at him blankly. He had so much to learn. Was he a newly arrived long term expat, just out for a bit of shore-leave? Or was he based in the USA, just over to Moscow for a short visit? In any case, he had much to learn. Fairness and rules did not matter here. Arrogance and determination did.

I did not talk to him. I did not talk to anyone. I was focused on my one objective of getting through customs. Any other conversation would be a potential distraction and a potential threat to my end objective.

The crowds pushed in and I was shoved against the back of the *devushka*. She gave me an icy glare that said she would scratch my eyes out given half a chance. It was now their turn in line. The couple laid out their bags on the counter for check in. The potato fed *babushka* working the counter reached for the woman's handbag and began to unzip it. The man swiftly reached down and clasped the *babushka's* wrist and said "there is no need to examine her bag."

The customs clerk was not flustered, but calmly rezipped the bag and returned it to the owner. She then asked "do you have anything to declare?"

"Thirty thousand dollars American," the man said evenly.

This declaration had no obvious effect on the customs clerk. She did not pause or flinch. Just another standard day of people passing through her booth carrying a bag full of more cash than she would probably earn in a lifetime. She waved them on and turned her gaze to me. Her eyes narrowed and she stood up more rigidly as she recognized the face of an American. The last couple had breezed through due to an unspoken understanding that her life would be miserable otherwise. Now it was her opportunity to regain her authority.

This clerk in front of me was now assuming the posture that said that she would not tolerate any unusual paperwork. I reached for my passport and was thankful of the years of experience with Russian government officials. Nothing would stop me now. I felt a wave of self-assurance protect me from the clerk's expanding black aura.

The day I arrived in Moscow, two years earlier, I had watched an American businessman cheerfully jog up to Russian passport control and hurdle the barrier into the arms of certain arrest. He had understood the Russian way well enough to assess his options and decide on the most expedient approach to enter the country. Whatever path he took he would be breaking the rules, so might as well go for the option that would likely get him through the process faster with less hassle. This memory inspired me to make the split second decision to smuggle my cat out of the country rather than declare her. I placed my carry on travel bag in front of the clerk and then expertly spilled all the contents onto the table in a "clumsy" effort to find my passport. Lipstick, books, comb, passport, spare socks all tumbled out of the bag onto the table in a pile of confusion. I scrambled to clean up the mess while deftly kicking the cat carrier from left to right below the table, circumventing customs for the kitty entirely.

The customs clerk looked at me with a stern glare of disapproval. A clumsy American. She took my passport and proceeded to slowly examine every page, pausing her finger on the various stamps that had accumulated.

My passport was in order. It was a close call, however, as the last time I entered the country, the passport clerk had initially not stamped my visa. I had forced my passport back at the clerk and insisted on the stamp. Everything is about the stamp. You must stamp my passport. She had shrugged and obliged with a bored air of indifference.

Today the clerk handed me back my passport and without a word waved me and my pile of stuff onwards. I swept everything along the table with my arm and rapidly collected the combs and socks and books into my carry-on bag. The American behind me handed the clerk his passport.

She looked at the passport for a moment before slapping the back of her hand on his visa page and crying out with indignation "You do not have an entry stamp on your visa. You have not entered the country legally."

The American clearly did not understand one word of Russian. He did grasp the fact that he was in trouble for something having to do with his passport. I smiled to myself for having my own passport in order. For having the foresight to have purchased a cat carrier that looked like a gym bag (with some breathing mesh on one end). For having the good sense of sliding my cat under the table rather than presenting the somewhat questionable exit certificate. For not having befriended this American who now definitely needed assistance. He was crying out, but I turned my back and moved away.

There was a point when I would have allied myself with this stranger as an act of camaraderie against the octopus that is the Russian way. But now I was in self-preservation mode. And I had barely enough energy left to fight my own battles.

Even the act of leaving my apartment for the last time and driving to the airport had been a struggle. As much as I relied on hitch-hiking as a standard form of transport, for going to the airport with all my worldly possessions I had organized for my dear driver, Vanya, to deliver me to the airport. He had been a faithful ally over the past years and I wanted him to be the one to deliver me to the airport for my final departure. Of course, I was certain that things would not go as per plan so of course I organized for pick up time to be 45 minutes before what was actually required. The designated time had come and passed and I called the office to track down the whereabouts of Vanya.

A quiet voice answered the phone. A new *devushka*, Anna, was working reception. Our previous receptionist had moved on to the booming banking sector and now a fresh recruit was manning the front desk.

"*Da, slushayu Vas*" — Yes, I'm listening. It was a sweet gentle voice, but the words reflected the old abrupt ways of the Russian government offices. The previous girl had been trained in the western way of doing business and was out hopefully helping to make Russia a better place. And now there was a new one at the starting blocks. I was about to launch into a coaching session for how she should answer the phone in a more professional manner, but then took a deep breath. Time to focus on the goal here. Must get to airport on time.

"Vanya was supposed to pick me up 15 minutes ago to go to the airport and he isn't here yet. Do you know if he is on his way?"

"I don't know," Anna answered after a pause.

"Can you see if Vanya is there?" I prompted her.

"Okay," she put down the phone and there was a pause of a few minutes. "No, Vanya is not here." No other information offered. No analysis of the problem.

"Do you know if he is on his way to pick me up?" I asked.

"I don't know," the girl answered.

"Could you see if Oleg or any of the other drivers can pick me up? Someone was supposed to pick me up 15 minutes ago."

"Okay," she put down the phone and there was a pause of a few minutes. "No. Oleg says that he is busy." No sense of urgency. No ability to problem solve. No alternate solutions.

I was about to launch into a set of questions – do you know who has reserved Oleg? Can I have Oleg instead and whoever has reserved Oleg can sort something else out? What about the other drivers? I did not want to hitchhike with all my luggage and cat.

Total silence on the other end of the line. Anna was awaiting the next request. This conversation was going to go nowhere fast. In the meantime I had a plane to catch.

"Thank you Anna. I have to go now."

"Okay, goodbye." The phone was hung up per my cue. She was probably sitting at the desk satisfied that she had answered every question correctly. In my time in Russia I had coached how many young women? Dozens? How many hundreds of thousands were there still out there totally oblivious to the basics of customer service. And Anna would have been one of the best ones in the latest rounds of interviews.

And so I left Moscow the same way that I entered it – hitchhiking. The moment I dropped the phone, I ran from my apartment block out to the Sadovoye Koltso and flagged down a rusty Lada. The grizzled driver was thrilled at the offer of $40 for helping to haul my luggage down from my flat and then driving me out to Sheremyetovo. He was courteous and friendly and optimistic about the future. And he coexisted in the same city as the veterinarian who insisted that my cat needed to be rabies free to leave the country and Anna, who would be sitting at her desk waiting for her next line of instructions.

The escape exercise from the point where I was drinking my vodka tonic on the floor of the waiting room to the point where I was happily settled in my aisle seat was mercifully painless. I was able to slip the cat onto the plane and under my seat without further incident and had prime real estate near where the flight attendants were stocking the bar. The prior year I had been on a Moscow to New York flight where the bar had been drunk dry by the Russians and American expats. Not an easy feat on a Boeing 767. On this flight I was pleased by my easy access to the alcohol and was planning to be semi-comatose in a matter of hours.

Then I noticed the girl sitting next to me – intensely reading each word of the laminated flight safety sheet, looking up every few words in her English to Russian dictionary. Clearly her first flight ever. Clearly her English was not very strong. And she was very alone.

In the course of a few minutes I learned that the girl's name was Anya. She was 16 years old and from a small village in the heart of Siberia. She was on her way to be a high school exchange student in Ohio for the next year. In the past week she had left Siberia for the first time and traveled by train to Moscow with an uncle. Anya was totally overwhelmed by the bright lights and big city of Moscow and couldn't stop talking about the beautiful women and extravagant shops and how many people and cars there were.

And now this sweet innocent girl was going to Ohio. She was so excited to meet me. The first American that she had ever met! And so great that I spoke Russian. But she paused and then continued her monologue in halting English. She had a real opportunity to practice speaking English with a real American! She was about to explode with excitement and nerves.

Young sweet innocent Siberian girl goes to Ohio as her first American experience. What would her next year be like? Imagine the adventure of daily activities. The adrenaline rush of an American freeway interchange. Feeding a parking meter. Seeing a fire truck rushing down the street with its sirens blaring. The overflowing shelves of a Midwest shopping mall. Even watching the baggage carousel in action at the Cleveland airport would be a new experience. Customer service.

Imagine the reverse. An American girl from the Midwest on her first trip to Russia. And of course I laughed. Yes, that was me just a few short years ago.

I looked at Anya and tried to peel away layers of cranky cynicism that had built up as a protective shell. How would she survive the experience of being plunged deep into the American Midwest – where surely no one around her would understand the context of her childhood in Siberia? She would be totally on her own to maintain her own sense of identity, reality, and balance in life.

Anya held a Russian edition of *Cosmopolitan* in her hands as a coveted prize and beamed with joy. She was having a big adventure now and was an international jet-setter. Anya pointed to photographs of glamorous women with matching luggage and supple gloves as evidence that America was the promised land. Everyone is beautiful and has such wonderful *things*.

Perhaps it was a bit evil, but I then pulled the Duty-Free Shopping catalogue out of the seat pocket and showed it to the Siberian girl. Her eyes grew wide as she looked at page after page of beautiful objects for sale. Necklaces and perfumes and chocolates. And all of it was available right here on this plane. Just to add to the sensory overload, I asked a flight attendant to show us one of the necklaces. Not that either Anya or I could afford it. The girl fell silent in reverent awe as the box was opened in front of her, exposing gleaming pearls on a black velvet lining. Imagine what her friends would say back home. Here she was sitting on a plane and shopping and looking at pearl necklaces!

Having exhausted the Duty-Free Shopping catalogue, Anya next turned to the Sky Mall catalogue. Now this would be an interesting first exposure to real American excess. The bright eager expression soon changed to a perplexed furrowed brow as she inspected advertisements for automated pet feeders with programmable timers. Heated pet beds – in a variety of fabrics and sizes. Page after page of massage therapy devices for back, for neck, for feet. Resistance weights for use in the pool. Different sets of weights for use in a home gym. Weights to fill with water for use when traveling. Garden gnomes.

"I do not understand," she said slowly and correctly in English. "Do people need such things?"

I could barely restrain my laughter in appreciation of the moment. On my arrival to Moscow exactly two years earlier, an American businessman had given me the sage saying "In Russia there are no rules – only suggestions." This became a core theme of my entire Russian experience. Here, on my departing flight, this Siberian girl was having her own first glimpse into her future life in America and establishing her own personal theme for the next year in the American Midwest.

Good luck, Anya. You will need it!

"Do people need such things?" The question echoed as I took my first steps to establish a new life back in San Francisco.

A walk to the local grocery store. Per the advice of friends who had returned to the US before me, I had brought a short shopping list and I intended on sticking to it. "Keep focus. Don't get distracted by the bright lights and variety of salad dressings," they had advised me. Bananas. Milk. Breakfast cereal. The bananas were easy and I had them ticked off the list in a matter of moments. Milk was more complex. Whole milk. Fat Free milk. Vitamin D added. Soy milk. Different dairies. Calcium added. Fine – I'll take the fat free with extra minerals.

Everything became far more complex in the breakfast cereal aisle. Boxes lined approximately 100m of shelf space. All different colors, pictures, sizes. Smiling cartoons. Stern advice about fiber and fat. On what basis could I possibly make a decision? I then did the unthinkable – I started reading the ingredients and nutrition labels on every box of cereal. Starting on one end and working my way methodically down the shelf. Toasted. Roasted. Puffed. Dried. Wheat. Corn. Oats. Rice. Walnut. Almond. Assorted nuts. Granola. Baked. Natural. Raw. Cinnamon. Chocolate. Strawberry. Blueberry. Apricot. Sugar-crunch. Sugar-free. Naturally sweetened. Honey-drizzled.

My head was spinning and I was only about 1/10 of the way down the aisle. My vision blurred and the unfamiliar sterile smell of cleaning fluids overwhelmed my senses. I was used to scavenging and then being delighted when I found something that came close to meeting my needs. Where was the thrill of the hunt – to find boxes of 100% pure orange juice labeled in German sold next to car batteries at a temporary table near the Metro station? Then the pride with which we would share our discovery with our friends. The struggle. The raw struggle for daily existence – to find food to feed my cat. To find something to eat in Tyumen other than boiled eggs and tea. All of that was behind me now.

Here – 200 types of breakfast cereal – the challenge was completely different. How to make a rational choice when supply and variety was plentiful. This was the beauty of the American system. Everything and anything was available.

The store was part of a larger American supermarket chain. They would have existing relationships with reliable suppliers. The goods on the shelf were the results of planned orders and deliveries, not just what was able to be bribed to pass through customs this week. Order processes and suppliers who were happy to provide anything – knowing that payment would be swift and a satisfied client would return for more.

I took a deep breath and closed my eyes to appreciate the raw benefits of the American system. The shop keeper would not have his passport and several thousand dollars on him at all times – just in case someone with the right connections wanted a piece of his business and showed up unannounced with either a baseball bat aimed at the shopkeeper's kneecaps or an arrest warrant and the backing of the city. The clerks smiled and said "Have a nice day". If you liked the shop you would come back. If not – there were other places to go. I am buying groceries – the shopkeeper gets my money, I get my groceries. Both can go away happy. Such a far cry from the Russian system where every necessity became a holy crusade to locate, capture, and bring home to the safety of my lair. The struggle for existence was over. I could buy my groceries and go home. And have confidence that this store would be here tomorrow if I wanted to return.

I was drifting into a pleasant warm calm state with all my senses blending into a general comforting collage. The hum of the industrial refrigerator housing an astonishing selection of fresh cheeses sourced from Australia, Denmark, Italy, and of course the United States. The clickety clack of shopping carts being pushed purposefully up and down aisles. A faint aroma of fresh bread broke through the overwhelming scent of cleaning fluids. Children called out to their mothers. Children – in public! When was the last time I saw that? A kaleidoscope of color and forms slowly turned in a pleasant blur.

An irate female voice broke through the gentle hum.

"I cannot believe this place," she said with unrestrained hostility. "Look, is this all that they have for Swiss muesli cereal? How totally lame."

My eyes slowly came into focus to find two college age girls staring at the breakfast cereal shelves with obvious disdain. Their hair was carefully styled to give the appearance of casualness. Their immaculate shoes clearly indicated that these were women who drove everywhere rather than walked.

Her friend picked up a cereal box, read the label, then added her own complaint in support. "Ugh. Look at how much fat is in this. Who would eat this crap?"

The first girl put a manicured hand in the pocket of her supple lambskin leather coat and pulled out her car keys. "Come on. This place sucks. Let's get out of here."

The second woman quickly stuffed the cereal box back on the shelf in agreement and the two girls marched away, and out of the store.

I stared after them in total amazement. Did they have any idea of how extraordinary their lives were compared to their Russian counterparts? Did they have any awareness about the vast engine of the American system that meant that as college age girls they could buy leather coats, stylish shoes, and a car? They didn't like the selection (of 200+ cereals) at this grocery store and now could just walk outside, and find their car in the parking lot, drive down the street and take a look at the selection at a different store. A parking lot! Where lines were painted and drivers parked their cars in a civilized manner. They probably had drivers' licenses – which were obtained by completing a test, paying a fee, and obtaining a license – rather than the years of bribery and extortion required in Moscow to obtain a license. But no, they were not aware of any of this. They would just critique the absence of their favorite brand of Swiss muesli and note that this grocery store obviously sucks.

I paid for my groceries and stumbled out of the store into the foreign land that was San Francisco. Clean air blowing in from the ocean. I breathed deeply and enjoyed the faint tang of salt in the crisp wind. The fog was starting to roll in and droplets of moisture clung to my coat. The misty air was fresh and invigorating – not like the Moscow air which left a thick film of green slime on my desk each day (and who knows what else in my lungs).

I walked along the sidewalk back towards my apartment. I reached the first street corner and saw an approaching car on the cross street and paused. The car actually stopped at the neatly painted cross walk and waited patiently while I crossed the street. I looked uneasily at the driver, convinced that he may decide to lunge at me after all. But no, cars are supposed to wait for pedestrians and he actually waited for me to cross. A manhole cover. I walked around it out of habit, drawing a few peculiar glances from other passersby. The corner had a sloped grade from the street to the sidewalk to accommodate wheelchairs. The curb was neatly formed and a storm drain was poised ready for the next rain. Crosswalk. Manhole with cover intact. Wheelchair-accessible curb. Storm drain. I was on full mental alert and aware of every detail of my surroundings. The things Americans take for granted.

A crowd of 20-somethings sat on the pavement and milled around outside a taqueria, eating burritos, smoking, and drinking beer loosely hidden by brown paper bags. They all had carefully spiked hair, pierced noses, ears, tongues. Heavy mascara, leather collars and wristbands with little silver spikes. Torn jeans. The uniform of the American radical youth who must be different just like everyone else. "Fight the power!" Exactly who were they fighting and why? Were they vaguely aware that virtually any Kazakh kid would have given their right arm to be sitting here in San Francisco, eating a burrito on the street corner, with all the opportunities of the United States available – if they were to take the initiative. One of the kids rolled up the aluminum foil from his burrito and tossed it aside on the street beside him. A city garbage bin sat neglected just a few feet away.

An older Asian couple walked towards me arm in arm, smiling and quietly talking to each other. The man held the leash of a very happy, fluffy, and energetic Maltese terrier. I laughed to myself to notice that the man was wearing a t-shirt printed with a large blow up photo of the very same dog. Proclaim the love for your dog while walking him down the street! As I passed the couple I caught brief bits of their conversation – in Mandarin, I believe. An immigrant couple who were clearly appreciating and enjoying the positive aspects of the American way of life.

I reached the next intersection – where a red light of a little man stopped all the pedestrians in an orderly fashion. I overheard two women near me share their latest troubles. "So now the black tie event is next week and I *still* don't have decent shoes to go with the dress. The ones I bought last week at Nordstrom really make my legs look fat, so I am going to have to return them…(big sigh)" The red standing man switched to a green walking man and the two women stepped off the curb, engrossed in the analysis of their stressful lives. Unaware that the cars near them had stopped obediently. No ladies, the perfect pair of shoes is not the ticket to happiness.

Back at my apartment I decided to watch the evening news on television. I was clearly out of touch with America and needed to find some common ground with my compatriots if I were to re-integrate into society.

The lead story on the evening news was on a local Bay Area man who had just received a patent for an innovative bird feeder that he claimed was 100% squirrel-proof. Apparently squirrels raiding bird feeders was a serious problem and this man thankfully had found a solution. The man poured some tasty sunflower seeds into the hopper of the feeder. The footage then showed a daring squirrel climbing up the pole of the bird feeder, enticed by the fresh seed. The squirrel sniffed the tray where the seed was displayed, but as he shuffled his weight a little higher on the pole and reached the tray, a cover snapped shut – denying the little animal of his treat. The news correspondent congratulated the inventor on his cleverness and contribution to society. Reporting from Danville, this is Action 6 News.

Meanwhile, in the alternate reality of Russia, the Chechen rebels were launching a major offensive on the Russian stronghold in Grozny, killing hundreds of Russian soldiers, civilians and Chechen rebels. I, however, was blissfully unaware of this fact, as now the news program broke to commercials where a smiling woman advised me how to freshen the air in my bathroom. Just use this disposable device that plugs into any electrical outlet and *voila* – the device releases a pleasant scent. Lavender or rose or fresh sea breeze. Her children were happy and hugged her, delighted by their fresh-smelling bathroom.

I had known that entry into American society would be difficult for dear Anya, and worried about her somewhere in Ohio. I had been completely unprepared, however, for the fact that my own country could seem so foreign.

30   BORN IN THE USA

September 1996 – San Francisco, California, USA

Months later I sat in the reception area of one of the major management consultancies awaiting the signal that it was my turn for a job interview. I breathed deeply and rehearsed to myself the correct phrasing that I had planned to describe my accomplishments in Russia. Partnership with local stakeholders. Strategic projects to support development of the private sector. Management of issues to achieve program goals on time and on budget. It all sounded so grand and noble and easy really when stated in such simplistic terms.

My shoes were now polished. My suits that had been shredded by Soviet-era splintering office furniture had been retired and I was wearing a fresh crisp jacket with a skirt that had been altered to fit just right. My hair had been cut by an American stylist and was looking distinctly healthier – now that it was no longer exposed to the mineral cocktail that came out of the St Petersburg water pipes. I sat on a sharply tailored modern sofa that undoubtedly was cleaned nightly. A fresh bouquet of flowers sat on a coffee table together with an assortment of magazines. The receptionist smiled and asked if I would like a glass of water or some tea. The phone rang and she answered with a pleasant even demeanor and put one caller on hold while the next call came through. Then apologizing to the first caller for the inconvenience and "how can I help you?"

The receptionist was the only visible resident in the office. The rest of the population was obscured in a labyrinth of six-foot-high beige cubicles that extended and twisted out of sight. Dull hum of a printer or copier in the background. A man walked by purposefully carrying a notebook and a pen before disappearing into the soft fabric maze. Two women entered the office from the elevator lobby, laughing, and carrying steaming takeaway coffee cups and a paper bag of bagels. Fluorescent lighting gave a yellow even glow to the scene. Not too harsh not too dim, just an even standard tone to the surroundings.

Reflexively I reached for a magazine and opened it randomly. A women's health magazine. Travel tips for the busy modern executive woman. Don't let business travel negatively impact your healthy lifestyle! This is a trap that too many people fall into. Here are some tips to keep in mind with your next business trip:

1. Order the vegetarian option on the flight. This is generally the healthiest meal selection. Give the potatoes a miss, however.

2. Investigate your hotel options in advance and stay at the hotel with the best fitness center available. Don't let travel interfere with your fitness routine!

3. At the end of a stressful day, reward yourself with a massage. If your hotel does not have an in house masseuse, the concierge should be able to organize one for you.

4. Bring your favorite bath oils and unwind with a therapeutic hot bath.

5. Keep in close touch with friends and family. Do call home every day. Your emotional health is just as important as your physical health.

6. Business dinners are fraught with dining hazards. Just say no to that second glass of wine.

The article might as well have been written by space travelers describing an alien culture. It had no relationship to the reality of business travel that I knew. Would the author even have understood that in regional Russia there was no such thing as "choice" in hotels? Could the author comprehend that I was at the mercy of the local government officials to even obtain a reservation? In the end I would be happy to have hot water, a door that locked properly, and a manageable number of insects. A massage organized through the concierge would be a delusional fantasy.

And then the advice of "just say no" to the glass of wine. This is a business trip we are talking about, right? The tone of the entire relationship would be established, revealed and maintained over vodka diplomacy. If I just said no to the alcohol, then I would be essentially handicapping my ability to accomplish my goals.

I closed the magazine and stared blankly at the receptionist who now was sitting with professional poise at her desk and typing with expert efficiency.

Nervous energy turned me back to the table of magazines. I picked up a newspaper and flicked to the "international page". Something to help remind me that the world I just left still existed.

And then there it was. A headline over a small article tucked away in the international section: "St Petersburg mafia claims latest victim." The story was all too familiar. A prominent St Petersburg figure gunned down at a restaurant. But wait. This time the name was Yuri Mikhailovich. There it was in print. Yuri was dead. The article continued how mafia entanglements were suspected. There was a statement from the city that it mourned the loss of such a prominent civil servant and the city would be investigating the incident and taking a tougher stand against organized crime.

I felt physically ill as I re-read the article. Just simple words, but they condemned Yuri with every letter. He was "suspected to be entangled" with organized crime. The city would investigate. The reporter had obviously just simply taken the statement from the city and put it into print. Would it possibly occur to the reporter that perhaps the city was part of the problem, not the solution? I had no doubt that Yuri had continued his quest to attempt to loosen the city's bureaucratic grip. He had understood that true grass roots economic growth and prosperity required individuals to have control over their private property rather than curry favor with those in positions of influence.

When I last saw him, he had declared his intent to continue his struggle to weaken the all-encompassing control of the St Petersburg bureaucracy over individuals' lives. Who was it exactly that he had crossed? It could have been anyone. The article offered no clue. The statement from the city was incredibly vague – just quoting a generic "spokesman of the city administration." Yuri was now condemned for posterity with allegations of mafia connections, while the city would be praised for taking a firmer stand against organized crime. All very neat and logical according to the western press.

As a summary of our situation in St Petersburg, Sergei had said "the fish rots from the head." He had noted this in the context of the pressure from Vincent and Big Boris and I initially interpreted this to mean the rot was sourced from the next level up. But upon reflection I had realized that the "head" did not necessarily refer to a person, but more to the overall structure of our situation. Our project may be signed off. Vincent may go, but another would fill his place. As long as there are power and money in a central structure, there will be people striving to influence the use of this power and money. Yuri Mikhailovich understood this and had been a champion of individuals in their quest to gain control over their lives, reducing the favors required of those in power. His efforts had challenged those with power and influence. And now he was gone.

And here I was, sitting in an office of an American management consultancy, preparing to explain how I could be a valuable member of this team. And then I gasped, recalling violently the article in the *Moscow Times* my first weekend in Moscow – during the half time of the Moscow Mustangs vs Kiev Destroyers football game. A lifetime ago. What was the article again? An American manager of a major consultancy had been found shot dead in his own bathtub. What was our response? He must have deserved it. He should have known better than to get himself entangled with shady characters. Then what did we say next? Pass the beer. And the paper was discarded and the article forgotten. If we, living in Russia, had not understood the plight of this expat, then how could I possibly expect anyone here to understand what I had been through? What the whole of Russia was going through?

A few minutes later I was escorted to a large private office for the interview. The heavy door swung closed behind the retreating, smiling receptionist. An American man invited me to be seated in an armchair. He sat behind a massive desk that could have doubled as a bomb shelter. His tailored shirt was crisply pressed and he casually fingered a fountain pen. A silver-framed photograph of a woman (presumably his wife) was positioned on a corner of the desk so that she smiled both at me and him.

Somehow I was supposed to convince this man that I would be a good fit into his organization.

The opening volley of questions was predictable enough. Why was I interested in this role? What value would I contribute to the consultancy? I took a deep breath and worked on sounding natural and enthusiastic. I deliver results in challenging environments and thrive on creative problem solving. I strive to understand what motivates my clients and approach projects with an orientation towards the client's own strategic goals. I enjoy mentoring junior members of the team and helping them to recognize their own strengths and weaknesses.

Such nice words. Such soothing generalities. Yes, I was avoiding specifics. How could I possibly describe my "challenging environment" without sounding like a complete lunatic? I had learned to drink professionally over the past few years. One of my principal allies on the project was just shot. We had our phones tapped and we were being followed. We were management consultants, not government operatives. We were not exactly trained for how to work in these sorts of circumstances, yet somehow we figured out how to get through and complete the project with the stamp of "successfully completed".

"So you were managing an $11M project," the man was now reading my resume. "Take me through your project management methodology and how you measured the success of the project with the key stakeholders."

I tried not to laugh. Project management methodology. Measuring success of the project. Expectations management of key stakeholders. The senior people in the St Petersburg government would not even talk to me except to call and insult us. We were tongue-lashed every time we made contact with the government agencies that we were supposed to be supporting. Did he understand that with aid projects, the core concept of "client" was virtually unrecognizable? In a normal commercial relationship a client has identified an issue and is engaging a consultant to assist with the resolution of the issue. The client is putting real money into the exercise, therefore is focused on the success of the project. With an aid project, however, the "client" neither has really identified a problem nor has paid money out of their budget to resolve it. The senior stakeholders for the project would have their own agendas, which at times might actually overlap with the stated goals of the project, but quite likely would not.

Such concepts would be foreign to this American consultant that wanted to hear about project plans and performance metrics and other documentation that would provide evidence that my project was successful. I took a deep breath and buried my opinions and recited a carefully rehearsed speech about an agreed statement of work, milestones, and key deliverables. I explained how we managed the program budget against forecast and actuals and completed the program exactly on time and on budget with all milestones signed off by the City of St Petersburg.

The man interviewing me pushed his chair back and kicked his feet up on his desk and folded his hands behind his head. His half-smile said that I had nothing to teach him. He was the experienced management consultant with a proven methodology. His shoes said that he had no idea that in many cultures it is a huge insult to show the soles of one's feet to another.

"And how do you know that the client was satisfied with the outcome of the project?" the consultant asked.

Because I managed to leave Russia with both my kneecaps intact – I bit my tongue to keep the words from slipping out of my mouth.

"The best indicator of success is if the client invites you back for the next phase of the project," I heard myself saying. "As the project in St Petersburg was being completed, USAID and the relevant Russian government agencies invited my company to roll out the title registration program to three additional cities. I was personally invited to continue on as the project manager."

Put in those terms it almost sounded like a one-way ticket to Siberia is something one should strive for.

The attention of the interviewer was focused over my shoulder and out the window. We were on the 30th floor and he had an expansive view of the San Francisco Bay Bridge. The sun was shining and wind blowing and undoubtedly there would be a swarm of yachts frolicking on the water in the glorious late summer afternoon. His attention was fading. The interview was coming to an end.

I suddenly felt nauseous. I had travelled to Russia with bright eyed optimism that I was going to change the world for the better. Economic development, private property, individual liberty and financial independence, foreign investment – I had read my project work orders from USAID with passion and commitment to these noble goals. Now, as I recited the simplistic declarations of success, the man interviewing me nodded with disinterested approval. I was following the model correctly for what he wanted to hear. Further details were unnecessary.

But then again, why should I let the value of those years be defined by people like this interviewer? He might just want the nice clean statement so as to validate his prior assumptions and move on. But somewhere out there would be the next generation of optimistic young kids – in search of adventure and an abstract goal to make a positive difference on the world around them. Certainly *they* would be interested in learning from others who had gone before them?

We were now in the chit-chat closing moments of the interview. This man had already made up his mind about my future. His attention was now directed over my shoulder and out the window.

"So, what was Russia really like?" he asked me casually. "How much vodka do Russians really drink? Is Aeroflot really as bad as they say?" He then looked at me with a conspiratorial half smile. "Were you a spy?"

I was half tempted to tell the interviewer about the newspaper headlines that had proclaimed "American spy arrives in Krasnoyarsk". But looking at his smirk and arrogant pose at the desk I realized that he could easily interpret the story as being a sign that I did not manage my stakeholder relationships that well after all.

The man's body language said that he was not actually interested in a substantive discussion at this point. It was up to me to come up with some amusing final comments. Some lessons from Russia apparently would be just as applicable in the United States. He was asking a question – but did he really want a thoughtful answer? I would give this man a nice entertaining sound bite. The whole story, however, I would share some day with those genuinely interested in making a difference in the world.

"Ah yes, vodka," I sighed. "Yes, this is a skill set we had to develop in order to work effectively with our Russian partners. I call it vodka diplomacy."

ACKNOWLEDGEMENTS

This book has been simmering in the background for many years and would never have reached completion if it were not for the ongoing encouragement and support of friends and family. Many thanks to all of my early readers and everyone who provided encouragement and advice along the way, including (but in no way limited to): my family including Vanessa Harkins, P. David Fisher, Philip J. Fisher, Christine Fisher, and Kathryn Fisher and all the rest of the Fisher Cousins; the ladies in my book club – especially Gretchen Ayer and Deborah Lightfoot; friends who have published before me, including John J. Miller, James Workman, and Kevin Buckholtz; early readers of very rough partial drafts over the years who provided much needed feedback and encouragement to continue with this project – Perry Devetzakis, Valerie Hunting, Alisa Zapp Machalek, Rebekah Jardine-Williams, and Karen Waterston. And thank you to all the amazing people who I met and worked with in Russia and Kazakhstan. You definitely impacted my life for the better – I can only hope that our time together resulted in a positive difference in your lives as well.

CREDITS

Cover and interior design by Vanessa Maynard (*http://vanessanoheart.net*)

Quote on expatriates is from Ernest Hemingway, *The Sun Also Rises* (1926).

Full text of "Ozymandius" by Percy Bysshe Shelley (1818) is available in the public domain without copyright.

Photo of Author by Nina Genikis.

ABOUT THE AUTHOR

Phaedra Fisher completed her Master's Degree in International Economics and Russian Studies at the Johns Hopkins University Paul H. Nitze School of Advanced International Studies (SAIS). From 1993 to 1996 she worked on a number of US government-funded projects throughout Russia and Kazakhstan. Although she has not returned to Russia since 1996, her life continues to offer new adventures and lessons.

Made in the USA
San Bernardino, CA
10 February 2014